ntive **Mansion,**

Washington,   , 186

ago our fathers brought

a new nation, conceived

to the proposition that

al"

a great civil war, testing

any nation so conceived,

ong endure. We are met

of that war. We have

w of it, as a final rest-

 need here, that the nation

American Presidents and the Presidency

Former President Herbert Hoover chatted with John F. Kennedy shortly after the young Democrat from Massachusetts had been elected Chief Executive.

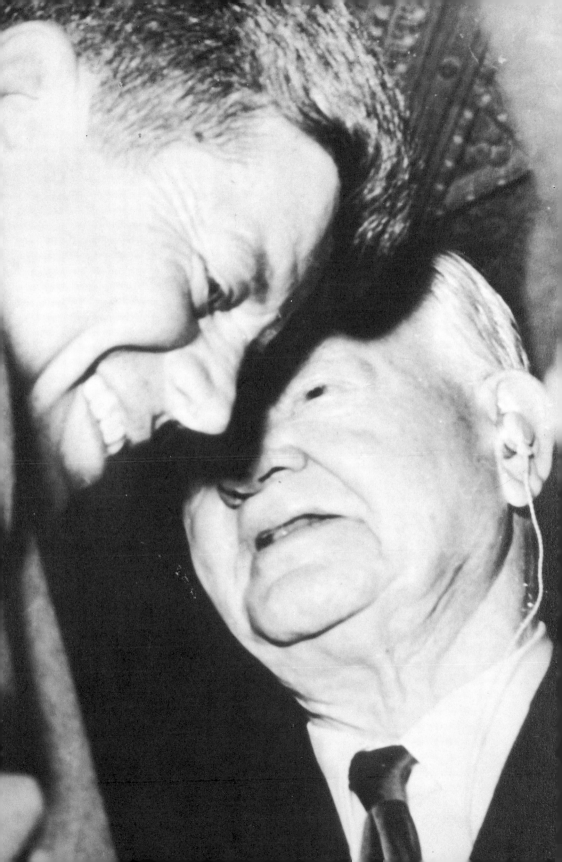

American Presidents and the Presidency

Marcus Cunliffe

AMERICAN HERITAGE PRESS

A Division of McGraw-Hill Book Company

New York   St. Louis   San Francisco

Düsseldorf   Mexico

Book design by Elaine Gongora

This book was set in Baskerline by University Graphics, Inc.

Library of Congress Cataloging in Publication Data
Cunliffe, Marcus.
    American Presidents and the Presidency.
    1968 ed. published under title: The American heritage
history of the Presidency.
    Bibliography: p.
    1. Presidents—U.S.   I.   Title.
JK511.C83   1972   353.03'13   72-925
ISBN 0-07-014935-6

To My Parents

Foreword

My aim with this book, written initially for the American Heritage Publishing Company in 1968, was to give a chronological and also a thematic view of the American Presidency. Hence the division into three sections, each with some overlap, covering the formative decades of the office up to the mid-nineteenth century; the period of latency or abeyance during the second half of the nineteenth century; and the vastly enlarged scope and problems of the twentieth century.

It has been quite substantially enlarged and revised, so as to keep abreast (so far as possible) of the extraordinary events of 1968–72. Even the most self-assured political commentators have had to confess their inability to prognosticate. Rules and probabilities have gone into the discard. The candidacy of Senator Robert F. Kennedy, and then his murder; the atmosphere of violence signalized also by the murder of Dr. Martin Luther King; the totally unexpected withdrawal from the 1968 contest of President Lyndon B. Johnson; the success of Richard M. Nixon, a figure often hitherto lumped with such forgotten men as Harold Stassen and Thomas E. Dewey, in capturing the Republican nomination; the remarkable early triumphs of Senator Eugene McCarthy; the perhaps inevitable yet unlooked-for nomination of Vice-President Hubert H. Humphrey as the Democratic candidate; Nixon's victory in 1968, the initial decline of his already-clouded reputation followed by his domination of the political scene in 1972: all these have confounded expectation, and cast into doubt familiar assumptions that the American democratic process follows predictable patterns.

Thus, few students of American politics have taken seriously the insistence of recent Presidents that the Vice-Presidency was a truly important office. Except for flukes it still seemed a dead end. Yet in 1968 the major parties nominated respectively the existing Vice-President and a former Vice-President; yet each chose for his running mate the traditional kind of nonentity—two little-known governors from minor states—as if to reinforce the traditionally low estimate of the Vice-Presidency; and yet, for a period at least, Vice-President Agnew and Muskie remained remarkably prominent in the public eye.

A two-term Presidency was accepted as the norm for the twentieth century. Yet Johnson denied himself almost certain renomination; journalists began to suggest[1] that in view of the terrible strain of office, single-term presidencies might become usual; and many commentators in 1969–71 suggested that President Nixon could well go down to defeat in 1972.

Political writers have ordinarily treated party conventions with indulgence. Even a cynic like H. L. Mencken thought of them as an enjoyably ridiculous American ritual: "One sits through long sessions wishing heartily that all the delegates and alternates were in hell—and then suddenly there comes a show so gaudy and hilarious, so melodramatic and obscene, so unimaginably exhilarating and preposterous that one lives a gorgeous year in an hour." Or they have pointed to the unifying and democratic purpose underlying the ballyhoo. But the spectacle of the 1968 conventions depressed and dismayed large sections of the public; they were conscious of the obscenity, not the exhilaration. In neither convention was there an opportunity for a genuine contest; the Republicans were sealed off in their vacationer's paradise at Miami Beach, and the Democrats were walled in at Chicago by Mayor Daley's policemen—a sight that evoked comparisons with the Russian coercion of Czechoslovakia.

Psephologists had proved that the Republicans were the minority party, had been ever since 1932, and might long remain so. The Republican choice of Barry Goldwater appeared to have done the party irreparable harm. Yet in 1968 division over Vietnam and the grotesque assassination of Robert Kennedy, followed by the Chappaquiddick scandal involving his younger brother, Senator Ted Kennedy, seemed to threaten wreck to the Democrats instead. Where was the stability, where the rationality, of a system in which neither major party appeared to stand for anything meaningful, and either might be shattered by the accidental loss of a potential leader or two? Never had the illogic of the American political-presidential mechanism stood out in a more uncharming and vulnerable light.

Again, political historians had long explained the futility of third and fourth parties in the American context.[2] But so shaken were pundits by the erratic shifts of 1968 that some speculated earnestly on the possibility that the white-supremacy, state-rights campaign of ex-Governor George Wallace of Alabama might prevent either major candidate from securing a popular majority, and so thrust the election into the House of Representatives—an emergency provision that had not had to be put into effect since the election of 1824. Though this did not happen, Wallace did not fade away either: in 1972 he was still a figure to be reckoned with.

Is the Presidency, along with the rest of the American political system, about to return to the turmoil of the early decades of the republic? Certainly the recent emphasis, like that of the formative years, has been quite as much upon the sorrows and frustrations as upon the splendors of the office. There is a curious appositeness in the allusions to the Presidency to be found in Ignatius Loyola Robertson's old book, *Sketches of Public Characters* (New York, 1830). Consider his description of the White House of Andrew Jackson's era:

> In the yellow drawing room there is . . . a French piano, which it is said cannot be kept in tune. In the days of omens, when Memnon's harp responded to the rays of the sun, or Aeolus first breathed among the reeds, this might be thought to have a mysterious bearing on the jars of the Cabinet councils or at least, a Greek Poet would have said that the Genius of the place was not always happy, and tuneful.

And he mentions a stone arch, in the southeast wall surrounding the White House, with a weeping willow on either side:

> It is said that an accomplished lady of the *Great House* in former days when congratulated upon her elevation remarked with a smile, "I don't know that there is much cause for congratulation; the President of the United States generally comes in at the iron gate, and goes out at the *weeping willows.*"[3]

More than most books on the Presidency mine has dwelt upon the failings of the office. Recent happenings have lent such an approach an added relevance. But of course upheaval in the 1960's was not confined to the United States. Only a biased observer could pretend for example that contemporary France or Russia or China presents a picture of greater stability and harmony. Or if disturbance is a sign of vitality, as some radicals believe, then the United States can be regarded as healthy rather than sick — at least by the same yardstick.

America is going through a bad patch. But a certain qualified comfort may be drawn from the experiences of the past. Bad patches have occurred before. In retrospect they have not looked as cataclysmic as they did at the time. Nor, it must be said, have successive generations of reformers and radicals managed to make any very lasting impression upon the resiliently flabby *status quo*. For good and for ill, Americans of all political persuasions have amazingly short memories.

The White House is still in operation, even if its *genius loci* is unhappy and will probably never be otherwise. However wretched the lot of subsequent Presidents, none has had a blacker crisis to contemplate than Abraham Lincoln at the beginning of 1861. He consoled himself with the reflection "This too shall pass." So perhaps might have Lyndon Johnson in 1968. So might some of the men who follow him in through the iron gate of 1600 Pennsylvania Avenue.

MARCUS CUNLIFFE

American Presidents and the Presidency

PART ONE

BASIC EVOLUTION

GEORGE WASHINGTON 1789-1797

JOHN ADAMS 1797-1801

THOMAS JEFFERSON 1801-1809

JAMES MADISON 1809-1817

JAMES MONROE 1817-1825

JOHN QUINCY ADAMS 1825-1829

ANDREW JACKSON 1829-1837

MARTIN VAN BUREN 1837-1841

WILLIAM HENRY HARRISON 1841

JOHN TYLER 1841-1845

JAMES K. POLK 1845-1849

ZACHARY TAYLOR 1849-1850

MILLARD FILLMORE 1850-1853

FRANKLIN PIERCE 1853-1857

JAMES BUCHANAN 1857-1861

ABRAHAM LINCOLN 1861-1865

CHAPTER ONE

The Invention of the Presidency

FIFTY-FIVE delegates arrived in Philadelphia in May, 1787, empowered to propose revisions to the Articles of Confederation under which the newly independent United States was governed. When they departed in September they had instead drafted an entirely new Constitution. There had been a good deal of disagreement and moments of near-deadlock. Several delegates had serious doubts as to the wisdom of the final document; a few, including Luther Martin of Maryland, even refused to sign it.

The discussions in Independence Hall had been carried on in secret (our knowledge of them derives largely from the daily notes kept by James Madison, which were not published until 1840, when he and all the other delegates were dead and buried). As word of them spread to the outside world reactions were mixed. The new Constitution was debated all over again, in newspapers and pamphlets, in conversation and in correspondence, in state legislatures and in state ratifying conventions. To take effect the document had

---

In Philadelphia's Independence Hall the delegates to the Constitutional Convention of 1787 created a new office—the Presidency.

to be ratified by at least nine of the thirteen states. Not until June, 1788, was the necessary total secured. Rhode Island, which had sent no delegates to Philadelphia, voted heavily against the Constitution in a popular referendum. Antifederalists—men opposed to the Constitution in whole or in part—put up a stout fight in other states. The Federalists—supporters of the Constitution—carried the day by only 57 votes to 47 in New Hampshire, and only 89 to 79 in George Washington's Virginia, though he had lent his great prestige to the Philadelphia Convention by attending, with some reluctance, and by consenting to preside over its sessions. New York, the eleventh state to ratify the Constitution, followed the example of Virginia and Massachusetts in indicating that various amendments must be given prompt consideration. North Carolina was so much concerned about these additions that ratification was withheld pending proof that the first Congress convened under the Constitution would respect its obligation.

One of the novel features of the Constitution which aroused alarm was the provision for an executive in the shape of a single person, the President. Under the Articles of Confederation there was also a President, a President of Congress; but the office was merely a chairmanship, not to be held for more than one year in any three. The immediately acceptable notion was of a "plural" executive, in which power was shared among some sort of committee or council. When the idea of a single executive was first mooted at Philadelphia by James Wilson of Pennsylvania, Madison noted that it was greeted with an embarrassed pause. Edmund Randolph of Virginia then voiced the objection that was evidently in the minds of a number of delegates. The temper of Americans, he said, was "adverse to the very semblance of monarchy"; a single executive figure would be "the foetus of monarchy."

Though the Convention swallowed its misgivings and approved the proposal, the cry was taken up again in the ratification controversies. In Virginia Washington's old friend George Mason, who had been at Philadelphia but declined to put his name to the Constitution, argued against the executive as against other clauses. The President would have far too much scope, he said, in being (under Article II, Section 2) "Commander-in-Chief of the Army and Navy of the United States, and of the Militia" when called into federal service, and in being empowered to make treaties and appoint public officials with the advice and consent of the Senate. Mason disliked the overlapping of executive and legislative functions entailed in such provisions. There should, he thought, have been a small council of state to give "proper information and advice," the chairman of which could serve as Vice-President. Without such a council, Mason warned, the President will "be directed by minions and favorites; or he will become a tool to the Senate—or a Council of State will grow out of the principal officers of the great departments." From this defect too had sprung "that unnecessary (and dangerous) officer the Vice-President, who for want of other employment is made president of the Senate, thereby dangerously blending the executive and legislative powers, besides always giving to some one of the States an unnecessary and unjust pre-eminence over the others." In short, George Mason saw the proposed Constitution as a scheme for "an elective monarchy." So did his fellow-Virginian, the eloquent patriot and ex-Governor Patrick Henry. It "squinted toward monarchy," Henry asserted in the Virginia ratifying convention. James Monroe, speaking against the Constitution in the same convention, was worried by the method of electing the President. He assumed that candidates would seldom gain the clear majority of votes which would enable the proposed Electoral College to decide the matter. The election would then according to the Constitution be thrown to the House of Representatives, with one vote for each state. How easily, Monroe speculated, could the "chair of the United States . . . be approached and achieved, even contrary to the wishes of the people." Given the prevailing "ardent spirity of liberty," treason and subversion were improbable; but anyone capable of digesting the lessons of history could not help but be uneasy for the future of the United States.

Others echoed these objections. Rawlin Lowndes, a South Carolina legislator, described the Constitution as "the best preparatory plan for a monarchical government he had read." A colleague, who like George Mason was worried by the President's re-eligibility for office at the end of his four-year term, declared that "this mighty, this omnipotent governor-general" could well sit in office for "fourteen times four years," and "may hold it so long that it will be impossible without a revolution, to displace him."[1]

Thomas Jefferson, receiving news of the Constitution at his post as American minister in Paris, liked some provisions but was ex-

POGHKEEPSIE
July 2d, 1788.

JUST ARRIVED

BY EXPRESS,

The Ratification of the New Conſtitution by the Convention of the State of Virginia, on Wedneſday the 25th June, by a majority of 10 ; 88 agreeing, and 78 diſſenting to its adoption.

"WE the Delegates of the People of Virginia, duly elected in Purſuance of a Recommendation of the General Aſſembly; and now met in Convention, having fully and fairly inveſtigated and diſcuſſed the Proceedings of the Federal Convention, and being prepared as well as the moſt mature Deliberation will enable us to decide thereon, DO, in the Name and on Behalf of the People of Virginia, declare and make known, that the Powers granted under the Conſtitution being derived from the People of the United States, may be reſumed by them whenſoever the ſame ſhall be perverted to their Injury or Oppreſſion, and that every Power not granted thereby remains with them and at their Will : That therefore no Right, of any Denomination, can be cancelled, abridged, reſtrained or modified by the Congreſs, by the Senate, or Houſe of Repreſentatives, acting in any Capacity, by the Preſident, or any Department or Officer of the United States, except in thoſe inſtances where Power is given by the Conſtitution for thoſe Purpoſes: That among other eſſential Rights, the Liberty of Conſcience, and of the Preſs, cannot be cancelled, abridged, reſtrained or modified by any Authority of the United States :

With theſe Impreſſions, with a ſolemn Appeal to the Searcher of Hearts for the Purity of our Intentions, and under the Conviction, that whatſoever Imperfections may exiſt in the Conſtitution, ought rather to be examined in the Mode preſcribed therein, than to bring the Union into Danger by Delay, with a Hope of obtaining Amendments previous to the Ratification :

We the ſaid Delegates, in the Name and in Behalf of the People of Virginia, do by theſe preſents aſſent to and ratify the Conſtitution, recommended on the 17th day of September, 1787, by the Federal Convention for the Government of the United States; hereby announcing to all thoſe whom it may concern, that the ſaid Conſtitution is binding upon the ſaid People, according to an authentic copy hereunto annexed, in the Words following:"—

[Here comes in the Conſtitution.]

A Letter from Richmond adviſes, that a Motion for previous Amendments was rejected by a Majority of Eight; but that ſome days would be paſſed in conſidering ſubſequent Amendments, and theſe, it appeared, from the temper of the Convention, would be recommended.

Virginia's ratification of the new Constitution was far from unanimous, as the broadside at left reveals. New Yorkers were also bitterly divided over the issue. The drawing below shows a parade sponsored by advocates of the Constitution in New York City; the float bears the name of Alexander Hamilton, one of the document's most influential supporters in the North.

tremely uneasy at the possibility of presidential re-election. "Reason and experience," he wrote to John Adams in November, 1787,

> prove to us that a chief magistrate, so continuable, is an officer for life. When one or two generations shall have proved that this is an office for life, it becomes on every succession worthy of intrigue, of bribery, of force, and even of foreign interference. It will be of great consequence to France and England to have America governed by a Galloman or Angloman. Once in office, and possessing the military force of the union, without either the aid or the check of a council, he would not easily be dethroned, even if the people could be induced to withdraw their votes from him. I wish that at the end of the 4 years they had made him for ever ineligible a second time. . . .

A few weeks later in a letter to James Madison, Jefferson reiterated that "I greatly dislike . . . the abandonment . . . of the necessity for rotation in office, and most particularly in the case of the President. Experience concurs with reason in concluding that the first magistrate will always be re-elected if the constitution permits it. He is then an officer for life."[2]

There was strenuous opposition to the proposals for a President in some of the northern states. One of the most influential of the Antifederalists was Governor George Clinton of New York. Writing a series of articles for the *New-York Journal* over the pen-name "Cato," Clinton predicted in accents of horror and woe that the President "will be surrounded with expectants and courtiers'." His patronage power; his control over the armed forces; his "unrestrained power of granting pardons for treason, which may be used to screen from punishment those whom he had secretly instigated to commit the crime, and thereby prevent a discovery of his own guilt"; his entrenchment in office for four long years: these factors proved to Clinton that "if the president is possessed of ambition, he has power and time sufficient to ruin his country." Taking another tack, Clinton asked whether there was any essential difference in power and prerogative between the American President and the "king of Great Britain." The President, said Clinton (enlarging on the clause of the Constitution which merely stipulates that he "shall . . . receive . . . a compensation"), was bound to be

13

paid enough "to appear with the splendor of a prince." He was also "a constituent part of the legislative power," since his approval was required for all federal legislation. He had great latitude of action in foreign affairs. "Therefore these powers, in both president and king, are substantially the same."

The Founding Fathers were more violently assailed for their work at Philadelphia in a series of articles published in February-April, 1788, in *The Freeman's Journal; Or, The North-American Intelligencer.* Their author, "Philadelphiensis," is believed to have been one Benjamin Workman, a tutor at the University of Pennsylvania. He detected a "conspiracy," devised by "an infernal junto of demagogues," to consolidate "our thirteen free commonwealths" into a *"despotic monarchy."* Lacking precise evidence for the charge, he argued that its truth was self-evident: "Who can deny but the *president general* will be *king* to all intents and purposes, and one of the most dangerous kind too—a king elected to command a standing army? Thus our laws are to be administered by this *tyrant;* for the whole, or at least the most important part of the executive department is put in his hands." This *"president general"* was vested with powers "exceeding those of the most *despotic monarch* . . . in modern times." Why had the conspirators thrown away the chances of American happiness by framing "a system of oppression that must involve in its consequences the misery of their own offspring"? Like other subsequent imaginers of conspiracy, the writer found corroboration, and further proof of depravity, in apparently unpromising material. The Founding Fathers, so mean and dastardly were they, had betrayed their country and their own children merely in "hopes of obtaining some lucrative employment, or of receiving a little more homage from the rest of their fellow creatures."[3] A strange diagnosis of a gathering that embraced old Benjamin Franklin, the austerely dignified Washington, and the scholarly James Madison, even if the later careers of a few of the delegates—the financier Robert Morris, or the imperiously ambitious Alexander Hamilton—perhaps lent a little color to such suspicions.

In fact practically all the gloomy forebodings of the Antifederalists are more likely to amuse than to impress us. Looking back with the hindsight of nearly two centuries, we know that things worked out very much better. The Presidency seemingly did *not* turn out to be an elective monarchy. Its incumbents have *not* proved to be in "office for life." The interfusion of executive and legislative functions, while sometimes a cause of friction and confusion, has justified itself as a wise improvement upon the theoretically ideal but practically unworkable plan of a perfect separation of powers. Not surprisingly, more attention has been devoted to those who analyzed the new Constitution sympathetically than to those who assailed it. We have been understandably impressed by the eighty-five letters contributed by Hamilton, Madison, and John Jay to *The Federalist* series of 1787–88. Thus Hamilton appears as an easy winner over Monroe and Clinton. Monroe wrings his hands at the opportunities for corruption (and worse) created by the method of electing the President. In *The Federalist* No. 68, Hamilton at his most sweetly reasonable points out how the mechanism of the Electoral College will give the people a say in the process, and exclude from it Senators and Representatives:

> This process of election affords a moral certainty that the office of President will seldom fall to . . . any man who is not in an eminent degree endowed with the requisite qualifications. Talents for low intrigue, and the little arts of popularity, may . . . suffice to elevate a man to [the governorship of a state]; but it will require other talents, and a different kind of merit, to establish him in the esteem and confidence of the whole Union. It will not be too strong to say that there will be a constant probability of seeing the station filled by characters preeminent for ability and virtue.

Too rosy a picture? Perhaps. But in the main accurate, which is more than can be said for Monroe's prophecy.

Clinton insisted that the Presidency would hardly differ from the British monarchy. Hamilton's devastating answer, in *The Federalist* No. 69, is worth quoting at length:

> The President of the United States would be an officer elected by the people for *four* years; the King of Great Britain is a perpetual and *hereditary* prince. The one would be amenable to personal punishment and disgrace [through impeachment]; the person of the other is . . . inviolable. The one would have a *qualified* negative upon the acts of the legislative body; the other has an *absolute* negative. The one would have a right to command the military and naval forces of the nation; the other, in addition to this right, possesses that of

declaring war [a right reserved to Congress in the Constitution], and of *raising* and *regulating* fleets and armies [likewise, a responsibility of Congress] by his own authority. The one would have a concurrent power [with the Senate] in the formation of treaties; the other is the *sole possessor* of the power of making treaties. The one would have a like concurrent authority in appointing to offices; the other is the sole author of all appointments. The one can confer no privileges whatsoever; the other can make denizens of aliens, noblemen of commoners; can erect corporations with all the rights incident to corporate bodies. The one can prescribe no rules concerning the commerce of currency of the nation; the other is in several respects the arbiter of commerce. . . . The one has no particle of spiritual jurisdiction; the other is supreme head and governor of the national church! What answer shall we give to those who would persuade us that things so unlike resemble each other? The same that ought to be given to those who tell us that a government, the sole power of which would be in the hands of the elective and periodical servants of the people, is an aristocracy, a monarchy, and a despotism.[4]

We can see that if some of the Federalist arguments smacked of special pleading, so did those of the Antifederalists. Clinton, for example, was the powerful governor of a powerful state. His disapproval was not directed toward executive authority as such, but toward federal, centralized executive authority. We are aware that the Antifederalists were on the whole less opposed to a single Executive than to some other aspects of the Constitution—notably the absence of a bill of rights, when this was a common feature of the post-Revolutionary state constitutions. We are aware, too, that most of them overcame their scruples fairly quickly once the new Constitution took effect. Some years before his death in 1799 Patrick Henry, reversing himself, had become a vehement Federalist. Jefferson told his friend Francis Hopkinson in March, 1789, that on the re-eligibility rule he would not wish to make further criticisms while George Washington was at the helm, having full confidence in "our great leader" who was about to be inaugurated. He hoped the potentially dangerous provision would be amended as soon as Washington had stepped down from the Presidency. But Jefferson himself was President a few years later, and he then saw no harm in imitating Washington's example of what he called "voluntary retirement after eight years."[5] James Monroe in the same way ceased

Four very vocal opponents of the new Constitution (clockwise from top, left): George Clinton of New York, and Patrick Henry, George Mason, and Edmund Randolph, all from Virginia.

to be apprehensive at the dreadful problem of election to the Presidency; he too was to have eight years in office.

By the same token, we are puzzled by the anxiety over the President as commander-in-chief expressed by Antifederalists in what Hamilton called their "parade of imaginary horribles." The New York ratifying convention suggested that the President should be prevented from taking the field at the head of his troops "without the previous desire of Congress." But the standing army of the United States numbered less than a thousand men in the 1780's. A generation later, despite America's increase in population and territory, it was to be not much over ten thousand. Nor were Presidents to show much enthusiasm for assuming personal command. The only instances in America's long history were to be "little Jemmy" Madison's somewhat farcical appearance at the inglorious encounter of Bladensburg, outside the nation's capital, in 1814, and one or two brief prodding exercises attempted by Abraham Lincoln.

As for the President's "unrestrained power of granting pardons," it is true that the Constitution gave him the right (Article II, Section 2) to "grant reprieves and pardons for offences against the United States, except in cases of impeachment." But this privilege of clemency was if anything to be invoked too sparingly by Presidents. When Eugene V. Debs was sentenced to ten years' imprisonment in 1918 for seditious opposition to the war, President Wilson let him stay in jail; the war had been over for three years when President Harding pardoned Debs with the genial observation that "personally he is of a very clean and lovable character."

We *know*, then, that the Presidency evolved into a wholesome and stable institution. It has been a great success, as success is commonly measured. Accepting this as a commonplace of history, we are apt to underestimate or misunderstand the problems facing the Constitution makers during that hot summer in Independence Hall.

Their task—one that most of them had probably not intended to undertake—disclosed itself as the invention of a new form of government. It was to be novel in several ways, not all of which concern us here. Like the Articles of Confederation, it was to be a dual or federal system conceding some powers to the central executive-legislative government and reserving others to the thirteen semisovereign states. It was to be looser and more democratic than the monarchical-aristocratic governments of Europe, yet was to furnish the "energy"—a favorite word among the Federalists—that men such as Washington, Jay, and Hamilton thought alarmingly absent in the Articles. A majority of the Philadelphia delegates were "Federalists" in the broad sense of wishing to impart more "energy" to the central government. Beyond that, certainty and unanimity ceased. They were venturing into dangerous country. The maps of this country were conjectural and daunting: "Here Be Wild Beasts" was, so to speak, inscribed in the blank spaces.

The Founding Fathers could seek inspiration from two types of material. There were the actual examples of other peoples, historical and contemporary, and of the former colonies that made up the United States, and there were the theoretical commentaries on government, above all those of John Locke, William Blackstone, and Baron Montesquieu. None of these provided reassurance. History seemed to show that loose federations such as those of the Greek city-states were too parochial and too jealous of one another to survive. On the other hand, well-knit societies like that of ancient Rome slid into corruption: the Republic became the Empire of the twelve Caesars. In modern times the picture was equally dismal. Almost every country in the known world from China to Portugal was ruled by a hereditary monarch. Some—Victor Amadeus II of Savoy-Sardinia, Ferdinand I of Naples, Gustavus III of Sweden, Frederick II of Prussia (who died the year before the Philadelphia Convention, having occupied the throne for forty-six years)—were absolute or would-be absolute rulers. Others—Louis XVI of France, Charles II of Spain, Leopold I of Tuscany, Catherine the Great of Russia—were known as enlightened or benevolent despots. Whatever the type of monarchy, there tended to be a tussle between the ruler and the aristocracy, each seeking power at the expense of the other.

The few exceptions yielded no comfort to the Founding Fathers. In Switzerland, where there was no king, there was instead a jostling collection of cantons, split over religious issues and controlled by a small group of rich families. In Holland there was a qualified monarchy in the shape of the Stadholder; but the current ruler, William V, was mournfully ineffectual. For a hundred and fifty years Poland had had an elective monarchy. The results were lamentable, as Jefferson knew when he complained in 1787 that the proposed American President "seems a bad edition of a Polish King." In Poland every election was an open invitation to conspiracy, within the country and on the part of neighboring nations. The nobility in the Polish Diet, or parliament, held the power, but so irresponsibly that they could not use it: they refused even to be bound by majority rule.[6]

The example of Britain might have seemed more relevant. In different ways Locke, Blackstone, and Montesquieu all praised the real or supposed features of British government: a monarch capable of ruling, yet restrained by Parliament from behaving despotically, a sensibly balanced and mixed constitution embodying a separation of functions, a vigorous tradition of libertarianism reinforced by a body of common law. At the outset of the Revolution, some Americans had allowed themselves to believe that the British king, George III, would use his prerogative to uphold their liberties. Swiftly disillusioned, they convinced themselves that neither the British nor any other monarchy would be desirable for the United States. The hereditary principle was objectionable; so were the inevitable accompaniments of monarchy—titles, sinecures, ecclesiastical hierarchies, "expectants and courtiers." Many Americans became convinced that this was so through reading Tom Paine's rousing pamphlet *Common Sense,* which is said to have sold 120,-000 copies within three months of its publication in 1776. Paine is one of the first and one of the most effective debunkers of the then-hallowed institution of kingship. "There is something exceedingly ridiculous," he announced, "in the composition of monarchy." It "excludes a man from the means of information, yet empowers him to act in cases where the highest judgement is required." A few pages later he asked:

> Why is the constitution of England sickly, but because monarchy hath poisoned the republic, the crown hath engrossed the commons?
> In England a king hath little more to do than to make war and give away places; which in plain terms is to impoverish the nation and set it together by the ears. A pretty business indeed for a man to be allowed eight hundred thousand sterling a year and worshipped into the bargain![7]

The lessons of history and the examples of other contemporary nations demonstrated that America must avoid both a monarchy and the rule of a clique—whether known as an aristocracy or an oligarchy. But could the word "rule" logically be applied to the rule of the many: to a government without "energy," without the vesting of authority in the hands of a small group of men, presided over by one supreme figure? Some believed the experiment was worth making, if only because the alternatives were so ominous. Some felt that the United States under the Articles of Confederation was healthy and reasonably strong. Why be alarmed by one small uprising—that of Daniel Shays, a dissatisfied Massachusetts farmer —in 1786? "A little rebellion, now and then, is a good thing, & as necessary in the political world as storms in the physical," Jefferson assured Madison in January, 1787. The Philadelphia Convention, he insisted in November of the same year, had been "too much impressed by the insurrection of Massachusetts: and in the spur of the moment they are setting up a kite to keep the hen yard in order."[8]

Others read the signs very differently. Madison received another letter, from George Washington, who was becoming convinced that his dreams of peaceful retirement at Mount Vernon were about to be shattered. Commenting on Shays's Rebellion, he took it as proof of "the want of energy in our governments. . . . Thirteen sovereignties pulling against each other, and all tugging at the foederal head," he warned, "will soon bring ruin to the whole." To another correspondent Washington exclaimed: "We are fast verging to anarchy and confusion!"[9]

He and men of his outlook were sure that the Articles were to blame. The "foederal head" was toothless. Executive power was in the hands of Congress, and they were feeble hands. Originally the executive departments were run by committees, such as the board of five members which superintended the treasury. By degrees separate departments came into being, with officials at their head: foreign affairs emerged as one such department in 1781. But government by committee continued, without any formal separation of executive from legislative functions. In consequence individual states did much as they pleased.

Nor were the states as a whole in strong executive hands. They had begun to draft new constitutions for themselves in 1776. To some extent they repeated the structures of colonial days, replacing the royal or proprietary governors with chief executives—known as

Commonwealth of Maſſachuſetts.

By His EXCELLENCY

JAMES BOWDOIN, Eſquire,

Governour of the Commonwealth of Maſſachuſetts.

A Proclamation.

HEREAS information has been given to the Supreme Executive of this Commonwealth, that on Tueſday laſt, the 29th of Auguſt, being the day appointed by law for the ſitting of the Court of Common Pleas and Court of General Seſſions of the Peace, at *Northampton*, in the county of *Hampſhire*, within this Commonwealth, a large concourſe of people, from ſeveral parts of that county, aſſembled at the Court-Houſe in *Northampton*, many of whom were armed with guns, ſwords and other deadly weapons, and with drums beating and fifes playing, in contempt and open defiance of the authority of this Government, did, by their threats of violence and keeping poſſeſſion of the Court-Houſe until twelve o'clock on the night of the ſame day, prevent the ſitting of the Court, and the orderly adminiſtration of juſtice in that county :

AND WHEREAS this high-handed offence is fraught with the moſt fatal and pernicious conſequences, muſt tend to ſubvert all law and government ; to diſſolve our excellent Conſtitution, and introduce univerſal riot, anarchy and confuſion, which would probably terminate in abſolute deſpotiſm, and conſequently deſtroy the faireſt proſpects of political happineſs, that any people was ever favoured with :

I HAVE therefore thought fit, by and with the advice of the Council, to iſſue this Proclamation, calling upon all Judges, Juſtices, Sheriffs, Conſtables, and other officers, civil and military, within this Commonwealth, to prevent and ſuppreſs all ſuch violent and riotous proceedings, if they ſhould be attempted in their ſeveral counties.

AND I DO hereby, purſuant to the indiſpenſible duty I owe to the good people of this Commonwealth, moſt ſolemnly call upon them, as they value the bleſſings of freedom and independence, which at the expence of ſo much blood and treaſure they have purchaſed—as they regard their faith, which in the ſight of G O D and the world, they pledged to one another, and to the people of the United States, when they adopted the preſent Conſtitution of Government—as they would not diſappoint the hopes, and thereby become contemptible in the eyes of other nations, in the view of whom they have riſen to glory and empire—as they would not deprive themſelves of the ſecurity derived from well-regulated Society, to their lives, liberties and property ; and as they would not devolve upon their children, inſtead of peace, freedom and ſafety, a ſtate of anarchy, confuſion and ſlavery,—I do moſt earneſtly and moſt ſolemnly call upon them to aid and aſſiſt with their utmoſt efforts the aforeſaid officers, and to unite in preventing and ſuppreſſing all ſuch treaſonable proceedings, and every meaſure that has a tendency to encourage them.

GIVEN at the COUNCIL-CHAMBER, in BOSTON, *this ſecond day of September, in the year of our* LORD, *one thouſand ſeven hundred and eighty-ſix, and in the eleventh year of the* Independence *of the* United States *of* AMERICA.

JAMES BOWDOIN.

By his Excellency's command.

JOHN AVERY, jun. Secretary.

BOSTON : Printed by ADAMS and NOURSE, Printers to the GENERAL COURT.

Shays's Rebellion—a short-lived uprising by poor farmers in Massachusetts in 1786—convinced many Americans that a strong central government was a necessity. Here is the proclamation issued by James Bowdoin, the governor of Massachusetts, concerning the revolt.

"presidents" in Delaware, New Hampshire, and Pennsylvania, and in the 1776 though not the 1778 constitution of South Carolina; and elsewhere styled as "governors." There had been acute friction between the colonial governors and their legislatures, with the latter hanging on grimly to their control of appropriations. These memories, and the augmented distaste for British institutions brought about by the Revolution, made the drafters of state constitutions determined to emphasize the primacy of the legislative over the executive branch. In eight states the governor was actually chosen by the legislature. Pennsylvania's "president" was elected by the legislature from among an upper chamber or council of twelve, which collectively formed the executive. Such councils were provided in other states: for example in New York, where the governor had to share his veto power and other powers with a council of revision. In North and South Carolina he was allowed no right of veto. Ten of the thirteen states limited the governor's term of office to one year. Only in two states, New York and Delaware, was he allowed a three-year term. The governor of Virginia, Edmund Randolph, regarded himself simply as "a member of the executive." Jefferson remarked of the Virginia constitution: "All the powers of government, legislative, executive and judiciary, result to the legislative body." As in the national Congress of the 1780's, the outcome of legislative supremacy was—at any rate in the opinion of those of the Federalist persuasion—muddle, inefficiency, bad feeling. In reacting against executive encroachments, the states had gone to the other extreme of legislative overlordship.[10] If the new Constitution could be criticized for seeking to establish a "Polish King," America in the 1780's could be portrayed as a country at the mercy of one principal Polish Diet and thirteen subsidiary ones.

This was the heart of the problem for the delegates at Philadelphia. Murphy's Law of Politics—"if anything bad can happen, it will"—had not yet been formulated. But they would have known exactly what he meant. History, the state of affairs in Europe, and their own experience of government in America combined to admonish them that the correct mixture of elements might be as hard to arrive at as the alchemists' elixir of eternal life. To change the metaphor, one might say that government in relation to the competing needs of a nation was like a single sheet for a double bed. It could not cover the whole surface: the art was to dispose it as equitably and effectively as possible. Or, to return to the actual words at Philadelphia, the problem of a rightly balanced Executive was, according to the shrewd Gouverneur Morris of New York, the most difficult of all: "Make him too weak: the Legislature will usurp his power. Make him too strong: he will usurp on the Legislature."[11]

Almost every conceivable answer was put forward in Philadelphia before the weary delegates settled upon the Constitution in its final form. The most audacious came from Alexander Hamilton in the course of a five-hour speech. He wanted a stronger central government and Executive than anything that had yet been suggested. Indeed he advocated a replica of the British system, "the best in the world." There should be a single Executive, or "Governour," who would be virtually a monarch, an upper house to hold office for life (or during good behavior), and a popularly elected lower house. No one gave an immediate favorable response to his plan. He had come near to saying the unsayable. Yet the notion of monarchy survived in curiously clandestine ways. In May, 1782, one of General Washington's officers, Colonel Lewis Nicola, had hinted to his commander that bearing in mind "the weakness of republics" and the "benefits of mixed government," something on the lines of the British monarchy could be "readily adopted" in the United States; and who better fitted to wear that crown than Washington himself? Washington at once quashed the suggestion as being "big with the greatest mischiefs, that can befall my Country." It is certain that he had no yearning for a throne. Nevertheless the idea of an American monarchy reappeared, as a fear if not as a hope. The young lexicographer Noah Webster feared a military *coup d'état* in 1785.

"Shall we have a king?" John Jay asked Washington in the following year, after analyzing the weaknesses of the existing government. In 1787 Mrs. Mercy Warren, sister of the Massachusetts patriot James Otis, maintained that "many of the younger Class, particularly the students of Law and the youth of fortune and pleasure, are crying out for a monarchy and a standing army to support it." It is conceivable that Nathaniel Gorham, one of the Massachusetts delegates to the Philadelphia Convention, might have been prepared at one stage to back a plan for a monarchy, at least for New England. While the Convention was in progress, wild rumors circulated that the delegates were about to recommend a

"Hanoverian bishop," Frederick Augustus, the second son of George III, as king of the United States. Though the rumor was totally unfounded, it was thought to have emanated from a band of Connecticut royalists. In later ratification controversies, the non-signing Luther Martin claimed that no less than twenty of the fifty-five delegates had been in favor of a consolidated national government of a monarchical nature.[12]

At the opposite pole from Hamilton's scheme stood sundry proposals that envisaged the executive as a separate branch of government but differed as to the shape it should have. The most cautious proposals, typified by the early remarks of Roger Sherman of Connecticut and the plan introduced by William Paterson of New Jersey, leaned towards a plural Executive, or else a single Executive held in check by an advisory council. Congress would select the Executive, who would be debarred from immediate reappointment and would be subject to removal at the hands of Congress. The Executive would have no veto power. Congress would determine appointments to civil and military office, and control foreign policy by retaining the treaty- and war-making powers. Such formulas drew upon the Articles of Confederation, and more especially upon those state constitutions that applied drastic curbs to executive authority—Georgia's for instance, which restricted the governor to one term of one year in any three-year period.

The intermediate proposals that won acceptance called for a single Executive, not chosen by Congress and re-eligible for appointment. If removable, he must be so only through impeachment on specific charges. He should have the right to veto legislation, a prime voice in the choice of judicial, diplomatic, and other important figures, a comparable though not absolute power in the management of foreign affairs, and various additional prerogatives, including the power to pardon offenders for all except the gravest crimes against the state. The delegates who advocated an "energetic" executive branch had taken a close look not only at the British government but at the situation of those states, notably New York and Massachusetts, in which the governor was in fact a figure of considerable authority. Indeed, by drawing selectively from the state constitutions it was possible to argue from precedent that sanction for every feature of a strong national Executive could be found in one or another of these charters of Americanism.

New York was the best case of an active, efficient, popular administration. The governor, re-eligible indefinitely, held office for a term of reasonable length. The constitution vested in him "the supreme executive powers and authority of the State." He was declared to be commander-in-chief of the militia, and even admiral of New York's navy; he could pardon offenders; he could call the legislature into special session, or dissolve it; he was required to present a miniature "State-of-the-Union" (or rather "State-of-the-State") report to each session, and to "take care that the laws are executed." He had fairly generous appointive and veto powers. He was popularly elected. By the test of experience, New York was a well-governed state. Its executive head, George Clinton, who had been first elected in 1777, was re-elected in 1780, 1783, and 1786—and would continue for a total of eighteen years. Nor did it seem to matter greatly what term of office was prescribed. A competent and well-liked governor would remain firmly in office. This was borne out in Connecticut, where Jonathan Trumbull was chief executive from 1769 to 1786 under a system of annual elections, and in New Jersey, where Governor William Livingston had been returned to office every year since 1776—and would be until 1790.

Emboldened by such considerations, the group of delegates who believed in a strong Executive found that week by week the Convention was more inclined to listen sympathetically. Once they could agree on the idea of a single Executive, and once they perceived the advantages of a system that mingled executive and legislative operations ("ambition must be made to counteract ambition," as Madison nicely put the point in *The Federalist* No. 51), the initial premises shaped the evolution of the debate.

The presiding presence of George Washington did much to encourage the process, although Washington himself played no active part in discussion. His standing was unique. He had served as commander-in-chief of the Revolutionary army for eight and a half years, accepting merely his expenses as financial return. Entrusted with extraordinary powers, he had quietly tendered his commission to Congress and gone back to private life as a planter at Mount Vernon. Everyone knew him to be above suspicion and without overweening ambition. Everyone knew too that with the ratification of the new Constitution it would be unthinkable to name any man but him as America's first true President. Gazing at this large,

Among the leading proponents of a strong Chief Executive were James Wilson (top, left) and Gouverneur Morris (bottom, left) of Pennsylvania, Rufus King of Massachusetts (top, right), and Alexander Hamilton.

imposing, reticent personage as he took the chair each day, the Philadelphia delegates saw in him the living embodiment of their groping efforts to define the presidential essence. When the Constitution had been completed, signed, and sealed and the delegates had gone home, one of them—Pierce Butler of South Carolina—candidly admitted that he did not think the powers vested in the President "would have been so great had not many of the members cast their eyes towards General Washington as President, and shaped their ideas . . . by their opinions of his Virtue."[13]

There were other reasons why the delegates moved toward the conception of a single and potentially strong Executive. One was that in the later stages of the Convention an identity of interests developed between the "Federalist" bloc and the representatives of small states. From different motives both were willing to uphold the position of the centralized Executive against that of large states reluctant to surrender the privileges of wealth and population. A second reason was that the advocates of a strong Executive, once they had got around the accusation that they were cryptomonarchists, had a more positive and compelling brief than their opponents. They exhibited also most of the talent at Philadelphia, although they were by no means unanimous on every issue. Men of the caliber of Madison of Virginia and Oliver Ellsworth of Connecticut might have misgivings: they were nevertheless capable of a dispassionate insight that led them to prefer the risks of autocracy to those of anarchy. Assailed by fewer doubts, James Wilson and Gouverneur Morris of Pennsylvania, Rufus King and Elbridge Gerry of Massachusetts, Charles Pinckney and John Rutledge of South Carolina, and of course New York's glitteringly talented Alexander Hamilton, all urged their colleagues toward the ultimate goal of a rejuvenated national government.

Gradually the Convention's business was broken up among committees, in each of which the Federalist contingent played a crucial role. Ellsworth, Wilson, and Rutledge were members of the five-man Committee on Detail, whose task was to frame a tentative draft constitution. (It was this body, and more particularly James Wilson, who probably made the decision to describe the executive as "President" instead of "Governor" or "Governour"—the designations favored by Hamilton and followed in the first rough outline prepared for the Committee on Detail by Edmund Randolph. Wilson was no doubt influenced by the use of the term "President" in a previous plan submitted by Charles Pinckney, and by consulting the constitution of his own state of Pennsylvania, which then described its executive as "president."

At a subsequent stage several important loose ends were referred to the charmingly named Committee on Postponed Matters and Unfinished Business. This body put forward sympathetic recommendations on such intricate problems as the method of electing and removing the President, his appointive powers, and the extent of his authority in negotiating treaties. In the last ten days of the Convention's life its provisional decisions were given a polish by a Committee on Style and Arrangement headed by Gouverneur Morris. Indeed he imparted more than polish to certain sections. By choosing the precise phraseology that he wanted (in company with Hamilton, Madison, and Rufus King), Morris was able to express "my own notions" without "alarm [to] others": namely, to steer the document in as Federalist a direction as he dared. Thirty-nine delegates were both present and willing to attach their names to the finished Constitution on September 17, "in the Year of our Lord"— who was not otherwise mentioned in the text—"one thousand seven hundred and Eighty seven and of the Independence of the United States of America the Twelfth." Some disaffected delegates had already gone home. Three who were still in attendance refused to sign.

So, in the course of inventing a new government, the Founding Fathers invented a new head of government, the President.

As many historians have remarked, and as the men of Philadelphia were abundantly conscious, the Constitution was a medley of compromises. The single sheet had been pulled to and fro across the double bed. Its final resting place was determined by sheer fatigue as well as by wisdom. At least the delegates could feel that they were exhausted because they had debated the problems of government exhaustively. For example, Article II simply stated that the President "shall hold his office during the term of four years." A letter from Madison to Jefferson, written a month after the delegates adjourned, reveals how much discussion had preceded the bare wording of such clauses:

As to the duration in office, a few would have preferred a

tenure during good behaviour—a considerable number would have done so in case an easy & effectual removal by impeachment could be settled. It was much agitated whether a long term, seven years, for example, with a subsequent & partial ineligibility, or a short term with a capacity to be reelected should be fixed. In favor of the first opinion were urged the danger of a gradual degeneracy of re-elections . . . into first a life and then a hereditary tenure, and the favorable effect of an incapacity to be reappointed on the independent exercise of the executive authority. On the other side it was contended that the prospect of necessary degradation would discourage the most dignified characters from aspiring to the office, would take away the principal motive to the faithful discharge of its duties—the hope of being rewarded with a reappointment . . .—and instead of producing an independent administration, . . . would render the [President] more indifferent to the importance of a place which he would soon be obliged to quit forever, and more ready to yield to the encroachments of the Legislature of which he might again be a member.[14]

Involved prose, for one of several involved and "much agitated" issues. Madison could have added that only at a late stage was the re-eligible four-year term substituted for a single seven-year term.

The Chief Executive was not given as much power as some of the delegates would have wished. Not all were satisfied with the provisions that enabled Congress to override the President's veto, or with the extent to which the Senate might assert its views on foreign policy. On the other hand the Executive was stronger than some thought desirable. More than a century of "Constitution worship" elapsed before the historian Charles A. Beard felt the need to remind Americans that their Founding Fathers had after all mostly been men of property, prominent in their communities, and conservatively inclined. This would not have been news to the Antifederalists. We need not impute wicked designs to the Founding Fathers if we stress that their Constitution was a product of its time—of a particular moment in American history when a significant number of influential and articulate citizens thought their country had reached a crisis. Diagnosing an emergency, they managed to incorporate in the Constitution what might almost be called emergency powers for the Executive.

In much the same way, New York happened to have a strong executive because conditions in the state during the years of the Revo-

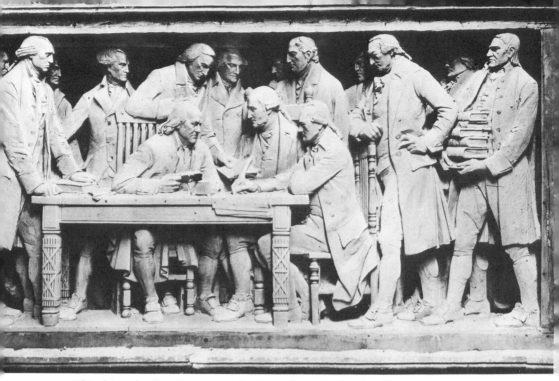

*This frieze by Lee Lawrie at the State Capitol of Nebraska is entitled
"Drafting the Constitution." Seated left to right are Benjamin Franklin,
George Washington, and Alexander Hamilton; James Madison of the
Virginia delegation stands fourth from left.*

lutionary War had been extraordinary, and because the leading
patriots were substantial, conservative persons. If the Philadelphia
meeting had taken place twenty or even ten years later, and the
country had continued to rub along under the Articles of Confederation, it is quite likely that the changes recommended would have
been much less sweeping and would have still accepted the principle of legislative supremacy. True, the powers of the President outlined in the 1787 Constitution were *in posse* rather than *in esse,*
potential rather than actual. The Founding Fathers, as befitted
serious-minded innovators, had an exceptional sense of posterity.
They wanted their work to last. The Constitution, like Washington's Farewell Address and the Monroe Doctrine, has achieved a
sort of timeless fame, as if it and they were conceived out of timeless wisdom. No doubt the Constitution makers were right, given
the later development of American history, to create an executive
branch and allow it the opportunity to display "energy," just as
Washington's and Monroe's pieces of advice have proved highly
relevant to later generations. Yet in common with these examples of

statecraft, the Constitution was produced in response to the urgent demands of its day. It was the happy, somewhat fortuitous outcome of prescience and jitters. If Washington, Hamilton, and the rest had not believed the "American empire" to be in imminent danger of "disunion, anarchy and misery" (Hamilton's words at the end of June, 1787),[15] the Constitution would probably not have worn anywhere near as well. A related paradox: those who, like Jefferson, kept calm, seeing no reason for jitters, have seemed to posterity not dispassionate or imaginative enough. They would, in declining to be stampeded into emergency measures, have bequeathed to posterity an instrument of government altogether too time-bound.

This is not to assert that the 1787 Constitution was entirely new. Though they were innovators, the men of Philadelphia did not regard themselves as revolutionaries. They had no interest in novelty for its own sake: their concern was to fashion a system of government that would operate efficiently and that would be supported by Americans. One way of enlisting support was to draw upon the immediate precedent of state constitutions such as that of New York. Yet even if they had desired to fabricate an utterly new system, they would not have been able to move beyond the dominant conceptions of the age. The writings they consulted—Locke, Blackstone, Montesquieu, the just-published *Defence of the Constitutions* by John Adams of Massachusetts—all affirmed the same eighteenth-century doctrine: checks and balances, mixed governments, separation of powers, the entrusting of an indefinable amount of prerogative to the Executive. The Philadelphia Constitution may be seen as a classic sample of the thinking of the Enlightenment. It is useful to consider the role of the President within the Constitution as a figment of the imagination of the Enlightenment: an equivocal, dream-personage who could lay claim to immortality only by taking on mortal flesh and undergoing the ordeal by experience that began in 1789 and is not yet ended.

The Constitution was not brand-new. Nor was it a complete guide to American federalism. Napoleon once said that constitutions should be "short and obscure." A certain guile worthy of Napoleon was apparent in some of the tantalizingly brief statements of the Founding Fathers. Gouverneur Morris was content to let future generations puzzle out everything that might be implied in his Delphic utterance, "The executive Power shall be vested in a

President . . ." and to let them weigh this against the equally oracular declaration that "all legislative Powers herein granted shall be vested in a Congress. . . ." The overlapping of executive and legislative functions was a deliberate application of eighteenth-century theorizing. So was the distinction drawn between them. (As Montesquieu observed in his *Esprit des Lois,* "When the legislative and executive powers are united . . . there can be no liberty; because apprehensions may arise, lest the same monarch or senate should enact tyrannical laws. . . .")[16] But much in the Constitution was vague, either because the delegates covered up disagreement with a form of words open to multiple interpretation, or because they were not able to anticipate the vast range of difficulties that would arise when the Constitution was tested. They built friction into the document, intentionally, as a safeguard against corruption and dictatorship. Some of the friction generated later they did not foresee and would not have deemed healthy. Some difficulties would be met by constitutional amendments. Four of the twenty-five changes sanctioned by amendment were to deal with election to and tenure of the Presidency—though many commentators feel that the Twenty-second Amendment, restricting the President to two terms, creates more difficulties than it solves.

The Constitution, praised all over the world for its wisdom and longevity, was not a perfect document. Its Antifederalist opponents, though sometimes foolish, inconsistent, and shortsighted, raised questions that have lingered on disquietingly. Could or should one man have the possibility of so much power? Was he entitled to it? Was he superhuman enough to carry such a burden? As the final chapter of this book indicates, a good many experts on American government wish to reopen the old debate as to the viability of a single Executive. Nor were critics of the Constitution entirely unjustified when they grumbled that the Federalists recommended their handiwork in divers ways to divers audiences. Abraham Lincoln once said that the incompatible arguments of a rival politician reminded him of the claim of a Yankee peddler that the clothes he was selling were "large enough for any man, small enough for any boy." In the same way, the Antifederalists could point out that whereas *The Federalist* papers ridiculed Clinton's comparison of the President with the British king, Alexander Hamilton had according to well-founded rumor recommended a strong American

Executive on exactly those grounds. Could the nonsigner Edmund Randolph, remembering Madison's vital role at Philadelphia and in the ratification moves, believe his colleague wholly sincere when Madison told him in May, 1789, that "I see and *politically feel* that [the Presidency] will be the weak branch of the Government"?[17] If Madison was sincere, how could he remain closely associated with the new Federalist administration? How could Jefferson become one of the executive heads, as Secretary of State, in the administration? Were there two or more conceptions of the power of the Presidency, ranging from strong to weak, beneath the apparent consensus of Philadelphia?

The critics of the Constitution were apt to harp tiresomely on the theme of monarchy. The word was often merely a catchall, a convenient term of abuse. Yet they were right to draw the parallel, as Edward S. Corwin stresses. In his words, the Presidency was in fact "designed in great measure to reproduce the monarchy of George III with the corruption left out, and also of course the hereditary feature."[18] In part because the eighteenth century could not imagine a totally nonmonarchical executive, in part because of their reading, in part because they wished to emulate the best features of the British system, and in a few cases because they secretly admired the pomp and circumstance of a mixed monarchical government, the Founding Fathers actually devised a type of elective monarchy, just as critics said. It was as if they had placed the Polish king in the British context, modified in turn by the American context.

The President, though the Constitution nowhere said so, was meant by some of the delegates to symbolize the United States, much as the British crown symbolized the British realm. A President is supposed to *preside,* with dignity and detachment, over affairs from which he is somewhat removed. This quasi-monarchical dream was ideally personified in the shape of George Washington, the "Father of His Country." Better still, he was not an actual father. Having no sons of his own he could never be the founder of a dynasty. Instead Americans could and did name their own sons after him. One such inheritor, the writer Washington Irving, caught the truth of the transfer of regality in his tale of Rip Van Winkle. Rip, falling asleep for twenty years on the eve of the Revolution, returns to his village in bewilderment. He discovers among other alterations that the old Dutch inn is now the Union Hotel. On

BOSTON ALMANACK, OR, THE FEDERAL CALENDAR, For the Year of our REDEMPTION, 1788. Being BISSEXTILE, or Leap-Year, and Twelfth of INDEPENDENCY.

Representation of the FEDERAL CHARIOT.

[See the Explanation, in the next Page.]

Printed by E. RUSSELL, at his Office next Liberty Pole

THERE EDITION.

Pulled by thirteen freemen representing the states, Washington and Franklin are depicted above escorting the Constitution and "Cap . . . of American Freedom" to ratification and the country's "Political salvation."

the inn sign "he recognized . . . the ruby face of King George, under which he had smoked so many a peaceful pipe; but even this was singularly metamorphosed. The red coat was changed for one of blue and buff, a sword was held in the hand instead of a sceptre, the head was decorated with a cocked hat, and underneath was painted in large characters, GENERAL WASHINGTON."

There is a story that at the close of the Philadelphia Convention Benjamin Franklin returned to his lodgings to be greeted by his landlady with the query: "Well, Mr. Franklin, what have you given us, a republic or a monarchy?" His enigmatic answer was: "A republic—if you can keep it."

Almost every book on the Convention or the history of the Presidency cites Pierce Butler's confession that delegates were stimulated to grant "full great" powers by shaping their ideas around the virtuous and awesome figure of General Washington. The conclusion of Butler's letter is less often quoted: "So that the Man, who by his Patriotism and Virtue, Contributed largely to the Emancipation of his Country, may be the Innocent means of its being, when He is lay'd low, oppress'd."[19]

An alarming observation, indicative of quite profound unease.

Above is an invitation to dine with President and Mrs. Washington at their mansion in Philadelphia in 1797. Their formal levees were criticized as being too reminiscent of royal receptions.

Had the Constitution makers invented a workable mechanism of government or a monster—or possibly a mere figurehead behind whom the real struggle for control would be carried on by heads of executive departments, members of the Senate, or others? Only time would show. No matter how ingenious and theoretically perfect the Constitution might be, the office of the President could develop beneficially for the nation only if George Washington accomplished a miracle of discretionary firmness, if his fellow countrymen displayed more than average good sense and harmony, and if luck or Providence smiled upon the risky scheme. Nearly every precedent of history taught that the plan would fail, or at any rate be transformed into a creature unpredictably strange in its lineaments.

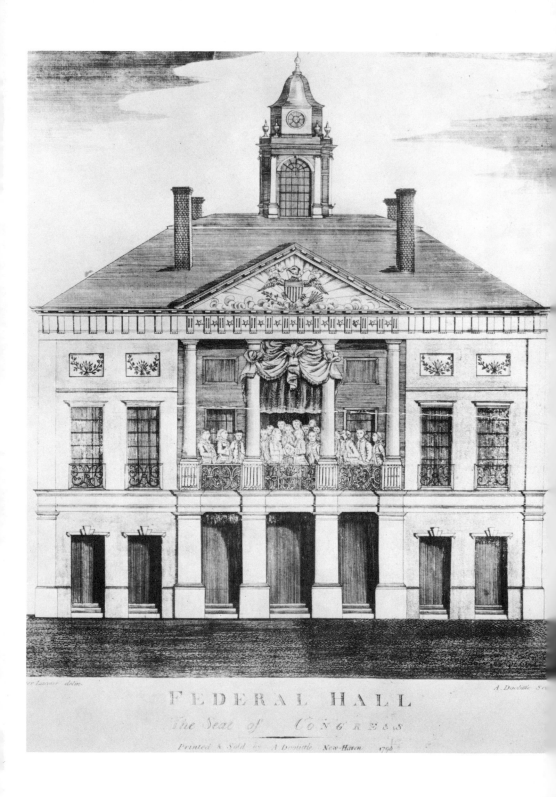

FEDERAL HALL
The Seat of Congress

Printed & Sold by A Doolittle New-Haven 1790

CHAPTER TWO

The Office Defined
and Tested

REXFORD GUY TUGWELL, a former adviser to Franklin D. Roosevelt, says that when the Philadelphia framers approved Article II of the Constitution, the one that describes the President, "none . . . could have had any very definite picture of the official they had created—except that he would be very much like Washington."

Washington himself, to judge from his correspondence, was much impressed by the level of debate at Philadelphia. It was, he told his French friend the Marquis de Lafayette in February, 1788, "little short of a miracle" that delegates from so many different states should have been able to reach agreement on a system "so little liable to well-founded objections." He thought the distribution of responsibility ingenious and prudent. Unlike Lafayette and Jefferson he was not worried by the possibility that a President might continue in office for more than one term. "I can see no

---

Washington's first inauguration took place on the balcony of New York City's Federal Hall on April 30, 1789. After administering the oath, Chancellor Robert R. Livingston cried out, "Long live George Washington, President of the United States," and the spectators echoed his words.

propriety," he informed Lafayette a couple of months later, "in precluding ourselves from the services of any man, who on some great emergency shall be deemed universally, most capable of serving the Public."[1]

General Washington was under no illusion that for the moment he was regarded as the indispensable person for the post. "Indispensable" was the word Alexander Hamilton used. "It is to little purpose," Hamilton went on, "to have *introduced* a system, if the weightiest influence is not given to its firm *establishment,* in the outset." Lafayette among others begged him "not to deny your acceptance of the office of President for the first years. You only can settle that political machine." Every finger pointed at Washington.

His own reactions were understandable. He was flattered to be held in such universal esteem. With more good sense and perhaps a greater freedom of maneuver than some of his successors, he determined—and announced to acquaintances—that he would take up the Presidency "unfettered by promises": he would not feed the expectations "of *any man living* for my assistance to office." He well knew, as he wrote to a correspondent, that "the first transactions of a nation, like those of an individual upon his first entrance into life, make the deepest impression, and . . . form the leading traits in its character."[2] In short, neither he nor any other patriot could decline to lend his services to the new government. When the electors made their choice known, the result was an extraordinary demonstration of confidence, of an order that would never be vouchsafed to any other American Chief Executive. Each elector had two votes. Each gave one of his votes to Washington, making him the unanimous choice for President. (The second in the list of preferences, some way behind, was John Adams of Massachusetts, who would thus become Vice-President.) When Washington considered that among the electors were such Antifederalist warhorses as Patrick Henry, he could indeed feel gratified.

Otherwise he was one of the most reluctant men ever to become President. Some of his reasons were personal. Too much of his life had already been spent in public service, away from his beloved Mount Vernon. He was fifty-seven years old. Though this was only slightly above what was to become the average age of Presidents at inauguration—fifty-four—Washington was weary and in poor health. Above all he was nervous. At Philadelphia he had heard more learned men than he expound the drawbacks of constitutional government. He did not feel he was equipped to deal with the "ocean of difficulties" that lay ahead. It was one thing to practice elementary plantation bookkeeping, quite another to contemplate the tangled mass of America's national and state debts. The strength of local and factional feeling displayed in some of the ratification controversies gave promise of a stormy passage. There were dozens of opportunities for wrangling over the new Constitution: for example, in the reference to "such District (not exceeding ten Miles square) as may, by Cession of particular States, and the Acceptance of Congress, become the Seat of the Government of the United States."

Being human, George Washington had snatched at the faint chance that the government might "be just as happily and effectually carried into execution without my aid." When he received the formal notice of his election and saw that all escape routes were barred, he "bade adieu to Mount Vernon, to private life, and to domestic felicity," he confided to his usually matter-of-fact diary, "with a mind oppressed with anxious and painful sensations."[3]

Within a few weeks he was feeling his way forward, cautiously and amid general acclaim. He was installed in reasonable comfort in a rented house in New York, the temporary Capital of the reconstituted Union. He had taken the oath of office prescribed in the Constitution: "I do solemnly swear that I will faithfully execute the Office of President of the United States, and will to the best of my Ability, preserve, protect and defend the Constitution of the United States." He had read out an appropriately modest yet dignified ten-minute inaugural address. Since Congress was assembling with a dilatoriness characteristic of the old days under the Articles of Confederation, there was no sudden press of business. Washington, and Congress, therefore had time to deal with sundry matters of protocol.

None of these was of tremendous consequence, but in the early stages it seemed important to get things right. Washington consulted the Vice-President and two newly appointed figures, Chief Justice John Jay and Secretary of the Treasury Alexander Hamilton, by inviting their answers to a set of written queries:

1st. Whether a line of conduct, equally distant from an association with all kinds of company on the one hand and from a total seclusion from Society on the other, ought to be adopted by [the President]? and, in that case, how is it to be done?

2nd. What will be the least exceptionable method of bringing any system, which may be adopted on this subject, before the public and into use? . . .

4th. Whether it would tend to prompt impertinent applications and involve disagreeable consequences to have it known, that the President will, every Morning at eight O'clock, be at leisure to give Audience to persons who may have business with him?

5th. Whether, when it shall have been understood that the President is not to give general entertainments in the manner the Presidents of Congress have formerly done, it will be practicable to draw such a line of discrimination in regard to persons, as that Six, eight or ten official characters (including in the rotation the members of both Houses of Congress) may be invited . . . to dine with him on the days fixed for receiving Company, without exciting clamours in the rest of the Community?

6th. Whether it could be satisfactory to the public for the President to make about four great entertainments, in a year on such great occasions as . . . the Anniversary of the Declaration of Independence. . . .

8th. Whether, during the recess of Congress, it would not be advantageous to the interests of the Union for the President to make the tour of the United States, in order to become better acquainted with their principal Characters and internal Circumstances, as well as to be more accessible to numbers of well-informed persons, who might give him useful information and advices on political subjects? . . .[4]

Hamilton's answer, more or less in line with that of Adams and Jay, was that "men's minds are prepared for a pretty high tone in the demeanor of the executive, but I doubt whether for so high a tone as in the abstract might be desirable. The notions of equality are . . . too general and too strong. . . ."[5] This probably accorded with Washington's own sentiments. He had always liked to live in style, dressing handsomely and entertaining on a generous scale. As President he felt that a still higher style, and a more formal one, was necessary. He decided that because of his office he could no longer accept private invitations. In lieu, he and "Lady" Washington (as she was sometimes called) invited others to levees, dinners, theater parties, and ceremonial receptions. Some recipients of these invitations, such as the scornful Senator William Maclay of Pennsylvania, complained that they had too much of the atmosphere of a royal court. The President bowed to his guests—there were no handshakes—and at the dinner table, Maclay reported, conversation was stiff and desultory, since initiative was left to the President, who was not a sparkling conversationalist.

No doubt some of these functions were too solemn and punctilious. Maclay and other critics were however unfair in not realizing that the Presidency was more than the man who occupied it. It was a symbolic office, which the majority of Americans then and later expected to see maintained with a degree of decorum. The striking feature of Washington's queries is the awareness he revealed of public sensitivity. What he was asking was how he might best reconcile the elevation of the office with American ideas of equality, and with the necessity to be accessible to "persons who may have business" with the President.

He was certainly less agitated by problems of protocol than John Adams, who was more of an American democrat than he was given credit for. Adams' writings were often misinterpreted. With his diplomatic experience in London and elsewhere, Adams had no doubt that a monarchy would be wrong for America. As a connoisseur of political systems, however, he appreciated the British solution; he considered European countries not yet ready to dispense with royal government; and he was honest enough to admit that the kings he had met were not more stupid than other men. Nevertheless Adams, the "Duke of Braintree," amused and irked certain members of the Senate over which he presided. He was satisfied when the Senate suggested that the President be officially known as "His Highness, the President of the United States of America, and Protector of their Liberties." He was dismayed when the House of Representatives opted for the simple title—"President of the United States"—used in Article II of the Constitution. "What," he asked, "will the common people of foreign countries, what will the sailors and soldiers say, 'George Washington, President of the United States'? They will despise him to all eternity." Adams was not as silly as the remark makes him sound. He was not talking of the *American* reaction but that of foreigners. People who insist on giving their stay-at-home companions bits of wisdom culled from travel overseas are never popular. But Adams was correct in his own terms. European society, especially that of courts, teemed with titles and ranks. American prestige might be jeopardized without such protective coloration—as American diplomats were to discover when, attending functions in plain clothes instead of court dress, they were now and then mistaken for servants. Nor were complimentary designations unimportant inside the United States. Foreign travelers were to claim that Americans, while lacking in some forms of deference or courtesy, were amazingly pretentious in other ways: for instance, in addressing one another as "Major," "Colonel," even "General"—and of course as "Judge." In this galaxy, "Mr. President" acquired the glamour of understatement.[6]

In his inaugural address Washington announced that he would prefer to receive no salary, although the Constitution spoke of a "compensation": he wished only to be reimbursed for expenses as when he had been commander-in-chief. Perhaps he had been impressed by Benjamin Franklin's argument at Philadelphia against a presidential salary. Franklin maintained from British precedent that if a "Post of Honour" become a "Place of Profit" it would make America's Chief Executive a greedy schemer. The framers rightly believed that this would be more likely to happen if he was *not* paid a reasonable salary. In 1789 Congress fixed the President's annual salary at $25,000. Heads of executive departments were to receive $3,500, and the Vice-President $5,000. The figures were to remain fixed until 1873, when the President's and Vice-President's emoluments were doubled to $50,000 and $10,000 respectively. John Adams, always touchy and a good deal less wealthy than George Washington, no doubt meditated on the apparent conclusion that Congress estimated the value of a President at five times that of his deputy.

Washington's advisers concurred in his view that it would be useful for the President to make extensive trips while Congress was recessed. He undertook a swing around New England in the summer of 1789 (omitting Rhode Island, which he did not visit until it had ratified the Constitution in 1790), and made a long tour of the Southern states in 1791. The performance never became standard for Presidents. John Adams, for example, headed home to Braintree (Quincy) each summer—staying so long that he was accused of neglecting his job. But Monroe imitated Washington by touring the

John Adams was the first but certainly not the last Vice-President to feel that his abilities were being wasted.

North in 1817, the year of his inauguration, and Andrew Jackson went among the Yankees in 1833—receiving an honorary degree from Harvard in the process. To their delight both men were welcomed by immense, applauding crowds. For them as for Washington and for nearly all the Presidents who came after, there was a peculiar thrill in these contacts with the mass of ordinary Americans. In some almost magical way, as if the President were like the giant Antaeus—whose strength depended upon contact with the earth—Presidents who traveled about the Union usually found that they were more refreshed than fatigued by the journeying, the hubbub, and the succession of banquets and testimonial speeches.[7]

Before he was able to set out on his New England visit, Washington began to establish more workaday precedents. Congressional enactments provided for the first executive departments and for the judiciary apparatus of a Supreme Court and a number of federal district and circuit courts. The Department of State absorbed and extended the functions of the former Department of Foreign Affairs. Thomas Jefferson was appointed Secretary of State, though he was still in France and not able to take office until March, 1790. Henry Knox of Massachusetts, a congenial associate of Revolutionary War days, was named Secretary of War. State, War, and Treasury (with Hamilton at its head): these made up the modest total of executive departments in 1789. Congress also created the office of Postmaster General, to control the postal service which Benjamin Franklin had once supervised. It was not an overwhelming task in that formative time. The Postmaster General, Samuel Osgood, was recommended to occupy a desk in the same room with his couple of clerks, so as to be able to keep an eye on their handling of the mails. A more important office in the executive circle was the Attorney Generalship, a post established along with the Supreme Court by the Judiciary Act of 1789. Washington's choice for Attorney General was his fellow Virginian Edmund Randolph, who had got over his objections to the new Constitution. He had been helped to do so by the President's prompt allusion, in the inaugural address, to the obligation of the government to encourage additional guarantees in the shape of amendments. Twelve amendments were in fact proposed in the House of Representatives. Ten were eventually ratified by the states and incorporated in the Constitution as the Bill of Rights in December, 1791.

The executive branch began modestly. Even in 1800, when Adams' administration was nearing its end, the accumulation of paper was so frugal that for the move to the new federal Capital, the entire archives of the executive departments could be stowed in seven packing cases.[8] But this did not mean there was no work to be done. The President was able to employ experienced secretaries, such as William Jackson, who had acted as secretary to the Continental Congress and the Philadelphia Convention. Even so the press of business was considerable, whether with routine involvements such as the signing of commissions or with more intricate questions.

Washington often invited Jefferson, Hamilton, and others to discuss over the breakfast table papers he had sent to them the previous day. Sometimes he would ask officials to report to him individually. Leonard D. White, who has made a close study of these first years, concludes that Washington was a capable, hard-working administrator. His wartime years, when he was after all largely concerned with humdrum matters of supply, equipment, promotion, recruitment, and the like, had obliged him to maintain a copious correspondence. He now seemed very much the master of administrative detail—signifying formal approval of schemes submitted by executive heads, sending outlines of plans to be expanded, seeking opinions on the constitutionality of acts of Congress or on policy matters, and requesting drafts of his various public papers.

When Jefferson became President in 1801 he outlined the system initiated by Washington as a model to be followed by his own heads of department (whose number had been increased by the formation in 1798 of a Navy Department). Every item of business, said Jefferson, had been seen at some stage by President Washington, whether addressed to him or to a particular executive head.

> If a doubt of any importance arose, he reserved it for conference. By this means, he was always in accurate possession of all facts and proceedings in every part of the Union, and to whatsoever department they related; he formed a central point for the different branches; preserved an unity of object and action among them; exercised that participation in the suggestion of affairs which his office made incumbent on him; and met himself the due responsibility for whatever was done.

In part Washington was instituting a mechanism for dealing with the miscellaneous matters of executive government. In part he was seeking guidance on problems that might be of greater import. During his first administration he initially made use of James Madison, who was then a member of the House of Representatives. It was Madison who drafted the first version of Washington's intended Farewell Address, when the President anticipated retirement in 1793. Their contacts became less frequent as Madison developed views in opposition to those of the administration.

Washington also sought the advice of the Supreme Court—only to be told that the Court meant to preserve its separation from the executive branch. When, for instance, he asked the Court to assist him in untangling the legal problems of the Neutrality Proclamation of 1793, he was told that the justices did not consider it their function to advise the Chief Magistrate. It had seemed possible that Washington would form a close liaison with the Senate. As the upper house of Congress, the Senate was somewhat analogous to the governors' councils of colonial days; it numbered only twenty-six men until new states began to be added to the Union—a reasonably intimate circle; and its constitutional duty to "advise and consent," especially on foreign policy questions, required it to have regular dealings with the President. But the separation of powers also envisaged in the Constitution proved stronger than the potential affinity between President and Senate. When the first test came there was a fiasco. Washington wished to make a treaty with Indian tribes. He duly notified the Senate and appeared before it. The treaty was read out. There followed an uneasy silence broken by muttering, while the President waited for senatorial approval and his audience fidgeted until its less bashful spokesmen intimated that they would like time (and privacy) in which to make up their minds. According to Senator Maclay, Washington behaved irritably and impatiently. If so, he quickly learned the lesson. Returning to the Senate after an adjournment, he was elaborately polite—but he never repeated the experiment. Thereafter Presidents would deal with the Senate indirectly, each keeping its distance.

The conferences that Jefferson recalled took place between Washington and his four executive heads: the Secretaries of State, War, and Treasury, and the Attorney General (the Postmaster General was not brought into the circle until 1829, under Andrew Jackson; and he was not officially deemed to be the head of an executive department until an act of 1872). The Vice-President and the Chief Justice had dropped out of the picture. John Adams, after one meeting in 1791 at which he deputized for the absent President, was never again brought in to these high-ranking deliberations. The Attorney General was invited because of the appearance of crucial legal problems—such as the constitutionality of the Bank of the United States, chartered in 1791—and because Edmund Randolph was a gifted man whom the President had known for many years.[9]

In 1792 and 1793 the group met with increasing frequency. Not that they were bosom friends. Jefferson recollected that Washington's executive heads were "equally divided by as marked an opposition of principle as monarchism and republicanism could bring

The first presidential Cabinet consisted of Henry Knox, Secretary of War; Alexander Hamilton, Secretary of the Treasury; Thomas Jefferson, Secretary of State; and Edmund Randolph, Attorney General. This Currier and Ives print was made in 1876.

into conflict." He and Hamilton, he also remembered, were "daily pitted . . . like two cocks." Henry Knox had usually sided with Hamilton, and Randolph was somewhat more independent.

The vital point is that a new governmental body, not mentioned in the Constitution or conceived by the framers, was evolving: the Cabinet. In a way it had been foreseen and was an inevitable outcome; for as Washington himself wrote at the end of the Philadelphia discussions: "The impossibility that one man should . . . perform all the great business of state I take to have been the reason for instituting the great departments, and appointing officers therein to assist the supreme magistrate in discharging the duties of his trust."[10] Charles Pinckney had talked of a "cabinet council" during the debates on a plural executive. In a sense Washington's "Cabinet"—the word seems to have been first applied to the group by Madison in 1793—was such a plural body. The nearest analogy in the President's own mind may have been to the councils of war which he had summoned when he was General Washington. It was military custom not to undertake a major operation without the advice *and* consent of the senior officers in any army. More than once Washington, though commander-in-chief, had rejected his own plan in the face of adverse comment from his generals.

His latter-day habit was to consult his executive heads, require them to vote, and arrive at a sort of collective decision. However, as in his military career, President Washington in Cabinet was much more than *primus inter pares*. Indeed there was an important difference. His generals had been appointed by Congress: his Cabinet was appointed by himself, and could be removed at his sole decision —a power of which he dramatically if sadly availed himself in 1795 when he dismissed Edmund Randolph on suspicion of improper dealings with a French diplomat. Jefferson, too, for all his democratic airs, was clear that the American Cabinet system had proved a success because unlike the Directory in revolutionary France it had a genuine head. Looking back from the perspective of 1811, when he had ceased to be President, Jefferson claimed that his own eight-year administration "presented an example of harmony in a cabinet of six persons, to which perhaps history has furnished no parallel." Yet he doubted whether this rapport would have been possible but for "the power of decision in the President."[11]

So the federal government acquired a Cabinet. By 1800 the institution and its name were accepted without question. It underwent changes while Washington was still President. He had not enjoyed the cleavage between Hamilton and Jefferson. He enjoyed still less the emergence of a party, or "faction," which, coalescing around Madison and Jefferson, was opposed to the general policy of his administration. After Hamilton and Jefferson resigned their offices, and after perhaps wrongly condemning Randolph, Washington announced that if possible he would no longer if he could help it "bring a man into an office of consequence . . . whose political tenets are adverse to the measures which the general government are pursuing." To do so would be "political suicide."[12] This development was to be permanent. Since 1795 Presidents have occasionally appointed Cabinet members who were affiliated to a rival party, but rarely at the risk of creating dissension within the ranks of the government. One exception was the period between 1815 and

1825, when there was no discernible two-party system. Even here, though, John Quincy Adams suffered by retaining men appointed by his predecessor.

Other aspects of the Cabinet were less permanent. Occasionally a Cabinet officer has exerted great influence over a President. But on the whole the Cabinet, an extra-constitutional body, has had a fluctuating existence and has tended to be replaced by other advisers chosen at presidential will either from within a select group of Cabinet favorites or from among men who, like those in Andrew Jackson's "Kitchen Cabinet," held no executive office at all.

In federal appointment as a whole Washington had to reckon with a federal necessity that would govern the calculations of all his successors. The art was to spread appointments geographically, in an effort to placate different sections of the country. For Washington and his immediate successor, John Adams, a more pressing problem was to persuade good men to accept federal posts. According to Stephen G. Kurtz, none of the major figures who served the first two Presidents could avoid financial hardship.[13] At the outset there were floods of applicants for federal employment. Within a few years, however, the cost of living doubled. Alexander Hamilton resigned from the Treasury at the beginning of 1795 mainly because he could no longer support his family, and had to stave off bankruptcy by returning to private law practice. John Marshall of Virginia, having no independent source of income, was forced to decline the invitation to become Attorney General in 1795. Patrick Henry and Charles Cotesworth Pinckney were other prominent Southerners who had to refuse invitations from the President. One result was that the chief posts tended to be filled by men who like Jefferson were relatively well-to-do. But they too were as anxious as Washington to escape the ordeal of office, some because they felt they had already served their time in the Revolution or in the Continental Congress, some because they found government at the state level more rewarding. There might have been a disastrous deterioration in the quality of federal administration had salaries not been increased by the Jeffersonian Republicans. This measure helped to sustain the prestige of federal service. So did various intangible factors, including the social pleasures and the chances for forming connections provided by life in the federal Capital. At any rate, all but the most menial places in the executive bureaus came to be filled by Americans who prided themselves on good family and superior education. Even Andrew Jackson with his zeal for rotation in office did not make much of a dent upon the genteel hierarchy of the District of Columbia. Central bureaucracies, and bureaucrats' wives, do not differ much from generation to generation or from country to country.

President Washington's relations with Congress began with almost an excess of formality on both sides. He benefited, however, from the initial deference paid to him. One issue, that of the President's prime responsibility for appointing to office, might have been thorny. Instead Congress readily conceded him the right to choose his own officials, judges, and diplomats—and the still more crucial right to dismiss appointees without explaining his reasons. In later decades the Senate hardly ever rejected Cabinet nominations, though it sometimes contested the President's will on other appointments. As for the removal power, it had been firmly specified in the statutes establishing the first executive departments and was underlined by the precedents of the first six Presidencies. Though the Senate was to censure Andrew Jackson for having dismissed Treasury Secretary William J. Duane, there is no doubt that he got the better of the purely constitutional argument. The summary of the historical background in his protest to the Senate of April, 1834, is worth quoting. The original debate in Congress, in 1789, said Jackson,

> covered the whole ground, embracing the Treasury as well as all the other Executive Departments, [but] arose on a motion to strike out of the bill to establish a . . . Department of State, a clause declaring the Secretary "to be removable from office by the President of the United States" . . . [It] was perceived that these words did not convey the sense of the House of Representatives in relation to the true source of the power of removal. With the avowed object of preventing any future interference that this power was exercised by the President in virtue of a grant from Congress, when in fact that body considered it as derived from the Constitution, the words . . . were struck out, and . . . a clause was inserted in a provision concerning the chief clerk of the Department, which declared that "whenever the said principal officer shall be removed from office by the President . . . or in any other case of vacancy," the chief clerk should . . . have charge of the papers of the office.

In other words, the change was made "for the express purpose of declaring the sense of Congress that the President derived the power of removal from the Constitution."

An apparently straightforward matter. But not even this point was settled forever. As John Quincy Adams remarked, the American system of federal government with checks and balances was the most complicated in the world. Adams conceded in his *Jubilee of the Constitution* (1839) that the right of removal, "like all other discretionary powers, is susceptible of great abuse." Here he could not resist the temptation to take a sidelong swipe at his old enemy Jackson. But having once been President himself, Adams was quick to defend the office by adding that any procedure curtailing the presidential preogative would be still more liable to abuse.[14] (No matter how negative their conception of the Presidency, every one of the predecessors of Andrew Johnson must have turned in his grave in 1868 when Congress impeached that luckless chief executive on the ground that he had dismissed his Secretary of War in violation of a congressional law.)

One reason Andrew Jackson's critics in the Senate challenged his removal power was that the Secretary of the Treasury occupied a special position among the executive heads. The beginning of this story, like that of so many, harks back to President Washington's time. The underlying truth of the story is still argued about by historians. It concerns the role of Alexander Hamilton as envisaged by himself, Jefferson, Congress, and his President. In all likelihood Hamilton did think of, and try to encourage, a pattern of American executive government based on that of Britain, in which Washington would represent the king and himself the prime minister. He was encouraged to hold some such view by the knowledge that England's vigorous young prime minister, William Pitt, also directed financial policy as chancellor of the exchequer and first lord of the treasury. The act of Congress creating Hamilton's department seemed to require him to maintain a special relationship with the House, which he interpreted as requiring him to be present at debates like a minister in Parliament. Problems over debts, banks, currency, and the like were both urgent and fundamental. The President was no expert on economics. Hamilton, while financially honest, was an unscrupulous as well as an extremely industrious and quick-witted person who could not resist

GEORGE   WASHINGTON
PRESIDENT.
1792.

This medal commemorated an Indian treaty signed in 1792.

meddling in Jefferson's domain of foreign affairs or attempting to run the War Department. With all this he was elaborately courteous to Washington.

According to Jefferson, who made his views clear to the President, Hamilton was sheltering behind the Washington prestige and treating the President as a ceremonial figure of no real substance. This theory would seem to be borne out by Hamilton's famous remark, after the President's death, that Washington was "*an Aegis very essential to me.*" Among recent historians, Joseph Charles, Jr., considers Hamilton to have been the dominant figure among Washington's advisers. Certainly Washington accepted Hamilton's main proposals, despite the opposition of Jefferson and of numerous thoughtful Americans including Madison. A second historian, Alexander DeConde, portrays Washington as "slow of mind," and says "he took his ideas and theories, without much question, from Hamilton."

It is intriguing to consider how the Presidency might have evolved if Hamilton had been able to take himself at his own valuation. An exceptionally ambitious and brilliant sequence of Treasury secretaries might have assumed executive initiative, relegating the President to a mainly honorific role like that of the president in other republican systems. Or, of course, the Secretaryship of State might have become the focus of real power; it was the senior executive post, and especially in the first years was thought to embrace not only foreign but sundry domestic responsibilities (such as the new federal mint). Two factors appear to have regulated matters differently. One reinforced by the unequivocal statement in the Constitution was the chilly response of Congress to Hamilton's overtures, (Article I, Section 6) that "no Person holding any Office under the United States, shall be a Member of either House during his Continuance in Office." Hamilton's efforts to present his recommendations on the floor of the House were rebuffed. In January, 1790, Congress decided that all future reports from the Secretary of the Treasury were to be submitted in written form.

The second factor, already touched on, was Washington's hold over his executive heads. Those who ridiculed him as ignorant and ponderous took care not to do so within reach of his formidable wrath; indeed most of them waited until he was dead. He had too commanding a presence to allow familiarity, let alone condescension. He was too experienced to be taken in by flattery or specious arguments. Where he failed to grasp the subtleties of a problem he was careful to listen to contrary opinions. And while he depended upon Hamilton, Hamilton undoubtedly depended upon him. As Jefferson testified, the first President held the balance between bitterly incompatible viewpoints. The position was uncomfortable, yet oddly enough it gave him additional stature. Neither group could afford to do without him at the head of affairs. Both begged him, wholeheartedly if for complex reasons, to remain for a second term. In consenting he settled the future pattern of the Presidency in several ways. One of these was to ensure that the President was master in his own executive domain. In Washington's second term the splenetic divisions of party politics perhaps made him more susceptible to the opinions that Hamilton—now a private citizen— voiced in his letters to the President. But that situation may be left until Chapter 4, which deals with politics and the Presidency.

Relations between Washington and his legislature developed politely in various ways. He vetoed only two congressional bills during his eight years of power, confining himself to a couple of minor issues and explaining that they conflicted with the Constitution or were undesirable. There seemed little cause here for alarm over entrusting the President with this semi-regal attribute (though incidentally, if those who sought to draw a parallel between the President and the British monarch had wished to make the comparison favorable, they could have disclosed that the royal veto had lain unused since the early eighteenth century). The next five Presidents were equally sparing in their reliance upon vetoes.

Nor was there much trouble over the annual State of the Union messages that Presidents Washington and Adams delivered in person before Congress. The only initial awkwardness came from exaggerated formality: Congress at first tended to answer messages from the President by tendering messages of appreciation in return. Later, as partisan feeling became intense, there were grumblings that the ceremonial of Washington's annual addresses too closely resembled the British "Speech from the Throne" that opened each session of Parliament. With this criticism in mind, Jefferson abandoned the Washington-Adams precedent and simply transmitted his messages to Congress to be read aloud by a clerk. His method was to be followed for more than a hundred years, until in 1913 Woodrow Wilson reverted to the ancient style—not to revive a ritual but to demonstrate his conception of a re-energized Presidency.

Congressional prickliness sometimes took mean and foolish shapes. On some early issues, however, their jealousy of presidential style was to prove wiser than they realized. For instance, Alexander Hamilton's draft in 1792 of an "Act for Establishing a Mint" stipulated that Washington's head should be stamped on all coins of the United States. A gracious gesture, for which there was plenty of precedent. But it was the wrong type of precedent, the type applied to reigning monarchs. The act was amended. Thenceforward, with an aversion to "over-mighty" symbols that other new nations would have been well advised to imitate, the United States commemorated rather than celebrated its Chief Magistrates. Not until they were dead might their likenesses be reproduced on currency or (a later, consequential decision) on postage stamps. It

After his unsuccessful, one-term Presidency, John Quincy Adams became a congressman and for many years was an eloquent and uncompromising opponent of slavery. This daguerreotype was made shortly before his death in 1848.

could be added that the nation carried caution to an excess of parsimony in not making financial provision for ex-Presidents. Washington was no pauper and lived only two and half years after he relinquished the Presidency: John Adams had to scrape along for a further quarter of a century. Jefferson, Madison, and Monroe, who survived after office for seventeen, nineteen, and six years respectively, were far from prosperous. Not until 1958 were pensions authorized for former Presidents. And even if money was no problem, a suitable occupation was. For a long while to come the majority of ex-Presidents either buried themselves in retirement, some to write justificatory memoirs, or hung about the corridors of power in hopes of re-election. John Quincy Adams was one of the few to plunge into a second active career—in his case as a redoubtable member of the House of Representatives.[15]

The precedents set by Presidents Washington and Adams in the field of foreign policy are hard to interpret, because both men were challenged within their own circle of advisers and because party feeling was as violent as it has ever been in American history. Both Presidents, it may be said, acted promptly, intelligently, and courageously—Adams in such a spirit of defiant rectitude that he alienated most of his Federalist supporters as well as his Republican opponents, and so denied himself the chance of re-election in 1800. There was by no means universal acceptance of the powers they appeared to be claiming on behalf of the executive branch. But then the situation was dangerous and intractable. The United States owed an actual and a figurative debt to France for assistance in the Revolutionary War, and was allied to France by the treaty of 1778. When the French Revolution erupted, all men of liberal views rejoiced. When the Revolution became more extreme and the French not only established a republic but guillotined their king, Louis XVI, and his queen, Marie Antoinette, Washington had to mediate between furiously divergent lines of policy. To recognize the French republic in its new phase was to sanction extremism and jeopardize American neutrality. To withhold recognition, entirely or in part, was to incur the enmity of the only other republican creation of the modern world, and to favor monarchical England in the Franco-British war which had broken out and which was to continue with only two short interruptions until the final overthrow of Napoleon at Waterloo in 1815.

Washington did not manage to solve the insoluble problem of presidential control of foreign policy. His Neutrality Proclamation of 1793, however, was the first of many such presidential directives to the nation. His decision here, like his decision not to receive the French republican-revolutionary minister Citizen Edmond Genèt, amounted in the eyes of Jefferson and Madison to an infringement on the privileges of the legislature. Congress was the branch that decided whether to declare war. A presidential neutrality proclamation prejudged the issue. A presidential claim that the duty of formally receiving representatives included the power to refuse to receive them, if allowed, would mean that the Executive could present Congress with a *fait accompli,* by having prejudged whether or not to enter into friendly relations with another country.

Washington did not entirely carry the day; Congress asserted itself by passing the Neutrality Act of 1794—again, the first of several such demonstrations of congressional control over war and peace. Nor was Hamilton's far-reaching analysis of presidential authority well received at the time. He claimed that there was a vital and intentional difference between legislative and executive powers in the wording of the Constitution. Legislative power was limited by the words "herein granted." Since there was no similar qualification in the grant of executive power, Hamilton said, the President was therefore empowered to do anything not specifically prohibited in the Constitution. Gouverneur Morris' "joker" had come to the surface. It remained a joker in the pack, though some players of the federal government game would insist that it was not a true card at all.

Nevertheless, with the emphatic underpinning of Hamilton, President Washington held his general position. In his second administration he emerged successfully from an angry challenge by the House of Representatives. He had sent John Jay to make a treaty with Britain. The resultant document, signed in 1794, was highly unpopular. The House demanded that Washington furnish copies of Jay's instructions and all other papers relevant to the negotiation. Of the arguments advanced the most plausible was that of Albert Gallatin, a man almost as resourceful as Hamilton, who was to serve as Jefferson's Secretary of the Treasury. Gallatin contended that according to the Constitution treaties had the force of law and therefore were a form of law. The House was a lawmaking body; hence it must have a say in the ratification of treaties or would be surrendering its legislative authority. A little perplexed, and annoyed by the truculence of Congress, Washington consulted Hamilton. The answer he got was what he no doubt wished to hear, though with an additional theory which must have stiffened his resolve—that the opposition might be collecting material in order to consider impeaching the President. At any rate he used Hamilton's words to reply impenitently that he could not furnish the papers. The concurrence of the House was not required to validate a treaty; he was obliged to maintain "the boundaries fixed by the Constitution."

In the early inconclusive struggles between Executive and legislature Washington and Adams were aided not merely by the pseudonymous writings of Hamilton but also by such Federalist stal-

Western Pennsylvanians, rebelling against a tax on whiskey in 1794, jeer at a tarred and feathered federal agent in this drawing. Washington proved

warts as John Marshall. At the height of Adams' troubles over his policy toward France, Marshall declared forthrightly in the House that "the President is the sole organ of the nation in its external relations, and its sole representative with foreign nations." Fighting words at the time, they were gradually to become a commonplace of American constitutionalism. One consideration that weakened congressional intransigence was that ordinary American citizens were showing a disturbing aptitude for conducting private diplomacy. Congress actually passed a law against such enterprises—and in so doing weakened its own case, for the law (popularly known as the "Logan Act" and still, incidentally, on the statute book) was entitled "An Act to Prevent Usurpation of Executive Functions."[16]

In domestic as in foreign affairs, Washington upheld the dignity of his office. His critics alleged that, egged on by Hamilton, he took altogether too strong a stand in suppressing the "whiskey rebels"— western Pennsylvanians who revolted against a tax on their chief product. Washington called out the militia, threatened to march at

the strength and determination of the new federal government by sending troops to quell the insurrection.

their head, and personally inspected the force before it went off (though not after all under his command). But he had done nothing unconstitutional. What he had done was to demonstrate the power of the federal government—and thereby, the power of the Presidency. Similarly, in the period of strained relations with France between 1797 and 1799, when war seemed imminent, John Adams displayed the inclinations of a strong President despite derision and abuse. He called Congress into special session and requested an increase in the size of the regular army. Though he was an unpopular and little-respected figure when his term ended, he could feel that he had sustained the honor of his family and that of the presidential office. Being an Adams, he rated the one as highly as the other. But then, so had George Washington; and he was not going to be outdistanced by George Washington if he could help it.

Among the Founding Fathers, Pierce Butler had feared that George Washington might be the innocent means by which his country would be "oppress'd." Too much trust was being placed in the office of President because he would occupy it: no one would be able to succeed him. Looking back on the evolution of the Presidency, we are impressed by the smoothness of succession. Washington was followed by his Vice-President, John Adams, in 1797, Adams by his Vice-President, Jefferson, in 1801. Then came a run of "inheritance"—Madison from Jefferson, Monroe from Madison, John Quincy Adams from Monroe—in which each President was followed by his Secretary of State. All but the Adamses had two terms in office; all but the Massachusetts Adamses were from Virginia.

The succession *was* smooth, considering what opportunities for discord there were and how abrupt and fearful, at least for the Federalists, was the so-called Revolution of 1800, when their party had to yield office to the Jeffersonian Republicans. The tact and the indication of a basic harmony in Jefferson's inaugural address of 1801 ("We are all Republicans, we are all Federalists") have been properly emphasized in surveys of American history.

But we should not forget how intricate was the problem of succession, and in particular how indeterminate was the role of the Vice-President. As Lucius Wilmerding, Jr., explains in *The Electoral College,* the framers of the Constitution gave much thought to the question of what should happen if the single Executive, in the person of the President, should fall ill or die. Their solution was to fasten upon the Vice-President. The Constitution (Article II, Section I) makes this plain: "In Case of the Removal of the President from Office, or of his Death, Resignation, or Inability to discharge the Powers and Duties of the said Office, the Same shall devolve on the Vice President. . . ."

The difficulty was that a Vice-President might suddenly find himself burdened with the full responsibility of the Chief Magistracy. The United States could not afford to let such a burden devolve upon a person of mediocre ability. It was imperative to ensure that the Vice-President would be a man worthy of the Presidency. The method adopted was in theory brilliantly effective. Article II of the Constitution defines the mode of choosing the Chief Executive:

> Each State shall appoint . . . a Number of Electors, equal to the whole number of Senators and Representatives to which the State may be entitled. . . .

The Electors shall meet in their respective States, and vote by Ballot for two Persons, one of whom at least shall not be an Inhabitant of the same State with themselves.

The Article goes on to specify the procedure by which, if no candidate should have the necessary majority, or if there should be a tie, the ultimate choice should rest with the House of Representatives (or with the Senate if there were a tie in the votes for candidates in line for the Vice-Presidency after the President had been chosen). Despite these intricacies, the intention is clear: "In every Case, after the Choice of the President, the Person having the greatest Number of Votes of the Electors shall be the Vice President."[17]

In short, the framers deliberately refrained from distinguishing between the President and Vice-President, at least so far as election was concerned. The electors would each vote for two men, either of whom they would be happy to see as President. As Senator Uriah Tracy of Connecticut defined the system in 1803, the runner-up "can have no existence until the first character is designated, and then seems to be discovered, not elected." By this beautifully simple mechanism they would obtain, the New Jersey Federalist Elias Boudinot said, "the second best character in the Union to fill the place of the first, in case it should be vacated by any unforeseen accident." The succession would be immediate and smooth. Not only would the Vice-President be a man of parts: through his previous activity as president of the Senate he would be familiar with the working of the government.

The mechanism failed. John Adams was the first of a long line of "second-best characters" who felt they had been consigned to limbo. After less than a year in office he confided to his wife: "My country has, in its wisdom, contrived for me the most insignificant office that ever the invention of man contrived or his imagination conceived."[18] He was a nobody, and an embarrassing nobody, mistrusted by the Senate and superfluous in the executive branch. It was not out of rudeness but simply because the Vice-President had no useful role that Washington excluded John Adams from the intimate discussions of the Cabinet.

Worse still for Adams' self-esteem, a few more years disclosed that the electors took the job at his own valuation. They did not plump for the two best men they could think of. Instead they began to discriminate sharply between the man they wanted for President

In 1800 the House of Representatives decided that Jefferson, not Aaron Burr (above), should be President; they had received an equal number of electoral votes, although Burr had been a vice-presidential candidate.

and the other figure for whom they were also obliged to expend a vote. The elections of 1789 and 1792 worked satisfactorily because all were agreed on their candidate for the Presidency. In 1796 and 1800 there was no such unanimity: when the nation was split between Federalist and Republican camps, the system disclosed its weaknesses. If the electors of one party gave all their votes equally to two men, and they turned out to be the stronger party, things could still go badly wrong. A few additional votes from other electors might give the Presidency to the victors' second choice. Or, as happened in 1796, the Presidency might go to a leading figure of one party (Adams) and the Vice-Presidency to one of his chief rivals (Jefferson). The first of these two unwelcome alternatives threatened the country in 1800, when the Republican electors gave an equal number of votes to Jefferson and to Aaron Burr, and the decision passed to the House of Representatives. Burr had been placed on the ticket only as a gesture of gratitude for his labors on behalf of the party in New York. At most he was to be Vice-President. The Republicans as a whole were as dismayed as the Federalists at the prospect of having him as President.

When Jefferson was at last installed in office—the Federalists in Congress had decided to support him rather than Burr—the Republicans began to press for a constitutional amendment. Their worry was that in the 1804 election the Federalists would, by juggling electoral votes, secure a Federalist Vice-President and so repeat the Republican maneuver of 1796. The Federalists argued for abiding by the intentions of the framers. Senator James Hillhouse of Connecticut, for example, said: "Your amendment proposes to persuade the people that there is only one man of correct politics in the United States. Your Constitution provides a remedy against this, and says you must bring forward two."[19] In vain: the Twelfth Amendment—specifying that the electors were to cast two distinct ballots, one for President and one for Vice-President—was fashioned in Congress, passed on to the states, and duly ratified, in time to ensure that Thomas Jefferson was re-elected to the Presidency in 1804, and that his Vice-President was of the same political persuasion. On this occasion the oft-renewed precedent was set: the Vice-President (George Clinton of New York), while a man of reasonable standing, was selected not because he was considered of presidential timber but because he could lend geographical or other support to the ticket.

In 1797 Jefferson, who never relished the public exposure of high office, wrote to an acquaintance that he nevertheless enjoyed being Vice-President. "The second office of the government is honorable and easy," he said, "the first is but a splendid misery."[20] He and Adams were undoubtedly distinguished holders of the "second office." But after 1804 its stature dwindled. With a few exceptions, Vice-Presidents would be picked because they came from such-and-such a state, or because the party wished to put some old warhorse out to graze. After Jefferson (until 1968) only one ex-Vice-President, Martin Van Buren, would gain the Presidency by election instead of inheritance through death. The names of some of the Vice-Presidents illustrate the decline. Only a scholar would be likely to have much to say about Daniel D. Tompkins, who entered office in 1817, or Richard M. Johnson (1837), or George M. Dallas (1845), or William R. King (1853). The contrast between the renown of Abraham

*The White House was still unfinished when John Adams moved in in 1800
and out a few months later. Here is architect James Hoban's design for
the President's Mansion.*

Lincoln and the obscurity of his first Vice-President, Hannibal
Hamlin, speaks for itself.[21]

Among other significant developments during the first fifteen to
twenty years of the new government was a change in its location.
After some debate and bargaining the site of the federal district
was settled upon along the Potomac, between Maryland and Virginia. The first two sessions of Congress were held in New York.
From 1791 until 1800, while the new site was being laid out, Philadelphia was the national Capital. The move to the permanent Capital, named Washington, D.C., in honor of the "Father of his
People," took place in the autumn of 1800. To some of its pioneering inhabitants it seemed a good deal less permanent than New
York or Philadelphia. John Adams arrived there at the beginning
of November, in the melancholy closing months of his Presidency.
His wife joined him a couple of weeks later. She reported to their
daughter that though the Executive Mansion was habitable, it was
barely so: "There is not a single apartment finished. . . . We have
not the least fence, yard, or other convenience 'outside,' and the
great unfinished audience room I make a drying-room of, to hang
up the clothes in. The principal stairs are not up, and will not be
this winter."[22]

A cheerless winter for the Adamses, on top of their other disappointments. Perhaps it is no wonder that he vacated the White

House (as it was soon to be known) with such unseemly haste that he did not wait to attend the inaugural ceremony for his successor Thomas Jefferson but hurried away northward to his native Massachusetts. (Twenty-eight years later his son John Quincy Adams also left the Capital without attending the inauguration of Andrew Jackson. They have been the only two Presidents thus to reveal the exasperation that several have nourished inwardly.) For a good many years the federal Capital, especially to foreign observers, would seem peculiarly rural and makeshift. Washington, D.C., was the Brasilia of its day.

Still, by degrees it took on life and form. Less than four years after Abigail Adams hung the washing in "the great unfinished audience room," Jefferson entertained a hundred guests there at a July Fourth celebration. Instead of bowing, like his Federalist predecessors, he shook hands to indicate the informality of the Republican regime. The change was bound to come, in a society that was growing demonstratively more egalitarian. But it was to leave all those who occupied the White House after him with an occupational ailment, the penalty of official cordiality, whose symptoms were aching arms and swollen fingers.

Jefferson's informality on this occasion symbolized an attempt to put the ship of state "on the Republican tack." He did not for example end his Presidency as Washington had done by issuing a Farewell Address: that had too regal a style for the Jeffersonians. In dress, in general behavior, and in his close contacts with his associates in Congress, Jefferson showed that he did not believe the presidential mold had hardened.

In some respects he was correct, though it remained to be seen whether his experiments would conduce to an efficient government. Some problems awaited a future crisis. There was, for instance, the question of what would happen when a President died in office. This happened in 1841, only a month after the inauguration of William Henry Harrison. Perhaps the Whigs had made a mistake in picking a candidate who was then sixty-eight years of age—the oldest on record. Perhaps Harrison had made a mistake in exposing himself to the elements for an hour and three quarters while he read the longest inaugural address on record—and caught a cold that developed into pneumonia. At any rate the Whigs found themselves with a Vice-President, John Tyler, who subscribed to

John Tyler became the first Vice-President to take over the Presidency upon the death of a Chief Executive. In the broadside at right mourning President William Henry Harrison, Tyler is unequivocally called President, but at first some officials regarded him as acting President only.

none of their policies. The country found itself confronted with a constitutional riddle: what was the status of Tyler?

Students of American constitutional history have maintained that the Founding Fathers did not intend that the Presidency should actually devolve upon the Vice-President, but simply that the "powers and duties" of the office should be entrusted to him as an emergency measure. Ex-President John Quincy Adams was among the contemporaries who asserted that Tyler had no right to call himself the President when he was only "Acting President." Tyler did not hesitate, however, to assume the office. He was sustained in his view by Secretary of State Daniel Webster; eight weeks later Congress recognized him as full President; and the issue soon died down, although it left a bitter taste in the mouths of such Whig spokesmen as Henry Clay. No subsequent Vice-President was chal-

A NATIONAL HYMN

TUNE CHINA.   BY L. GRIFFING

Composed to be sung on the 14th. of May 1841: the day recommended by the PRESIDENT, to be set apart as a day of fasting and prayer, by the people of the United States, on account of the death of Gen. Wm. H. Harrison.

1.

ALMIGHTY GOD! Oh, hear our moan!
　We lift our voice in prayer;
Oh! make our country's cause thy own,
　Take us beneath thy care.

2.

We mourn our Chieftain laid in dust;
　We feel thy chastening rod:
We know thy judgments all are just:
　But oh! have mercy GOD!

3.

Be thou our council, thou our guide,
　Keep us from every ill;
And may the man call'd to Preside,
　Learn, and obey thy will.

lenged in assuming the presidential office.[23]

The office in fact was to be the center of seemingly endless controversy. Nevertheless the first few incumbents, sometimes consciously and sometimes unwittingly, defined its basic nature. Their successors, whether or not they were fully aware of the process, and whether or not they liked what was happening, were to be fixed within certain intangible yet real modes. There was a genetic element in the office. The business of protocol is a case in point. The Federalist initiators approved of a degree of ceremony: Jefferson and Madison did not. Yet with James Monroe the White House saw a level of formality and even magnificence that no Federalist President could have surpassed.

President after President was to discover that the post was beset with cares. After the measured succession of the Virginia Dynasty, the Presidency was in theory open to all comers. The desire to be President afflicted American men by scores and hundreds. The handful who gained the prize found it, as Jefferson had foretold, a "splendid misery." There were the major battles with Congress and the constant lesser guerrilla clashes. There was the aggravation of attack by waspish journalists and pamphleteers. There was the sickening importunacy of office seekers, the lack of privacy, the strain of social functions (sometimes, as Rexford Tugwell has remarked, the social aspects impose an almost intolerable strain on presidential couples unused to entertainment on the grand scale; several Presidents' wives have cracked up).[24] There was the grind of routine, and the swamping of small office staffs whenever an emergency increased the press of business. There was the dense, clammy heat of the Washington summer climate. Almost no President who was re-elected had a second term as popular as his first. This was true of Washington, of Jefferson, of Madison, and of Jackson. Euphoria yielded to acrimony. The knowledge that no President would care to challenge Washington's precedent after eight years had much to do with this recurrent phenomenon of second-term gloom. Once the end was in sight for a President and his power was waning, criticism became sharper and more open, applause briefer and more perfunctory. Then there was the final anticlimax of being out of office—a relief, but so sudden a relief that some Presidents seemed to languish afterward and die prematurely.[25]

Jefferson was once present at a meeting in 1793 at which George

Washington exploded with anger on hearing of a recent piece of scurrility aimed at him. The President declared that he had "never repented but once the having slipped the moment of resigning his office, & that was every moment since, that by god he had rather be on his farm than be made *emperor of the world,* and yet they were charging him with wanting to be a king." Near the end of his life John Adams reflected that "no man who ever held the office of President would congratulate a friend on obtaining it." Adams added, repeating an aphorism of Louis XIV's: "He will make one man ungrateful, and a hundred men his enemies, for every office he can bestow." In 1807 Jefferson said: "I am tired of an office where I can do no more good than many others, who would be glad to be employed in it. To myself, personally, it brings nothing but unceasing drudgery and daily loss of friends."[26]

Those who followed Jefferson have left similar testimony. One consolation did buoy up the Adamses and Jeffersons and bring them together again, although they were not able to savor it until the calm of old age. They were the forerunners, the Founding Fathers. They had known bitter rivalry; they had not always been discreet or sensible. But they could finally believe that they had fought together in more than one sense. Through their strife they had fashioned a nation and a government, a government of laws whose precise meaning was open to debate but whose import was beyond question. Believing this, the veterans of Philadelphia and primordial Washington, D.C., could believe that posterity would thank them even if their contemporaries failed to do so.

CHAPTER THREE

The Presidency Consolidated

In the early days of the American republic Alexander Hamilton predicted that a time would come "when every vital question of state will be merged in the question, 'Who will be the next President?'"[1] His prediction was borne out, in large part because the Presidency became the apex of the politcal contest between excited and organized national parties. But there were other factors.

Among these the first in time and perhaps also in significance was the Presidency of George Washington. In his second administration he was the target of considerable criticism. For some years after his death Jeffersonian Republicans hesitated to sing his praises, since his name and reputation were being appropriated by the Federalists for partisan purposes—for example, in the Washington Benevolent Societies, which they promoted. These were political clubs despite their pretense of benevolent patriotism. Soon this

---

Washington's unequaled prestige was a key factor in the initial success of the Presidency. He was not without critics, however, a fact forgotten by those who deified him after his death. At left is one elaborate memorial to the first Chief Executive.

factionalism dropped away: thenceforward his name would be associated with the national Capital, with towns, counties, lakes, and mountains, or with the blameless "Washingtonian" temperance movement. Washington was once more the Father of his Country. In retrospect, all Americans were ready to pay tribute to him. His birthday was a national holiday; his Farewell Address was read aloud each year in Congress.

With the decades these rituals would become automatic and lose some of their impact. But they were not empty gestures, even if those who participated gradually forgot exactly whom, or rather what, they were honoring. They were in truth honoring the establishment of a stable society—a society created through the necessarily disrupting process of a revolution. In *The First New Nation* Seymour Martin Lipset illuminates the situation by relating the history of the young United States to that of the many subsequent countries, particularly those in twentieth-century Africa, that have likewise, on achieving independence, had to face the less dramatic but more complex task of existing and thriving under a new instrument of government. There is, as Lipset says, an acute difficulty in legitimizing the new authority hard on the heels of repudiating the old. Authority cannot be created overnight, nor can it be imposed: it must be willingly recognized by those subject to it, through their active participation. Success is possible only where the population is broadly united and sympathetic to parliamentary mechanisms. If these conditions are lacking, the result will be an authoritarian government with no organic base of support.

A further complication is that new countries also need symbols around which to rally decisive leadership, and a sense of an actual *transfer* of authority from the former ruling power. A daunting set of conditions, rarely fulfilled. They were fulfilled, however, for the United States; and George Washington was, next to the general high level of American political sophistication, the prime agent. Having seen him, Abigail Adams enthused that he looked more like a king than George III, whom she had also seen.

His actions as President were commendable. Yet as a symbol of new sovereign authority he was almost more important to the United States for what he was than for what he did. The hiatus was over, the machine was running again, the movement was forward. We can begin to see how much his presence did for the United

States by conjecturing what the Constitution would have looked like, and whether it would have been ratified at all, if he had clung to his initial unwillingness to attend the Philadelphia Convention. We can guess what a jolt the new government would have suffered if President Washington had died from either of the two serious illnesses that laid him low during his first term. Or if he had felt too much like a king, or an angry party chieftain bent on revenge, and had determined to offer himself again for election in 1800—as a few desperate Federalists urged him to do—what chaos might not have befallen America?

Instead there came the healing, bandaging influences of mere usage, the lulling of repetitious ritual, the absorption in the daily detail of government, the increment of folklore and precedent and tradition. (The long continuance of John Marshall at the head of the Supreme Court helped greatly in forming what Bagehot called the "cake of custom." The Court's decisions were not welcomed by everyone, but they were accepted, and in emphasizing the centrality of the federal government, they indirectly asserted the centrality of the executive branch. Though Jefferson detested Marshall, he never made a frontal attack upon him—knowing that like Washington, John Marshall was a person who by virtue of his office was enveloped in an impersonal dignity.) Familiarity of this kind bred not contempt but acceptance and respect.

An interesting conversation took place between Adams and Jefferson in 1800, at a moment when it was becoming clear that Jefferson had won the presidential election. Adams said to him: "Well, I understand that you are to beat me in this contest, and I will only say that I will be as faithful a subject as any you will have." Jefferson replied: "Mr. Adams . . . this is no personal contest between you and me. Two systems of principles . . . divide our fellow citizens into two parties. . . . Were we both to die today, tomorrow two other names would be in the place of ours, without any change in the motion of the machinery. Its motion is from its principle, not from you or myself."[2] Neither man was perhaps entirely sincere or candid. Adams' comment sounds double-edged; he may have used the word "subject" sarcastically and have intended to imply that perhaps Jefferson would have no real following. Yet both men found it convenient to believe in the continuity of systems.

In his *Democracy in America,* written on the basis of a visit during Andrew Jackson's administration, Alexis de Tocqueville said that the Presidency was not of great importance, since all legislation was controlled by Congress. This we may take as one of Tocqueville's errors, or at least failures of vision, caused by relying too much on the views of such anti-Jackson men as Daniel Webster. But he was correct when he pointed to the nationwide interest in political issues, and to the remarkable American propensity for setting up voluntary organizations. Americans were, so to speak, addicted to such involvements: a healthy addiction greatly encouraged by the profound constitutionalism of George Washington and those who immediately followed him. He and they continually emphasized that their nation needed time in which to take shape. Every year counted. Each administration added to the fabric. Those who watched Abraham Lincoln in 1861, as he faced the gravest crisis since 1776, were not greatly impressed. Henry Adams recalled the spectacle of Lincoln at the inaugural ball, where he was made awkward by his white kid gloves. Seeing the President's "plain, plowed face," Adams said that he needed all the experience he could get, and that it would not be enough.[3] Perhaps no other Presidents have suffered the full dread of unexplored hazards that Washington and Lincoln had to overcome. But at least Lincoln knew that there *was* a Union to revere and defend. There was comfort, if only a limited comfort, in the awareness that fifteen Presidents had held office before him. Several had confronted and survived possible disaster. Several had ennobled the office—or perhaps it was the office that ennobled them.

The sequence had been maintained thanks to a certain amount of good luck. Washington did *not* die in 1789 or 1790. There was no sudden transfer of the Presidency until Harrison's death in 1841. But Tyler, Harrison's newly elevated Vice-President, was in a somewhat precarious position. Luck preserved "His Accidency," and the stability of the Chief Magistracy, in 1844, when he narrowly missed death through an explosion aboard the frigate *Princeton,* which killed the Secretary of State. Luck had attended President Jackson nine years earlier: when a madman armed with two pistols tried to shoot him at pointblank range, both weapons misfired. It is possible that luck, and prudence, saved the life of President-elect Lincoln. There were strong rumors of a plot to kill him. If there was a plot it was circumvented. Although he was jeered at for having

John Tyler, who had become President when Harrison died, was almost killed himself in 1844 when a gun exploded aboard a frigate he was visiting. Fortunately, Tyler was belowdecks at the time, but as this lithograph shows, several people in his party were fatally injured, including the Secretary of State, Abel P. Upshur.

taken undignified or cowardly evasive action en route to Washington, he was quite right to be cautious. His death before he was inaugurated might have brought about the collapse of the Union. Precarious enough in 1861, the national government would have been further weakened if any of these previous alarms had ended fatally.

The example of George Washington and the stature of some of his successors, the organic rooting of the government over the decades, a measure of sheer luck: these contributed to the consolidation of the Presidency. But was consolidation continuous, or was it promoted by the "strong" Presidents and set back by "weak" ones? One difficulty in offering an answer is that a great man such as Jefferson was not necessarily a great President. Or he may be deemed a great President because his posthumous prestige increased the renown of the Presidency. Another problem is to decide how any one individual can ever be said to define the character of his era. In his book *Andrew Jackson: Symbol for an Age* (1955), John William Ward presents a persuasive interpretation of a man who embodied rather than set the tone of his times. Some historians believe that America's history, at least for the nineteenth century, has been distorted through being portrayed as a history largely of the federal government and of presidential administrations. They would concede that Americans were often engaged in political controversy and were excited by the quadrennial drama of presidential elections. But these historians argue that such concern was intermittent and that it was in fact usually a concern with local issues and the attention to be paid to them in the otherwise remote purlieus of the federal Capital. Or it could be claimed that after its initial establishment the Presidency was, except for occasional interludes, not dominant and not even particularly visible for most of the next hundred years.

There is a valuable degree of truth in these views.[4] The case of Thomas Jefferson illustrates the need to define terms. His reputation has had some startling ups and downs—charted in Merrill Peterson's *The Image of Jefferson in the American Mind* (1960). The imposing monument to Jefferson in Washington, D.C., was not built until the early 1940's—under a Democratic administration. Though he now figures in all selective listings of outstanding Presidents, most scholars distinguish between his intellectual and his executive accomplishments. They frequently quote John Marshall's comment to Hamilton in a letter written during the presidential campaign of 1800:

> Mr. Jefferson appears to me to be a man, who will embody himself with the House of Representatives. By weakening the office of President he will increase his personal power. He will diminish his responsibility, sap the fundamental principles of the government, and become the leader of that party which is about to constitute the majority of the legislature.

Marshall's forecast was shrewd. Jefferson's sway depended upon intimate contact with Republican adherents in Congress. Gone were the lonely, trenchant assertions of John Adams. Jefferson dealt with the here and now, not with some abstract vision of the Executive to be vindicated decades or centuries hence. In the less skillful hands of Madison, and in more critical circumstances, presidential authority appeared to wane. The elections of 1804, 1808,

1812, 1816, and 1820 revealed little of the tension and uncertainty of 1800. This was not to be wondered at, since the succession was hardly in doubt. Jefferson's public pronouncements invariably stressed the modesty of the executive function. In his first annual message he meekly promised: "Nothing shall be wanting on my part to inform, as far as in my power, the legislative judgement, nor to carry that judgement into faithful execution."[5]

In these respects the Presidency under the Republicans did go into partial eclipse. The astronomical metaphor is helpful. It suggests the alternation of light and shadow that has characterized the stages of the Presidency. It suggests too that there was something ordained, or at any rate normal, in the alternation. Jefferson and his Virginian successors, Madison and Monroe, did not press for recognition of executive supremacy because they genuinely did not believe in it. They were reacting to the theories advanced by Alexander Hamilton—the most comprehensive claims made for the Presidency in the whole of America's first century under the Constitution. But they were not simply resisting Hamilton. They themselves had an equally clear, though by its nature negative-sounding, view of the limits of federal power in relation to the states, and of executive power in relation to Congress.

In yet another respect the metaphor of "eclipse" is apposite. Eclipses are temporary. Jefferson was by no means the last President to pay assiduous courtship to Congress as the best method of getting his own way. He himself was no negligible figure. Hamilton disagreed with his friend John Marshall's estimate of their opponent. It was wrong, he said in a letter of January, 1801, to suppose that Jefferson "is an enemy to the power of the Executive," or that he favored the concentration of power in the House of Representatives: "It is a fact . . . that, while we were in the administration together, he was generally for a large construction of the executive authority and not backward to act upon it in cases which coincided with his views." Here Hamilton's memory was defective, or he had special motives for wishing to portray Jefferson as a decisive person. But he was not altogether wrong. As Secretary of State and as President, Jefferson was "not backward . . . in cases which coincided with his views."[6] The most famous example, his initiative in arranging the Louisiana Purchase, was a less resounding executive gesture than is sometimes stated. He had not anticipated the outcome and was embarrassed at having committed the nation without congressional approval. Still, his embarrassment was on a reasonable scale. Other instances of his executive inclination were his astonishing feat in rushing the unpalatable Embargo Act through Congress in a single day, and his occasional brushes with the federal courts. He was particularly incensed when a judge remarked that "the President's duties as chief magistrate do not demand his whole time, and are not unremitting." Jefferson retorted:

> If he alludes to our annual retirement from the seat of government, during the sickly season, he should be told that such arrangements are made for carrying on the public business . . . that it goes on as unremittingly there, as if it were at the seat of government. I pass more hours in public business at Monticello than I do here [in Washington], every day; and it is much more laborious, because all must be done in writing.[7]

Certainly he was not idle. He probably worked harder, and gave more active guidance in promoting legislation, than many later Presidents. True, his techniques were devious; and many of the Jeffersonian dicta that impress us as forthright were, as his biographer Dumas Malone observes, not even noticed at the time because they were confined to private correspondence. If the Presidency is conceived of on the Hamiltonian model, as conspicuous assertion of prerogative, the Virginia triumvirate was inadequate. The War of 1812 was frequently referred to as "Mr. Madison's War." But this was a doubtful compliment: his name was attached to the conflict not in honor but in blame for having let the nation slide into an unnecessary and inglorious struggle from which, according to his critics, he was rescued only by the unlooked-for triumph of General Jackson at the Battle of New Orleans. The Monroe Doctrine, through which James Monroe's name is primarily known to mankind, actually owed more to Secretary of State John Quincy Adams than to its nominal author.

It is then not feasible to pretend that the Virginia Dynasty notably strengthened the Presidency, either by intention or in effect. The national luck carried them through a number of painful crises. But of course "luck" is not enough of an historical explanation: it is an excuse for not offering proper explanations. We may say that the United States was lucky in the first third of the nineteenth century if we mean that it was fortunate in being remote from the European

Three Virginians—Thomas Jefferson, James Madison, and James Monroe—held the Presidency from 1801 to 1825. The Jefferson portrait is by Rembrandt Peale, the other two by Gilbert Stuart.

trouble center. Once the Union had got through the first parlous decade of the new Constitution—a decade that was probably more a "Critical Period" than the 1780's, for which the term was coined—an interval without great shocks and controversies was needed. There have been few tranquil interludes in the nation's history. President Warren G. Harding has been ridiculed for his message of 1920, in which he said: "America's present need is not heroics but healing; not nostrums but normalcy; not revolution but restoration; not surgery but serenity." Yet this craving for uneventfulness, for being left in peace, was understandable in 1920, and still more in 1810 or 1820. Americans have revealed a considerable appetite for social change, in the shape of new homes, new jobs, new ways of living. Their appetite for intellectual or institutional change has been far smaller. The strain of the one form of change has produced a longing for stability in the other realm.

In these respects, whether or not they deserve the credit, Jefferson, Madison, and Monroe can be thought of as providing an element of "normalcy" for the system of government over which they presided. The administrations of the first two were not very serene, but at least they seemed not to add unnecessarily to the problems of their age by raising fundamental difficulties. When Jefferson retired from the Presidency in 1809, the lawyer-author William Wirt prepared a handsome and maybe fulsome tribute on behalf of the

Virginia state legislature. We have learned to mistrust the slogan that the Democratic party of Jackson's day took as a legacy from Jefferson and put at the masthead of the Washington *Globe:* "The world is too much governed." Nor do the majority of twentieth-century Democrats lay stress on Jefferson's supposed dictum: "That government is best which governs least." But Wirt's theme of tolerance, tranquillity, and prosperity caught the essence of the Jeffersonian dream. He was in earnest, if not completely accurate, when he thanked the ex-President

> for the model of an administration conducted on the purest principles of republicanism;
> For pomp and state laid aside;
> Patronage discarded;
> Internal taxes abolished;
> A host of superfluous offices disbanded;
> The monarchic maxim that a national debt is a national blessing, renounced. . . .
> Without the guilt or calamities of conquest, a vast and fertile region added to our country. . . .
> Peace with the civilized world, preserved through a period of uncommon difficulty and trial. . . .[8]

Or, reverting to the Constitution, it might be said that in general the Virginia Dynasty considered themselves more bound by the Tenth Amendment than given *carte blanche* by the preamble to the document, which says:

> We the People of the United States, in Order to form a more perfect Union, establish Justice, ensure domestic Tranquility, provide for the common defence, promote the general Welfare, and secure the Blessings of Liberty to ourselves and our Posterity, do ordain and establish this Constitution for the United States of America.

Jefferson was congratulated by Wirt for preserving the blessings of liberty. What else he was credited with could be thought to promote the general welfare. But he had not achieved this by declaring that as the official entrusted with special care for national well-being he was authorized, indeed obliged, to interpret his responsibilities broadly. Rather he had respected the spirit and the letter of the final amendment in the Bill of Rights: "The powers not delegated to the United States by the Constitution, nor prohibited by it to the

States, are reserved to the States respectively, or to the people." In the same spirit Madison and Monroe declined to sponsor schemes for internal improvement, which they believed must constitutionally be left to the states.

Under John Quincy Adams there was an attempt to build upon an older conception. We may call this Federalist, though the maverick Adamses prided themselves on not having been orthodox Federalists. Perhaps Henry Clay's phrase, the "American System," is more appropriate. In his first annual message to Congress, in 1825, Adams insisted that "the great object of civil government is the improvement of the conditions of those who are partners to the civil contract." He therefore recommended a national university, an astronomical observatory, and (he spoke just before the railroad boom) a network of roads and canals. There was no extraordinary novelty in what he proposed. Less than ten years earlier John C. Calhoun had been an enthusiastic advocate of internal improvements. Speaking in the House of Representatives in 1817, Calhoun had said:

> The more enlarged the sphere of commercial circulation — the more extended that of social intercourse — the more strongly we are bound together — the more inseparable our destinies . . . . Let us, then, bind the republic together with a perfect system of roads and canals. Let us conquer space.[9]

Adams in similar language said that roads and canals, "by multiplying and facilitating the communications and intercourse between distant regions and multitudes of men, are among the most important means of improvement." Nor was Adams the first to mention a national university. George Washington was as keen as Jefferson on providing higher education for American youths at home, instead of obliging them to go to Europe, where they jeopardized their sense of nationality. Washington left a bequest to help launch a federal university in the District of Columbia.

Yet Adams' schemes were derided or ignored. He had no party organization to back him. He lacked the personal magnetism to fire the national imagination and impose his will. There is a revealing story that, turning the first sod of a new enterprise on a hot day, he removed his jacket to ease his work with the spade, and was surprised when this homely gesture was applauded. It would not have occurred to him to court popularity by taking off his jacket to begin with. He made a double tactical error in his first message:

> While foreign nations less blessed with that freedom which is power than ourselves are advancing with gigantic strides in the career of public improvement, were we to slumber in indolence . . . and proclaim to the world that we are palsied by the will of our constituents, would it not be to cast away the bounties of Providence and doom ourselves to perpetual inferiority?

In trying to stimulate national pride he offended it by appearing to suggest that the United States was backward. (He also incidentally reminded the public that he, like his father, had spent a good many years abroad on foreign service—a patriotic duty in his eyes, but to the more chauvinist of his countrymen an absence casting doubt on his Americanness.) And the appeal to American leaders not to be "palsied" by the parochialism and sluggishness of their constituents alienated an electorate that was beginning to expect of its leaders not rebuke but the assurance that the people were the fount of wisdom.

But there are deeper reasons for Adams' failure. He was not merely the last representative in the Presidency of an outmoded style of social behavior: he was anachronistic in advocating a plan that was both ahead of and behind its time. His farsightedness, together with a forgivable tinge of exaggeration and self-pity, is apparent in a summary he prepared in 1837 for a Massachusetts author who was contemplating a biographical account.

> The great effort of my administration was to mature into a permanent and regular system the application of all the superfluous revenue of the Union into internal improvements . . . . In ten years from this day the whole Union would have been checkered over with railroads and canals. It may still be done half a century later and with the limping gait of state legislature and private adventure. I would have done it in the administration of the affairs of the nation. . . . The great object of my life, therefore, as applied to the administration of the government of the United States, has failed. The American Union, as a moral person in the family of nations, is to live from hand to mouth, and to cast away instead of using for the improvement of its own condition, the bounties of Providence.

Only a few days before his death Adams reproached himself in his private diary for his inability to convey his vision to others: "I should have been one of the greatest benefactors of my country. . . . But the conceptive power of mind was not conferred upon me by my Maker, and I have not improved the scanty portion of His gifts as I might and ought to have done."[10]

In common with other shy, gifted people John Quincy Adams was a compound of self-doubt and vanity. In his heart he may well have felt that the fault lay less with his Maker and himself than with his obtuse fellow citizens. If so, he was not far wrong. The neglect of what John K. Galbraith has called the "public sector" in favor of the "private sector" has become a matter of urgent relevance to the twentieth-century United States. The aim of Adams was to realize something recognizable to our generation under other names—of which the Great Society is one. He was not, it should be added, interested in his vision for the sake of aggrandizing the Presidency. He did not closely consider how his scheme was to be carried out. In this he revealed himself not to be a practical politician. Later Presidents who would have sympathized with his general objectives would also regard him as a man with no real grasp of how his office operated. No President can afford to march out of step with his time or with his potential following. The Adams plan had no chance of success. But it deserved a better fate than to be merely an isolated signpost to a road not then taken—a road to power and dignity for the federal government as a whole, and so indirectly for the man in the White House.

Then came Andrew Jackson, one of the half-dozen major figures in the history of the Presidency. Some accounts have made him even more important than he was. Jackson was not swept into power by a tidal wave of newly enfranchised democratic voters. The first decisive increase in presidential voter participation came, as R. P. McCormick has shown, with the 1840 contest between Van Buren and Harrison.[11] Nor did Jackson invent, or enter the Presidency by means of, the new device of the national nominating convention. Nor did his backers or the general public think of him in 1824 and 1828, the first two elections in which he was a presidential candidate, as a passionate democrat, an energetic leader, a man of firm political convictions. His initial reputation was that of a military hero, a courageous patriot, a successful Tennessee planter-judge, a

Andrew Jackson was sixty-six years old in 1833 when Ralph E. W. Earl painted him in military uniform. That was the year of Old Hickory's second inauguration.

person with a fairly long and wide experience of public life who had been a member of both houses of Congress as well as a onetime military governor of Florida. The alarm expressed by men like Daniel Webster at the prospect of having him in the White House was based on uncertainty rather than on any definite knowledge of what he might do. Nicholas Biddle, the clever and debonair head of the Second Bank of the United States, was confident that Jackson would do nothing very drastic and so voted for him in 1828. Those who watched the inaugural ceremony in 1829 saw an old, thin, white-haired man, an apparently extinct volcano, so feeble that he had to be held up by a pair of flanking servants. Some wondered whether the new President had enough stamina to endure the fatigues of office.

Even when the frail old gentleman had begun to reveal that there was plenty of fire left in him, his actual policies were in the main either circumscribed or negative. It was not he who claimed to be ushering in a new dispensation. In his own view he was restoring America to the purity of the old Jeffersonian ideal. With this aim he recommended in his first two annual messages that Presidents should be restricted to a single term by means of a constitutional amendment. His vetoing of internal improvements bills was avowedly Jeffersonian. His opposition to Biddle's Bank was that of an oldline Republican; he knew how strenuously Jefferson had fought against Hamilton's First Bank of the United States, whose charter had been allowed to expire in 1811. The second creation was too much modeled upon the original one, and was—its critics alleged—established in 1816 only because the costs of the War of 1812 provided arguments for the supporters of a central banking system. Even in his most defiantly "executive" messages there were often passages that taken in isolation sounded like Jeffersonianism: agrarian, libertarian, hostile to "consolidated" government. Thus in his Bank Veto of July, 1832, Jackson said: "Our government is [not] to be maintained or our Union preserved by invasions of the rights and powers of the several States. . . . Its true strength consists in leaving individuals and States as much as possible to themselves. . . ." And in his Protest to the Senate of April, 1834, Jackson spoke of his "anxious desire" to persuade his countrymen "that it is not in a splendid government supported by powerful monopolies and aristocratic establishments that they will find happiness or their liberties protection, but in a plain system, void of pomp, protecting all and granting favors to none, dispensing its blessings like the dews of heaven, unseen and unfelt save in the freshness and beauty they contribute to produce."[12] In this traditional, Jeffersonian idea of a "plain" administration intended for a yeoman society, the operations of government were to be so minimal that they were virtually "unseen and unfelt." It was a world away from John Quincy Adams' vision of a government of talents, enlightening the people and embellishing the land. It was a long way also, apparently, from the image of "Old Hickory," the vigorous democratic ruler whose example has been cited by every subsequent strong President.

There is no contradiction, Andrew Jackson presents the case, as John Tyler was to do in a minor degree, of a forceful Chief Executive who does not approve of a forceful federal government. In the twentieth century it has seemed impossible to divorce the one from the other. In the Jacksonian Era, when the main aim of the President was not to reform but to restore, his admirers saw no contradiction.

For them Andrew Jackson was a phenomenon to delight in. No matter what qualifications scholars may suggest, they are still prepared to agree that with Jackson a new element was added to the role of the Chief Executive. He was, as contemporaries claimed, the "People's President." The United States witnessed a modulation, in the phraseology of the sociologist Max Weber, from government by a "party of notables" to government by a "party of politicians." Jackson was—again in Weber's terminology—an outstanding example of "charisma." He was in other words a leader whose links with his supporters were intimate, unself-conscious, and reciprocal. Jacksonians identified themselves with him and he with them. J. G. Baldwin caught the essence of Jacksonism in a sketch written in 1855. In the direct, impatient world of Tennessee, said Baldwin,

> As face answereth to face in water, so must the popular favorite answer to the genius and character of the people. Only a bold, frank, decisive man could rise to power in such a community. He must shrink from no danger; he must fear no responsibility; he must wear no mask; he must wait for no cue; he must be able to appeal to the strong feelings and the manly common-sense of the people.

Baldwin noted that Jackson had almost no formal education (all his predecessors except George Washington had been to college). He lacked the ability to write lucidly and elegantly, and so entrusted the composition of his principal statements to subordinates such as Roger B. Taney, who drafted part of the Bank Veto, and Edward Livingston, who was the author of the Nullification Proclamation. He was no orator, unlike his great Senate adversaries Clay, Webster, and Calhoun, or his wordy lieutenant Senator Thomas Hart Benton. Platform skill helped Lincoln and James Garfield into the Presidency, and secured William Jennings Bryan the Democratic nomination in 1896; in an earlier day it was less vital. Indeed none of the Presidents before Jackson was celebrated for oratory. Jackson had a more compelling asset. As Baldwin put it:

> Swords, not words, were his arguments. . . . He had neither the temper nor the abilities to parley. He could speak tersely, vigorously, movingly, but his words were the brief words of command. Action followed speech, as thunder the lightning. . . . With him, to think and to do were not so much two things as one.[13]

Another perceptive observer, Jackson's biographer James Parton, said that the way to understand him was to remember his Scotch-

Irish ancestry. His was the world of the clan. He was the clan chieftain, bound to his following by mutual ties of kinship and interest. In this intense camaraderie, loyalty was almost the highest virtue; betrayal, actual or fancied, was the worst crime, to be answered with implacable hatred. Jackson's enthusiasms and antipathies were simple, direct, and wholehearted. He could be worked upon by astute advisers; it was probably Van Buren who persuaded him to go against expectation by vetoing the well-lobbied Maysville Road Bill in 1830. On this and other occasions he responded to lofty as well as to personal arguments. He believed in the Republican-Democratic cause while he also relished the notion of frustrating his enemies. The Maysville veto satisfied both his sense of doctrine and the desire to punish his enemy Henry Clay, whose state of Kentucky would have benefited particularly from the bill. However, once his mind was made up no amount of political counsel could convince him to change it.

Van Buren was fascinated by the power that could be wielded by a man of Jackson's temperament. The clan was an admirable paradigm for the American political party. It did not preclude planning and organization of a highly professional order; the technique was to hit upon a popular issue that would generate zeal and provide a rallying cry, and then to channel this surging combative spirit into the party apparatus. Van Buren was also intrigued by the latitude allowed their leader by the clan members. Perhaps his discussion of the matter, in the works he began to write in retirement, was a little wistful; for Van Buren was too dispassionately intelligent not to acknowledge that he himself had been a colorless successor to Jackson in the Presidency. It was splendid to be known as the People's President, or as the Hero of New Orleans. It was less gratifying to be dubbed the Kinderhook Fox or the Wizard of the Albany Regency. Old Hickory was a gloriously sturdy appellation; but what of the sting of being referred to as the Mistletoe Politician—a parasite entwined about the Jackson tree? It was more flattering to be assailed as a tyrant than lampooned as an artful dodger—in the way that some Whig journalist masquerading as Davy Crockett said of Van Buren, "He could take a piece of meat on one side of his mouth, a piece of bread on the other, and cabbage in the middle, and chew and swallow each severally while never mixing them together."[14]

The discovery which interested the equable Van Buren was that the people demanded of a popular leader that he be like themselves, on a larger scale. They did not blame him unduly for inconsistency or for making mistakes. These after all were human foibles, of the kind imputed to their gods by the ancient Greeks. What the people loved and warmed to was vitality, color, even idiosyncrasy, combined with courage and certitude. They did not ask too carefully how or where they were being led so long as they had confidence in the leader. Andrew Jackson's errors were forgiven and forgotten, or chuckled over, because his supporters could feel that he was at one with them.[15] An identification so complete made him irresistibly appealing—at least to those who identified with him. The anger of the opposition, the rival clan, only heightened the invigorating sense of Jacksonian solidarity. "The people believed in General Jackson," testified one contemporary, "as the Turks in their prophet." Thomas Hart Benton did not greatly exaggerate when he described Jackson's departure from federal Capital at the end of his Presidency. According to Benton a great shout went up from the assembled crowd, a shout "such as power never commanded, nor man in power received. . . It was the acclaim of posterity, breaking from the bosoms of contemporaries." In Baldwin's view, Andrew Jackson "impressed his name and character upon the country more deeply than any man, the father of his country only excepted, ever did. . . . He gave a fresh . . . influence to the popular mind. . . and started the government and the people onward in a new and more impulsive career. He opened a new era in American politics. . . . He found a confederacy—he left an empire. . . ."

We may add that as a young congressman Jackson had joined a small group in attacking a proposal to deliver a valedictory address of thanks to the retiring President Washington. He was to be a different sort of President. Yet the office too had its traditional loyalties, its cohering effect upon the holders. Jackson did not object when his followers campaigned for him as the "second Washington." And he took the opportunity, near the end of his administration, of issuing his own version of the Farewell Address. The man who had involved himself in more political controversy than the republic had known for a quarter of a century solemnly warned his countrymen against "systematic efforts publicly made to sow the seeds of discord between different parts of the United States."

Jackson regarded himself as the People's President, and the people were always welcome in the White House. This drawing shows an enormous 1,400-pound cheese—a gift to Jackson—being devoured by the voters at one of his public receptions in the White House.

Whether Jackson's activities as party leader and pugnacious President had quite the wholesome grandeur that Baldwin attributes to them will be considered in future chapters. It should be apparent from his Jeffersonian feeling for state rights that the "empire" he sustained was, so far as he was concerned, still a "confederacy." But there is no doubt of the essential if partial truth of the assessments quoted above, or of the essential novelty—within limits—of what he represented as a charismatic leader.

No President before him, not even "Long Tom" Jefferson, had come anywhere so near to basing his conception of the Presidency upon the proposition that the Chief Executive ruled of, for, and by the people. Wherever the people were mentioned in the Constitution—in the preamble or in the Tenth Amendment—Jackson claimed to be their voice. He was, he said in his Protest to the Senate, "the representative and trustee of the American people."[16] As such he claimed the right, in fact the duty, to defend his office against Congress and the Court, to strike down the Bank, to defeat the Nullifiers, to establish the principle of rotation in office, to advance his views through the medium of an administration newspaper, the Washington *Globe,* which (in Baldwin's phrase) was "a whole troop of cavalry and a pack of flying artillery besides." He was the popular will incarnate. But who were the people? How did Jackson know he represented them? Could a party leader speak for more than half, or a little over, of the people? Was such a leader liable to confuse the national welfare with his own prejudices? Was he in danger of mistaking coercion for persuasion? Did the rhetoric of popular democracy lend itself to cynical abuse? The answer to these questions would long be debated. What was beyond question, as Jackson rode off in his carriage toward The Hermitage in 1837, was that—for good or ill—the Presidency had changed its quality. Henceforward any assertive Chief Executive would be armed with additional weapons. By the same token, more weapons could be turned against him.

James K. Polk, President from 1845 to 1849, was a faithful Jackson man in thought and deed. He too was from Tennessee. The Democrats (as the former Jeffersonian Republican party was now known) dressed him up as Young Hickory, the heir of Old Hickory. Like Jackson he seized the opportunity of a final message to present his testament of faith. In keeping with the man and his time, it was in large part a doctrinaire exposition of the excellencies of the Democratic ensemble. However, he also underlined the creed of his master, in the course of justifying his use of the veto to cover major policy issues:

> If it be said that the Representatives in the popular branch of Congress are chosen directly by the people, it is answered, the people elect the President. If both Houses represent the States and the people, so does the President. The President represents in the executive department the whole people of the United States, as each member of the legislative department represents portions of them.

There was a double implication in Polk's words. The Senate, not being the "popular" house of Congress, was less authentically representative than the President or the lower house. And congressmen were less representative than the President, since they—he said—were only "responsible to the people of particular States or districts," while he was responsible to "an enlightened public opinion" and to "the people of the whole Union." As such Polk found the veto a dramatically effective device. It was, Tocqueville noted, "a sort of appeal to the people."

Democratic contentions were not accepted by the Whigs. Answering Jackson in the Senate in 1834, Daniel Webster poured scorn on "the idea of this airy and unreal responsibility to the public." He went on to attack the Jacksonian claim *that the President is the direct representative of the American people*":

> Now, Sir, this is not the language of the Constitution. The Constitution nowhere calls him the representative of the American people; still less, their direct representative. It could not do so with the least propriety.[17]

An apparent flaw in the Jackson-Polk reasoning was that the President was not directly elected. How could a man picked by a few hundred members of the Electoral College—or, as in the special circumstances of 1801 and 1825, by a handful of Congressmen—be thought of as the embodiment of anything so large and impalpable as "enlightened public opinion"? Jackson had a ready and indignant answer. The Electoral College was an unreliable device. Through its malfunctioning, and the further unrepresentativeness of the House of Representatives, he had been cheated of the Presidency in 1825. He had secured more popular votes than John Quincy Adams; both he and the American public had been thwarted. In consequence he had proposed to introduce a more democratic system of presidential election, but Congress had undemocratically refused to put the matter to the test of a constitutional amendment.

However, neither the Electoral College nor Congress was able long to withstand the general will of the American people. In 1828 they placed Jackson in power, beyond quibble. In 1832 he tested the efficacy of the responsibility of the President to the whole people by vetoing the Bank recharter, although it had passed the House by 107 votes to 85 and the Senate by 28 to 20. Jackson was vindicated at the election: some 688,000 voters rallied to him, as against 530,000 for the coalition of enemies led by Henry Clay and William Wirt. Here was his mandate. Clay and Biddle in private correspondence saw that Jackson's victory did amount to "a popular ratification" of his stand on the Bank issue.

By Polk's day there was the further sanction of the national nomi-

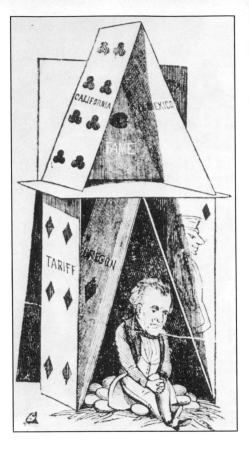

James K. Polk (above), a protégé of Jackson's, was sometimes called Young Hickory. In an 1846 cartoon (left) titled "This Is the House That Polk Built," the President sits brooding over—and dangerously under—his tenuously balanced young administration. He seems to be planning ways to prevent the Oregon boundary dispute, the conflict with Mexico, and tariff problems from collapsing on his head.

nating convention, in place of the old narrow congressional caucus. Grass-roots sentiment found expression through the convention delegates. Politicians claimed that the candidate could not help but be the man the people wanted. In Polk's case there was the inconvenient fact that his name had been hardly mentioned for the Presidency in the Democratic newspapers. At the Baltimore convention in May, 1844, he was not put in nomination until the eighth ballot, and not nominated until the ninth. Still, he was declared to be the party's unanimous choice, and on winning the election soon made clear that he too felt he had a mandate. Even before he was inaugurated he told a crony that whether or not he managed to achieve harmony among the Democratic factions that had preferred other candidates, "in any event I intend to be *myself* President of the U.S."[18]

The Polk mandate came partly from the knowledge that Andrew Jackson accepted him as a worthy Democratic standard-bearer, but mainly from the evident appeal of a party platform that called for a vigorous policy toward Oregon and Mexico. His own stubborn, ungenial temperament reinforced the conviction that he had received a directive from the United States. In office he created difficulties for himself by behaving deviously and by annoying his supporters in Congress, to a degree surprising in one who had learned the ropes as Speaker of the House of Representatives. He made the settlement of the Oregon boundary question with Britain more complicated than was necessary.

Nevertheless his record of accomplishment in one term was astonishing. For us his performance in the Mexican War is especially significant. In the words of Leonard D. White, "Polk gave the country its first demonstration of the *administrative* capacities of the Presidency as a war agency. He proved that a President could run a war."[19] He also made mistakes. Leaving aside the question of whether the war with Mexico need have been fought at all, Polk managed to offend many of his subordinates, especially in the Army and Navy. He was ungracious and mistrustful toward those who were Whigs. He behaved abominably, though not without some provocation, to Nicholas Trist, the State Department chief clerk whom he dispatched to Mexico as his peacemaking agent. At times he seemed to conceive of the administration, and of the war effort, as though it were on the local scale of the fairly recent days when he had been governor of Tennessee. He wore himself almost literally to death in the White House, but the fault was in some degree his own. He would not devolve responsibility on his executive heads. He preoccupied himself with filling the hundreds of offices vacated as the result of a Democratic victory. He went to the same trouble in scrutinizing the score upon score of applications for appointments to new Army regiments. When his Secretary of War, William L. Marcy, escaped the summer heat, the President more or less assumed the direction of the War Department. In his four-year term Polk spent only six weeks away from Washington. "He works from 10 to 12 hours in every 24," said an acquaintance. "He holds two Cabinets a week. He sees visitors two hours every day when the Cabinet is not employed. . . . He is also in frequent communion with his [department] secretaries." When the days' labors ended Polk recounted them in his diary, often at length, and brooded over his problems. A sympathetic Democrat urged Mrs. Polk to make the President take some recreation, for example by going out with her for a drive. "I did so," she replied, "and the carriage waited and waited. . . . It would have been obliged to wait all day, for somebody was always in the office, and Mr. Polk would not, or could not, come." Polk's own explanation, near the end of his term, was: "No President who performs his duty . . . conscientiously can have any leisure. If he intrusts the details . . . to subordinates constant errors will occur. I prefer to supervise the whole operations of the Government myself . . . and this makes my duties very great."[20]

But even an administrative genius, no matter how brilliant and decisive, would have found the task almost overwhelming. Since Washington's era the population of the country had increased from four or five million to twenty million. By the end of 1845 the original thirteen states had grown to twenty-eight. The press of public business expanded accordingly. Administrative arrangements, however, remained primitive. Presidents in search of secretarial assistance usually paid sons or nephews out of the executive salary. Not until 1857 did Congress authorize additional expenditure to give the President his own private secretary. Whenever there was an unusual amount of activity in Washington the Executive was swamped. In this respect Polk's desperate labors to keep abreast of the material that poured in were a miniature prefiguration of Lincoln's nightmarish struggle during the Civil War. The executive branch, having no margin for sudden expansion, was always on the edge of collapse. The lessons of Polk's administration were not pondered. Indeed it was not only Lincoln who suffered the consequences. As late as 1898, confronted with the Spanish-American War, McKinley's Secretary of War Russell A. Alger was even more beset than Marcy had been; and in 1899 McKinley himself was ready to cry, with Polk, "I have had enough of it, Heaven knows! I have had all the honor there is in the place, and . . . responsibilities enough to kill any man."[21]

There was a further lesson of Polk's administration, likewise ignored. Though by later standards the executive branch was still minuscule, it had proliferated enough to make strict supervision as difficult as it was necessary. The War and Navy departments were extreme cases because of the intrusion of the service mentality. But in each department the bureau heads contrived to follow their own inclinations and routines, whatever the White House or their immediate chiefs might ordain. Incurably suspicious and pertinacious, Polk was horrified to encounter the curious combination of laxity and inflexibility that has been noted in "Foggy Bottom" long after his day. His Secretaries were sometimes unaware of decisions taken (or not taken) in their own departments. Orders were ignored, shelved, reinterpreted. Expenditure was on occasion slack to the point of corruption; each bureau exaggerated its needs as a matter of course. For a man of Polk's frugal outlook, the administration was scandalously wasteful.

In comparison with some European governments, that of the United States was in fact reasonably honest, efficient, and economical. Yet Polk made a valuable contribution when in the midst of all his other burdens he formed himself into a one-man investigatory commission. His principal discovery was that there was no budgetary mechanism. In the Treasury Act of 1789 Congress had required the Secretary of the Treasury, not the President, to compile and submit estimates of income and expenditure. Hamilton, according to Leonard D. White, set the precedent of not consulting the President. Monroe complained in vain that he was being kept in the dark by his Secretary. John Quincy Adams insisted on seeing the draft annual report of the Treasury Department. It is doubtful though that Adams or any of his predecessors had scrutinized the estimates of the various departments for their respective fields.

In the general prosperity of the country such casualness went unnoticed. A different mood began to appear with the severe depression of 1837. Polk, worried by the expense of the Mexican War, and devoted to the old Republican principle of freedom from public debt, tried to institute a regular, thorough scrutiny of executive expenditure. In his view no one but the President could do this. He was more prescient than he realized. But his opening salvoes died away. With his departure the problem went back into limbo—one more task to be deferred until the period half a century later when the executive branch would begin to orchestrate the themes that rare compulsive men like Polk had striven to play on a single instrument. The problem of course was that the symphony would still have to be conducted by one man—the President.

In fairness to Polk we must also say that he got results. He used his Cabinet more, and more effectively, than anyone else had done. He kept the entire administration on the alert with his probings. If they had been as energetic and competent as he, his task would have been appreciably lighter. He took the lead, within the Cabinet, in planning strategy, logistics, finance, diplomacy. Though he was not always judicious he was invariably vigorous; and that, as Van Buren said of Jackson, was at least half the battle. His predecessors had learned that the Presidency was, even in supposedly normal times, a demanding office. "Dignified slavery," Jackson called it; "toilsome and anxious probation" was Van Buren's phrase. Polk sighed that it was "no bed of roses."[22] At least he could reflect that with Oregon and California and New Mexico in American hands, Young Hickory had deserved his nickname. There was no doubt that the Mexican conflict was "Mr. Polk's War."

The inertia of the system, the institutionalized vendetta of party politics, and Polk's lack of personal charm, however, meant that what he had consolidated went largely unrecognized. The great crisis in the nation's history, and the great leap forward in the demonstration of executive authority, came in 1861 with the accession of Abraham Lincoln. Ironically enough he was, as David Donald emphasizes in a brilliant essay, a "Whig in the White House." As an Illinois congressman, he had in January, 1848, voted for a resolution that maintained the Mexican War had been "unnecessarily and unconstitionally begun by the President of the United States." Being a faithful Whig he believed that Jackson and Polk had exceeded the limits of executive authority. Yet this same man as President said, "I conceive that I may in an emergency do things on military grounds which cannot constitutionally be done by Congress," and told a committee in 1862 that "as Commander in Chief of the Army and Navy, in time of war I suppose I have the right to take any measure which may best subdue the enemy."[23] Though Polk had been an aggressive war leader, who showed how a President might display his talents as commander of the armed forces, he had not explicitly derived his claims to authority from the Commander-in-Chief clause of the Constitution. Edward S. Corwin says that until the Civil War it was "the forgotten clause." Then Lincoln, leaning also on his duty "to take care that the laws be

---

Lincoln posed for this daguerreotype in 1860, the year he was elected to the Presidency and South Carolina seceded from the Union.

faithfully executed," envisaged something known as "the war power," which he thought entitled him to take amazing liberties in his first three months in office—a period when Congress was not yet in regular session and had not been summoned by him into special session. He created a ninety-day national army out of the state militias, having maneuvered over the provisioning of Fort Sumter and so in a way launched a civil war. He called out forty thousand volunteers for three years' service, more than doubled the regular Army and Navy, declared a blockade of Southern ports, expended Treasury funds for unauthorized purposes, and in other respects behaved—so his critics alleged—as if the Constitution did not exist.

Lincoln's justification, of course, was that in dire emergency it was necessary to act in order to save the country. Without a country there would be no Constitution. In the light of the war powers exercised by twentieth-century Presidents his conduct seems understandable, and even circumspect except for the umbrella of martial law that permitted him to hold several thousand civilians in jail without due process. In the light of the Whig theory of the Presidency, his behavior was ominously reminiscent of Jacksonian "despotism." A legal brief contesting his assumptions argued that they made the President "the impersonation of the country" and empowered him to do whatever he pleased to "*save the life of the nation*":

> This is to assert that the Constitution contemplated and tacitly provided that the President should be dictator, and all constitutional government be at an end whenever he should think that "the life of the nation" is in danger.

In the abstract, such misgivings were reasonable. There were disquieting denials of individual liberty during the Civil War years, in the name of emergency. Constitutionalists were rightly concerned lest they somehow acquire the sanction of usage—much as, for example, temporary buildings are apt to become permanently occupied. Nor could Congress lightly accept the apparent marauding by the President in the no-man's-land between those two branches of government. Why, demanded Senator Charles Sumner, should "these vast War Powers" not pertain also to Congress? The President "is only the instrument of Congress, under the Constitution." Unless Congress upheld its rights, the American republic would be degraded "to one of those short-lived, vulgar despotisms appearing occasionally as a warning to mankind." Lincoln would have been delighted if he had known the opinion that Jefferson had expressed in a letter of 1810: "In time of peace the people look most to their representatives; but in war to the Executive solely."[24]

But he would probably not have quoted the letter in any public answer to his critics. He was too clever to give offense where he could avoid it; and he agreed with the theoretical position of the Sumners and Wades and other vehement Republicans. He agreed because he had carried his old Whig views into the new Republican party. The paradox of Lincoln's Presidency is revealed by the kind of abuse that greeted him. He was assailed both as a dictator *and* as "timid and ignorant," "a political coward," "an awful, woeful ass," a man "without any spinal column." In other words he was accused both of having exceeded his authority and of having failed to exert his authority.

Some of the criticism came from radical Republicans who thought the administration far too hesitant on the slavery issue. Some came from persons who felt that he lacked the magisterial presence they associated with his office. Ralph Waldo Emerson complained in 1863 that "you cannot refine Mr. Lincoln's taste, extend his horizon, or clear his judgement; he will not walk dignifiedly through the traditional part of the President of America . . . Some criticism, was of the random variety that every President must learn to tolerate if he is to preserve his sanity. At moments Lincoln felt near the end of his tether. His friend Ward Lamon (if we can rely on him) reported an outburst from Lincoln similar to one by George Washington: "In God's name! if any one can do better in my place than I . . . am endeavoring to do, let him try his hand at it, and no one will be better contented than myself."

All such testimony points to the dual character of Lincoln's Presidency. As Commander in Chief he acted the part of an almost ruthless Chief Executive. In pursuit of his aim of preserving the Union and restoring the peace, he behaved almost mediumistically, as if some spirit—the spirit of the office—were speaking through him. Otherwise he spoke very much in his own voice—that of a colloquial, wryly humorous, innately intelligent, half-deprecating Western politican, who had like all successful politicans dreamed of becoming President (and since he was a Whig, President in the style of, say, Henry Clay). Half of him still visualized the office on Whig lines. It was this Lincoln who left to Congress most of the initiative in developing legislation: as President-elect he had said he thought Congress "should originate, as well as perfect its measures, without external bias." For the same reason he made little use of the veto power; here his only challenge to Congress was his pocket veto —allowing a bill to die by leaving it unsigned—of the Wade-Davis reconstruction bill, which he thought infringed the executive zone of responsibility. And possibly, though this is less clear, his Whig political education accounts for his failure to dominate his Cabinet, or indeed to bring it into any regular system. Whatever the explanation, he gave his department heads far more scope for independent action than had Jackson or Polk.

Abraham Lincoln wielded more power than any predecessor, because he had to. His Emancipation Proclamation is an example of his calm assertion of prerogative in the face of whatever Congress or his Cabinet might deem the proper course. In any survey of the Presidency these assertions earn him a prominent place as an "aggrandizer." They were a high-water mark not reached again for almost half a century. In other respects he was a Jefferson rather than a Jackson. Unlike Jackson he did not stamp his name and his personality upon his era. Like that of Jefferson, his reputation was to a considerable extent posthumous. Only when he was dead, and the extraordinary quality of his thoughts and actions became evident, did Lincoln join the ranks of the elect among the presidentially elected. He enriched—and so consolidated—the office from the grave. His soul, in company with John Brown's, went marching on. Emerson and a multitude of others forgot their strictures and began to marvel.

In this Civil War sketch, a group of Union soldiers—about to go to the front lines—are startled to see President Abraham Lincoln coming forward to shake their hands and encourage them.

City Point /65

"good God you goin to shake with me Uncle Abe"

MAD TOM in A RAGE

CHAPTER FOUR

The Place of
Party Politics

THE President's Cabinet is one example of an institution nowhere mentioned in the Constitution. Another, more important example is the growth of political parties and their effect on the Presidency.

Though the Constitution was silent on the matter, the framers and the nation's early leaders had decided views: they were against "parties" and "factions" and did not want them in the United States. At best, as in eighteenth-century England, parties were seen as cynical and shifting alliances controlled by a circle of powerful families. Their atmosphere was venal; lackeys and "placemen" jockeyed for recognition by the party of the "King's Friends" or that of his no less aristocratic opponents. (The contemptibility of this world is brought out in *Gulliver's Travels*. Dean Swift mocks the pretensions of the rival factions in Lilliput—perhaps with an element of self-contempt, since his own career depended largely on turning out political journalism on behalf of the Tory party.) At worst, the appearance of such groupings spelled the doom of a society by

---

In this Federalist cartoon, titled "Mad Tom in a Rage," Jefferson and a devil try to destroy the government built by Washington and Adams.

splitting it into irreconcilably hostile segments. Gouverneur Morris seemed to discern the future when he said in a speech at Philadelphia in 1787 that "in all public bodies there are two parties. The Executive will necessarily be more connected with one than the other. There will be a personal interest therefore in one of the parties to oppose as well as in the other to support him." But the point of the argument was that the President ought not to be elected by Congress; for if that happened, "some leader of party will always covet his set, will perplex his administration, will cabal with the Legislature, till he succeeds in supplanting him."[1]

Astute American theorists such as John Adams and James Madison were of course aware that mankind was not basically different in the United States, though they believed American society was more simple and more wholesome than that of the Old World. In the famous tenth essay from *The Federalist,* which Madison wrote in 1787, he addressed himself to the problem of "factions" or "parties" as they might appear under the Constitution. He perceived that "a landed interest, a manufacturing interest, a mercantile interest, a moneyed interest, with many lesser interests, grow up of necessity in civilized nations, and divide them into different classes, actuated by different sentiments and views." The United States would be no exception—in fact would be divided geographically or sectionally as well. He added, with impressive foresight, "The regulation of these various and interfering interests forms the principal task of modern legislation, and involves the spirit of party and faction in the necessary and ordinary operations of the government."

Yet taken as a whole Madison's essay is hardly a prediction of, still less a welcome for, the parties that were within a few years to burst upon the American scene. He regarded them as factions, and defined "faction" as "a number of citizens, whether . . . a majority or minority of the whole, who are united and actuated by some common impulse of passion, or of interest, *adverse to the rights of other citizens, or to the permanent and aggregate interests of the community"* [my italics]. To Madison parties were, if necessary, a necessary evil. They could not be avoided altogether, so they must be brought under control by means of checks and balances. Madison's hope was twofold. First, discord would be muted by the calmer, wiser counsels of elected legislatures. Second, the abundance of rival interests within a republic so large would cause them to minimize one another. Here, striving to develop consolatory arguments for the new Constitution, Madison stumbled upon a crucial reassurance. But in general his essay is pessimistic so far as the actual parties are concerned. Even a minority interest, he conceded, might "clog the administration" and "convulse" society, though it could not accomplish total overthrow. Wise legislators ought to emerge: on the other hand, "men of factious tempers, of local prejudices, or of sinister designs, may, by intrigue, by corruption, or by other means, first obtain the suffrages, and then betray the interests, of the people." In short, Madison's *Federalist* No. 10 does not give three ringing cheers for the prospect of the party system. And nowhere does he mention the prospect of two major parties, as distinct from an assortment, contending for the Presidency as well as for the legislative branch.[2]

After a few years of government under the Constitution, prominent Americans seemed to share the apprehensions expressed by Madison, without any inclination as yet to discern therapeutic effects. In March, 1798, Jefferson told Francis Hopkinson that he had never been willing to align his views on religion, philosophy, or politics with those of "any party of men. . . . Such an addiction is the last degradation of a free and moral agent. If I could not go to heaven but with a party, I would not go there at all." When Vice-President John Adams spoke of parties he specifically meant political units; and he was emphatic in his disapproval: "There is nothing I dread so much as the division of the Republic into two great parties, each under its leader. . . . This, in my humble opinion, is to be feared as the greatest political evil under our Constitution." The outcome, he thought, would be spleen and destructiveness. "As soon as one man hints at an improvement," he said, "his rival opposes it. No sooner has one party discovered . . . any amelioration . . . than the opposite party belies it . . . misrepresents it, ridicules it . . . and persecutes it." In the Farewell Address of 1796 George Washington warned his countrymen "in the most solemn manner against the baneful effects of the spirit of party":

> It serves always to distract the public councils and enfeeble the public administration. It agitates the community with ill-founded jealousies and false alarms; kindles the animosity of one part against another; foments occasionally riot and insurrection.[3]

To their surprise and dismay, Washington and Adams were faced by the very phenomenon that was so widely deplored. No wonder that they were slow to recognize it as unavoidable, and quite unable to consider it a potential benefit. While he was in office Washington never thought of his administration as that of a party but as national in outlook. True, in his second term he took care to appoint to executive offices only men whose sentiments were, like his own, "Federal." But this did not mean he accepted the role of an opposition party. The Jeffersonian Republicans, sometimes known as Democratic Republicans, who challenged his conduct of affairs were not to him "*the* opposition" but simply "opposition": "faction," and disloyal faction at that. He knew very well that the Republicans identified him with the "Federalists," Jefferson informed him in 1792 that Alexander Hamilton's Federalist scheme was to "dismount" Washington from the Chief Magistracy and place him at the head of a party—the Federalist party. But Washington, reluctant to place the Federalist persuasion on a footing with the subversive "mobocracy," was still less prepared to agree that he might be in danger of losing his presidential impartiality. Only when he was out of office did he begin to show signs of acknowledging such an affiliation. He was still sure in 1798 that a "profest Democrat" was a man who "will leave nothing unattempted to overturn the Government of this Country." A year later—the last year of his life—Washington went a little further in his political education. By then he appeared to see what was in train. Explaining why he would not become a candidate for the 1800 presidential election, he observed that "principle, not men, is now, and will be, the object of contention." Even if he were to consent, "I should not draw a *single* vote from the Anti-federal side; and of course, should stand upon no stronger ground than any other Federal well supported."[4]

John Adams as President had an even more unsavory experience of the incipient spirit of party. Less elevated than Washington in the nation's regard, he caught the full blast of Republican opposition; and of an opposition quite tightly organized from inside Congress. Feeling between Republicans and Federalists was intense: witness the three stringent Alien and Sedition Acts passed by the Federalist majority in 1798 and approved by Adams in the hope of giving him some protection from the barrage of "Antifederal"

This poster, disseminated by Jefferson's opponents, portrayed him as a disgracefully inadequate successor to the godlike Washington.

abuse. He had—in Jefferson—a Republican Vice-President. Worse still, Adams had to contend with the "Ultras" or "High Federalists," who looked to Hamilton for guidance and urged the President toward extreme policies. Adams had misguidedly continued his predecessor's Cabinet in office; and the principal Secretaries were markedly Hamiltonian. Vilified throughout his four years in office, and defeated at the election of 1800 by a combination of Jeffersonians and Hamiltonians, Adams retired more firmly convinced than ever that parties might be the ruin of the United States.

The Jeffersonian opposition was understandably quicker to visualize parties as a legitimate mechanism. By 1792 Madison was convinced. Jefferson himself, initially hesitant, was beginning to grasp the point. At the end of 1795, still less partisan in mood than some of the admirers who were about to push him for the Presidency, he somewhat cautiously declared himself:

> Were parties here divided merely by a greediness for office, as in England, to take a part . . . would be unworthy . . . but where the . . . difference is as substantial . . . as between the republicans & the Monocrats of our country, I hold it . . . honorable to take a firm & decided part. . . .

Three years later Jefferson had arrived at a surprisingly "modern" assessment:

> In every free and deliberating society there must . . . be opposite parties and violent dissensions and discords; and one of these must for the most part prevail over the other for a longer or shorter time. Perhaps this party division is necessary to induce each to watch and [relate] to the people the proceedings of the other.[5]

Being the "outs," anxious to be "in," the Republicans showed more enterprise than the Federalists, both in Congress and in the country as a whole. Their more avowedly libertarian and egalitarian creed made it easier for them to broaden the base of their support. Both tactics and ideology led them to seek a grass-roots following, and to link this with sundry devices—canvassing, newspaper articles, slogans, tickets—that foreshadowed the present-day structure. The passion of their beliefs and their genuine distrust of one another induced both parties to compete ferociously for office.

The origin of the American party system is a matter of great interest and complexity. Two points are of particular relevance: the role of the Presidency and the attitude of the various Presidents. Herbert Agar, Joseph Charles, William N. Chambers, and other students of American political history all agree that the Presidency was the vital prize in the system. Richard P. McCormick goes so far as to suggest that the contest for the Presidency was the prime function of American politics.[6] Perhaps this was not why parties originated; but once they were in being, circumstances oriented political groups in this direction. The 1787 Constitution created a *national* political environment. In order to gain a hearing, local groups now had to find representation within the federal government. To do this they had to coalesce with other groups. Such loose coalitions were ineffective and wasteful of effort unless they could be bound

John Randolph of Virginia (left) clashed with President Jefferson and lost his political power. Albert Gallatin, Jefferson's Secretary of the Treasury, served as liaison between the President and his supporters in Congress.

together by more permanent ties of organization and animated by larger enthusiasms and antipathies.

In European countries, as McCormick points out, political parties have been oriented toward the legislature, not the executive. Why did this not happen in the United States, especially when the first two Presidents revealed their distaste for parties? The answer obviously lies in the conception of the Presidency. In Europe the executive was usually a hereditary monarchy, not accessible to the competition of politics. In the United States, the fact that the Presidency was an elective office held for a relatively short term made it automatically subject to competition. If the Chief Executive had become a merely ceremonial figure, submissive to the dictates of Congress or of his Cabinet, the competition might have taken other forms. Instead, Washington and Adams unwittingly thrust the office to the forefront of party politics by upholding its dignity. If the President was not to be a cipher, then he was a person of incalculable potential. Even at a modest estimate, a political party primarily active in the legislature needed the concurrence of the executive branch. The emotions stirred by the elections of 1796 and 1800 ensured that these quadrennial contests would grip the national imagination. The fight for the Presidency became inextricably involved with other aspects of a nationwide battle—a battle for a whole administration, all the seats in the House of Representatives, one third of those in the Senate, and a large number (growing steadily as the principle of popular election replaced legislative selection) of governorships and other state and local offices. The "coattail" phenomenon was soon apparent. A minor candidate had more chance of recognition, and victory, if he could be associated with a national campaign. In 1796, for example, Massachusetts men were stimulated to re-elect Governor Sam Adams by being reminded that the issue was tremendous: "MONARCHY or REPUBLICANISM." The introduction of the Twelfth Amendment in time for the 1804 election conferred a constitutional sanction upon an evolution not at all desired in 1787.

The Presidency of Thomas Jefferson set the seal on the involvement in politics of the Chief Executive. Unlike Washington and Adams he entered office, and won re-election, through the operation of a system of which in the main he approved. In office he worked closely and smoothly with his congressional following. The man who in 1789 had proclaimed his intention to think for himself as an undegraded "free and moral agent" was now impatient of Republican legislators who would not stay in line. They were "wayward freaks," liable to "disturb the operations."[7] The network of relationships that had been created in the 1790's by such pioneer politicos as John Backley, Clerk of the House in Washington's administration, was spread wider. Jefferson's devoted Secretary of the Treasury, Albert Gallatin, communicated to the Republican caucus in Congress the detail of what Jefferson wanted done. The executive branch likewise made use of key members of the standing congressional committees, which were beginning to multiply. Legislation was shepherded by unofficial but nonetheless active "floor leaders." Executive patronage was liberally applied throughout the nation to reward the faithful.

Punishments were meted out to those who had lost favor with the President. A celebrated—some would say flagrant—case was that of John Randolph of Virginia. A master of sarcastic oratory, Randolph was at the age of twenty-eight singled out as House floor leader and chairman of the important Ways and Means Committee.

During Jefferson's first administration his reputation stood high. He dined regularly with the President and was in almost daily touch with Gallatin or others of the Cabinet group. As floor leader he directed the repeal of the Judiciary Act and the impeachment of the vituperative Supreme Court Justice Samuel Chase—a chief villain in Republican eyes. As committee chairman Randolph secured vital appropriations for the President, for instance to purchase Florida and to reduce the national debt.

However, he and Jefferson fell out, partly because he failed to secure the conviction of Chase at the impeachment trial. The dinners ceased; the President found other channels of communication; Randolph was ousted from his floor leadership and his chairmanship. He had, so the President thought, become one of the wayward freaks—and indeed his subsequent, idiosyncratic career seemed to bear out the accusation. In 1813 another Republican contested Randolph's seat in the House and defeated him. By an odd coincidence Randolph's successful rival was a son-in-law of Thomas Jefferson's. Although Randolph regained his seat in 1815 he was never again entrusted with responsible party office in Congress.

Jefferson maintained his hold over the Republican party because he was so clearly its most distinguished figure, because indirect leadership suited his talents, and because the Federalist party was in decline. Circumstances, however, worked against his successors Madison and Monroe. To the extent that they owed their nomination to the Republican caucus, they were regarded by Congress as its beneficiaries. And the gradual disappearance of the Federalists as a coherent, formidable opposition had the unanticipated effect of weakening discipline within the Republican ranks. John Randolph, who for a quarter of a century after his own relegation to political impotence lost no opportunity to point to the same feature in other men's careers, said of Madison in 1811: "He is President *de jure* only; who exercises the office *de facto* I do not know." By the end of Madison's first administration the executive office, or the power attached to it, was parceled out among the Speaker of the House (Henry Clay), the caucus in Congress, and the heads of congressional committees. Madison was not a complete nonentity; but there was an uncomfortable edge of truth in Randolph's gibe. John Adams had been denied a second term because there was too much resistance, inside and outside his party. It could be said that Madi-

King George and Napoleon beat and rob Jefferson in this cartoon, which personified the plight of the young United States, caught between warring England and France.

son's second term was a proof either that even second-rate Presidents could be sure of re-election in wartime, or else that the office did not seem important enough to warrant putting someone else in his place.

The afflictions of Madison were those of Monroe, in more painful form. Outwardly all was well in the "Era of Good Feelings." The Republican caucus followed expectation in nominating Monroe: as Madison's Secretary of State he was the heir apparent. In the presidential election of 1816 he secured 183 electoral votes to the Federalist candidate's 34. In 1820 Monroe was unopposed, a thing that had not happened since 1789 and would never happen again. Every electoral vote except one went to him. With the collapse of the Federalists as a party capable of putting up a plausible candidate, the spokesman of a definite viewpoint, it appeared that perhaps the previous epoch of violent party spirit had been an aberration. After all, the emergence of parties and their subsequent disintegration covered almost exactly the period when Europe was in the grip of the Revolutionary and Napoleonic wars. This prolonged crisis might have determined the entire course of American politics. The cleavage between the "Anglomen" of the Federalist group and the

Republican "Gallomen" could be interpreted as evidence of the need for the United States to respect Washington's advice to have "as little *political* connection" with foreign nations as possible, and Jefferson's identical warning against "entangling alliances." The happy conclusion of the War of 1812, and the return of peace to Europe, guaranteed America the immunity she sought. If an additional statement of intent were needed, it was provided in the Monroe Doctrine.

Now was the time to rejoice in America's harmony. Washington, it seemed, had been correct also in warning the nation against the "baneful effect of the spirit of party." The Presidency might regain its full dignity as an honorable station raised far above petty faction. It could be what the Founding Fathers intended. In this lofty frame of mind no less a figure than Andrew Jackson, the hero of New Orleans, recommended magnanimity to the newly elected Monroe in 1816:

> Now is the time to exterminate the monster called party spirit. By selecting characters most conspicuous for their probity, virtue, capacity and firmness, without any regard to party, you will go far to, if not entirely eradicate those feelings which, on former occasions, threw so many obstacles in the way of government; and perhaps have the pleasure of uniting a people heretofore divided. . . . Consult no party in your choice. [8]

Jackson's views were in accord with those of Monroe. The new President wished to demonstrate the complete truth of Jefferson's old conciliatory assertion, "We are all Republicans, we are all Federalists." He deliberately discounted party membership in distributing patronage. Though Monroe did not know it, he was following an opinion uttered by ex-President John Adams in a letter of 1811. The President, Adams had said, "ought to select the men best qualified . . . for offices at his own responsibility," unimpeded by any other agency. Unless he could do so "he must be the slave of the party that brought him in. He can never be independent or impartial." [9]

There was, it appeared, a prevailing notion among high-minded Americans that parties were dead—and good riddance. Monroe therefore reverted to Washington's early practice in offering executive posts to the most eminent men in the land. The result, on paper, was a Cabinet of exceptional merit. Though Clay and Jackson refused office, Monroe succeeded in picking John Quincy Adams for his Secretary of State, John C. Calhoun as Secretary of War, William H. Crawford as Secretary of the Treasury, and William Wirt as Attorney General. When Adams succeeded Monroe in 1825 he adhered to the same dignified assumption. In his inaugural address Adams announced:

> There remains one effort of magnanimity, one sacrifice of prejudice and passion, to be made by the individuals throughout the nation who have heretofore followed the standards of political party. It is that of discarding every remnant of rancor against each other, of embracing as countrymen and friends, and of yielding to talents and virtue alone that confidence which in times of contention for principle was bestowed only upon those who bore the badge of party communion.

In obedience to his own ideals Adams retained some of Monroe's Cabinet, brought in Henry Clay as Secretary of State, and offered posts to Jackson and Crawford, though neither would accept.

It is worth repeating that of the first six Presidents, none, not even Jefferson, was wholly committed to the belief that political parties were essential to the United States. All except Jefferson and possibly Madison disliked most aspects of the party system, and strongly disliked the effect of politics upon the Presidency. Most of their successors have at one time or another regretted the partisan features of the office. Several have renewed the early effort to rise above politics, in the sincere conviction that there is something anomalous in being both President of the United States and a party chieftain. A distaste so deeply rooted and so recurrent deserves to be studied sympathetically—though the consequences of the attempt at presidential impartiality have nearly always been unfortunate.

They were certainly unfortunate for Monroe and J. Q. Adams. Both failed to appreciate that when major parties disappeared they would be replaced by minor factions. Whatever the defects of the party system, it possessed a chain of command, a sense of purpose, a unifying quality. Factions, on the other hand, were fluid, personal, divisive, and conspiratorial. When issues were no longer at stake, and no longer presented through the device of contending national organizations, there would still be contention among ambitious individuals. As before, the grand prize was the Presidency; but there was little semblance of grandeur in the struggle to attain it. In Monroe's cabinet Adams, Calhoun, and Crawford were all keenly interested in becoming President. Outside the Cabinet, so were Clay, Jackson, and others. In the absence of party discipline the succession could no longer be regulated by the Republican caucus; support had to be intrigued for, and tended to form geographically, each section responding to the appeal of a particular native son. Congress rather than the executive branch held the initiative. Clay remarked to Adams, after the re-election of Monroe, that the President "had not the slightest influence on Congress. His career was considered as closed. There was nothing further to be expected by him or from him."[10]

Poor Monroe knew that something was amiss. When the country was at war, or stirred by some internal controversy, he said plaintively, "the course is plain, and you have something to cheer and animate you to action, but we are now blessed with peace, and the success of the late war has overwhelmed the federal party, so that there is no division of that kind to rally any persons together in support of the administration."[11] If he had been versed in the ancient techniques of unstable regimes he might have applied the principle of *divide et impera*—divide and rule—by setting his rivals at loggerheads. But he had no such guile. By declining to play the patronage game he lost all influence.

Looking back on the Era of Good Feelings, Martin Van Buren observed:

> In the place of two great parties arrayed against each other in a fair and open contest for the establishment of principles in the administration of Government which they respectively believed most conducive to the public interest, the country was overrun with personal factions.

He blamed Monroe for aggravating the situation. His solution to the problem of the Presidency, and of the whole nation, was not to rejoice in the disappearance of parties but to work for their restoration. A rising young professional politician in the 1820's, Van Buren did not feel apologetic for his craft. On the contrary, he saw it as the way to rescue the United States from futile animosities. The lesson was clear to another of the new breed of specialists in man-

management, for whom politics was an endlessly absorbing and not entirely cynical occupation. This was Thurlow Weed, one of Van Buren's professional rivals in New York. Weed saw the need for a revision of the party system. He also saw the potential appeal of John Quincy Adams, who in New England at any rate could command a handsome block of votes. But, he noted, sadly, "Mr. Adams during his administration failed to cherish, strengthen, or even recognize the party to which he owed his election [the National Republicans]; nor, as far as I am informed, with the great power he possessed did he make a single influential friend."[12]

Personal and fortuitous factors have to be taken into account. Monroe could have at least shown an interest in the protracted debates over the Missouri Compromise (or compromises) in 1819–21, instead of being so inert. He could have asserted himself more in the field of foreign policy. Adams blundered after the disputed election of 1824. Appointed to the Presidency in the House of Representatives when he had in fact got fewer popular and electoral votes than Andrew Jackson, he appeared to indulge in a "corrupt bargain" by rewarding Clay, who had turned the House in his favor, with the Secretaryship of State. Though there was almost certainly no "bargain" as such, the aggrieved Jackson could attract widespread sympathy as the victim of secret machinations, deprived of his rightful office by a palace guard. After this nothing went right for Adams. Jackson men inside his Cabinet were almost openly disloyal. The theory even began to develop, thanks to Monroe's and his own retention of previous executive officers, that the Cabinet's tenure might not end with each outgoing administration but be continued in some semi-independent fashion. Halfway through his Presidency, Adams confessed in his diary that while he could not conceive what retirement would be like, it could not be "worse than this perpetual motion and crazing cares. The weight grows heavier from day to day."[13] Andrew Jackson felt and showed his weariness at the very outset of his administration, which got off to almost as wobbly a start as Adams'. But he took command.

These were differences of personality. But Monroe and Adams were at the mercy of circumstance. Jackson had guessed wrong along with them when in 1816 he had offered the conventional disparagement of party politics. His pronouncements as a candidate in 1824 and 1828 were equally conventional and demure, not out of

Martin Van Buren, shrewdest of politicians, supported Andrew Jackson in 1828. To help Jackson carry New York, Van Buren ran for governor there himself; but after just two and a half months in office he resigned to become President Jackson's Secretary of State—and eventually his successor in the White House.

cunning but rather because he and his managers had no clear idea of the new look in politics. The experts in what Van Buren called the "art and business of President-making" were feeling their way toward some fresh dispensation. Van Buren put his talents for the 1824 election at the disposal of Crawford of Georgia. He may have been shrewd; but Crawford suffered a serious stroke and dropped behind in the competition. By 1828 Van Buren was ready to back Andrew Jackson; and this time Jackson won. Within a fairly short period the clever men in politics perceived that the art of President making was inseparable from the art of party making.

They reached this conclusion without forming any particular conception of the Presidency as such. They were not concerned with nice constitutional arguments as to the Chief Executive's relationship to the legislature and the judiciary, or his authority in the realm of foreign affairs. They were interested in a "strong" Executive only to the extent that a forceful President might be a popular President, and could be looked up to as a party leader instead of being cold-shouldered as Monroe and Adams had been. In a sense they did not intend to innovate, but to get back to the good days when Thomas Jefferson had been in office and the Republican machinery had revolved with a contented hum. The lessons of Jeffersonian Republicanism were not mysterious. The desired formula comprised a President with a national reputation (which of course might also mean that he had a quantity of enemies); a well-knit party, able to reward the deserving and castigate the disloyal; an issue or two large and vital enough to arouse interest in all corners of the union, and "democratic" enough to satisfy the Jeffersonian ideology; and an opposition that was, while not sufficiently powerful to win, sturdy enough to put up a reasonable fight.

The task was easier for the Republicans, or for what remained of the party by the 1820's, than for the scattered and dispirited Federalists. The Republicans had retained whatever dominance and initiative were left. A revived party would be in tune with the impetus toward political democracy that was already manifesting itself in the abolition of suffrage restrictions, the allotment of legislators to smaller electoral districts, and the growing habit of subjecting governors and officials to popular election. Such a party could also claim direct inheritance from the Jeffersonian party. In fact Jackson frequently still called himself a Republican when his party was officially styled Democratic. Opponents of "the Democracy" were on the other hand distinctly unwilling to admit descent from discredited Federalists. (It was a mark of James K. Polk's instinctive partisanship that he referred to the Whigs in his diary, as late as 1848, as the "Federal party.")

In other words conditions were favorable for a fresh demonstration of a Jeffersonian approach to politics, though probably only a man of exceptional force could have contrived to take matters as far as did Andrew Jackson. The virtual collapse of the congressional caucus in 1820 showed that some other device was needed. Jackson's defeat in 1824–25, when he had already won a sizable vote of confidence, dramatized the issue and filled him with an energizing desire for revenge. On this particular issue, majoritarian democracy and the victory of Jackson became synonymous for him. In his first annual message of December, 1829, and again a year later in his second message to Congress, Jackson revealed that he still felt the sting of his earlier frustration. "To the people," he declared in 1829, "belongs the right of electing their Chief Magistrate; it was never designed that their choice should . . . be defeated, either by the intervention of electoral colleges or by . . . the House of Representatives." In both messages he recommended a constitutional amendment to permit the free expression of the popular will. He was on familiar ground; amendments of this nature had been proposed several times in Congress in the previous decade, and very nearly carried. They, and Jackson's recommendations, never got anywhere for one cogent reason: the party in power preferred to stick to the known system, with all its manipulative possibilities, rather than take chances on a less controllable method. In 1829–30 Jackson still spoke as an outsider, a plain man unacquainted with political wiles.

In this guise he was more attractive to the populace than the Clays, Crawfords, and Calhouns. All three major groups contending for the Presidency in 1832—the Democratic party (now formally labeled as such), the National Republicans (who soon became known as Whigs), and the short-lived Antimasonic movement —chose their candidates by means of national nominating conventions. King Caucus was dead. Much of the credit for the demise went to Jackson, though in actuality the Antimasonic party convention preceded that of the Democrats by several months. Moreover, both of the other parties pioneered the introduction of party platforms in this election: the Democrats did not produce one of their own until 1840.

The Democrats had nevertheless done much to evolve a body of doctrine that cemented the party together, furnished ammunition against enemies, and again found a symbol in Andrew Jackson. The first great manifesto came in Jackson's 1829 message to Congress, on the problem of "rotation in office": in other words, whether men ought to hold governmental appointments indefinitely or be subject to removal. Once more he had Jeffersonian sanction, both in theory and in practice.[14] He had the more recent support of the Tenure of Office Act of 1820, by which Congress had limited certain appointments to a maximum of four years as a check against corruption. And he was consistent in recommending that the Presidency itself be bound by the same principle of rotation, through restriction to a single four- or six-year term in office. Among the arguments produced by Jackson in favor of rotation was his celebrated assertion that

> The duties of all public officers are, or at least admit of being made, so plain and simple that men of intelligence may readily qualify themselves for their performance; and I can not but believe that more is lost by the long continuance of men in office than is gained by their experience.

No man, he said, had any "intrinsic right" to an official post. He wished to destroy the notion that an appointment was a form of property. He conceded that there might be cases of individual hardship. But on balance, rotation—"a leading principle in the republican creed"—would give "healthful action" to the whole system of government.

The personal factor that lent force to Jackson's words was obvious. He himself had succeeded in several careers—legal, military, political—without ever undergoing a laborious apprenticeship. This Tennessee outsider had been thwarted in 1824 by the coteries of the federal Capital. Even Cabinet members were beginning to assume that they held office almost indefinitely, like federal judges. One of Jackson's rivals for the Presidency, William H. Crawford, occupied Cabinet posts continuously from 1815 to 1825. William Wirt, the Antimasonic candidate for the Presidency in 1832, was Attorney General from 1817 to 1829. The rot spread downward from the overprivileged few; or so the Jacksonians alleged.

What Jackson did not admit in his 1829 message was the influence of rotation upon political parties. He was not a simpleton, or a hypocrite. It is reasonable to suppose that politics was a secondary concern for him. Not so for his lieutenants, whose operating rule was baldly stated by William L. Marcy: "To the victor belong the spoils of the enemy." Jackson himself warmed to the idea of politics as warfare, with no quarter given to unworthy foes. But he would have preferred the less crass discussion of the problem that went on in a correspondence of 1828 between Postmaster General John McLean and young Edward Everett of Massachusetts. What, McLean asked, binds parties together? "The hope of office," was his answer, with its "honors and emoluments." Administrations could not afford to neglect this prime political truth. John Quincy Adams had followed an opposite rule, "from pure motives," but "the People will not sustain it." The earnest, respectable Everett, destined to become the nation's most admired public orator, agreed and added that in the United States, since there were no other badges of honor such as titles, "office" was everything that men sought in the public sphere. "Truly incredible," he said, "are the efforts men are willing to make, the humiliations they will endure, to get it. . . . While office is so passionately coveted, no party will sit still and see themselves postponed to their opponents in politics.[15]

This candid and intelligent exchange reveals the variety of motives that impelled men to seek presidential office or to rally around those who did. Jackson did not abuse the "spoils system" during his administrations. Though the figures are disputed, it seems that he removed between 10 and 20 per cent of the approximately ten thousand holders of federal offices, and something over a third of the six hundred officials whose appointment was the direct concern of the President. By later standards the total was modest and the application was in general honest. The wholesale massacre feared by anti-Jackson alarmists did not occur. The danger lay in the extension of the system to the indiscriminate degree practiced by Jackson's Postmaster General William T. Barry. Until Barry's incumbency the Postmaster General was not a member of the Cabinet, and local postmasters were removed only for negligence or misconduct. Whig congressmen maintained that in six years of "Barry-mongering" there had been nearly thirteen hundred removals of postal officials, usually without any explanation being given.

Barry was an exceptionally incompetent appointee, whom Jackson eventually replaced. But rotation was a double-edged weapon, apt to hurt all who wielded it. Old-style Republicans were worried by its implications. Ex-President Madison wrote in a private letter that the business of bribing and threatening entailed in the practice of wholesale rotation "could not fail to degrade any Administration." John Tyler, a future President, had similar misgivings. So did Thomas Ritchie, editor of the Richmond *Enquirer* and a sturdy Jeffersonian. "I go for reform," he assured Van Buren in March, 1829, when Jackson had been President less than a month, "but what is reform? . . . It surely is not to put out a good and experienced officer, because he was a decent friend of J. Q. Adams, *in order* to put in a heated partizan of the election of Gen. Jackson. . . . I trust that such a spirit of Reform will not come near to us in Virginia."[16] Reform or abuse, no single development would cause Presidents more headscratching, or bind them more closely to the party apparatus, than the application of the rotation principle.

The Democratic-Republican party under Jackson boasted as President a figure of national repute who had not been associated with caucus politics. They had resourceful men like Van Buren to plan strategy and distribute patronage. The next great step was to agree upon some issue that would arouse the martial enthusiasm of the whole party from the President downward. Politicians well knew the value of such issues. One of W. H. Crawford's congressional friends sighed in 1821 that if they could only "hit upon a few great principles and unite their support with that of Crawford," victory would be certain. The Jackson movement laid a general claim to be the democratic party, and intermittently professed a Jeffersonian attachment to state rights. But the big issue they hit upon was the status of the Second Bank of the United States. It was a real issue, although an intricate one. Reduced to simple terms, the battle lay between Andrew Jackson, the People's President, and the "Monster Bank." Jackson was the ideal leader in the campaign, for he shared the fairly widespread American distrust of banks and made the fight vividly personal. Old Hickory was the democracy's champion against the entrenched barons of the Bank; he was throwing down the gage at the feet of the Bank's chief henchman, Henry Clay of the "corrupt bargain." Senator Benton was delighted by the controversy. "The B.U.S.," he exulted, "is the turning point. The political engine of the federal monarchical party, will draw the lines between parties again."[17]

And so it happened. Although the Democrats had no party platform in 1832, their campaign speeches hammered away at the Bank question. Jackson's Bank Veto message was understandably denounced by his opponents as an incitement to class warfare. It was not quite that but it was certainly excellent material for party propaganda. His victory in the 1832 election showed that the country was once more grouping into rival camps, and that the Jacksonians were in a winning position. They were on the attack and they held the Presidency.

It is tempting to speculate that the national game of politics has

Jackson attacks the National Bank with his veto stick in this cartoon. Van Buren, standing at center, helps kill the monster, whose many heads represent Nicholas Biddle, director of the Bank, and the directors of the controversial institution's various state branches.

influenced the development of the American version of football, which is elaborate, ritualized, episodic, somewhat arcane, and therefore difficult for a novice to follow, and has a sort of jackpot quality in which a sudden profusion of points may be scored. Possession of the ball is highly important; fumbling may be disastrous and give possession to the other team (party). The side that has possession must give proof of the ability to gain ground or it will automatically lose possession to the other side. The most important performer in these games is a nonplayer, the coach, whose direction is, according to temperament, sometimes flamboyantly apparent and sometimes coolly concealed. The contract of an unsuccessful coach is not renewed. One might add further analogies: for example that, other things being equal, the richest team is the likeliest to rise to the head of the table.

During Jackson's Presidency one feature of old- (or new-) style politics was missing. Van Buren's later writings refer to "two great parties" as the desideratum of a healthy system. This condition was not fulfilled in 1832 or in 1836. The Democrats were more or less unified: their opponents were not. Indeed in 1836 the coalition of anti-Jackson men who now called themselves Whigs decided not to put forward one candidate but to let several run, partly in the hope that the election would have to be referred to the House of Representatives. As for Jackson, his 1829 and 1830 messages to Congress leave the impression that in those days he did not anticipate a straightforward division between two major national parties. The United States was liable, he said, to have a "multiplication of candidates for the Presidency."

By 1836 the situation was that the Democrats were proud of their national standing as a major party; and quite naturally they saw no reason to assist their enemies in consolidating to the same extent. Theorists might recommend an almost exact parity of strength between two (and no more than two) parties. The party in possession was not eager to oblige the theorists by building up its rivals. Nor, so long as the President might be picked in the House of Representatives, were the Whigs persuaded of the need to emulate the monolithic structure of the Democrats, especially since they were committed to the proposition that a powerful Executive was a national hazard.

The election of 1836 taught the Whigs a number of lessons. The negative lesson was that the multiple-candidate strategy had failed, even against the Democrats' relatively unimposing nominee Van Buren. A positive lesson was that the Whigs stood a good chance of winning in 1840 by emulating what the Democrats had done. They must capitalize upon the weaknesses of their foes. After eight years in office Jackson had alienated a good many powerful politicians. Van Buren had to be forced upon the reluctant Southern Democrats as the 1836 nominee. By 1840 a total of twelve years of Democratic rule would be bound to leave voters with a vague feeling that it was time for a change—since the millenium would as usual have failed to arrive under the current administration.

The result of Whig cogitations was the choice of a Middle Western candidate of Southern birth, whose manner was dignified and who was portrayed as the hero of Tippecanoe—a battle against the Indians fought in 1811. William Henry Harrison was the nearest

William Henry Harrison dispenses cider to voters outside his log cabin while Jackson and Van Buren try vainly to stop him.

thing to Andrew Jackson, with Whig overtones. The successful campaign waged on his behalf against Van Buren marked the full emergence of what R. P. McCormick calls the second party system. Most accounts of the "Log Cabin" saturnalia of 1840 stress the emptiness and imitativeness of the Whig campaign. There is the implication that in their lust for office they cynically outbid the Democrats. It is true that they did lust for office, and that having won they snatched at the spoils even more avidly than Jackson's or Van Buren's followers. It is also true that a few of the more austere Whigs expressed regret at the vote-catching vulgarities of the campaign season. Much more significant, however, is the readiness and skill of the Whigs in pitching their appeal at a popular level. This was not blind imitation of the Democrats but shrewd recognition of the political facts of life. The second party system, like the first Republican-Federalist system, produced national coalition-organizations whose primary effort went into the capture of the Presidency. What differentiated the second system was the elaboration and professionalism of these organizations, the small (though still not trivial) zone of disagreement as to party platforms, the dramatizing of the contest through the press, the state and national party conventions, and the campaign itself, with its plethora of speeches, songs, and slogans. The voting figures reveal the effect on the American public. In 1840, in an election supposedly rendered meaningless by farcical claims and accusations, 78 per cent of those eligible to vote turned out to register their preference. The figure was easily the highest recorded up till then in a presidential contest. It was not to be surpassed until the McKinley-Bryan battle of 1896. In other words, the lines had been drawn again. Willy-nilly, Presidents were —at least for the period between winning nomination and leaving office—the standard-bearers of their parties. As before, not all of them welcomed the role, which exposed them to indignity and additional controversy. The separation of powers implanted in the Constitution isolated them from their congressional cohorts, as if they were generals trying to command an army by remote control. As soon as the next election loomed, their authority began to dwindle unless they were clear favorites for renomination. As soon as they retired from the White House, unless like Jackson they had an exceptional hold over the party, they were apt to be put out to graze. They were in such cases symbols whose magic had evaporated. The scratched buttons and faded ribbons and yellowed newspaper clippings that had borne their names ended up with other miscellaneous relics of the past in old desk drawers. This was the near-oblivion of democratic politics: ruthless, wasteful, and in the main desirable.

Thenceforward party politics pervaded American life. In 1841 a Whig administration followed Van Buren's Democratic term in office. In 1845 the Democrats returned to power with James K. Polk. In 1849 Zachary Taylor brought victory for the Whigs. In 1853 the Democrats once more celebrated a presidential inauguration—that of Franklin Pierce. The rapid alternations created an irresistibly congenial climate for the spoils system. It spread so far and fast that every four years brought thousands of new faces into the post offices and custom houses and bureaus of the land, while the demand for places seemed always to outrun supply. In ceasing to be regarded as private property (if they had), the offices rotated in the whirligig of fortune had apparently become party property. The process affected an astonishing number of citizens, from the impecunious to the thrivingly ambitious. The writer Nathaniel Hawthorne is an example of one of the impecunious, thrust in and out of office with dazing rapidity. A Democrat and a classmate at Bowdoin College of the rising politician Franklin Pierce of New Hampshire, Hawthorne was helped by Pierce to secure a post in the Boston Custom House during Van Buren's administration. Harrison's victory left him unemployed in 1841: this is one of the reasons he went to live for a while at the Utopian colony at Brook Farm, near Boston. In came Polk; and presently Hawthorne was again a federal officeholder, this time as surveyor of the port of Salem. His removal in 1849, on account of Taylor's triumph, aroused some local protest, but he was still removed: a humiliation on which he spoke feelingly in the preface to *The Scarlet Letter.* He now wrote busily to replace his lost income. Among his literary products was a dutifully eulogistic campaign biography of Pierce, published during the election year of 1852. Pierce's success brought a reward for Hawthorne—as for thousands of deserving Democrats—in the shape of a consulship at Liverpool, which he held for four years.[18] At least a small part of his mournful withdrawnness during the Civil War may be seen as the response of a Democrat whose party was then in semidisgrace.

The most exasperating consequence of the identification of politics with the Presidency was experienced by the Presidents themselves. Filling posts in their administration had always been a delicate and sometimes a burdensome responsibility. It was now a nightmare. After Harrison's inauguration the White House was surrounded by a frantic crowd of office seekers. They invaded the building. The President, trying to hold a Cabinet meeting, could not find a vacant room. He could not persuade the throng to leave him alone; they insisted that he receive their mass of papers on the spot and promise to attend to them. In desperation he agreed. He and an official were at least allowed to escape upstairs, laden with applications. Polk, who augmented his difficulties through a fiercely partisan interpretation of his duties, came to loathe a process of which he theoretically approved. The pages of his diary are full of self-commiseration. In March, 1846, he wrote, "I am ready to exclaim, will the pressure for office never cease! It is one year today since I entered . . . office, and still the pressure . . . has not abated." Two and a half years later he was just as exasperated:

> The office of President is generally esteemed a very high & dignified position. . . . I think the public would not so regard it if they could . . . observe the kind of people by whom I am often annoyed. I . . . must be accessible to my fellow-citizens, and this gives an opportunity to all . . . descriptions of people to obtrude themselves upon me. . . . There is no class of our population by whom I am annoyed so much, or for whom I entertain a more sovereign contempt, than the professed office-seekers who have besieged me ever since I have been in the Presidential office.

In fact Polk more than once recorded the view that no President would ever again be re-elected. "The number of office-seekers has become so large," he said in January, 1847, "that they probably hold the balance of power between the two great parties in the country, and if disappointed . . . under one administration they will readily unite . . . with the party and candidate of opposite politics . . . to increase their chances for place." In short, "the patronage of the Government will destroy the popularity of any President, however well he may administer the Government."[19] An alarming paradox: the absence of a vigorous party competition rendered the President powerless, but party competition, carried to its logical conclusion in the spoils system, had the same effect.

*Four Presidents (clockwise from top, left): William Henry Harrison,
Zachary Taylor, Franklin Pierce, and James Buchanan. The first two died
in office; Pierce and Buchanan were woefully inept.*

Polk was unduly despondent. Later Presidents learned to tolerate the system as an inevitable feature of life. Even Zachary Taylor, who had had forty years of continuous military service before reaching the Presidency, absorbed the notion from the American air he breathed. At the outset of his administration he assured Thurlow Weed that he did not intend to kick away the party ladder by which he had ascended—"colonels, majors, captains, lieutenants, sergeants, and corporals are just as necessary to success in politics as they are to the discipline and efficiency of an army." Despite this robust attitude, Taylor no more learned to enjoy the pressure than did other Presidents. A caller at the White House early in Taylor's term found that sixty or seventy persons were ahead of him. The majority had come on harmless if tedious ceremonial errands; but there were "knots gathered in corners" of anxious supplicants.[20] In the argument over ratifying the 1787 Constitution, Governor Clinton had once predicted that the President would be "surrounded with expectants and courtiers." He was right, except that the former far outnumbered the latter.

The only reasonable compromise open to Presidents was to tackle the unsavory task with dispatch and humor (with the consoling knowledge that some of the "career" federal bureaus were immune to these recurrent evictions), and to avoid becoming unnecessarily embroiled. A delightful deadpan note from President Lincoln illustrates the secret amusement to be extracted from a wretched business. It is an answer to one of thousands of people who pestered him for jobs:

> *My dear Madam*
> The most I can say is that when the time comes, if it be made to appear that the appointment of your friend to the Post-Office at Oskaloosa, will be as satisfactory to the people there, as would be that of any other person, he will probably receive it; otherwise not.[21]

At the other extreme was the conduct of Lincoln's predecessor James Buchanan. Buchanan, who had been in politics for as long a spell as Taylor had been in the Army, tried to carry the rotation principle beyond the permissible limit. He offended against party ethics by maintaining that although he was a Democrat who followed another Democrat, his administration was nevertheless new

This Whig cartoon, drawn during the presidential campaign of 1852, shows General Winfield Scott pulling the President's chair away from Democrat Franklin Pierce, who complains, "Do you want to knock a feller's brains out?" But Pierce won the election that November.

and ought to be given a free hand in removals and appointments. Even the spoilsmen objected to such a proposition. And Buchanan offended against presidential ethics by urging federal appointees to secure his renomination in 1860. The attempt failed: again he had gone too far.

It is not surprising that civil service reform became almost an obsessive concern of righteous Americans in the generation after the Civil War. As Polk suggested, the spoils system not only took up too much of the President's time, but it had a dangerous tendency to cheapen the executive office and to reintroduce an element of faction that often set the President at odds with members of his party in and out of Congress. When scholars discussed the history of the Jacksonian Era during the next three quarters of a century, few gave high marks to the People's President. Moisei Ostrogorski, William Graham Sumner, and others blamed him for setting in train the disastrous deterioration of American governmental service. They were too hard on him as a person, and not sympathetic enough to the conundrum of how to make government both popular and elevated. But they were justified in expressing disquiet. The ideology of democracy sounded perilously close to hypocrisy.

Other political aspects of the Presidency deserve a mention. One problem was the choice of an appropriate candidate. Most of the men who nursed presidential ambitions were politicians. Their labors in the party cause entitled them to expect consideration. Yet the Presidency had an aura of remoteness, of symbolic majesty. Politicians were men who rolled up their sleeves and got their hands dirty. If they were smooth, like Van Buren, they incurred suspicion as trimmers, artful dodgers, men without principle. In Calhoun's view, Van Buren was not "of the race of the lion or of the tiger; he belonged to a lower order—the fox."[22] But certain politicians such as Calhoun were not foxy enough. Their tigerish assertions of principle made them unacceptable. They were not "available." The search therefore, out of expediency and out of some more elevated desire, was for candidates who were "available" in not having made enemies, and also distinguished in some national sphere. The President was to be in and yet not of the political scene. He was to be introduced to it, not—if possible—spawned by it. Hence the attractiveness of military heroes: Washington, Jackson, Harrison, Taylor, Winfield Scott. Available soldiers must also be civilian enough in outlook to refute the charge that they were fond of military despotism, standing armies, and social hierarchies. The professional politicans of the pre-Civil War decades might have felt frustrated and resentful if the stock of suitable military candidates had been abundant enough to fill the office in continuous succession. They could take heart from the defeat of General Scott at the hands of Brigadier General Pierce, who was more of a politico than a warrior. Like Pierce, however, they were quick to see the advantages of a military reputation. When a war came, ambition as well as patriotism set them scrambling for officers' commissions.

In the Mexican War James K. Polk probably played politics too hard. His dilemma was ironical. As President of the United States

---

This songsheet honored Zachary Taylor's role in the victory at Buena Vista during the Mexican War; two years later Taylor became President.

"General Taylor never Surrenders"

→ BUENA VISTA ←

GRAND TRIUMPHAL MARCH

Composed in Honor of

MAJOR GENERAL TAYLOR'S

VICTORY IN MEXICO

February 23d 1847

Philadelphia J. G. Osbourn 112 So. 3rd Street.   Nett 25 Cts.

he wished to encompass the defeat of Mexico. As head of the Democratic party he wished to secure the credit for victory to his own chosen people. He did his best by appointing Democrats to nearly all the new brigadier and major generalships—including his former Tennessee law partner Gideon Pillow. He was prepared to let a reasonable number of junior commissions go to the Whigs, but when he found the congressional Democrats unwilling to yield the point he did not press it unduly. The great problem was that the Army's two most senior active generals, Taylor and Scott, were both Whigs. He did not think highly of them as soldiers: he detested them as Whigs. If they were permitted to win resounding victories, Polk would be presenting the rival party with a ready-made presidential candidate, perhaps two. If he withheld supplies and men he would have behaved despicably—and the disgrace might well rebound on the Democrats. The only solution, which he adopted with some eagerness, was to put a Democratic general in supreme command. The suggested warrior was Thomas Hart Benton, senator from Missouri, who had seen brief service in the War of 1812. To make Benton senior to Scott and Taylor he would have to be given the then nonexistent rank of lieutenant general. The plan was submitted to Congress and rejected only through strenuous Whig efforts, though it was a preposterous plan. Polk, chagrined and tormented, had to watch the two Whig generals bring the war to a triumphant close. As he had feared, one of them—Taylor—stepped into the Whig presidential nomination in 1848. Polk vented his frustration upon his diary, denouncing Taylor and Scott as unscrupulous politicians. When news reached him of each victorious battle, he merely complained that he ought to have been notified more promptly. He developed the peevish theory that generals did not win battles, and ought not to be lauded: the real heroes, Polk said, were the volunteer soldiers, most of whom happened to be Democrats.

Polk allowed political feelings to warp his judgement. What of Lincoln in the Civil War? He had the stigma of being a professional politician of unheroic antecedents; and of course he was a minority President, the nominee of a newly formed and miscellaneous party. Most of the prominent Republicans distrusted or even despised him. Yet according to David Donald, Lincoln showed great political finesse in controlling his party, in securing renomination when

no one seemed enthusiastic for him, and in winning re-election—
the first President since Jackson to accomplish the feat. Some
historians would not lay so much stress on Lincoln's political sophistication. But David Donald is right to emphasize Lincoln's
canniness, his ability to play off factions hostile to him by making
them fight one another, his adroitness in avoiding controversial
statements of policy, and his Buchanan-like manipulation of patronage to turn votes his way. The difference between him and
Buchanan was that he succeeded in his maneuver.

There were of course other differences, which also set him above
Polk in political mastery. He played the political game with
shrewdness but without pettiness or rancor. He had the sagacity to
convert his weakness into a kind of strength by establishing himself
at the head of a coalition government. In 1864 he spoke of himself
not as the Republican but as the "National Union" party nominee,
and underlined the notion by welcoming the nomination of Andrew Johnson of Tennessee, a Union Democrat, as vice-presidential
running mate. He was not repudiating the idea of political parties,
as Monroe and John Quincy Adams had misguidedly done. Rather,
he was seeking to pull into his orbit everyone who would give him
support—and perhaps eventually a vote. His relations with Congress were sometimes strained; he was not a President on the Jefferson model, hand in glove with the legislative branch. The pros
and cons of Lincoln's political strategy could be debated indefinitely. So could the advantages and disadvantages of an evolution that
through the decades brought the Presidency into the arena of party
politics. It might be argued that the process was one of deterioration. The best answer is that if the political ruck could produce a
Lincoln for President, and if he could so skillfully deploy his political experience without surrendering any of the essential grandeur
of the executive office, then the history of the Presidency up to
1865 was on the whole a history not of decline but of successful adap-
tation.

PART TWO

"BORN TO COMMAND."

OF VETO MEMORY.

HAD I BEEN CONSULTED.

KING ANDREW THE FIRST

LIMITING FACTORS

ABRAHAM LINCOLN 1861-1865
ANDREW JOHNSON 1865-1869
ULYSSES S. GRANT 1869-1877
RUTHERFORD B. HAYES 1877-1881
JAMES A. GARFIELD 1881
CHESTER A. ARTHUR 1881-1885
GROVER CLEVELAND 1885-1889
BENJAMIN HARRISON 1889-1893
GROVER CLEVELAND 1893-1897
WILLIAM McKINLEY 1897-1901

CHAPTER FIVE

Suspicion of the Presidency

THE previous three chapters have described how the Presidency became "legitimized," and how the office took on reality and vitality. Americans unable to imagine in 1789 what the Presidency would be like were within thirty years or less unable to remember what the country had been like without a Presidency. Most historians of America's Chief Magistracy chart its development as an intermittent yet irreversible increase in prestige and authority. Power once successfully wielded by "strong" Presidents is in their view jeopardized or left unused by "weak" Presidents, but never quite lost. Assessments of "strong" or "great" Presidents seem to agree that several of the first dozen incumbents fall into this honorific category. A collection of essays entitled *America's Ten Greatest Presidents* (1961), edited by Morton Borden, pays the high compliment to no less than five among the first twelve: to Washington, John Adams, Jefferson, Jackson, and Polk.

In the anti-Jackson cartoon at left, the President gaily dons Napoleon's clothes as Van Buren and Roger B. Taney encourage his despotism.

Moreover, such estimates invariably assume that what has been good for the Presidency has been good for the country. Edward S. Corwin is by no means condemning the tendency when he remarks that "by and large, the history of the presidency has been a history of aggrandizement." He and other distinguished political scientists, generally speaking, see the cumulative expansion of executive power as an index of national unity and national power.

No doubt they are correct. But it is important to remember that the process has not been continuous, nor has it been uncontested. The growth of presidential power has perturbed many Americans who ought not to be dismissed as merely stupid or hysterical. Corwin sums up the basis of their uneasiness and resentment when he says in the same paragraph:

> The Constitution reflects the struggle between two conceptions of executive power: that it ought always to be subordinate to the supreme legislative power, and that it ought to be, within generous limits, autonomous and self-directing; or, in other terms, the idea that the people are *represented* in the Legislature versus the idea that they are *embodied* in the Executive.[1]

The struggle, he adds, has never entirely ceased.

For a corroboration we need look no further back than the 1964 presidential campaign. Here are the words — extraordinary in the circumstances — of one of the contenders, Senator Barry Goldwater, in "My Case for the Republican Party":

> We hear praise of a power-wielding, arm-twisting President who "gets his program through Congress" by knowing the use of power.
> Throughout the course of history, there have been many other such wielders of power. There have even been dictators who regularly held plebiscites, in which their dictatorships were approved by an Ivory-soap-like percentage of the electorate. But their countries were not free, nor can any country remain free under such despotic power.
> Some of the current worship of powerful executives may come from those who admire strength and accomplishment of any sort. Others hail the display of Presidential strength . . . simply because they approve of the *result* reached by the use of power. This is nothing less than the totalitarian philosophy that the end justifies the means. . . . If ever there was a phi-

losophy of government totally at war with that of the Founding Fathers, it is this one.

To be a constitutionalist, it is at least as important that the use of power be legitimate as that it be beneficial.[2]

This was a dominant theme of Goldwater's campaign. Elsewhere he asserted that America's traditional and essential balance of power was being upset "by the trend toward increasing concentration of power in the Presidency. . . . *The more complete and concentrated executive power becomes, the greater will be the temptation to employ it to wipe out all opposing power.* . . ."[3]

It could be said that Goldwater was resoundingly defeated, and that he lost partly because he dealt in such hoary platitudes. He could not hope to scare the American people by warning them of dangers that had long ago disappeared, if indeed they had ever existed, in the United States. It could be noted, too, that he spoke as a senator: complaints of executive encroachments have been a standard feature of congressional oratory since 1789. He spoke moreover as an upholder of state rights—another ancient source of hostility to centralized government. The significant point, however, is that after one hundred seventy-five years of the Presidency, an honest though somewhat ingenuous nominee for the office could gain the confidence of a major party, and the enthusiastic if confused agreement of millions of fellow citizens, by reiterating the old cry of "executive encroachment," of presidential despotism. In fact the Republican party was no stranger to the cry. Throughout his successful campaign of 1952, General Eisenhower had stressed the need to end "executive usurpations of power" and to "restore the Congress to its rightful place in the Government."[4]

The persistence of this fear deserves to be taken seriously. A central clue is provided by Corwin's reminder that there have been two rival conceptions of executive power. The "strong" Presidents, their admiring biographers, and perhaps a majority of Americans have preferred the "autonomous and self-directing" conception. But a sizable number of "weak" Presidents and a numerous minority of Americans have preferred the conception of a limited Executive, acting negatively in response to the initiative of Congress and taking no step to weaken the authority of individual states. The Founding Fathers appeared to tip the balance toward the first con-

This cartoon of 1951 depicts a pint-sized Harry Truman asking Congress for powers he is not big enough to handle.

ception. Not all the Founding Fathers agreed, however, nor did many of their supporters. They were disposed to fight for their conception, and to believe all aspirants to the Presidency guilty of nefarious designs until proved innocent. For men who actually achieved the Presidency, this meant that they were regarded with suspicion until the moment they left office. At the back of men's minds was the dread of monarchy, tyranny, despotism, usurpation — a vocabulary of doubt and resentment employed again and again.

Of course the critics of Presidents often exaggerated, and knew they were exaggerating, for partisan purposes. Politicians avail themselves of whatever weapons are to hand. The fiercer the contest the less scruple they have in choice of weapons — including brickbats. "Waving the bloody shirt" against the Democrats (associating them with Southern secession) was to be a favorite tactic of Republicans after the Civil War.[5] In the same way, the opposition party in the first half-century of American nationhood could always hope to attract votes (partly through appealing to xenophobia) by accusing the administration of un-American inclinations towards monarchism.

Much of the criticism of George Washington was deliberately exaggerated along these lines. Could the more scurrilous journalists and pamphleteers who attacked him really have believed that he wanted to be king, or was behaving like a hypocrite and an autocrat? They must, we feel, have been conscious of the unfairness of describing him as one who "thundered contempt upon the people with as much confidence as if he sat upon the throne of Indostan," or of grumbling that he "receives visits. He returns none. Are these republican virtues? Do they command our esteem?" Another assailant pretended that the "improper influence" of Washington had deceived and "debauched" the American nation. "Let the history of the federal government," he went on, "instruct mankind, that the masque of patriotism may be worn to conceal the foulest designs against the liberties of a people." The abuse heaped on Washington by Thomas Paine, the erstwhile hero of early Revolutionary days, had a demented quality. Paine, living in France, had convinced himself that the United States was sliding back into British monarchical-aristocratic ways, and that Washington was largely to blame. In a sixty-page open letter, written in 1796, Paine ranted that you commenced your Presidential career by encouraging and swallowing the grossest adulation, and you travelled America . . . to put yourself in the way of receiving it. . . .

John Adams has said (and John . . . was always a speller after places and offices) . . . that as Mr. Washington had no child . . . the Presidency should be made hereditary in the family of Lund Washington [a cousin]. . . . He did not go so far as to say, also, that the Vice Presidency should be hereditary in the family of John Adams. He prudently left that to stand on the ground that one good turn deserves another.[6]

The interest of such scurrility lies not in its truthfulness, for it is invariably inaccurate as well as malignant, but in the underlying motivation. Two points should be noted. One is that these onslaughts represent a complex though largely irrational hostility to any person who achieves the combination of high office and celebrity that define the Presidency. Merely to be President, no matter how deservingly or how modestly, is to attract venomous abuse. The second point is that this abuse reveals a less irrational dislike of the combination of power and social standing that make the Presidency actually comparable—even if the comparison is somewhat farfetched—to an elective monarchy. In the case of Washington, since he maintained a dignified style and since fear of a reversion to monarchy was still understandable, the element of rationality was more genuine than with subsequent Presidents. The vocabulary was inevitably a good deal more than mere rhetoric.

Three other factors help to account for the unpopularity that surrounded the Presidency along with the acclaim. The situation of Barry Goldwater, as we have seen, displays these factors, which are friction between Congress and the Executive, party politics, and state rights. Power must rival power: this was the condition of a government of separated branches, fully comprehended by Madison, Hamilton, and other Founding Fathers. Power acquired must necessarily be power acquired *from* some other branch. Each time a President successfully asserted an additional prerogative he laid up trouble for himself and his successors. Congress would be sure to strike back. Sometimes it would strike when no offense had been given, just to keep in training. Of thirty-three items of possible legislation proposed by the undemanding Calvin Coolidge in his first annual message, Congress deigned to pass only one. A newspaper, looking at the record of Coolidge's relations with Capitol Hill, said "Congress has devoted itself to bloodying the President's nose, boxing his ears, and otherwise maltreating him."[7] The contest was bloodier still when vital and controversial issues were at stake. So great has been the cleavage, and the resultant friction, that a modern political scientist, James MacGregor Burns, diagnoses what he calls *The Deadlock of Democracy*. In his book, first published in 1963, Burns argues that the United States long ago developed, and suffered from thereafter, not a two-party but a four-party system. Each of the two main parties, according to his analysis, has split into a presidential and a congressional bloc.[8]

Whether or not Burns is correct, it is undeniable that members of the opposition party, sometimes assisted by disaffected congressmen from the administration party, often voiced intense suspicion of nineteenth-century Presidents. This suspicion was particularly virulent at times of crisis. A major source of complaint, exacerbated in wartime by the historic distrust of standing armies, was the President's patronage power. James Madison was a mild, scholarly man with a deep aversion to "executive encroachments." When during the War of 1812 he asked for an increase in the size of the regular Army, John Randolph of Roanoke (a member of his own party) protested that Madison was building up a "mighty apparatus of favoritism." The rival Federalist party accused Madison of scheming to place James Monroe at the head of the vastly expanded army. Monroe, acting Secretary of War, was also Secretary of State, and the most likely successor to Madison as President. "What a grasp at power is this!" exploded the Federalist politician Josiah Quincy of Massachusetts. His party was doubly indignant because the new officers' commissions were given almost exclusively to Republicans.[9]

Similar fury was aroused during the Mexican War, by James K. Polk's endeavors to turn it to the advantage of his own party and to the disadvantage of the Whigs. At the beginning of 1848, when the war was virtually over, Polk asked for ten additional regular regiments and twenty volunteer regiments. A Whig congressman angrily maintained that the five hundred and forty new Army officers created by this move were meant to help purchase the coming presidential election for the Democrats. Polk, said his critic, "has already much greater patronage than Washington, Madison, Jackson, or any other of his predecessors . . . and I cannot . . . believe that the interests or honor of the country would be advanced by increasing it."[10] Compare the Whig complaint in eighteenth-century England that the king's power "has increased, is increasing, and ought to be diminished."

The state rights controversy likewise fomented hostility toward any President who had asserted the supremacy of the central government. In the days of the Virginia Dynasty of Presidents the issue was on the whole dormant. Jefferson, Madison, and Monroe genuinely believed in preserving the sovereign rights of the states. On several occasions they vetoed or discouraged bills providing federal funds for internal improvements, arguing that while such bills might be desirable they could not be sanctioned without the passing of a constitutional amendment. But Madison clashed with the governors of Massachusetts and Connecticut. Opposed to the administration over the War of 1812, the New Englanders denied that Madison was empowered to call out the militias and use them outside the boundaries of their own states.

This and other disputes were fought out mainly in the Supreme Court, where Chief Justice John Marshall served as champion of federal over state jurisdiction. But in 1832 there was a violent clash between Andrew Jackson and South Carolina caused by Southern objections to high tariffs. Jackson's prompt, unyielding response to the Palmetto State's defiance won him high praise from posterity and even from such unfriendly contemporaries as Daniel Webster. His Nullification Proclamation of December, 1832, is regarded as a key document in the history of federal control, and an example of his indomitable courage.

There is, however, another side to the story. One reason South Carolina persisted in defying the Washington government was that Jackson's previous conduct seemed to show that he too was a state rights man. He had vetoed the Maysville Road Bill of 1830 on strict-constructionist grounds. He had openly sympathized with the state of Georgia, and openly flouted John Marshall's Court, in the controversy as to whether Georgia had the right to remove the Cherokees within its borders or whether—as the Supreme Court ruled—the Indians were wards of the federal government. The surprise and outrage of South Carolina are revealed in the resolutions approved by the state legislature as a reply to his Nullification decree:

Resolved, That the proclamation of the President is the more extraordinary, that he had silently, and as it is supposed, with entire approbation, witnessed our sister state of Georgia avow, act upon, and carry into effect, even to the taking of life, principles identical with those now denounced by him in South Carolina.

How was his behavior to be explained? The obvious answer, according to John C. Calhoun and his fellow Carolinians, was that power had gone to the President's head. "King Andrew" was acting as capriciously and arrogantly as any European despot:

Resolved, That the opinions of the President, in regard to the rights of the States, are erroneous and dangerous, leading not only to the establishment of a consolidated government in the stead of our free confederacy, *but to the concentration of all powers in the chief executive. . . .*
Resolved, That the declaration of the President . . . is rather an appeal to the loyalty of subjects, than to the patriotism of citizens, and is a blending of official and individual character, heretofore unknown in our state papers, and revolting to our conception of political propriety.

Historians have rightly stressed the importance of Jackson in making the Presidency a far more vivid, personal, popular, dynamic institution. Something new began with Andrew Jackson. Clinton Rossiter hints at the reverse side of the coin when he remarks that "more than one such President a century would be hard to take." To see why Jackson's enemies saw him as a baleful influence it is necessary to review the events of his administrations critically instead of admiringly: in other words, as they appeared to such opponents as Calhoun, Daniel Webster, and Henry Clay.

Charles M. Wiltse, the biographer of Calhoun, is one of the few modern scholars to have undertaken this valuable task. The record of Jacksonian usurpation, he points out, contained several weighty charges.[11] Thus, over the Peggy Eaton affair Jackson had behaved (in the view of his enemies) with savage indiscretion. Mrs. Margaret Bayard Smith, a fairly sympathetic Washington hostess, reported that "the only excuse his best friends can make for his violence and imbecilities, is, that he is in his dotage." In the affair he treated his Cabinet and his Vice-President with contempt. Indeed he replaced every member except one, his Postmaster General. Even before this

A grotesque caricature of President Jackson, obviously drawn by someone who detested him

he had formed the habit of relying on a "Kitchen Cabinet" of editors and politicians. He established the Washington *Globe* as an administration newspaper, and used it and other Democratic publications to pervert the truth and coerce his followers into unswerving obedience to the party line. He wrecked the ideal of an impartial, permanent civil service by sanctifying the cynical practice of rotation in office. He brought the code of a frontier bully into the White House. His crude, implacable clansman's outlook impelled him to believe that John Quincy Adams and Henry Clay had stooped to a corrupt bargain in order to keep him out of the Presidency. He broke off relations with his own Vice-President when he discovered that Calhoun had disapproved of his highhanded activities as a military leader ten years earlier. He earned the enmity of former supporters, including Representative Davy Crockett and Senator Hugh Lawson White from his own state of Tennessee, and the strong-willed Senator George Poindexter of Mississippi.

In vetoing the recharter of the Second Bank of the United States, Jackson had defied well-informed public opinion and the wishes of both houses of Congress. In his eight years of office he used the veto twelve times—more than the eleven vetoes of all his predecessors. His Bank Veto appealed blatantly to the common man, stirring up class war with its allegations that the friends of the Bank were friends of monopoly and aristocracy.

In the Cherokee cases the President contended that he was not bound by decisions of the Supreme Court. The executive, in his view (as docilely expounded in administration newspapers) was an independent, coordinate branch of the government, with the right to "execute" the Constitution according to executive interpretation. He made the challenge explicit in his Bank veto message of July, 1832. Although previous Supreme Court rulings had held (as in *McCulloch v. Maryland, 1819,* and *Osborn v. Bank of the U.S., 1824*) that the Bank was constitutional, he refused to recognize such precedents:

> If the opinion of the Supreme Court covered the whole ground of this act, it ought not to control the co-ordinate authorities of this government. . . . Each public officer who takes an oath to support the Constitution swears that he will support it as he understands it, and not as it is understood by others. . . . The opinion of the judges has no more authority over Congress than the opinion of Congress has over the judges; and on that point the President is independent of both.

When Jackson vetoed the Bank recharter in 1832 it still had four years of life left. He decided to kill the Bank at once by removing the government deposits to which it was entitled in the original charter. He had to dismiss two Secretaries of the Treasury before he could find a third, Roger B. Taney, who was ready to do his bidding. The deposits were transferred to an assortment of twenty-three private or "pet" banks.

The President had in this instance as in the Peggy Eaton imbroglio made clear his contempt for his Cabinet. He had shown equal contempt for the judiciary. His opponents in Congress maintained that by vetoing so many of their bills, and by asserting in effect that he was the voice of the popular will, Jackson was guilty of similar contempt for the legislative branch. In an unprecedented step the Senate vented its displeasure by introducing two censure resolutions, one against Jackson and one against Taney, at the end of 1833. Both passed, after protracted debate. What was at stake, said Calhoun, was not just a struggle over a bank but "a struggle between the executive and legislative departments of the government."

Jackson's answer to the Senate was a lengthy message, by turns caustic and plaintive, which denounced the censure resolutions as unconstitutional, described them as an act akin to impeachment, and demanded that his reply be entered on the Senate's records. The request was refused. (The Senate took further vengeance by refusing to confirm Taney's appointment as Secretary of the Treasury and postponing confirmation of his subsequent appointment to the Supreme Court, though in 1836 he was eventually rewarded with the Chief Justiceship, upon the death of John Marshall.)

The Senate's display was vindictive. But Jackson's opponents could contend that it was he who had loosed the vendettas of partisan politics upon the United States, and they who were reluctantly obliged to follow suit. They saw proof of the vendetta instincts of the Jacksonian Democracy in the long campaign of Senator Thomas Hart Benton of Missouri (who had once fought a vicious duel-cum-brawl with Jackson before becoming a henchman) to have the censure resolution expunged from the Senate journal and—a vulgarly melodramatic touch—to have "black lines . . . drawn around the entry." Benton at last got his way in January, 1837, by 24 votes to 19. "And now, sir," he declared in triumph, "I finish the task which, three years ago, I imposed on myself. Solitary and alone, and amidst the jeers and taunts of my opponents, I put this ball in motion. The people have taken it up and rolled it forward, and I am not anything in the vast mass which now propels it. In the name of the mass I speak. . . ."[12]

Benton's demagogic cry rankled and lodged in the Whig memory. Apart from everything else, it was absurd to pretend that he had fought alone, sustained only by the people. In several states controlled by the Democrats, senators were "instructed" by the state legislatures to vote with Benton. Some meekly obeyed; some, like John Tyler of Virginia, resigned their seats in protest. Yet another grievance against "King Andrew" was that in his first and second annual messages, recommending a mode of popular election for the President, he also recommended that the "Chief Magistrate" should be limited to "a single term of either four or six years." The reasons he gave, in the second message, were that the President was the agent most subject to the temptation to exceed his powers. Was Andrew Jackson not convicted out of his own mouth? For he ignored his previous, reiterated dictum. He made sure that his followers nominated him for a second term. As this

"The ball a rolling on" for the Whig team was more than just a campaign slogan in 1840. Pushing a huge paper ball from city to city, Whig partisans gave posterity the phrase "Keep the ball rolling."

drew near its end, Calhoun was one of those who believed that Jackson was bent on a third term in office. Calhoun was wrong, of course, but he felt he was essentially right: Jackson picked his successor, Martin Van Buren, and forced him upon the party convention, together with a vice-presidential nominee, Richard M. Johnson of Kentucky, so distasteful to some of the party faithful that he was actually hissed by the Virginia delegation. In the 1836 election, Jackson's home state, Tennessee, indicated the extent of anti-Jackson feeling by handing its electoral votes to his antagonist Hugh Lawson White.[13]

Benton's victory was given an ironical twist in the election of 1840, when the Whigs settled part of the score against Jackson by engineering the defeat of his handpicked favorite Van Buren. "I put this ball in motion," Benton had bragged. Whig demonstrators retaliated in 1840 by rolling forward a giant sphere, to the accompaniment of a jeering campaign song:

> What has caused this great commotion, motion, motion,
>   Our country through?
>   It is the ball a-rolling on,
> For Tippecanoe and Tyler too, Tippecanoe and Tyler too.
> And with them we'll beat little Van, Van, Van;
>   Van is a used-up man.

The Whigs got their own back too by pretending that Van Buren, "King Matty," while not as fierce a tyrant as his predecessor, had at least developed a royal taste for gold dinner services, eau de Cologne, and expensive wine:

> King Matty he sat in his "big white House,"
> A curling his whiskers fine,
> And the *Globe* man, Blair, sat by his side,
> A drinking his champagne wine, wine, wine,
> A drinking his champagne wine.

The speedy adoption by the Whigs of Democratic techniques, including the spoils system as well as the carnival type of election campaign, makes it appear that the charges of executive despotism against Jackson had no real substance. Van Buren's explanation, in his *Autobiography,* is that the anti-Jackson men took up the cry because they had no other—once they discovered that the Bank contest was going against them. In his brilliant *Age of Jackson* (1945), Arthur M. Schlesinger, Jr., agrees that "executive despotism" was a rallying cry for enemies of Jackson's who otherwise had almost nothing in common. He concedes that "the fear of executive despotism . . . is no fancy, as the experience of the one-party states of the twentieth century clearly shows." But he thinks it unlikely that "many raised this cry against Jackson who would not have fought him anyway." The charge of tyranny, Schlesinger adds, "has been made against every strong Democratic President by those whose interests he threatens." This is borne out by the administrations of Franklin D. Roosevelt and John F. Kennedy, which Schlesinger has also explored with admiring insight.[14]

It may seem then that we are to discount the violence of language hurled against Andrew Jackson. It would appear to belong to the inflated currency of partisan rhetoric, and to testify more to envy and chagrin and congressional touchiness than to genuine alarm. This is certainly how most historians view the extreme instances of anti-Jacksonianism, during the period of the censure debates. A few well-known examples convey the tone of such indictments. Chancellor Kent of New York wrote to Justice Story, "I look upon Jackson as a detestable, ignorant, reckless, vain and malignant tyrant. . . . This elective monarchy frightens me. The experiment, with its foundations laid on universal suffrage and our unfettered press, is of too violent a nature for our excitable people." Daniel Webster, fulminating in the Senate, declared that "the President carries on the government; all the rest are subcontractors. . . . A

Briareus sits in the centre of our system, and with his hundred hands touches everything, controls everything." Henry Clay, also in the Senate, said: "We are in the midst of a revolution, hitherto bloodless, but tending rapidly towards a total change of the pure republican character of the Government, and to the concentration of all power in the hands of one man." Governor Erastus Root of New York wrote to Clay to compliment him on his speech and ask:

When will the mad career of the "military chieftain" be checked? Or is it never to meet with a check? Will a thoughtless multitude, led on by or encouraged by knavish politicians, always sing paeans of praise to the usurpations of a despot, if emblazoned with military renown?

Calhoun echoed Clay's insinuations:

The Senator from Kentucky read a striking passage from Plutarch, descriptive of Caesar forcing himself, sword in hand, into the treasury of the Roman commonwealth. We are in the same stage of our political revolution, and the analogy between the two cases is complete, varied only by the character of the actors, and the circumstances of the times. . . . The Senator said truly, and, let me add, philosophically, that "we are in the midst of a revolution."[15]

Those of the Whig persuasion, it could be said, derived their *raison d'etre* from the theme of "King Andrew." The very name of the party (originating in 1834) was an effort to draw a parallel between "Andrew I" and George III: in each case the cause of liberty was upheld by a "Whig" opposition. Or take Nathaniel Beverley Tucker's *The Partisan Leader*. This fantasy novel, published in 1836, is usually regarded as an expression of Southern state rights sentiment, and so it is. The work of a Virginian, it predicts a situation in which his state is driven into a future rebellion against the Washington government. But it also a novel about "usurpation." Written to prevent if possible the election of Van Buren, it treats him as though he would be certain to emulate King Andrew by becoming King Matty. In *The Partisan Leader* Van Buren has succeeded to the Presidency; moreover he has held office for twelve years, with no intention of retiring from his "palace," the White House.

Again, the successful Whig candidate in 1840, William Henry Harrison, produced a set of promises in December, 1838, that point by point are almost laughably non-Jacksonian.

An "Executive sincerely desirous to restore the Administration to its original simplicity and purity" would, Harrison said, "confine his service to a single term . . . disclaim all right of control over the public treasury . . . never attempt to influence the elections" at any level, limit his veto power, "never suffer the influence of his office to be used for purposes of a purely party character," give reasons for removals from office to the individual concerned and—if requested—to the Senate, and "not . . . suffer the Executive Department of the Government to become the source of legislation, but leave the whole business of making the laws for the Union" to Congress. [16]

In the 1840 elections the Whigs were still harping on the same tune. Henry Clay, speechmaking on behalf of Harrison, repeated that Presidents should be restricted to one term. His review of recent history, in a speech made in Hanover County, Virginia, emphasized what was by then Whig doctrine. "Executive encroachment has followed upon executive encroachment," Clay declared:

> The nation has been in the condition of a man who, having gone to bed after his barn has been consumed by fire, is aroused in the morning to witness his dwelling-house wrapped in flames. So bold and presumptuous has the executive become, that, penetrating in its influence the hall of a co-ordinate branch of the government, by means of a submissive or instructed majority of the Senate, it has caused the record of the country to be effaced and expunged, the inviolability of which was guaranteed by a solemn injunction of the Constitution! . . .

Clay concluded with the ominous statement that "if the progress of executive usurpation were to continue unchecked, hopeless despair would seize the public mind, or the people would be goaded to acts of open and violent resistance."

Edwin C. Rozwenc, who incorporates this speech in a collection of source material on Jacksonian America, points out a logical weakness in the Whig position. Like Barry Goldwater in 1964, the Whigs in 1836, in 1840, and again in 1844 sought to narrow executive authority while at the same time recommending vigorous action by the federal government. [17] There is a further interesting parallel. Goldwater struck an answering chord in his audiences when he expatiated on the spread of violence in America, and implied both that he would take firm action to end it and that the violence was in some way the fault of the Democratic administration. In the second term of Jackson's administration, and during the Presidency of Van Buren, there appeared to be a frightening eruption of violence in the United States. In the autumn of 1834 one New England periodical published an alarmist article entitled "The March of Anarchy"; another said that the previous year had produced "examples of outrage and violence altogether unprecedented in the annals of our country." *Niles' Register* claimed in September, 1835, to have recently clipped "more than 500 articles, relating to the various *excitements* now acting on the people of the United States, public and private! *Society seems everywhere unhinged* . . . ."[18] In 1838 a young Whig politician gave a talk on this subject to the Young Men's Lyceum of Springfield, Illinois. The speaker, Abraham Lincoln, who revered Henry Clay and yearned to follow in his footsteps, said that America faced serious danger from the "increasing disregard for law"—a disregard that could lead to the seizure of power by some exceptional man with the ambitions of "an Alexander, a Caesar, or a Napoleon." Edmund Wilson, pondering this utterance in his book *Patriotic Gore* (1962), suggests that Lincoln had unwittingly "projected himself" into this dashing, sinister role. Perhaps. It is just as likely that in 1838 Lincoln was thinking of Andrew Jackson.[19]

To blame the Democrats for the unrest of the 1830's was (as in the 1960's) as irresistible as it was unfair. Whatever the exact cause, many felt that something was wrong with America. Some believed the trouble lay with Andrew Jackson and his usurpations. It is not enough to dismiss this uneasiness as party maneuvering, although there was certainly a tinge of blatant partisan exaggeration. Van Buren's explanation does not tell us why complaints at King Andrew began *before* the Whigs had discovered their vulnerability on the Bank issue. In the 1832 election they were confident of defeating Jackson over the Bank. Even so, an anti-Jackson campaign booklet of 1832, a nursery rhyme paraphrase—"This Is the House that Jackson Built"—shows the monarchy accusation in full swing:

> And here is
> THE TYRANT
> Who, born to command,
> Is the curse of the country—the King of the land

Against whom the people have taken their stand—
The dotard of sixty—the plaything of knaves
Who would make us obey him, or render us slaves.[20]

Schlesinger's *Age of Jackson,* published in the year of Franklin
D. Roosevelt's death after being elected for a third and a fourth
term, could not help but be colored by the knowledge that F.D.R.'s
powerful and prolonged stay in office had brought America
through grave emergencies, domestic and foreign. It was natural
that Schlesinger should be more interested in the positive than in
the negative aspects of Jackson's reign. For this reason, no doubt, he
did not directly discuss the censure resolutions.

We do not need to commit ourselves to believing that Jackson
was a tyrant, still less that he or Van Buren had the faintest intention of becoming a king. But it is worth going into this much detail
on Andrew Jackson in order to see why many of his contemporaries
were prepared to believe the assertion. His somewhat inconsistent,
highly egocentric, and almost rabble-rousing Presidency after all
followed a sequence of quiescent administrations in which no large
demands were being made on behalf of the executive branch. Nor,
unlike Polk and Lincoln and Franklin D. Roosevelt, was he confronted with a war situation (even if he indulged in some saber-
rattling against the French over a minor matter of unpaid debts),
which would oblige him to take vigorous action. Nor could it be
said that the nation faced acute internal crises, with the possible
exception of the Nullification controversy. The Bank war was of
his own contriving. State rights sensitivity, party spleen, and congressional jealousy of the White House are not in themselves
enough to explain why a Clay, a Webster, and a Calhoun may have
honestly felt that Andrew Jackson was a menace to the nation. The
alarm they expressed and the vocabulary they employed to express
it drew upon deep American suspicions, not allayed by the apparently harmless evolution of the Presidency after Jackson.

This brings us to subterranean and frankly speculative problems.
They are barely touched on in the innumerable books that recount
the history of the executive office or analyze its functions. Let us
agree that Andrew Jackson was a figure of profound importance in
the presidential succession, a man who demanded and received
popular support on a scale never before experienced. Let us also
assume that he generated dislike and resistance of an intensity also

Three assassins (left to right): Lincoln's slayer, John Wilkes Booth; Charles Guiteau, who shot President Garfield in 1881; and Leon Czolgosz, who murdered William McKinley in 1901.

hitherto unknown. He did things no previous President had attempted. Something was also done to him, or almost done to him, that no previous President had experienced.

Niles' Register said in 1835 that *"society everywhere seems unhinged."* In his list of *"excitements* now acting upon the people of the United States" Hezekiah Niles could have included one episode of peculiar significance. Someone tried to assassinate Andrew Jackson with two pistols fired at pointblank range. In fact both misfired, although when tested afterward they worked perfectly. Only luck saved the President.

A fresh hazard had been added to the office. Thirty years later, in April, 1865, the next effort at assassination succeeded: in the moment of Union victory Booth shot Abraham Lincoln in Washington. In 1881 the same fate claimed the life of President Garfield. In 1901 it was the turn of President McKinley. The terrible tally was increased in November, 1963, with the slaying of John F. Kennedy in Dallas, the "Hate Capital of the Southwest." Not very long before, a man who had strapped some sticks of dynamite to himself failed to carry through a scheme to blow the President to pieces while he was vacationing in Florida.[21]

Between the assassinations of McKinley and Kennedy came a number of abortive attacks. Ex-President Theodore Roosevelt was wounded in the chest by a revolver bullet during his 1912 campaign for re-election as a Progressive candidate. An attempt was made on the life of President-elect Franklin D. Roosevelt in February, 1933. The bullets, missing him, killed Mayor Cermak of Chicago, who was sitting in the car next to him, and wounded several others. There was a flurry of shooting in a Puerto Rican plot that involved President Harry S. Truman in 1950. Though he escaped unhurt, one of the guards at Blair House (where he was then living) was killed and two were wounded.

These isolated acts of violence are generally regarded as meaningless events—wild gestures by wretched, unhinged creatures. Lawrence, the man who tried to kill Andrew Jackson, was an unemployed drifter, an English-born immigrant, who believed that he was the rightful heir to the thrones of England and America, and that Jackson stood in his way. Lincoln's murderer, John Wilkes Booth, was a flashy actor with delusions of grandeur. By the time he struck, allegedly on behalf of the South, it was too late for his assault to bring anything but harm: his section lay in ruins. Charles J. Guiteau, who shot James Garfield, was an unstable specimen of the breed known as "disappointed office seekers," and a member of the thwarted "Stalwart" wing of Garfield's Republican party. There was nothing very stalwart in shooting Garfield in the back while he waited for a train. The good-natured McKinley was fired on by a self-styled anarchist, Leon Czolgosz, who had no connection with the American anarchist groups that he had halfheartedly sought to contact. Giuseppe Zangara, Franklin Roosevelt's assailant, another unemployed drifter, seemed to have not even a confused idea of what he might accomplish by taking the President's life. As for the shooting of Kennedy, we are in a nightmare realm. We do not know and perhaps shall never know whether Lee Harvey Oswald acted alone. The very pointlessness of his behavior had induced critics in the United States and elsewhere to invent a conspiracy if they could not discover one. So far, the event remains without plausible explanation. In the light of previous American assassinations the meaning might be that it was meaningless.

Hence perhaps the fascination with coincidences attending death in the presidential office. Players of these mystery games point out that every President elected in each one of the twenty-year intervals starting with 1840 died in office, from Harrison to Kennedy; or that both Lincoln and Kennedy had Vice-Presidents named Johnson. But they are recognized as mere games: coincidence substitutes for significance.

In short the series of attacks on the President, from Jackson to Kennedy, would appear to be "nonpolitical" in origin. If any comparison exists, perhaps it is with England, another nation that in the past century or so has revealed no tendency to political or ideological killings. One might for example cite the attempt to kill the prime minister, Sir Robert Peel, in the 1840's. We remember the incident only in the context of insanity: the case of the would-be assassin, Daniel M'Naghten, who shot Peel's secretary by mistake, prompted the courts to formulate the "M'Naghten rule" on determining culpability for insane acts. Or there were the three attempts on the life of the young Queen Victoria between 1840 and 1842. One of these, like certain of the American instances, seems to belong to the genre of black comedy. The queen was fired upon by a hump-backed lunatic named Bean. In the melee he escaped arrest; before he was finally caught the police were rounding up every humpback in London.[22]

General reasons are, it is true, offered for the relative frequency of American assassination attempts. At least in comparison with Britain, the United States has accepted disorder and a high crime rate as a sort of endemic condition of a mobile, heterogeneous, and enormous country. England had its civil war more than three hundred years ago; the American Civil War, with all the deep unrest that occasioned, accompanied, and followed it, is in historical perspective a quite recent affair. Another obvious reason, given renewed prominence in the 1960's, is the availability of lethal weapons. Yankee ingenuity and early mass production techniques, it could be said, introduced the democracy of the pistol along with that of the ballot box: Colt and Derringer brought homicide within the reach of even the poorest citizen. (A Northern visitor to Dallas, Texas, shortly before the arrival there of President Kennedy was told by a local acquaintance: "God made big people. And God made little people. But Colt made the .45 to even things out.") A third obvious factor is the accessibility of the American President. A Secret Service bodyguard was not provided until after Czolgosz's fatal wounding of McKinley. Before (and since) the President was an easy target for assassination, not to mention personal insult, on the street, in travel, at the White House, on the platform of some crowded hall.[23]

A further though less obvious reason might be the effect of newspaper stories on the minds of potential American assassins. In the nineteenth and early twentieth century sensational attacks—sometimes by anarchists, sometimes by "patriots"—were made on heads of state all over the world. Orsini tried to kill Napoleon III in 1858, seven years before Booth burst into Lincoln's box at the theater. A quarter of a century before Theodore Roosevelt was wounded in the chest, the same thing happened to Bismarck in Germany. The list of actual killings, all of them front-page stories, is appallingly long. In 1868 the victim was Prince Michael of Serbia. In 1881, the year of Garfield's death, Tsar Alexander II became a mangled corpse from the throwing of a terrorist bomb. Anarchists dispatched President Carnot of France (1894), Empress Elizabeth of Austria (1890), and King Umberto of Italy (1900). In 1903, in Serbia, it was the turn of King Michael's son Alexander. The Russian minister of the interior, Plehve, was assassinated in 1904, the Portuguese king (Carlos) and crown prince in 1908. The prime ministers of Russia and Spain were murdered in 1911 and 1912. The killing of Archduke Ferdinand of Austria at Sarajevo in 1914 ignited the First World War. And in recent years the tally has been renewed with the assassination of Mahatma Gandhi in India, Prime Minister Bandaranaike in Ceylon, and a host of other attacks—including those of French extremists on President De Gaulle.[24]

Even so a puzzle remains. Including Lyndon B. Johnson and counting the two separate terms of Grover Cleveland as one administration, there have been thirty-five Presidents. Four have been assassinated; attempts have been made to assassinate at least four others: eight murders or near-murders out of thirty-five. The actuarial chances are thus more than one in five that somebody will try to kill an American President, and about one in nine that he will succeed. The risks could be argued to be greater still. No one made an attempt on the life of the first six Presidents, from George Washington through John Quincy Adams. The danger began with Andrew Jackson, for reasons perhaps already plain. Omitting the first six, we can take twenty-nine Presidents into account, and say that the odds on someone trying to kill them stand at more than one in four.

Why such high odds, when American Presidents are too hedged in by constitutional limitations to assume absolute power even if they wanted to? The vocabulary of the would-be assassins, lunatic though they may have been, tells us something. Lawrence brooded over the idea that Andrew Jackson was an actual king, though an usurper, who had in the pursuit of his wicked aims also killed Lawrence's royal father. The man who shot Theodore Roosevelt shouted out, "No third term!"

Though the application was insane the vocabulary was drawn from everyday American discourse. As Louis Brownlow observes:

> Every President . . . with but one exception, when he has been in office has been denounced as a despot, a tyrant, a dictator, as one who was using the power of the government . . . to achieve his own personal ambitions. The only President who was not so denounced was William Henry Harrison; he lived only one month after he was inaugurated.[25]

The vocabulary was suddenly and hysterically heightened in Jackson's time. Calhoun said in the Senate that Jackson's Bank depredations were "adding robbery to murder." Jackson claimed he had received five hundred letters from people threatening to kill him. So heated was the atmosphere that he himself believed the assassin had been hired by his enemies. Administration newspapers spread the theory. America witnessed an extraordinary moment when Calhoun, a former Vice-President and a member of the United States Senate, rose from his seat to deny that he had plotted to kill the President.[26]

Wild though Jackson's charges were, they contained a grain of truth. In a sense every enemy who called the President a tyrant or a Caesar was invoking the momentum of history. For the mentally unstable, or indeed for those literal-minded citizens who believed what they were told, America was succumbing to a despot. The lesson was plain, to Lawrence and to Booth and no doubt to others who were not quite prepared to translate thought into deed: the tyrant must be struck down, the murderer murdered. *Sic semper tyrannis!* as Booth shouted: *ever thus to tyrants!* Was that not after all the sacred motto of Virginia, the Old Dominion? Had not Virginia's Thomas Jefferson declared that "the tree of liberty must be refreshed from time to time with the blood of patriots and tyrants"? Such blood was "its natural manure."

Every strong President was subject to this sinister animus. Lincoln was stigmatized as a tyrant by Supreme Court justices and Northern editors as well as by the Confederacy. He was another Jackson, with his bypassing of Congress, his arrests of citizens who ventured to criticize him, his use of bayonets to enforce his decrees.

Senator Charles Sumner, indignant at Andrew Johnson's attempt to maintain Lincoln's initiative in determining Reconstruction policy, protested in 1865: "If something is not done the President will be crowned king before Congress meets." Johnson's retort to his critics, in February, 1866, was couched in the same extravagant idiom: "Men may talk about beheading and about usurpation, but when I am beheaded I want the American people to be witnesses. I do not want it, by innuendoes and indirect remarks in high places, to be suggested to men who have assassination brooding in their bosoms. . . ." William H. Crook, a White House bodyguard, recalled a couple of rabid incidents. One concerned a man by the name of Grapevine, who, trying to get an interview with Johnson, cried: "What are you all doing here? I am the President, and that man is an imposter." Struggling to force his way in to see Johnson, he was arrested—and found to be armed with a large bowie knife. Another man, the brother of a Union general, behaved so oddly in seeking admission to the President that Crook sought to put him off. He then produced a pistol, which was knocked aside by a soldier in the office. Crook added: "There can be no doubt that, since he was armed with a perfectly new pistol, and since he tried to shoot the man who kept him from the President, he had intended to shoot Mr. Johnson. Episodes of that kind were of frequent occurrence in the White House. We dealt with them quickly, and they rarely got into the newspapers."[27]

According to some observers, it was just as well that newspapers were deprived of such sensational items. The American press had never been noted for reticence. With the advent of "yellow" journalism, after the Civil War, comment was apt to go beyond scurrility. Early in 1900, indulging his appetite for the macabre, the journalist-author Ambrose Bierce contributed to the New York

---

Andrew Johnson's attempt to treat the defeated South magnanimously earned him the bitter enmity of the Radical Republicans and of the press, which printed vicious cartoons like this one.

Journal the following quatrain, on the recent murder of William Goebel, governor-elect of Kentucky:

> The bullet that pierced Goebel's breast
> Can not be found in all the West;
> Good reason, it is speeding here
> To stretch McKinley on his bier.

The *Journal* was one of William Randolph Hearst's papers. A year or so later another Hearst columnist, in the course of denouncing President McKinley, said: "If bad institutions and bad men can only be got rid of by killing, then the killing must be done." When McKinley was actually assassinated, in September, 1901, Bierce and his colleague disclaimed any inflammatory aim, and Hearst himself was horrified by the event. But he never spoke of the affair to Bierce, or gave new instructions to his staff. Other newspapers virtuously condemned the Hearst press; and Theodore Roosevelt told Congress that the assassin had probably been stimulated by "reckless utterances . . . in the public press. . . . The wind is sowed by the men who preach such doctrines, and they cannot escape their share of responsibility for the whirlwind that is reaped."[28]

In fairness to Hearst, it should be added that he was assailed as much for advocating radical ideas in his papers as for apparently inciting to murder. The problem of possible incitement through journalistic comment remained perplexing. A virulent example was provided in 1937. The confidential press reports of the Mc-Clure Syndicate (whose service was distributed each week to some two hundred and seventy American newspapers) quoted an official of American Cyanamid as typical of right-wing reactions to the Roosevelt administration. This official, in remarks made at a private dinner in New York, apparently "asserted in so many words that 'the paranoiac in the White House' is destroying the nation, that a couple of well-placed bullets would be the best thing for the country, and that he for one would buy a bottle of champagne as quick as he could get it to celebrate such news." In the 1960's the columnist Westbrook Pegler—one of Roosevelt's most bitter critics —said of F.D.R., with unrepentant vehemence:

> It is regrettable that Giuseppe Zangara hit the wrong man when he shot at Roosevelt in Miami. Roosevelt made many decisions in favor of Soviet Russia, beginning with his recognition of the Soviet Government [in 1933]. Thereafter he per-

F. D. R., an undogmatic believer in the "try-anything" style of government, was attacked as a fascist by the left and a Communist by the right. In this cartoon, Senate majority leader Alben Barkley advises Roosevelt to disguise his desire to be a dictator.

mitted the whole bureaucracy to be infested with spies. Anyone who opposed Roosevelt, or any of his henchmen, or designs, was labelled a "hatemonger." All right, if he acquired all this hate from people he set out to alienate, why deny it to him now?[29]

The idiom still had not changed by 1963. Five weeks before the Dallas catastrophe a Delaware newspaper announced with a hideous jocularity: "Yes, Virginia, there is a Santa Claus. His name right now happens to be Kennedy—let's shoot him, literally, before

Christmas." The editor who wrote this advice scandalized some of his readers. But he did write it, and did print it. The only crumb of comfort in the anecdote is that he may well have been too ignorant to know what the word "literally" literally means.[30]

In the early years of the twentieth century, when the Presidency was suddenly being reactivated, a number of fantasy stories appeared that were set in the future and dealt with notions of violence, oligarchy, and usurpation in the United States. In the case of the anonymously published novel *Philip Dru: Administrator; A Story of Tomorrow*, 1920–1935 (1912), written by Woodrow Wilson's friend and follower Colonel Edward M. House, the fantasy is enthusiastic. More often it is somber, as with a short story entitled "The Coup d'Etat of 1961," composed during the Presidency of Theodore Roosevelt. The author, Henry Dwight Sedgwick, was no crank but a respected man of letters. In his tale the American Presidency becomes the embodiment first of oligarchy and then of autocracy. A tycoon-superman named Campbell steps into the office and creates an absolute, quasi-royal dynasty of Campbells. Ruling with a pretense of constitutionalism, and backed by the Supreme Court, he is able to dispense altogether with sessions of Congress. Sedgwick concludes his coolly ironical sketch:

> Since then, however, both Senate and House have met regularly. They have authorized stock transactions in each chamber, and the principal business of the country is now transacted there. The President has assumed the titles of Lord Suzerain of South America, High Protector of China, Chief Ruler of the Pacific Archipelago, and has established the Orders of George, of Abraham, of Ulysses, and of William, in honor of Washington, Lincoln, Grant, and McKinley; the members are appointed by him after an examination and sworn inventory of their private fortunes. President Campbell was renominated and re-elected every four years; and since his death his son has succeeded to the party nomination. "The Constitution," as some famous lawyer says, "is like the skin of a great animal, that stretches, expands, and grows with its growth."[31]

To return from fantasy to fact, certain patterns begin to appear in the careers of those Presidents who have been special targets for suspicion. One would expect strong executive heads to be even more hated, and more subject to the charge of "usurpation," if they seek re-election. Sure enough, there is a correlation of sorts, though admittedly imperfect and conjectural. Four of the eight assassination attempts have been directed at Presidents—Jackson, Lincoln, McKinley, Truman—who had achieved re-election. In a fifth case, that of Kennedy, it is reasonable to suppose that he would have won the second term he would certainly have sought. Though Theodore Roosevelt was not in office at the time he was shot, and had not strictly speaking been re-elected for a second term in 1904, he was nevertheless attempting to return to power, and in effect for a third term. A cartoon of the period shows him leaping blithely over a high "Anti-3rd-Term Wall," which is marked "Built by George Washington." In another hostile cartoon he brandishes a scroll inscribed "THEODORE ROOSEVELT FOR EVER AND EVER"; in another he pins up a proclamation signed "TR REX," which says: "*I* am the will of the people. . . . *I* chose myself to be leader. . . . *I* will have as many terms in office as I desire."[32]

The other two intended victims, Garfield and F.D.R., give us less to go upon, since Garfield had been in office for only four months and Roosevelt was merely President-elect. It is at least worth speculating that their offense, in the minds of the crazed creatures who fired at them, was that they had not yet become "legitimate" rulers. In the same way, perhaps, it is significant that attempted assassinations of Queen Victoria were confined to the early years of her long reign. She followed the unpopular Hanoverian kings and was not even a male sovereign. Her "legitimacy" was therefore weak. Garfield, securing the Republican nomination at the thirty-sixth ballot in an unedifying contest with General Grant (who would thereby himself have violated the third-term taboo), was immediately bedeviled by party feuds. In Guiteau's eyes he was thus not yet endowed with the prestige of office, as the head of the state, but was simply the victorious head of a rival political machine. It was, lamented *Frank Leslie's Illustrated Newspaper*, "a thing of fearful omen that the assassin should have sought to justify the monstrous deed by considerations based on the spite and jealousy of a defeated faction, or the wrathful attitude of men whose sole grievance is their failure to share the spoils of office."[33]

Both the strong Presidents and their haters are curiously involved in the language of monarchy—a language that has undergone little change from Washington to Lyndon Johnson. A key word is "usurpation"—the act of seizing power illegitimately. Theodore Roosevelt, defending his conception of the Presidency in a letter to an English friend, boasted that "I have used every ounce of power there was in the office and I have not cared a rap for the criticisms of those who spoke of my 'usurpation of power'; for I knew that . . . there was no usurpation." John F. Kennedy developed a similar argument when he was campaigning for the office in 1960. He said that Woodrow Wilson "discovered that to be a big man in the White House inevitably brings cries of dictatorship. So did Lincoln and Jackson and the two Roosevelts. And so may the next occupant . . . if he is the man the times demand. But how much better it would be . . . to have a Roosevelt or a Wilson than to have another James Buchanan, cringing in the White House, afraid to move." Like Roosevelt, Kennedy drew a distinction between the "good" (or vigorous) Presidents and the "bad" (or inept), between the "Lincolns" and the "Buchanans."[34]

It is also possibly significant that no efforts have been made to assassinate Presidents in periods of war and other grave crisis. At such times the nation draws together. The charge of usurpation seems relatively unimportant in face of the demand for leadership. Lincoln was assassinated when the crisis of the Civil War was over, McKinley when America had emerged triumphantly from the Spanish-American War. One point of this chapter, however, is that Buchanan survived, in common with every other unaggressive President: Lincoln, in common with several other aggrandizing Presidents, was shot at. And after each bold assertion of executive authority, for reasons to be explored later, there followed a marked reaction. After Jackson no President until Lincoln had a second term. Lincoln's successor, Andrew Johnson, was vilified and nearly impeached. After Lincoln, with the exception of the unassertive Grant, no President until McKinley was re-elected for a second consecutive term. After the bold administrations of Teddy Roosevelt and Wilson came what Harold J. Laski called "the era of conscious abdication,"—another monarchical word—"from power" during the 1920's.[35]

All strong Presidents, no matter how grateful posterity may be, have quickened the undercurrent of hatred, the persistent fear that the Founding Fathers had bequeathed a potential "elective monarchy" to the United States. The Kennedys were frequently referred

In the play MacBird, *characters resembling President Lyndon Johnson and his wife plotted the murder of a young king who was unmistakably reminiscent of John F. Kennedy.*

to as a "royal family," sometimes with affectionate mockery, more often with malice and suspicion. A recent example of the literature of antipresidential fantasy, Barbara Garson's pastiche *MacBird,* is bound by the same queer compulsion. Portraying Lyndon Johnson as the Macbeth-like assassin of John F. Kennedy, it is a drama of monarchy and usurpation. The only novelty lies in the apparent assumption that *all* contenders for the throne would be illegitimate. In other respects it reveals kindred obsessions to those of such bizarre bygone items as *The Adder's Den: or Secrets of the Great Conspiracy to Overthrow Liberty in America* (1864). Its author, John Smith Dye, was a respectable if fanatical abolitionist, whose *bête noire* was not so much the Presidency as the Confederacy. He was convinced that Southerners, led by Calhoun until his death in 1850, had in fulfillment of their determination to overthrow the Union fatally poisoned Presidents William Henry Harrison and Zachary Taylor. According to Dye, Southerners were also behind the attack on Jackson in 1835, and had tried unsuccessfully to assassinate President-elect James Buchanan in 1857, and President-elect Lincoln in 1861.[36]

To Lawrence in 1835 "King Andrew the First" was Andrew the usurper, the false king. All Presidents who are assertive are false kings in the peculiar yet intrinsic vocabulary. The assassins may be insane, but they act out deep convictions and resentments, shared with many of their countrymen.

There is a final reason why talk of "usurpation" and "legitimacy" seems appropriate in the profoundly republican American context. The President has a dual function. He is monarch and prime minister rolled into one. His task is both to rule and to govern. As head of state he symbolizes the American union and speaks for every person within it. As head of government and party chief he must provide active direction, but as the leader of a political machine. This development was inevitable. Yet it added to the inner doubts of Americans about the validity of presidential authority; and the first serious qualms came with Andrew Jackson. The President, this "elective monarch," upon inauguration becomes a part of the sacred fabric of national identity. Like a king, he never dies because the succession is automatic and instantaneous. But what is his legitimacy? There is a revealingly cynical definition in Ambrose Bierce's *Devil's Dictionary:*

> PRESIDENT, n. The leading figure in a small group of men of whom—and of whom only—it is positively known that immense numbers of their countrymen did not want any of them for President.

A man for whom many Americans did not vote, a partisan politician *against* whom many voted, suddenly becomes their almost regal representative. In no less than fifteen contests up to 1968 the President has been elected without a popular majority:

1824	John Quincy Adams
1844	James K. Polk
1848	Zachary Taylor
1856	James Buchanan
1860	Abraham Lincoln
1876	Rutherford B. Hayes
1880	James A. Garfield
1884	Grover Cleveland

1888	Benjamin Harrison
1892	Grover Cleveland
1912	Woodrow Wilson
1916	Woodrow Wilson
1948	Harry S. Truman
1960	John F. Kennedy
1968	Richard M. Nixon

The margin in these and other elections has often been remarkably small. In 1864 Lincoln beat McClellan by only 400,000 out of 4 million votes, though his advantages were considerable (and, unknown to him, probably included tampering with soldiers' ballot boxes).[37] In 1880 Garfield squeaked by with a majority over his Democratic opponent Winfield Scott Hancock of fewer than 10,000 votes out of a total of more than 9 million. In 1888 Benjamin Harrison actually received fewer popular votes than his defeated opponent Cleveland. In 1960 Kennedy secured 49.94 per cent of the popular vote, a mere one sixth of 1 per cent more than the Republican candidate Richard M. Nixon. It is a testimony to the soundness of American democracy that the results of contests so close are usually accepted with a display of good-humored resignation by the defeated. It would be surprising, though, if an embittered minority did not brood over the outcome—especially in the knowledge that in certain districts the vote-counting is not overscrupulous, and that the tally of popular votes is distorted by the anachronistic workings of the Electoral College. Frustration is heightened in a country so wedded to a two-party system for those already discontented citizens who voted for forlorn-hope nominees of third (or even fourth and fifth) parties.

To sum up:

—The presidential office is disliked, feared, and suspected as well as admired and sought after and venerated.

—Strong Presidents, beginning with Andrew Jackson (though with premonitory rumblings even in the case of George Washington), have by being strong stirred up deep resentments, which invariably express themselves as attacks on monarchical pretensions.

—The strong Presidents have been the ones most in danger of assassination.

—The danger is increased if they prolong their tenure through re-election.

After Congress had declared Rutherford B. Hayes the winner of the disputed election of 1876, supporters of Samuel Tilden threatened armed rebellion. Tilden urged them to support the congressional decision.

—These resentments, which lie beneath the surface but bubble up periodically, aggravated perhaps by political opponents and the press, may act upon the minds of the unstable, the failures, the men sick with anonymity. The assassins are to be understood not as people behaving inexplicably but within a national climate of opinion sometimes heavy with anger and accusation.

—Two lines in Walt Whitman's "Starting from Paumanok" may serve for an epigraph:

> And I will make a song for the ears of the President, full
> of weapons with menacing points,
> And behind the weapons countless dissatisfied faces.

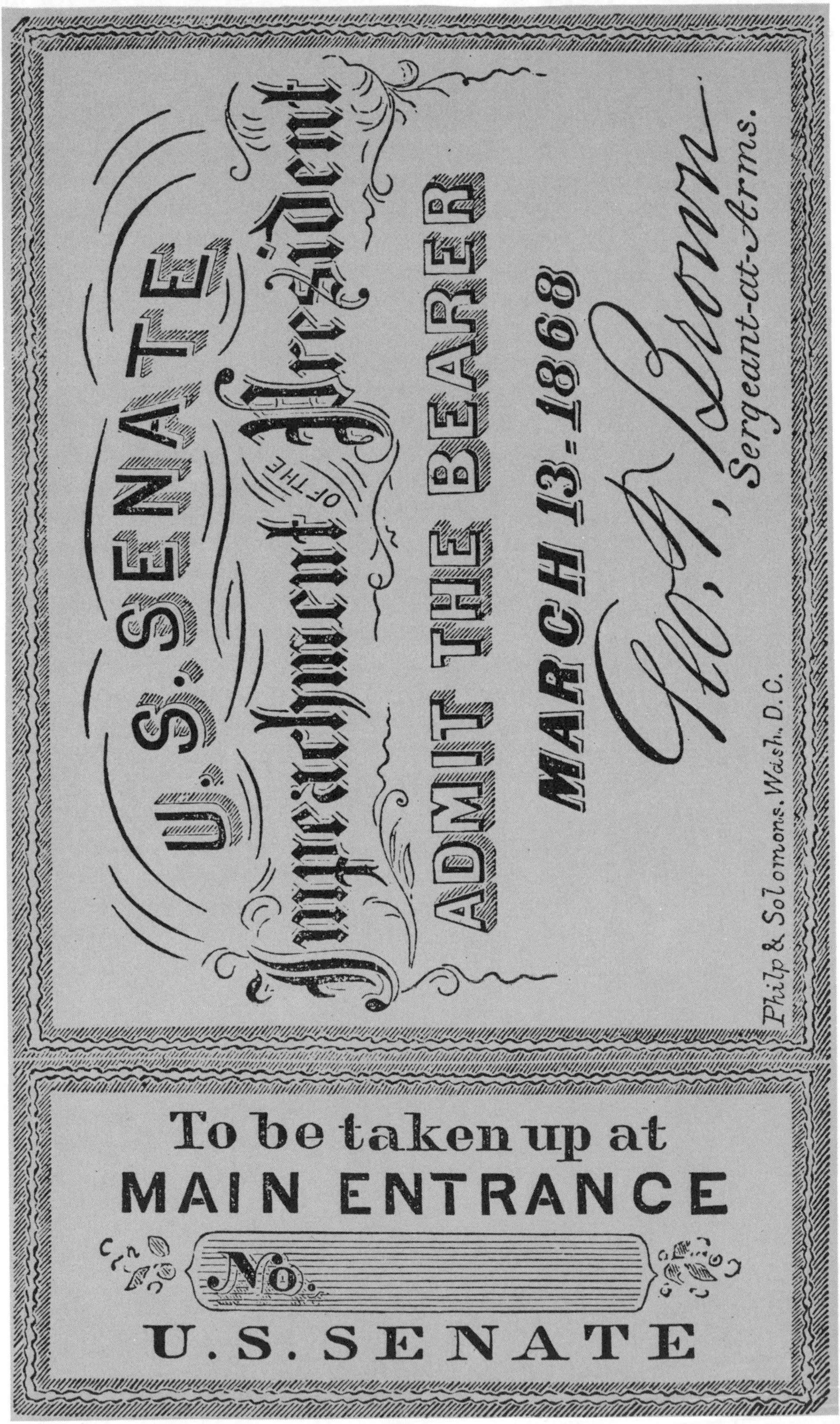

U. S. SENATE

Impeachment of the President

ADMIT THE BEARER

MARCH 13 = 1868

Geo. T. Brown

Sergeant-at-Arms.

Philp & Solomons. Wash. D.C.

To be taken up at

MAIN ENTRANCE

No.

U. S. SENATE

CHAPTER SIX

Authority
in Abeyance

In 1848, the year of revolutions and fresh aspirations in Europe, the Swiss people framed a new republican constitution. They drew upon the American Constitution for several features. But they did not provide for a President because it seemed to them an invitation to dictatorship. Their suspicion was based to some extent on what they had read of American experience. They could, for example, have consulted an essay entitled "Federal Government," published in 1840 by Abel Upshur, who was to become Secretary of State in Tyler's Cabinet. Upshur said the "most defective part" of the American Constitution was that relating to the executive branch; the prerogative of the President was described in dangerously "loose and unguarded terms," enabling him to claim far too much authority.

A generation later, in 1884, another American, Henry C. Lockwood, wrote a book entitled *The Abolition of the Presidency*, in

---

Tickets admitting spectators to the Senate during President Andrew Johnson's impeachment trial in 1868 were hard to come by; thousands poured into Washington, hoping to watch the spectacle. The trial lasted for three months and resulted in Johnson's acquittal.

which he argued that the only way to rescue American liberty was to get rid of the Presidency—in other words, the single Executive—and replace it with an executive council on the Swiss pattern. There was, he maintained, a universal but perilous tendency to entrust rulership to one man:

> Let a person be chosen to an office, with power conferred upon it equal to that of the Presidency of the United States, and it will make but little difference whether the law actually gives him the right to act in a particular direction or not. . . . He acts. No argument that the law has been violated will avail. . . . He is a separate power in himself. The lines with which we attempt to mark the limits of his power are shadowy and ill-defined. A party . . . stands back of him demanding action. . . . The sentiment of hero worship, which . . . prevails among the American people, will endorse him.[1]

The Swiss reaction of 1848 shows how seriously the rest of the world, as well as some Americans, took the criticisms of Jacksonian "usurpation." Lockwood's volume reveals that in 1884 there was still uneasiness in the United States at the extension of executive authority contrived by Abraham Lincoln, even though Congress had hobbled and almost impeached Andrew Johnson, Lincoln's successor, had controlled Grant, and had kept Hayes and Arthur on the defensive. Lockwood was worried too by the way in which his countrymen had unthinkingly accepted General Grant as President, knowing nothing about him except that he was presumably a strong man who would take command of the nation and issue orders for its salvation.

Lockwood's fears seem exaggerated, and—in the circumstances of his era—somewhat ludicrous. We know and feel he should have known that General Grant was a feeble President. Young Henry Adams, the grandson of President John Quincy Adams, had come to Washington after the Civil War in the hope of making a public career, possibly as a political journalist. As he said, all Adamses automatically gravitated to Washington. The laxity and mediocrity of Congress dismayed him. He and his friends were convinced that the country needed a "reform President" to bring "the Senate back to decency," that the task could be accomplished only by a man who was not a professional politician, and that Grant might be the man. If so Adams would back him up.

With this in prospect, said Adams (writing of himself in the third-

At left, Thaddeus Stevens, fiery leader of the Radical Republicans in Congress, exhorts the House to impeach President Johnson. Right, the Senate sergeant at arms serves a summons on Johnson, ordering him to appear for trial. Johnson's lawyers would not let him attend, so he remained in the White House, waiting anxiously for daily reports of the proceedings. He was cleared, but by only one vote.

person style), he went to hear the announcement of Grant's Cabinet. The list of names was so abject, so deplorable, that "within five minutes" it "changed his intended future into an absurdity so laughable as to make him ashamed." As for the senators, they "made no secret of saying . . . that Grant's nominations betrayed his intent as plainly as they betrayed his incompetence. A great soldier might be a baby politician."[2] General Grant, the hero of Shiloh, Vicksburg, the Wilderness, and Appomattox, was inaugurated in 1869. U. S. "Unconditional Surrender" Grant came into office on the heels of a disgraced President, Andrew Johnson, who the previous year had been arraigned by the Senate on charges which amounted to the assertion that the executive office was subordinate to the legislature. Thirty-five Senators voted to convict him, against nineteen for acquittal. Since a two-thirds vote was necessary, the proceeding failed—by one vote. Adams referred to this crisis when he said that he meant "to support the executive in attacking the Senate and taking away its two-thirds vote and power of confirmation, nor did he much care how it should be done, for he thought it safer to effect the revolution in 1870 than to wait until 1920." Though the impeachment was defeated, the executive branch had received the severest setback in its history. Instead of striving to restore the prestige of the Presidency, Grant virtually made an unconditional surrender to Congress. His Cabinet appointments, most of them prosperous nonentities, proved as much.

Lockwood's book was in fact less eccentric than it sounds. His general argument was that, powerful or impotent, a single-man Executive was unsatisfactory. Such opinions began with the creation of the office and have persisted as an undercurrent to the present day. A good many Presidents have themselves had misgivings about the power inherent in their position. Some have perhaps merely rationalized their own sluggishness or ineptitude. Others have believed in the necessary restriction of presidential authority not as an excuse for personal timidity but as a matter of genuine conviction. This "Whig" conception prevailed among Presidents in the years between Jackson and Lincoln, during almost the whole of the last third of the nineteenth century, again under President Taft (1909–13), and again under the Republican administrations of the 1920's and the 1950's. Even Jackson and Lincoln were in some respects leaders with a negative view of their functions. Jackson saw himself merely as resisting harmful developments; Lincoln left to Congress practically all the legislative programs that were not of immediate relevance to the war effort.

Another way of putting this is to say that active Presidents make things difficult for their successors. In the to-and-fro contest between the executive and legislative branches, Congress strives to recover territory it has lost. A regular alternation may be discerned. After the initial "executive" period of Washington and John Adams there came the "legislative" interlude of the Virginia Dynasty. After Andrew Jackson came a quarter-century of "legislative" dominance.[3] After Lincoln came the violent counterattack by Congress, of which Andrew Johnson bore the brunt. If a strong-willed President is succeeded by another one, the double dose produces a correspondingly fierce reaction from Congress—as happened after Lincoln and the contumacious Andrew Johnson, or after the administrations of Franklin D. Roosevelt and Harry S. Truman. The reaction is heightened when, as usually happens, it coincides with a change of party: the outs tend to adopt the "legislative" or "Whig" conception of the Presidency as an additional weapon in their arsenal of criticisms against the administration in power. But even when the succession remains in the hands of the same party, an incoming President may be at pains to disclaim the executive pretensions of his predecessor.

The most striking example is the attitude of William Howard Taft. Having inherited office from Theodore Roosevelt, he discovered that a number of intractable problems such as tariff revision had been neglected and bequeathed to him in aggravated form. Roosevelt's continued prominence on the national scene, even when he was trying to behave like a retired statesman, constituted a kind of interference with the new executive head. Moreover, in Taft's eyes, Roosevelt had weakened party unity by estranging the conservative wing of the Republicans. In claiming too much, and in basing his claim on personal qualities, he had left a legacy of unrest. Taft explained his disapproval with considerable asperity after he left the White House, in a book entitled *Our Chief Magistrate and His Powers* (1916). Annoyed that Roosevelt had compared himself to Lincoln, and Taft to Buchanan, Taft replied that this was sheer egotism and that T. R.'s doctrine was unsound and unsafe. Like Lockwood he feared the possible consequences of those Presidents who "played their parts upon the political stage with histrionic genius and commanded the people almost as if they were an army and the President their Commander-in-Chief." Fortunately, said Taft, "there have always been men in this free and intelligent people of ours, who apparently courting political . . . disaster have registered protest against this undue Executive domination . . . ." He revealed his own discomfort and resentment by adding that though the cry of domination was often unjustified, "the fact that Executive domination is regarded as a useful ground for attack, even when there is no ground for it, is itself proof of the dependence we properly place upon the sanity and clear perceptions of the people in avoiding its baneful effects when there is real danger." A peculiar statement, and the more peculiar because it emanated from a former occupant of the White House. Taft seems to be saying that Presidents should preserve harmony by not rocking the political boat. He also apparently meant that the risk of executive domination is to be taken seriously, and has great theoretical validity even when it is without actual foundation.

Although one must allow for a certain amount of pique, Taft's observations still merit attention. He had not become senile on retiring from the Presidency. He was a professor of law at Yale at the time when he wrote, and would later be Chief Justice of the Supreme Court. He had an unhappy four years in the White House, despite his administrative experience and his well-organized mind. He could not quite understand why things had gone so badly. Although he could not bring the problem into focus, he was correct in believing that it involved the question of how much power the President ought to have, and where it was prudent to draw the line. Within his "proper sphere," Taft went on to say, the President had "great responsibilities and opportunities."[4] But what were these?

The span of Chief Executives between Lincoln and McKinley faced the problem in more acute guises. Seen in one way, they were men of no particular distinction under whose stewardship the office reached the nadir of its power. Seen in another way, they fought courageously and saved the Presidency from ignominious subjection to Congress. There is no doubt of the weight of the challenge hurled at them. Andrew Johnson was denied the right to control his own Cabinet or have more than a passive, minimal role in legislation. To earlier generations of Presidents the executive right of appointment and removal had been settled beyond dispute. Yet under Johnson it was repudiated by the Senate. During the impeachment proceedings a congressional spokesman, Benjamin F. Butler, went so far as to say that the issue at stake was "whether the Presidential office (if it bears the prerogatives and power claimed for it) ought, in fact, to exist, as a part of the constitutional government of a free people."[5] If the impeachment had succeeded, Benjamin F. Wade would as president pro tempore of the Senate have become President in Johnson's place. According to rumor Wade would then have appointed the notorious "Beast" Butler as Secretary of State.

The threat went unfulfilled, but nothing in Grant's two administrations abated the challenge. In accepting the Republican nomination Grant defined his future role as that of a "purely administrative officer." He held the same opinion when he left office. As a soldier he had unquestioningly deferred to civil authority; while he was President he regarded Congress as the supreme civil authority. "The President very rarely appoints," he informed a companion, "he merely registers the appointments of members of Congress." Cocksure congressmen such as Roscoe Conkling treated Grant affably but with basic contempt. George F. Hoar, who was just beginning a long and honorable congressional career, said later that in those days Senators like Conkling, John Sherman, Simon Cameron, Charles Sumner, and John A. "Black Jack" Logan "would have received as a personal affront a private message from the White House expressing a desire that they should adopt any course in the discharge of their legislative duties that they did not approve. If they visited the White House, it was to give, not to receive advice." John Sherman approvingly summed up the congressional position when he explained that "the executive department of a republic like ours should be subordinate to the legislative department. The President should obey and enforce the laws, leaving to the people the duty of correcting any errors committed by their representatives in Congress."[6] Significantly, senators began to claim precedence over Cabinet members at social functions.

The first display of renewed presidential courage came with Rutherford B. Hayes, when he deliberately ignored the hints and hopes of the Senate by preparing his own list of Cabinet nominations. In retaliation the Senate referred the entire list to committee scrutiny. After a great deal of delay and uproar Hayes got his way. He went on to contest the congressional phalanx by assailing one of its chief strongholds, the New York Custom House. When a commission appointed by Hayes confirmed the corruption of the custom house, Hayes removed two of the principals, including the collector, Chester A. Arthur. Another struggle ensued, with Conkling in the van, before Hayes once more imposed his will. He persisted with other nominations, cheered by the discovery that large sections of the public were as exasperated as he by the cynical misuse of the spoils system. By July, 1880, he could write, "I have had great success. No member of either house now attempts even to dictate appointments. . . . I began with selecting a Cabinet in opposition to their wishes, and I have gone on in that path steadily until

Rutherford B. Hayes sits in a chair made from horns and hide, a gift from frontiersman Seth Kinsman, who poses with the President.

I am now filling the important places of collector of the port and postmaster of Philadelphia almost without a suggestion even from Senators or Representatives."[7]

Emboldened by Hayes's defiance, James A. Garfield began his Presidency by appointing an enemy of Conkling's to the collectorship of the port of New York. "This," he wrote to a friend, "brings on the contest at once and will settle whether the President is registering clerk of the Senate or the Executive of the Nation." Garfield won a famous victory. Not only was his nominee finally confirmed by the Senate, but when the two New York senators, Conkling and Platt, ostentatiously resigned their seats in order to seek a vote of confidence from the New York assembly, the state legislators rebelled against them. Conkling's power was broken forever. Running (in retrospect) with the hare as well as the hounds, John Sherman made the statesmanlike comment that if Conkling and Platt had been vindicated by their assembly, "the President would have been powerless to appoint anyone in New York without consulting the Senators, practically transferring to them his constitutional power."[8]

Murdered by a Republican "Stalwart" of the Conkling persuasion, Garfield was prevented from offering further proof of executive independence. The crime produced one benefit in the shape of the Pendleton (civil service reform) Act of 1883, which heralded the gradual rescue of federal offices from the stranglehold of the spoils system. There was too the pleasantly surprising discovery that Garfield's successor, Chester A. Arthur, abandoned his spoilsman's outlook on entering the White House and conducted his administration with dignity and some ability.

After Arthur, Grover Cleveland likewise displayed tenacity and shrewdness in resisting congressional inroads. The difficulty was that while the Presidency and the House of Representatives were in Democratic hands as a result of the elections of 1884, the Senate still retained a Republican majority. Cleveland, a product of New York local and state government, had only once visited Washington before his inauguration. The belief that he was a greenhorn in their world may have stimulated the Senate to try and shatter him. Their technique was to hold up several hundred of his appointments and to demand copies of the papers relating to these appointments. Cleveland refused in a ponderous but unmistakably decisive message, which ended:

> Neither the discontent of party friends, nor the allurements constantly offered of confirmation of appointees conditioned upon the avowal that suspensions have been made on party grounds alone, nor the threat proposed in the resolutions now before the Senate that no confirmation will be complied with, are sufficient to . . . deter me from following the way I am convinced leads to better government for the people.

Cleveland soon showed that he was nobody's fool. Even the vitriolic Senator John J. Ingalls of Kansas, while pouring scorn upon political reformers, conceded that President Cleveland was "a very extraordinary man" and a puzzle—"the sphinx of American politics." Stories of his brusque treatment of office seekers and lobbyists became common. One such visitor described ruefully how, after an hour of affable conversation with the President, he thought the moment was opportune to introduce his particular interest. But as soon as he began, "I could see the process of congelation; and before I had half finished . . . the President was a monumental icicle. I became so thoroughly chilled that I broke off, took up my hat and said, 'Good-night, Mr. President.'" A Western Democrat was so infuriated by Cleveland's refusal to dispense patronage on a generous scale that he erupted into verse:

> 'Tis better to vote for some billy goat,
> That butts for his corn and his hay,
> Than to vote for a man that has not the sand
> To stand by his party a day.[9]

President Cleveland was particularly impatient of the mass of private bills designed to afford relief to the greedy as well as the needy. Someone remarked that the American way in warfare was to take its soldiers straight from the plow and return them to the plow —with a pension. Most of the three hundred and one vetoes of Grover Cleveland's first term were of private pension acts. One or two of his vetoes, and several of Hayes's, were however concerned with more important matters. Cleveland, Hayes, and Arthur all vetoed acts restricting Chinese immigration. Hayes resisted congressional blackmail by stoutly vetoing seven successive appropriations bills to which "riders" were attached. By appending such riders to essential legislation, Congress tried to compel him to sanction repugnant provisions. Hayes's veto messages stressed what was at stake. In one he said:

> The new doctrine, if maintained, will result in a consolidation of unchecked and despotic power in the House of Representatives. A bare majority of the House will become the Government. The Executive will no longer be . . . an equal and independent branch of the Government.[10]

With the exception of Grant the postwar Presidents thus did their best to counter the extreme assertions of legislative omnipotence. They won significant struggles with the Senate and the House. The Tenure of Office Act, used with such savage force to humiliate

THE MAN WHO DARES.
ARTHUR (putting his foot down)—"*Our honor first !*"
UNCLE SAM—"*Stick to it, my boy—I'm behind you.*"

This cartoon, published in 1882, praises President Chester Arthur for his courage in vetoing a bill that forbade Chinese immigration to the United States for twenty years.

Andrew Johnson, was never afterward resorted to as a means of browbeating the executive branch, and was eventually repealed in 1887. They even on occasion employed the cherished argument of strong Presidents like Jackson and Theodore Roosevelt that the Chief Magistrate was the embodiment of the popular will. Andrew Johnson referred specifically to Jackson in a speech of April, 1866. Johnson too was "the Tribune of the people, and . . . I . . . intend to assert the power which the people have placed in me. . . . Tyranny and despotism can be exercised by many more rigorously . . . than by one." Hayes, vetoing an Army appropriation bill in 1879 because of its obnoxious rider, said: "The people of this country are unwilling to see the supremacy of the Constitution replaced by the omnipotence of any department of the Government." Cleveland

National Guardsmen fire into an angry mob of demonstrators during the Chicago Pullman strike of 1894. Grover Cleveland was sharply criticized for sending in the troops against the wishes of the governor.

had assured the Senate of his determination to seek "better government for the people"; and in his subsequent book *Presidential Problems* (1904) he reiterated that "the Presidency is pre-eminently the people's office."[11] Now and then there were episodes of a Jacksonian or Lincolnian drama. In 1877 President Hayes dispatched contingents of regular troops to restore order in several states after labor strikes had erupted into violence. Cleveland, ignoring the protests of Governor Altgeld, sent soldiers into Illinois during the Pullman strike of 1894.

It may be argued then that the majority of post-1865 Presidents did what they could against severe handicaps. Undoubtedly they were handicapped. In the first place, this was a period of bitter and close competition between the two major parties. Other things being equal, conditions might have favored the evolution of the President as a valued party generalissimo, directing the fight and using his personal and official magnetism to secure cohesion. Instead there tended to be a stalemate. Though the Republicans won three of the five presidential elections from 1876 to 1892, they secured a popular majority in none of these. Despite the apparent unevenness in party strength, and despite the apparent triumphs indicated in Electoral College votes, Republicans and Democrats ran almost neck and neck. In three of the five elections the gap between the winners and the losers in the two parties was under 1 per cent. The Republicans squeezed through with small margins in certain key states such as New York and Indiana. Under the circumstances, the temptation to bribery and fraud were irresistible. It may be impossible to buy all the votes all the time (and is in any case unnecessary): the possibility of buying some of the votes some of the time lured politicians who were otherwise fairly upright men. The political history of the era is therefore full of "Burn-this-letter" skullduggery. There are many instances of secret directives like the one sent in the 1888 election to loyal workers in Indiana from the National Republican Committee: "Divide the floaters into blocks of five and put a trusted man in charge of these five, with the necessary funds, and make him responsible that none get away, and that all vote our ticket."[12] The impudence of some of the frauds and the elaborate ingenuity of others seem amusing today. But it would be a mistake to suppose that the men involved were not in earnest. The race was too close and the stakes too high to permit frivolity. Mockery was left to the newspapers. It was a great period for satirical journalism because the sources of satire lay so richly to hand.

Worse still for effective government, the major parties rarely achieved simultaneous working majorities in both houses of Congress and control of the Presidency. The Democrats managed this for only two years, from 1893 to 1895. The Republicans, somewhat better off, were also often hamstrung through the loss of at least one element in the system. Coherent legislative programs were unattainable. The Republican Hayes faced a Democratic House for the whole of his four years in office, and a Democratic Senate for the last two years. He suffered crippling disadvantages in having entered the Presidency after an unsalubrious juggling with a few thousand crucial votes. In almost every sense a minority incumbent, though personally honest, "His Fraudulency," the "de facto President," could not hope to give clear leadership. Other Presidents, while less marginally installed, were acutely aware that they held office without the sustenance of a comfortable majority.

Nor did it make much difference when the President and Congress were of the same political hue. Friction between the executive and legislative branches was inevitable unless the President tamely acquiesced in congressional supremacy. He could purchase peace only at the expense of his prerogative, as Grant and Benjamin Harrison did. Harrison, having defeated Cleveland in 1888, allowed himself to be instructed in his forthcoming duties by Senator Sherman, who told him: "The President should touch elbows with Congress. He should have no policy distinct from that of his party; and this is better represented in Congress than in the Executive."[13] Less complaisant Chief Magistrates could have answered that it was not always feasible in a time of ferocious factionalism to know which of the rival wings constituted the true party. And patronage created monstrous difficulties. Even after the passage of the Pendleton Act and the extension of its merit system to cover more and more offices through the years, every administration was bedeviled with patronage squabbles. Over one hundred thousand posts were still up for auction when Cleveland entered the White House. The dilemma of each President was that if he declined to play the patronage game he would win the approval of a handful of civil service reformers and satisfy his own conscience, but he would forfeit all chance of working with Congress. Jacob Dolson Cox, a perceptive congressman, said: "The experience of President Hayes proved that an administration which seeks to abolish the spoils system must expect to lose that appearance of leadership in legislation which has been sustained by the farming out of patronage. . . . In ordinary affairs a President who will not so purchase help will find his recommendations treated with slight respect, or even ostentatiously overruled." Indeed the "appearance of leadership," Hayes added, was "in the main a sham."[14] Congress often paid little or no attention to the legislative suggestions contained in Presidents' messages. Chester Arthur raised urgent matters involving law and order without any response whatsoever. His third annual message listed eight important recommendations, including federal aid for education, a presidential succession law, and regulation of interstate commerce. Congress acted upon only one of the eight, territorial government for Alaska, probably because such action would eventually provide votes,

Four hirsute Presidents: James A. Garfield (top, left), who was assassinated; his successor, Chester A. Arthur (top, right), Grover Cleveland (bottom, left), the only Democrat of the four; and Benjamin Harrison (bottom, right), whose single term came between Cleveland's two administrations.

seats, and patronage. The much-quoted comment of the British observer James Bryce was not far from the mark in the 1880's. Bryce claimed that presidential messages might have no more effect on Congress than "an article in a prominent party newspaper."

In the 1840's James K. Polk had prophesied that the spoils system would prevent any future President from winning re-election; the struggle for loot would alienate him from Congress and commit power into the hands of the legislature. In the late nineteenth century it began to seem that Polk's prophecy had come true. Except for the untypical wartime administrations of Lincoln, and the retention in office of the pusillanimous Grant, no President was reelected for a second consecutive term until William McKinley in 1900. Chester Arthur, who became President through the death of Garfield, sought a nomination in 1884 but was denied it; Grover Cleveland in 1888 and Benjamin Harrison in 1892 were defeated.

James Bryce had a close knowledge of and a considerable admiration for the United States. The main thesis of his influential book *The American Commonwealth* (1888) was that the United States had to be seen as a whole, and that as a whole it worked extremely well. There were good reasons why the political and governmental systems had evolved as they had. But if the reasons were good, Bryce could not help but betray his conviction that the results were regrettable. Men of education and social standing no longer entered politics, because more wealth or prestige, or both, were to be found in business and the law. The deterioration was cumulative. The higher the proportion of politicos such as Roscoe Conkling and "Boss" Platt, "Coffee-Pot" Wallace and "Fire-Alarm" Foraker, the smaller the number of persons of integrity who could be induced to pass their lives in such company. To Bryce, it followed that great men would not occupy the Presidency. Those nominated were usually party politicians of limited horizons. Indeed he thought the horizons *were* limited. Great Presidents were thrown up by great crises; and compared with the beginning years of the republic or with the agonies of the Civil War, the administrations of the Gilded Age seemed an anticlimax. Foreign affairs were limited to a contretemps with Chile, a scene in Samoa, a happening in Honolulu: events that seemed improbably remote and theatrical to the average American.

Much of what Bryce wrote was true. As he correctly pointed out:

> An American may, through a long life, never be reminded of
> the Federal Government, except when he votes at presiden-
> tial and congressional elections, lodges a complaint against
> the post-office, and opens his trunks for a customhouse of-
> ficer. . . . His direct taxes are paid to officials acting under
> State laws. The State . . . registers his birth . . . pays for his
> schooling . . . marries him, divorces him . . . declares him a
> bankrupt. . . . The police that guard his house, the local
> boards which look after the poor, control highways, impose
> water rates, manage schools—all these derive their legal
> powers from his State alone.[15]

The United States was still mainly oriented toward the local
community and the state. There was no federal income tax. The
Army and Navy were tiny, obscure bodies. The majority of congressmen came to Washington to intercede for their constituents,
not to make national policy. The deficiency in Bryce's account—
one that he shared with his American contemporaries—was that he
underestimated the gravity of the nation's domestic problems, and
the muted, puzzled, sometimes foolish but nevertheless earnest and
growing belief that something ought to be done.

Perhaps the most alarming factor of all, a weakness apparent in
previous and in subsequent history, was that by its very nature
American federal government was ill-equipped to deal with complex, long-term issues. Weak executive leadership aggravated the
situation. But even when the executive branch was strong and resourceful, the separation of powers and the peculiar rules of party
government crippled policy making. If a problem could be solved
in one swift stroke, this was sometimes done. If it demanded sustained scrutiny and protracted, systematic remedial action, this was
almost invariably absent. Government direction was too divided
and discontinuous. Because the two major parties were loose coalitions they competed for public support mainly on matters calculated to please and attract the electorate. The spoils system was
merely the most conspicuous example of an entire conception of
federal party government: namely, a central agency for the distribution of rewards, bonuses, and concessions. Serious, unattractive,
nonrewarding matters of public policy were ignored, or covered
over by bland procrastinations that purported to be compromises.
The rules of the political game stimulated legislators not to tackle

such intractable areas but rather to make party capital out of them by pretending that the other party was to blame. It was the congressional equivalent of the children's party game of passing the hot potato, or handing some other object around as rapidly as possible to avoid being caught with it when the music stopped. (The entire field of race relations, from the 1820's to the present day, illustrates the evasive and impotent aspects of federal activity.) One result was the search for innocuous, "available" presidential candidates.

A pattern had emerged that still holds true. Those who would act positively are thwarted. The only room for maneuver lies with those who are skilled in the techniques of busy nonactivity. Third, "protest" parties spring up to dramatize the issues, but they have no hope of capturing the Presidency. Sometimes the knowledge that they are merely fringe movements makes them reckless; and their apparent irresponsibility alienates the general public. This weakness is not confined to the United States. It can be seen in all democratic societies whose government is mediated through political parties. Fortunately for the United States, a climate of reform eventually develops. When the need for change is at length recognized, the executive and legislative branches are capable of devising swift, decisive measures. But this is because the President has finally taken the lead, or because the parties have concluded that they will lose seats if they do not satisfy public demand. In either case the initiative has come from ordinary citizens, not from Capitol Hill or the White House. The party system had and has many virtues. But it suffers from a desire to please where it ought to exhibit a desire to instruct and correct. It has too often sought ephemeral popularity at the expense of permanent benefit.

In the Gilded Age federal government, executive and legislative, revealed these inadequacies as glaringly as at any time in the nation's history. Some of the reasons have been indicated. There were others. The problems arising in the United States were novel, intricate, and prodigious. The inevitable strains following upon a civil war were heightened by the struggle over the control of Reconstruction waged between Andrew Johnson and Congress. The predicaments of the South were then distorted by a contest between Republicans and Democrats for the possession of Southern votes. Larger questions of economic welfare and civil rights were lost to view in petty bargains over pork-barrel legislation, and in cynical assessments of whether the Negro vote was an asset or a liability. Grant's plea, "Let us have peace," became not the noble ideal it might have been but a formula to justify private and partisan machinations.

There would have been some excuse for neglecting the South's ultimate welfare if the federal government had been preoccupied with other, even deeper issues of national welfare. President Cleveland's annual message of December, 1888, near the end of his first term, revealed an awareness of what these amounted to:

> The fortunes realized by our manufacturers are no longer solely the reward of sturdy industry and enlightened foresight, but they result from the discriminating favor of the Government and are largely built upon undue exactions from the masses of our people. The gulf between employers and the employed is constantly widening, and classes are rapidly forming, one comprising the very rich and powerful, while in another are found the toiling poor. . . . Corporations, which should be carefully restrained creatures of the law and the servants of the people, are fast becoming the people's masters.

Here if ever was a summons to action. Nor was Cleveland springing a brand-new diagnosis upon the country. Nine years earlier Henry George's *Progress and Poverty* had eloquently analyzed the cleavage between the "house of Have" and the "house of Want." Books and magazine articles on the subject were beginning to come out with some frequency. Yet with few exceptions the entire United States—President, Congress, judiciary, populace—accepted the doctrines of laissez faire as an article of faith. An uncompromising scholar like Professor William G. Sumner of Yale might challenge various sacred cows; but he did not deplore the consequences of an unregulated economic order because he genuinely believed in nonregulation. Like certain other intellectuals of his generation, indeed perhaps in common with the majority of college-educated Americans, Sumner exhibited an interesting mixture of complacence and pessimism known to its possessors as right thinking ("Every right-thinking citizen will surely agree . . ."). He was complacent in that he could not conceive of a superior alternative to unbridled laissez faire. He was pessimistic in that he did not really consider democracy an admirable achievement. Not that he was stupid or malevolent. On the contrary, he was a man of

This Puck *cartoon praises Cleveland for placing thousands of federal jobs under the merit—rather than the spoils—system.*

intelligence and integrity. But he was enclosed—as of course most of us are—by the beliefs of his time. The key belief, reinforced by such miscellaneous American dogmas as self-help, libertarianism, and state rights, was still that in the United States that government was best which governed least.

The citizens most responsibly involved in improving the tone of government focused their energies on civil service reform. Note that it was the *tone* that preoccupied them, not the notion of vigorous *action*. Cleveland's 1888 message to Congress continued:

> The existing situation is injurious to the health of our entire body-politic. It stifles . . . all patriotic love of country, and substitutes . . . selfish greed and grasping avarice. Devotion to American citizenship for its own sake . . . is displaced by the assumption that the Government, instead of being the embodiment of equality, is but an instrumentality through which especial . . . advantages are to be gained.[16]

He went on to denounce the "communism of . . . capital" as not less dangerous than the "communism of oppressed poverty and toil." "Communism of capital" was an arresting phrase. Cleveland employed the word "communism," however, merely to indicate his distaste for any organization that threatened property rights. The aims of the "Goo-Goo," or Good Government, reformers, who commended his message, were limited to chasing the money changers from the temple. The temple itself, the shrine of federalism, was to be purified yet not energized. Their ideal was government as a sort of Hall of Fame stocked with frozen statues. Insofar as they confined themselves to condemning the spoils system, and uttering general reproofs at rascally businessmen and corrupt legislators, the reformers made it still harder for a would-be powerful President to offer a lead to his country. In a way the ward heelers and party bosses had more insight than the gentleman-reformers. They were right, if for the wrong reasons, in insisting that despite Cleveland and his admirers, government *is* an instrumentality through which advantages are to be gained. The solution was not to stop the government from dispensing aid, but to make its assistance more efficient, more humanitarian, and far more complete. The "pols" knew too that it was impossible for Presidents to behave with perfect neutrality. In attacking Conkling, the most Garfield could do was give a patronage plum to the rival Blaine faction.

Being average sensible Americans, the Presidents of the Gilded Age did not, except at occasional moments, recognize the opportunity that awaited them—or rather, that would await their successors in a more amenable climate of opinion. Hayes, Garfield, and Cleveland were surprised and delighted in their clashes with the congressional hegemony to discover that public sympathy was with them, and would not tolerate blatant excesses on the part of its elected representatives. The proper presidential tactic was to strike a responsive chord in the electorate, especially through bold use of the veto, and claim a popular mandate for thoroughgoing reform. However, this was easier said than done in an era of congressional supremacy and of minority Presidents. The point is that the Presidents themselves had no wish to attempt an extension of the executive function.

Their defiance of Congress was courageous, and provided an essential base for the operations of the Roosevelts and Wilsons of a later time. But they were fighting defensively to drive off their besiegers; they did not move on to seize the initiative. Hayes was impressed by the arguments of Horace Greeley and his supporters among the reform wing of the Republicans, in his 1872 campaign, that corruption in government was greatly increased if the President held office for two terms: unhealthily close links were forged between Executive and legislature. In accepting the Republican nomination in 1876, Hayes accordingly announced that he would never be a candidate for re-election—"believing that the restoration of the civil service to the system established by Washington and followed by the early Presidents can best be accomplished by an Executive who is under no temptation to use the patronage of his office to promote his own re-election." In his inaugural address of March, 1877, Hayes recommended a constitutional amendment on the lines (though he did not say so) of the Confederate constitution, limiting the President to a single term of six years. Cleveland also thought a single-term limitation would be wise. The idea was a solace to Chief Executives who hated the friction and uncertainty of the existing method. Ex-President Taft remarked in a 1915 speech that it would have been better, "as it was at one time voted in the [Philadelphia] convention, to make the term of Presidency seven years and render him ineligible thereafter."[17]

Another proposed reform, first suggested by the House of Representatives in 1864 and warmly endorsed by a Senate committee in 1881, was to allow department heads to sit in Congress. Two future Presidents were strongly in favor. Congressman James A. Garfield wanted to readjust executive-legislative relations "so that there shall be greater responsibility to the legislative branch than there is now." Woodrow Wilson, while still a student at Princeton, published an article in 1879 entitled "Cabinet Government in the United States," warning that the nation's political maladies might prove incurable unless Cabinet members were selected from Congress and played a full part in the legislative process.[18] There is no record of Garfield's attitude toward the idea when he was actually in the White House. Neither he nor President Wilson pressed it. The snag was that while the reform might make for greater legislative effectiveness, it would be almost certain to weaken the President. The plan came to nothing. The executive branch limped along. Though Presidents, starting with Grant, were equipped with private secretaries, the job was at first deemed too menial to appeal to men of real ability. No new executive department was created between 1849, when Zachary Taylor appointed a Secretary of the Interior, and 1889, when the Department of Agriculture came into being. The Department of Commerce and Labor, which one would have thought at least as important, was not established until 1903.

Grover Cleveland was the toughest of this run of Presidents. In his *Twenty Years of the Republic* (1905), Harry Thurston Peck quotes the story of an Englishman asked to explain the secret of Lord Palmerston's great political popularity:

> "Why," said he, "what the nation likes in Palmerston is his you-be-damnedness." It was something of the same quality in Mr. Cleveland that caused the American people [at a moment of adversity for him] to let their hearts go out to him. [19]

But Cleveland had not much more than obstinacy to offer. His impatience with office seekers and pension hunters was close to mere irascibility. They disturbed his existence. His central idea was that the President must maintain his distance from Congress. It was a kind of Monroe Doctrine for the White House: he would not interfere with Capitol Hill if its agents refrained from interfering with him. The rule was too inert to vitalize the Presidency—which in any case Cleveland did not wish to do. In between his two terms he lived comfortably as a Wall Street lawyer. He was a good deal closer in his second term to the Republicans than to the radical members of his own party. He had grown sententious and business-minded: "the Stuffed Prophet," an unkind journalist called him. As for Cleveland's sparring partner in the presidential ring, Benjamin Harrison was a person of good family and gentlemanly behavior, of no consequence. He was the perfect vehicle of machine politics: presentable, decent, obliging, and too naïve to realize that his victory had been manufactured by a labor force of a hundred thousand industrious Republican politicians taking orders from the party directorate. For Cleveland and Harrison, in the new era of Populist discontent of the 1890's, "the people" were a slightly suspect entity. The word had acquired a dubious connotation. The people were liable to be the troublemakers, the men with an insufficient regard for the sanctity of property.

Striking evidence of the slump in presidential authority is to be found in the polemical and imaginative literature of the era. The authors and intellectuals who might have been expected to rally to the side of the Presidency did not do so. They refrained for a variety of reasons. One response was cynicism, disdain, despair. Men of good will such as Carl Schurz, E. L. Godkin (the gifted editor of the *Nation*), Horace Greeley of the New York *Tribune*, Charles Francis Adams, and his son Henry Adams, made their bid through the Liberal Republican movement in 1872. Their candidate Greeley, also nominated by the Democrats, was resoundingly beaten. Though they made further efforts now and then to defy the party organization, the reformers were almost always frustrated.

They were quick to conclude that although the existing parties were beyond redemption, third parties and *ad hoc* coalitions were also doomed to failure. The President was the prisoner of his party. Having decided this, disillusioned figures like Henry Adams tended to conduct themselves as if they were an invited audience at a bad play. Adams himself lived in Washington, hobnobbing with the few members of Congress or the executive branch who could match epigrams with him and his somewhat patronizingly witty Bostonian wife. They thought Hayes a provincial nobody, and Mrs. Hayes even worse. Their friend Henry James probably took Adams for his model in a short story called "Pandora." The Adamsish character in the story, discussing a prospective dinner party, says: "Hang it, there's only a month left; let us be vulgar and have some fun—let us invite the President." Mrs. Adams, retailing Washington gossip in one of her weekly letters to her father, passed on with relish the absurd information that the Hayeses "suffer much from rats in the White House who run over their bed and nibble the President's toes." For her it filled out the picture of the gawky official couple with their morning prayers and their nonalcoholic entertainments.[20]

The fictional President in Henry Adams' anonymous novel *Democracy* (1880) epitomizes the contempt felt by American patricians for the succession of bores and boobies who had now occupied the office for several decades—indeed, according to the Adams canon, ever since John Quincy Adams had been President. In the novel, Adams' imaginary President begins his career as a stone-cutter in a quarry. Clumsy and inarticulate, he is unable to fashion his own inaugural address. Here Adams was probably aiming both at Grant and at Johnson, for he happened to know that his friend

CONTINENTAL HOTEL

But my dear they are for sale by all Hardware Stores in this country.

We cannot leave until we visit the Enterprise Mfg. Co. and order some of Mrs. Potts'

Cold Handle Sad Irons, like this.

PRESIDENT AND MRS HAYES VISIT TO PHILADELPHIA

Nineteenth-century advertisers felt free to use pictures of Presidents to tout their products. Above, President Rutherford B. Hayes and his wife, Lucy, discuss the desirability of an iron.

George Bancroft had composed President Johnson's first message to Congress. His account of a reception at the White House is a derisive parody of Rutherford and Mrs. Hayes; the fictional President's lady is a religious zealot who forbids wine, billiards, and cards in the White House and will not receive women unless their bosoms and arms are amply clothed.

Such ridicule could be dismissed as individual malice if it were not reinforced by so much other evidence that Presidents were regarded by well-informed Americans as nobodies. Adams' judgment was not faultless: he thought Benjamin Harrison had been a good President, presumably because Harrison's prose and table manners were refined. But on more serious grounds the Presidents failed to make an impact, unless an unpleasant one. In radical circles, for example, the few episodes in which Presidents asserted their authority decisively seemed to prove that they were no true friends of "the people." Andrew Johnson had appeared to most reformers not as a gallant Jacksonian but as an obstructionist bully. Hayes and Cleveland incurred dislike through using regular soldiers to intervene in labor disputes. No wonder that the Populist party platform of 1892 proposed to restrict the President to a single term.

For the most part, however, reformers simply ignored the Presidency, not out of spleen but because it did not occur to them that Presidents had any function in leading the nation to better things. Fertile though the reformers were in devising panaceas, they expected little or nothing of the federal government as a whole because they mistrusted it and because they too were bound by laissez-faire presuppositions. Henry George's *Progress and Poverty* offered a compelling view of the economic and social plight of the United States, and a plausible remedy in his "Single Tax." Nothing but the tax, he seemed to believe, was required to cleanse the national stables. Other executive action would be irrelevant, and probably harmful. In 1888, the year of Cleveland's moving yet negative message, Edward Bellamy published his enormously popular Utopian novel, *Looking Backward.* By portraying an ideal America of the year A.D. 2000, Bellamy delivered a powerful indirect indictment of the America of his own day, in which society is like a coach dragged along by the harnessed poor while the rich ride on top. His hero, returning to the Boston of 1887, is sickened by the spectacle of humanity "hanging on a cross" (a metaphor that may have been adapted by William Jennings Bryan for his "Cross of Gold" speech in 1896), in a world of vicious and meaningless strife. Again, though, Bellamy's vision of the future leaves the federal government virtually out of the scheme. A cooperative economy is introduced. Everyone is obliged to serve as a state employee in the "Industrial Army." Affairs are adminstered by a group of experienced businessmen. There is no mention of Congress, or of any federal administrative structure, or of the President. He is apparently not even the chairman of the executive group, not even as a figurehead.

A less familiar example is a novel by Francis Marion Crawford entitled *An American Politician.* Crawford, who thereafter specialized in romantic stories set in picturesque places, wrote his novel in 1884, no doubt under the stimulus of the presidential election of that year. It was the year when liberally inclined Republicans staged a limited revolt against the party candidate, James G. Blaine, the "Continental Liar from the State of Maine," by voting instead for the Democratic nominee, Grover Cleveland. The hero of Crawford's novel is a gentleman-reformer from Massachusetts, and a Democrat. His difficulty is that he does not approve of political parties, and cannot stomach the local breed of Boston-Irish Democrats with whom he is obliged to have dealings. It looks as though he will never win a campaign, since he will not compromise his principles. Crawford contrives an extraordinary piece of wish-fulfillment in order to console his hero and his readers. He maintains that America's destinies are still in the hands of the patriciate, though for reasons not made clear their activities are clandestine. The hero, having passed muster, is brought under the wing of a mysterious inner council of three. The triumvirate is apparently rich, worldly, and powerful. They can maneuver as effectively as any clutch of senators or monopolists. They will ensure that the hero plays a part in the federal government, for their organization is something like what the Society of the Cincinnati (an organization of former Army officers) was alleged to be by its critics when it was founded in the 1780's. The three secret leaders are, says Crawford, members of

> a small community, . . . which had existed from the earliest days of American independence. . . . It had frequently occurred that all three members of the council simultaneously held seats in the senate. . . . More than one President since Washington had sat at one time or another in the triumvirate; secretaries of state, orators, lawyers, financiers and philanthropists had given the best years of their lives to the duties of the council.

In this latter-day Hamiltonian dream the United States is thus still governed by the wise and well-born. The interest for us is that Crawford's dream was in 1884 pathetically at variance with the actual American situation, and that though his was a dream of power, it is power wielded by a sort of Cabinet of which the President is merely one member — if he is a member at all.

While Crawford was scribbling his novel, Woodrow Wilson, by then a graduate student at Johns Hopkins University, was busy with a doctoral thesis, *Congressional Government,* a lucid, confident exposition that was published in 1885. His views had not greatly altered since his essay of 1879. Wilson contended that since the Civil War the country had been "denied a new order of statesmanship to suit the altered conditions of government." But the very

alteration inhibited statesmanship: the chief issues were too humdrum "to enlist feeling or arouse enthusiasm." And the American
Constitution prevented leadership from being effective except in
times of crisis. The Speaker of the House of Representatives had as
much power as anyone, through his right to appoint committee
chairmen; but his prerogatives were "cramped and covert." The
Presidency was "too silent and inactive, too little like a premiership
and too much like a superintendency."

Wilson did not, however, deplore the lack of presidential authority: he took it for granted that "the business of the President, occasionally great, is usually not much above routine." Most of the
time it was "*mere* administration, mere obedience of directions
from the masters of policy, the Standing Committees." What concerned Wilson was a closer relationship, on the British pattern,
between the executive *departments* and Congress. Congress had
inevitably become the dominant branch, in part because the
standing committees had the time and means to acquire specialized
knowledge of multifarious issues. By the same token Cabinets collectively knew far more about governmental matters than Presidents, who lived "by proxy; they are the executive in theory, but
the Secretaries are the executive in fact." A modern President "must
content himself with such general supervision as he may find time
to exercise." Congress had become and must remain the central
force in federal government; Wilson apparently saw no function
for the President beyond a rather vague administrative role as the
superintendent of the executive secretaries, whom he should continue to appoint but whom Congress "should have the privilege of
dismissing . . . whenever their service became unsatisfactory."[21]

Later Wilson would change his tune. For the moment he was
fairly representative of the mood of the 1880's. One of the recent
works that Wilson mentioned appreciatively was Alfred Stickney's
A True Republic, which proposed to make the President a quasi-
ceremonial figure, responsible to the legislature, which could remove him by a two-thirds vote or continue him in office for life—
like a federal judge—providing he behaved himself. A century
earlier Antifederalists had feared that the President might become
an elective monarch. Opinion had now swung so far in the opposite
direction that he was being envisaged as precisely that—but a
monarch without potency who would reign but not rule.

McKinley worked well with Congress, but as this Puck *cartoon indicates, he too felt that the legislators moved too slowly.*

Some historians believe that in the 1890's the pendulum began to swing back again, thanks to the pugnacity of Cleveland and the more successfully genial administration of William McKinley, who seemed almost as skillful in working with Congress as Jefferson had been. If so, the liberal reaction was decidedly lukewarm. Serious magazines such as *The Arena* and *Century* carried a number of articles on necessary political reforms. For instance, an associate justice of the Supreme Court of North Carolina, referring to a sign of activity on the part of Grover Cleveland, made the surprising claim in *The Arena* that "the weakness in our government is in the overwhelming weight of the executive and its constant tendency to grow":

> But recently we have seen the unprecedented spectacle of the president, whose duty . . . is merely to execute the laws . . . publicly stating by a letter to a member of the legislative de-

partment, what legislation he desired. He appoints the judiciary. He can veto legislation. He can procure legislation by the use of patronage. Now, he goes further, and simply tells Congress what he desires them to do. From this to the Roman Empire, in which, under the emblems . . . of a republic, the executive was in fact the whole government, united in one person, is but a step.

The author, Judge Walter Clark, recommended the elimination of the veto, the suppression of patronage, and the popular election of senators, to oblige all branches of government to "understand their true positions as agents and servants of the sovereign people."[22]

True, radical opinion was beginning to argue that the federal government should own and operate the railroads and the telegraph, telephone, and postal services, and that possibly land ownership too should be nationalized. "We believe," declared the People's Party platform of 1892, "that the power of government—in other words, of the people—should be expanded . . . as rapidly and as far as the good sense of an intelligent people and the teachings of experience shall justify." But the emphasis was upon power exercised on behalf of the people. In the Populist vision "government" was to do all sorts of things that had not been done before. But there was evident suspicion of the dangers of increasing the national government's power through an increase of patronage appointments. No consideration seemed to be given as to how this "government" was to be manned, or what precisely the President and the executive branch could or should do. An addendum to the 1892 platform, calling for the direct election of senators, also proposed to limit the President to one term. Other Populist programs advocated the direct election of the President. Yet such participatory democracy was much more concerned for the rights of the people than for an extension of executive authority as such. As for the two major parties, the Republican platforms of the 1880's and 1890's said nothing about presidential authority, while the Democrats contented themselves with vaguely Jeffersonian allusions to the Republicans' abuse of centralized power.[22]

Such views were summarized and emphatically restated as late as 1897, in the Reverend W. D. P. Bliss's huge *Encyclopedia of Social Reform.* "Very many believe," he wrote sourly, "that the Presidents of the United States have too much power." Or if not that, then they were too feeble, too unrepresentative. Among the authorities cited by Bliss, to support his implication that the Presidency was unsatisfactory, were James Bryce and the distinguished civil service reformers Dorman B. Eaton and George W. Curtis. Eaton wished to confine the President to a single term of six years, Curtis to revive the Electoral College as a genuine President-choosing chamber. The article asserted that Presidents were *not* properly chosen, and offered figures to demonstrate that in the 1896 election a shift from McKinley to Bryan of just over 20,000 votes in six marginal states would have brought victory for the Democratic candidate. Bliss also quoted from a radical memorial to Congress petitioning for the abolition of the Presidency:

> It maintains the false, illogical, disorganizing theory—born in monarchy, and principally denying democracy—of the "partition of powers." In the democratic polity, all powers are derived from the people, and are no more capable of partition from and against each other than are the people! . . . It is a constantly menacing, constantly growing cause of danger to the republic—whose eventual ruin it must inevitably occasion.

The petitioners were almost back at the Articles of Confederation. They proposed, having got rid of Presidents, to transfer the executive functions to an "administrative commission, or congressional ministry, to be chosen by Congress from their own body, or from among other competent citizens."[23]

American history is full of surprises. One of the most intriguing is the process by which an office apparently despised or disliked by forward-looking citizens could within a few years leap into power and popularity. To judge from the literature of the Gilded Age, the change was neither desirable nor attainable.

1. He was a bright child; his face always wore a Mobile-leer.

2. He never stoned cats—always hung his.

3. Even when a boy he showed a great love of Liberty.

4. When sixteen he could not read or write, which made it very inconvenient when he went—skating.

5. His piety was such that he would say his prayers wherever he happened to be.

9. He left the army and ran for Congress.

7. As a preacher he fairly lifted his hearers from their pews, with his powerful sermons.

6. He was of great assistance to his father on the farm.

DE GOLYER PAVEMENT

8. The General was a man of peace, even in war times.

10. But it was not until he went to Washington as a Representative that he found his proper walk in life.

11. If elected, he may possibly make a few religious changes in the architecture of the White House.

CHAPTER SEVEN

The Folklore of
the Presidency

FROM the close of Andrew Jackson's administration to the end of the nineteenth century the Presidency was—except under Abraham Lincoln—basically defensive and undramatic. In comparison with the extraordinary developments of the twentieth century the office lacked eclat. Those who wished to abolish it were, however, in a tiny minority. If the Presidency was not accepted as the dominant element in the federal equation, it was nevertheless of great symbolic importance. Even a sluggish President was still the nation's first citizen, the ceremonial head of state, welcomer of distinguished visitors, receiver of deputations, signer of bills and commissions, maker of speeches.

The Presidency continued also to matter to political machines. Third parties with no hope whatsoever of being returned to power followed the pattern of the two principal parties: they built their organization around a presidential candidate who became their figurehead and leader. To the Democrats and Whigs (or Republicans) the selection of a presidential nominee was a task of absorbing

---

Puck's *"Life of Garfield"* satirized the idealized versions of candidates' lives that were part of every campaign.

interest and prolonged scrutiny, reminiscent of the laborious search through which Tibetans used to choose their Dalai Lama.

A fundamental difference between the American and the Tibetan rituals was that in the United States the whole process was at least theoretically democratic. In other words, the explorations and incantations were conducted in the open—theoretically, at least—with the maximum of participation at all levels. When Jackson left the White House the democratization of choice was well developed. The franchise was open to nearly all white males (though not to females or Negroes). National parties had elaborate structures linking every community in the land. The congressional caucus was gone. In its place were the national party conventions, each preceded by a mass of state and special-interest party conventions whose opinions were keenly observed by those politicians professionally involved in the art and business of President making.

The Presidency was of boundless interest, too, to the hundreds of Americans who with varying degrees of justification felt that the office might fall to them. Few of the outstanding congressmen of the century were able to renounce all thought of the Presidency. Ambitious wives nagged at them. Men from their own state sang their praises. Party followers hoping for preferment cast about for "coming men" around whom to rally. Hardheaded politicians might encourage a score of aspirants, in order to test the public response or sometimes for more devious reasons. Henry Clay, John C. Calhoun, Daniel Webster, Stephen Douglas, William H. Seward, and Salmon P. Chase were only a few among the well-known politicians of their day who thought they had the Presidency within their grasp. Abraham Lincoln typified innumerable Americans when he confessed to a friend that "from my boyhood up my ambition was to be President."[1] Nor was the dream confined to congressmen.

With the advent of Jacksonianism it became clear that there were several routes which might lead to the White House. The most obvious starting point was a career in the law. All six of the disappointed candidates mentioned above received a law training. Of the first twenty-four men who actually served as President, from George Washington to William McKinley, all but five (Washington, W. H. Harrison, Zachary Taylor, Andrew Johnson, Grant) had been admitted to the bar. The transition from law to politics was

The Presidency eluded many of the towering figures in American political history, including Henry Clay (top, left), John Calhoun (top, right), Daniel Webster (bottom, left), and Stephen Douglas (bottom, right).

easily made. Some men, such as Daniel Webster, were able to shine simultaneously in both fields, though the combination may have weakened his presidential appeal by giving him a reputation as the advocate of rich men's causes.

Many aspirants served an apprenticeship in state legislatures, as did Abraham Lincoln. It was also naturally important for possible candidates to have gained some experience of the federal Capital, either as congressmen or as Cabinet members, or both. Of the politicians nominated by one of the major parties for the Presidency or the Vice-Presidency, Clay, Polk, Schuyler Colfax, and James G. Blaine had all served as Speakers of the House of Representatives. Madison, Fillmore, Lincoln, Hayes, Garfield, and McKinley had also been in the House. Monroe, John Quincy Adams, Van Buren, and Benjamin Harrison had been in the Senate. Andrew Jackson could claim membership of both houses of Congress, as could W. H. Harrison, Tyler, Pierce, Buchanan, and Andrew Johnson. Congressman Garfield was elected to the Senate in 1880, the year in which he was elected President. After the end of the Virginia Dynasty, Cabinet membership was a less satisfactory entrée, though Van Buren strengthened his position by holding office as Jackson's Secretary of State. President Polk, who remembered the jostling for the Chief Magistracy that had characterized the tenure of the executive departments in the previous twenty years, made his Cabinet members pledge not to seek the Presidency while they were in his administration. Polk's Secretary of State, James Buchanan, bided his time and ended up as President in 1857. Otherwise, apart from Grant's brief spell as *ad interim* Secretary of War under Johnson, no Cabinet member rose to the White House until William Howard Taft, who, when nominated in 1908, was Theodore Roosevelt's Secretary of War.

Though a firsthand knowledge of Washington, D.C., was valuable, it was not essential. Lincoln could never have been nominated on the strength of his one unspectacular term as a Whig congressman. His attraction depended considerably more on the reputation he had built up in his home state, Illinois. In the same way Rutherford B. Hayes caught the eye of the Republican President makers not as a result of his two modest terms in the House of Representatives, in which his display of initiative was confined to recommending improvements for the Library of Congress, but through the record he established as governor of Ohio. His opponent in the 1876 presidential campaign, Samuel J. Tilden, likewise acquired renown in his own state of New York. Tilden had never served in Congress; his prowess at the bar and in state affairs brought him to the governorship of New York. One of his predecessors, Horatio Seymour, had also been chosen as the Democratic nominee, in 1868, because of his success as governor of New York. Grover Cleveland was a third Democratic nominee from the Empire State who rose to the top of his party without benefit of a spell in Congress. His fame was based on a succession of state offices—assistant district attorney and sheriff of Erie County, mayor of Buffalo—culminating in the governorship. Polk had been governor of Tennessee as well as a member of Congress; so had Andrew Johnson. McKinley, a protégé of Hayes's, followed the same path as his mentor, via Congress and into the governorship of Ohio. Indeed Woodrow Wilson speculated in his *Congressional Government* (1885) that since the Presidency was primarily an administrative office, those who held it could perhaps best prepare themselves by undertaking the essentially comparable task of governing a state. The careers of Cleveland, McKinley, Theodore Roosevelt, and Woodrow Wilson suggested that here was indeed a broad highway to the White House.

And there was the back-door method of entry through the Vice-Presidency. In an actuarial sense it was less of a gamble than any of the other possible ways. The accession of Tyler, Millard Fillmore, Andrew Johnson, and Chester A. Arthur within a period of forty years might have impelled presidential hopefuls to stake their chances on accident. It certainly should have led Americans to give more thought to the succession problem. When Garfield died there was no one to follow Arthur in the succession. There was no Vice-President available, and the Republicans, who had lost their Senate majority when Conkling and Platt resigned in the spring of 1881, had prevented the election of a president *pro tempore*, who would have been next in line for the Presidency. If Arthur too had died before entering office an appalling hiatus would have been created. After he had been sworn in, President Arthur continually reminded Congress of the need to clarify the process in anticipation of future difficulties. But Congress merely toyed with the problem; it contained too many conundrums, and too much jockeying for legislative or party advantage. Above all, the Vice-President was settled in national folklore as a sort of man without a country—"His Superfluous Excellency" in Benjamin Franklin's phrase. In *Congressional Government,* Woodrow Wilson devoted a mere paragraph of debonair flippancy to the Vice-President:

> His position is one of anomalous insignificance and curious uncertainty. . . . It is one of the remarkable things about him, that it is hard to find in sketching the government any proper place to discuss him. . . . He is simply a judicial officer set to moderate the proceedings of an assembly whose rules he has had no voice in framing and can have no voice in changing . . . . His chief dignity, next to presiding over the Senate, lies in the circumstance that he is awaiting the death or disability of the President. And the chief embarrassment in discussing his office is, that in explaining how little there is to be said about it one has evidently said all there is to say.[2]

Daniel Webster, rejecting the offer of the Whig vice-presidential nomination in 1848, had remarked: "I do not choose to be buried until I am really dead." The irony of his comment is that within two years it was the Whig President, Taylor, who was dead: Webster would have been resurrected into the office he coveted. But such mortuary calculations did not figure in the plans of active politicians, partly no doubt because the "Accidental Presidents" from Tyler to Arthur failed to add anything positive to the Chief Magistracy. The outcome was the relegation of the Vice-Presidency almost to a minor, sometimes perfunctory exercise at the national party convention. A name had to be found to add to the ticket in order to balance it geographically. Such was the fate that lifted Congressman William A. Wheeler of New York to be Hayes's running mate. An adviser had told Hayes in 1876: "The ticket and platform should be of such character as to give the Republicans New York, Pennsylvania, and Indiana, or the first two certainly. This ticket would do it: Hayes and Wheeler." Thanking his friend, Hayes was too inhibited in his reply to raise a question that he put instead to his wife: "I am ashamed to say, Who is *Wheeler?*"[3] In a later generation someone would invent the joke that the President lived in the White House, his deputy in the Dog House.

There was a final way to the Presidency far removed from the zone of politics: the way of the military hero. George Washington's glory grew from his eight and a half years as commander in chief, and Andrew Jackson's from his miraculous victory in the Battle of

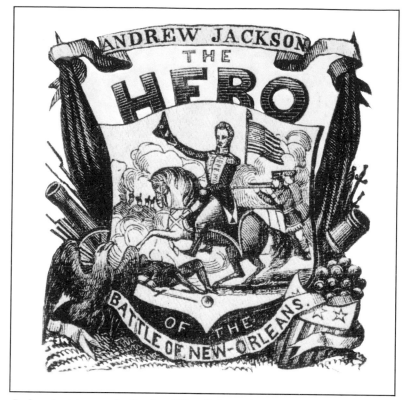

Jackson's victory at the Battle of New Orleans during the War of 1812 made him a national hero—and eventually President.

New Orleans. Zachary Taylor and Ulysses S. Grant were professional soldiers. So were a quartet of unsuccessful candidates: Winfield Scott, the Whig nominee in 1852; John C. Fremont, the candidate of the new Republican party in 1856; George B. McClellan, chosen by the Democrats to run against Lincoln in 1864; and Winfield Scott Hancock, the Democratic contender in 1880. Some analysts have stressed the fact that a majority of American Presidents had undergone military service. W. H. Harrison, Franklin Pierce, and James A. Garfield were presented to the electorate as General Harrison, General Pierce, General Garfield, on the strength of rank attained in three different wars. It has been maintained that far from being a disadvantage, a period of Army experience was a distinct asset for candidates. Certainly the Republican Presidents of the post-1865 era—Grant, Hayes, Benjamin Harrison, McKinley—had all made gallant records as officers in the Union army. Even Chester Arthur had been a general, if only a quartermaster general. The Republican charge against Cleveland in 1884, that he had ignominiously hired a substitute instead of fighting in the Civil War, might have cost him the election but for the fact that his Republican opponent, James G. Blaine, had also remained a civilian.

It has also been argued that a professional soldier was a vulnerable candidate unless he could demonstrate that he was really a "citizen" soldier. In support of this view, it has been pointed out that George Washington was a special case, and was without professional training; that Jackson too was unusual, and was to some extent identified as a congressman; that Zachary Taylor was a most unmilitary figure, who preferred not to dress in uniform and was not a West Pointer; and that Grant, the only graduate of the U. S. Military Academy to be elected President before General Eisenhower, was as unsoldierly as Taylor in appearance and outlook. Moreover it is possible to generalize from the defeated military candidates. Scott, "Old Fuss and Feathers," can be seen as too fond of uniform to appeal to American voters; and McClellan and Hancock as West Pointers more typical than Grant, and therefore less attractive to the electorate.

So many factors need to be taken into account that it is difficult to draw any reliable conclusions. Defeated or not, none of the nominees mentioned above would have been chosen by a major party if they had not seemed possible winners. Heroism on the battlefield stood any candidate in good stead, whether he was a professional soldier or merely a volunteer officer holding a temporary commission. It was assumed that a man who had been a general was a proven leader. Professionals like Taylor and Grant had the additional advantage of remoteness from the political scene. Their very innocence seemed a source of strength. They were uncontaminated by the political squabbles that titillated but also disgusted the American newspaper reader. Their hands would not be tied. Or, as the politicians could privately reflect, the Taylors and Grants might turn out to be malleable. The ideal military hero was a man with no previous political affiliation who, having suddenly burst

---

Hayes interrupted his legal career to lead Union troops during the Civil War; he was wounded five times. This engraving features his answer to a suggestion that he take a midwar furlough to campaign for a seat in Congress. He was elected anyway.

RUTHERFORD B. HAYES DURING THE WAR.

The man who would leave the Battle field to stump a State for Congress, while his Country is in danger, ought to be Scalped.

into the limelight, discovered that his lifelong principles were after all in harmony with those of one of the major parties. President Truman was to reveal a traditional politician's response when he hinted to General Eisenhower—then still a serving officer—that he might become the next (Democratic) President. The opportunity was too good to miss.

After the Civil War as after the Second World War, the victorious generals were at once sought out. Gideon Welles, the Secretary of the Navy, was one of those who did not warm to General Grant. He noted acidly in his diary that the Radical Republicans did not truly want Grant as their candidate when they began to pay him court, "but they are fearful he will be taken up by the Democrats." Whether or not they were aware of this at the time, Grant had voted for the Democrats in 1856. Still, the reason he gave was that he knew the Republican candidate, Fremont—and disliked him. At any rate, Republican scouts had to go and interrogate Grant's family before they were sure that he could be passed off as a Republican.[4]

It is doubtful whether Grant would have consented to run as the Democratic candidate if their scouts had reached him first, given the favors he had been shown by Lincoln, and the implication that the Democrats had been the disloyal party. But this very reason was an inducement to the Democrats to adopt soldier-candidates, so as to show that they had done as much as the Republicans to preserve the Union. In the fevered atmosphere of wartime McClellan was an irresistible Democratic choice. Many Americans still believed he was the Union's greatest general, deprived of his destiny by the folly of the Lincoln administration. The usually sober *North American Review,* recommending him for the Presidency in April, 1864, revealed that at least in emergencies a military hero was deeply appealing to the American public:

> The imagination needs a single figure which it can invest with all those attributes of admiration that become vague . . . when divided among a host. Accordingly, we impersonate in the general, not only the army he heads, but whatever qualities we are proud of in the nation itself. . . . There is nothing more touching than the sight of the nation in search of its great man, nothing more beautiful than its readiness to accept a hero on trust.

The nation very nearly did accept McClellan on trust, and of course did go the whole hog for Grant. The counterview, expressed by *Harper's Weekly* in March, 1864—"the school of the soldier is not the school in which a President of the United States should be trained"—was not in itself enough to deny the election to a McClellan.[5] The same thing had been said against Andrew Jackson, the "military chieftain," and against Taylor. The invariable riposte was that despite his military garb the man in question was still a citizen. In 1880 Hancock's managers were at pains to insist that he and his party had always acknowledged the supremacy of the civil over the military authority. The weakness of his position was that he faced in Garfield a contender who had also fought bravely in the Civil War, and who had achieved fairly high rank with no previous grounding in the military profession. That he had returned to Congress halfway through the war, while Hancock soldiered on, was considered no discredit to Garfield. In the folklore of the Presidency it was possible to gain a reputation as a hero, or in other fields, in a very short space of time. The most important quality to display, together with modesty and sterling worth, was versatility.

There was thus no innate prejudice against professional soldiers, so long as they conducted themselves with becoming modesty. The principal complaint against most of those who seemed prominent enough to be eligible for the Presidency was, oddly enough, not that they had no connection with politics but that they were apt to form a connection too readily. Like other Americans they were susceptible to the presidential enchantment. Once the magic dust had been thrown in the eyes even of a character as sturdily unimaginative as Zachary Taylor he was subtly changed. Winfield Scott, first proposed as a Whig possibility before the 1840 election, was on tenterhooks thereafter until the final fiasco of 1852, after which setback he was a sadder and wiser man. McClellan, though a West Pointer, resembled Grant in having left the Army before the Civil War.

The qualities sought in these military men did not differ fundamentally from the ones expected of candidates drawn from the orthodox avenues of party politics. These qualities are amply indicated in the torrent of campaign biographies that began to appear with Andrew Jackson. W. Burlie Brown shows in his fascinating analysis, *The People's Choice: The Presidential Image in the Cam-*

paign Biography (1960), that while they were often written in galloping haste and naturally tended to present each candidate in a rosy light, they tell us a great deal about features admired by successive generations of Americans. In the nineteenth century it was taken for granted that every candidate would be a Protestant of predominantly British (English, Scottish, Irish, Welsh) descent. The novelist William Dean Howells, who had already furnished a campaign biography of Lincoln, later volunteered to perform the same task for his fellow Ohioan Hayes, perhaps in hopes of being rewarded with a congenial diplomatic assignment in Europe. Howells produced his potboiler in three weeks, and here and there allowed himself a touch of humor unusual in the genre, as when he alluded to another prerequisite for presidential nominees: "It is necessary that every American should have an indisputable grandfather, in order to be represented in the Revolutionary period by actual ancestral service, or connected with it by ancestral reminiscence." Nathaniel Hawthorne's campaign biography of Franklin Pierce supplies a splendid all-purpose example of a candidate's patriotic ancestor:

> On the 19th of April, 1775, being then less than eighteen years of age, the stripling was at the plough, when tidings reached him of the bloodshed at Lexington and Concord. He immediately loosened the ox chain, left the plough in the furrow, took his uncle's gun and equipments, and set forth towards the scene of action.

Brown cites other unconsciously revealing passages. The candidate's father was almost always a plain, God-fearing, hard-working citizen like that of Van Buren, "a firm Whig in the Revolution" who instilled in his son "the maxims of piety, industry, economy and patriotism." The gentler virtues of filial generosity, kindheartedness, domesticity, and the like were inculcated by a procession of candidates' mothers. The first of these, a prototype for subsequent imitation, was the mother of George Washington. True, the young George was supposed to have confessed to his father rather than his mother the mischief wrought by chopping down the celebrated cherry tree. But a story which had equal currency in the nineteenth century was the frank admission by George, when a youth, that he had broken in a favorite colt of the Widow Washington's so vigorously that it dropped down dead. In the anecdote, his mother announced her pleasure that her son was incapable of falsehood. The candidate's mother, as he and his biographer wished to portray her and as the electorate was eager to believe, is touchingly described in this classic delineation of sweet old Mrs. McKinley:

> To see her, you must imagine a bright-eyed, motherly old lady, dressed in soft black, with a white lace collar around the throat and a cap of snow-white on her head. She is straight, well formed, and of medium height, and her hair is the color of frosted silver and combed so that the white strands curl just over the ears before they are tucked into the snowy cap.[6]

As for the candidate's boyhood, the folklore of campaign biography modulated with the shift in national tastes that took place in the last third of the century, from anecdotes of exemplary conduct to Tom Sawyerish tales of harmless pranks and physical activity. This shift is apparent in two different biographies of Rutherford Hayes. The first, written by the Reverend Russell H. Conwell, best known for his immensely popular lectures on self-help, is almost as unblushing as the picture of young George Washington presented seventy years earlier by the Reverend Mason Weems. Conwell says of Hayes:

> During his attendance at the common school, he was always waiting at the steps of the old stone schoolhouse when the door opened in the morning, and was never late in returning to his seat at recess. He did not splinter his desk with his penknife, nor throw paper balls or applecores at his neighbors . . . . He engaged in no quarrel with his schoolmaster, and he strictly obeyed every direction and command of his instructors.

The second biographer followed the newer line by stressing in Hayes's boyhood "his overflowing jollity and drollery more distinctly than his ardor in study."

The candidates, however, all respected education. Several credited their success to devoted teachers. Several others—Pierce, Fremont, Blaine, Cleveland, McKinley—themselves taught in school before beginning their political careers. None, though, was unduly given to scholarship. As one of Grant's biographers observed, "a President"—he might have said a presidential candidate —"should not be a theorist or a bookworm." The aim of education was to rise in life, not to become a recluse. A man worthy of a

William Henry Harrison had been elected President as a "log cabin candidate." Forty-eight years later his grandson, Benjamin Harrison, used mock log cabins as his campaign headquarters.

nation's votes ought to have had a wholesome, rural upbringing, which indeed was not difficult for candidates to claim in the nineteenth century: no President except perhaps Arthur was a thoroughly urban character, and he was in origin only a Vice-President. If possible the candidate must have been born poor, better still in a log cabin, like Pierce, Buchanan, Lincoln, and Garfield. *Log Cabin to White House* was the perfect title for a presidential biography. Many contain vignettes of the young hero, orphaned or otherwise alone, setting out to earn a living. Though Cleveland looked almost excessively prosperous when the Democrats nominated him, his chronicler conjured up a pathetic memory of young Grover, employed as an office boy at three dollars a week, obliged to walk through the snow to work in flimsy shoes and no overcoat.[7] Hancock was probably as handicapped by *not* having had an impoverished childhood as by having graduated from West Point. The biographer of Horatio Seymour tackled a similar difficulty with his elegant subject by declaring that despite his worldly polish he was "only a plain farmer after all . . . the proudest specimen of American yeomanry the world has ever looked upon." Playing his strong card, the biographer remarked that Seymour had, "while earnestly devoting himself to the tilling of the soil, been giving the best energies of his comprehensive mind to national affairs."[8]

It is easy to make fun of this type of campaign literature, produced in haste, sometimes as a commercial venture and always intended to beatify a presidential hopeful. Yet well-known writers readily contributed their talents, and upright candidates showed no hesitation in furnishing details of their early life. The entire nation in these quadrennial displays of sentiment longed to be told that the candidates were not as other men. The nominee of the other party, they were determined to believe, was incompetent, misguided, perhaps villainous. Their own leader was by contrast a magnificent yet representative American, a person like themselves raised by force of character and by the presidential lottery to the height of fame. He was their champion. If he was a politician, his supporters were anxious to be reassured, as they inevitably were, that he was not a "mere politician" but a patriot, a loyal party man who bore forward the banner of the true political faith—whichever one it might be. If the voters were deceived, it was because they wanted to be deceived into thinking that it was possible to escape from the trammels of the everyday. Rutherford B. Hayes was an honest man, though also a skillful politician. When Garfield emerged as the Republican candidate in 1880, President Hayes at once began to set down in his diary, in all sincerity, the series of clichés by which the party should boost the new leader:

> We must neglect no element of success. There is a great deal of strength in Garfield's life and struggles as a self made man. Let it be thoroughly presented. In facts & incidents, in poetry and tales—in pictures—on banners, in representations, in watchwords and nicknames.
> How from poverty and obscurity . . . he became a great scholar, a Statesman [note: *not* a "Politician"], a Major General, a Senator, a Presidential Candidate. Give the amplest details—a school teacher—a laborer on the canal—the name of his boat. . . .
> Once in about twenty years a campaign on personal characteristics is in order. Gen. Jackson in 1820-24—Gen. Harri-

son in 1840—Lincoln in 1860—now Garfield in 1880 . . . Such struggles with adverse circumstances and such success! . . . He is the ideal candidate because he is the ideal self made man.[9]

To Hayes the ballyhoo was beautiful because he was convinced that "we stand on the rock of truth." A campaign biography was like a secular sermon—a standing invitation to Americans to honor the nobility of their own transfigured existences. The poet Walt Whitman felt a kindred stirring of exultation mixed with exaltation. "I know of nothing grander," he cried, "better exercise, better digestion, more positive proof of the past, the triumphant result of faith in human kind, than a well-contested national election." The American preacher Henry Ward Beecher, when lecturing on current affairs, had a breezy knack of appearing to condemn while actually praising. He told an English audience in the 1880's that certain forms of American agitation had harmful aspects. Quadrennial elections were among these. The presidential election year was the time when "the most useless thing on God's earth is built on God's earth—namely, a political platform, which men never use and never stand on after it is built. Then the candidates are put forth, and every newspaper editor, and every public-spirited citizen . . . declares . . . that the further existence of the Government depends on the election of both parties." The excitement stirred up was prodigious, and some men felt "these wild excitements are not wholesome." Here Beecher shifts to his good-old-America key: "I say the best speeches of the community scattered through the land, discussing finance, taxes, education, are the education of the common people, and they learn more in a year of universal debate than they would in twenty years of reading and thinking without such help."[10]

Once a potential candidate had been identified he was propelled along on a mounting tide of enthusiasm. In 1867, for example, Grant Clubs sprang up all over the North. The National Union Club was formed in Philadelphia to secure him the Republican nomination. By the beginning of 1868 various magazines and newspapers—the *Nation, Harper's Weekly*, the New York *Tribune* and the *Sun*—had come out for him. A Central Grant Club was organized. In February, 1868, state conventions in New York, Indiana, and Wisconsin endorsed him. Immediately before the opening of

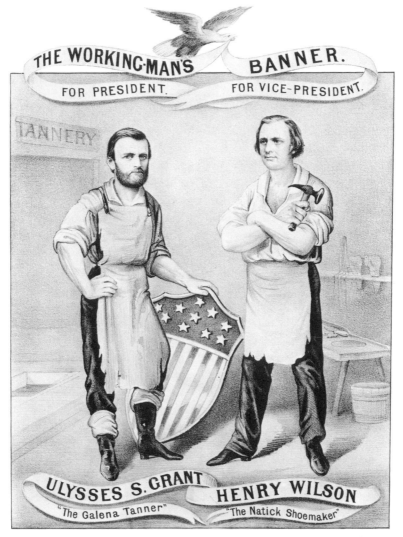

This poster emphasizes Grant's humble origins—a great political asset in those post-Civil War days.

the Republican National Convention, held in Chicago in May, 1868, a "Soldiers and Sailors Convention" was staged in the same city; the convention wildly applauded an address by Grant's aged father, and announced that everyone who had battled for the Union ought to be prepared to battle for General Grant.

When the Republican convention assembled, the delegates soon had the pleasure of gazing at a platform curtain specially decorated by the cartoonist Thomas Nast. In contest after contest Nast was to sway voters with his boldly repulsive caricatures of politicians such as Greeley, Tilden, and Hancock, of whom he and his editor disapproved. On this occasion he was in a more solemn mood. He had painted on the backcloth a huge White House flanked by two pedestals labeled "Republican Nominee" and "Democratic Nominee" (the latter would not be chosen for another six weeks, when the Democrats met in New York). Grant was already seated on the Republican pedestal. A figure of Columbia was pointing to the empty Democratic pedestal, with the words "Match him!" The six hundred and fifty delegates duly nominated Grant on the first ballot. A blank curtain covering Nast's design was at once raised to disclose the tableau—and produce an ecstatic pandemonium on the convention floor. "Match him!" became a Republican campaign slogan. The party message, in Hayes's words, was to be spread "in representations, in watchwords and nicknames." A more cynical party man might have added "and in misrepresentation—of the other side."[11]

Some aspirants, including Salmon P. Chase, weakened their chances of nomination by appearing too eager. In keeping with the style set by Washington and John Adams, and with the view that a candidate ought to stay above the fracas, the folklore of President making required possible nominees to behave as if hardly aware that their names were on everyone's lips. Trying in vain to offset the feeling that Blaine was too nakedly interested in the Presidency, one of his supporters declared, "He is not a coy candidate. It is an honest aspiration and he indulged it like a man." In the nineteenth century a few candidates genuinely felt the reluctance to run that perhaps only Adlai Stevenson has shown among twentieth-century nominees. Horatio Seymour, the Democratic choice for 1868, was in earnest when he insisted that he had "not the slightest desire to occupy the White House; there is too much trouble and responsibility." He made three public announcements to this effect, and sealed himself off by accepting the chairmanship of the convention, so that he would quite obviously be ineligible. When his name was nevertheless put forward Seymour stopped the ballot count and told the delegates, "I must not be nominated by this Convention, as I could not accept the nomination if tendered." Twenty-one ballots later, with the convention in a state of near deadlock, the Ohio delegation reintroduced his name "against his inclination," as the Ohio spokesman said, "but no longer against his honor." Seymour was frantic. He protested that "when I said I could not be a candidate, I *meant* it! . . . God bless you for your kindness . . . but your candidate I cannot be." However, while he was cooling himself in the foyer the convention nominated him in his absence. After that resistance was futile, though in later days he described his failure to persist in refusal as "the mistake of my life."[12]

Such total reluctance was rare. The problem was that the ritual of indifference and hesitation made it impossible to distinguish between genuine modesty or unwillingness and counterfeit versions. Potential nominees such as Seymour (or Grant and Tilden), who were honestly of two minds whether to enter the race, were accused of excessive coyness. Men who were sure that they would like to be nominated had to continue to disclaim and dissemble. A visitor from another planet confronted with the performance might have decided that every public figure in the United States was either a nervous imbecile or a scheming hypocrite. An unfriendly acquaintance of General Winfield Scott's happened to travel with him aboard a Hudson river steamboat in June, 1839, when Scott had just begun to be mentioned as a Whig candidate for the 1840 contest. The passengers gave three cheers as Scott finally disembarked. He responded with a polite word of thanks. His caustic acquaintance said the general "professed to deprecate being held up as a candidate for the presidency at this, or *any future time* —it is a hard part for him to play, but he does it with more discretion than some would have expected of him, and only overacts sometimes. . . ."[13]

It was a hard part for anyone to play, though the skepticism of this particular report was justified by Scott's subsequent ambitious behavior. More sophisticated and cooler-headed men than he learned to walk the narrow path of compromise by combining an air of personal detachment with judicious promotional activity on the part of their friends. At this distance, when we are accustomed to more candid avowals, it is not easy to assess the inmost thoughts of potential presidential nominees in a bygone era. The diary of Rutherford B. Hayes is more baffling than revealing, although he regarded it as confidential and was disturbed when he once thought it might have been mislaid. His editor, T. Harry Williams, says that Hayes was "a curious mixture of idealism and practicality," at times "too high-minded for his own advancement, and at others . . . the most adept of politicians." Hayes noted in October, 1875, that if he won re-election as governor of Ohio "I am likely to be pushed for the Republican nomination for President. This would make my life a disturbed and troubled one until the nomination six or eight months hence. If nominated, the stir would last until November a year hence." He appeared cool to the prospect — admittedly a remote one, since there were several other prominent candidates — and equally calm about the possibility of losing the gubernatorial election, which would remove him from the presidential list.

By February, 1876, reinstalled in the governorship, Hayes wrote that every day brought letters and callers on the subject of the Presidency: "I say very little. I have in no instance encouraged any one to work to that end. . . . I have said the whole talk about me is on the score of availability. Let availability do the work then." In other words, he was available if he was "available." At the beginning of April he told himself, "I would be glad if now I could in some satisfactory way drop out of the candidacy." A few days later he observed: "In politics I am growing more indifferent. I would like it if I could now return to my planting and books at home." However, this entry in his diary is followed by a copy of a letter he had sent to one of the Ohio delegates to the forthcoming national convention, affirming politely that he expected the courtesy of "the solid vote of Ohio," at any rate in the initial balloting. In subsequent entries he transcribed various letters of support, with his answers, all of them models of discretion. His aim, as he told Garfield, was "not to lose my head, and to get through it without doing or saying anything unjust or even uncharitable towards competitors or their supporters."[14] Luck was on his side. He had abided by the rules; the other Republican contenders stalemated one another, and the nomination was his. How much did he want it? The truth is veiled from us, and was perhaps veiled from Hayes himself. Consciously or not, he was the servant of a complex code that had evolved through several decades. In obedience to its subtle but nonetheless imperious etiquette he remained at home in Columbus while the delegates were in conclave at Cincinnati.

Party conventions too were — much as in the twentieth century — highly stylized affairs, blending emotion and guile, exuberant horseplay and episodes of an almost mystical gravity. America's big and growing cities vied for the honor, publicity, and profit of acting as hosts. To attract custom they built vast auditoriums such as the Chicago "Wigwam" (a wooden structure, not a tent), which witnessed Lincoln's nomination, and the new Tammany Hall in New York. Ten thousand people crammed into the 1880 Republican convention in Chicago. The noise, the heat, and the confusion were both insufferable and intoxicating. Somewhere in the midst of the platitudes and the bargaining the delegates glimpsed a vision of a united and regenerate party, to be led into the promised land by a spotless commander who had not sought the nomination but had been sought by it. "I nominate one whose name will suppress all faction and thrill the republic": these words in support of Hancock at the Democrats' 1880 convention embodied the universal formula. A national convention was a religious revival grafted on to a stock exchange. The vision, though it might prove a mirage, often possessed a strangely moving quality. As in revivalist meetings, it was compounded of penitence as well as hope. Past follies were washed clean. Every good party man longed to believe that the party candidate was as doughty and virtuous as his campaign biography said he was. The orator who called James G. Blaine a "plumed knight" in an 1876 nomination speech was certainly overvaluing a somewhat sordid politician; but the language of heroism seemed perfectly appropriate to him and to thousands of Blaine's devotees.

The convention mood could not have been sustained without minor rituals of reconciliation and unanimity. Hence the transfer of ballots to the winning candidate; hence the concern of defeated aspirants to congratulate the victor as rapidly and conspicuously as possible. If a man could not be a good winner, policy and party ethics enjoined on him the necessity of being a good loser. Party loyalty was esteemed a virtue almost beyond price. Young Theodore Roosevelt prided himself on having been a "regular" in 1884. When many of his fastidious friends bolted the party rather than vote for Blaine he stuck to his leader. He never doubted he had done the right thing. Once the army was on the march it was fatal to undermine the commander. Indeed, martial metaphors mingled with those of religion and commerce in the rich amalgam of President-making rhetoric.

Once nominated, a candidate was not expected to play an active part in the campaign. There were exceptions. William Henry Harrison set a precedent by making semipolitical speeches in 1836, and the fashion was repeated in 1840. Ex-President John Quincy Adams deplored this "revolution in the habits and manners of the people":

> Electioneering for the Presidency has spread its contagion to the President himself, to his now only competitor, to his immediate predecessor. . . . The principal leaders of the political parties are travelling about the country . . . and holding forth, like Methodist preachers, hour after hour, to assembled multitudes, under the broad canopy of heaven. [15]

Party chiefs continued to stump the country in subsequent presidential election years. The candidates themselves, however, and the existing President, reverted to an appearance of aloofness, leaving the orating and parading and fund-raising and distribution of handbills and ribbons to the party machine. They were of course busy behind the scenes. But most stayed at home. A misleading contemporary print showed Abraham Lincoln returning on horseback to his home in Springfield, Illinois, "after his successful campaign for the Presidency of the United States in October, 1860." He in fact did not stir from Springfield. The nearest he came to a campaign speech was to attend a local Republican rally in August and utter a few well-chosen words. He declared that "it has been my purpose, since I have been placed in my present position, to make no speeches." After thanking the crowd and stressing that the cause that brought them all together was far more important than any particular candidate, he excused himself and left the gathering in the hands of the orators of the day. Two other nominees in 1860, John Bell and J. C. Breckinridge, likewise maintained a gentlemanly silence. A fourth nominee, Stephen A. Douglas, hurled himself into the fray with an admirable wholeheartedness, knowing that he had virtually no chance of victory. He even penetrated into the South, which was by then enemy country for a Union Democrat. Some of his followers, though, felt that he had shown an indecent disregard of precedent. They put out the unconvincing explanation that he was on a lyceum lecture tour, en route to a visit to his mother in New York, Cartoonists drew mocking maps of Douglas' zigzag itinerary "In Search of His Mother."

For twenty years thereafter the rule of reticence prevailed. In 1868 Grant hid himself in Galena, Illinois, his home town, to avoid the hurly-burly. Although he was persuaded to take a tour

Candidate William McKinley greets visiting delegations on the front porch of his home in Canton, Ohio, in 1896. His opponent, William Jennings Bryan, traveled all over the country in search of votes, but the stay-at-home McKinley was victorious.

as far west as Denver, Colorado, in company with the popular generals Sherman and Sheridan, no political speeches were delivered during the trip. Grant's opponent, Horatio Seymour, made some able but belated speeches in October, 1868. In 1876 Hayes did not leave Columbus, Ohio, except to attend the Centennial Exposition at Philadelphia on "Ohio Day," less than two weeks before the election. He delivered a few short addresses at the Exposition, and was pleased that, as he put it, he had not "slopped over." In 1880 Garfield once more defied custom by undertaking an ambitious tour, during which he spoke seventy times. Since he was a first-rate orator his boldness was forgiven. It was also understood that underdog candidates such as William Jennings Bryan (another celebrated orator) might have to take the stump. In Bryan's case, there was the consideration that the predominantly Republican press of 1896 either maligned or ignored him. His exhausting travels in the North, West, and South were designed to bring a message to the electorate that they might otherwise never hear. But party funds and party organization were not yet geared to such campaigning. One of his associates complained that Bryan had to make his own arrangements as he went along. Since he had no special train he sometimes had to get up in the middle of the night to keep the next engagement. A newspaper reporter traveling with him said that "Mr. Bryan has often been forced to carry his heavy grips from the train some distance up the street" and that in one place he was obliged to "walk from the train up town, no arrangements having been made to have a carriage for him."[16] But Bryan lost, and McKinley—waging a front porch campaign from his home in Canton, Ohio—won. Not until 1928 did speaking tours by both major candidates become a regular feature of presidential elections. In any case, the politicos no doubt realized that other factors were more important than personal appearances—especially in an age when candidates were not required to be handsome and magnetic. By 1880, when campaign literature began to be produced in quantity, the torchlight era was over:

Oh, they marches in parades and they gets up hurrahs,
And they tramps through the mud for the good old cause—

The mood caught in this nineteenth-century doggerel would no longer quite apply. The printed word seemed even more crucial than the spoken word, and far more than a parade of "Wide-Awakes." In 1896 the Republican national committee alone sent out three hundred million leaflets—enough to supply four copies to every man, woman, and child in the country. Whatever was needed, from vote buying to processions, the Republicans had. That year a substantial campaign fund, raised by energetic touting of wealthy backers, paid the expenses of a mobile task force of fourteen hundred Republican organizers.[17] Without the intricate substructure of a major party a candidate could accomplish little, whether he barnstormed through every state in the Union or was content to sit tight and receive an occasional delegation in his own parlor.

Cleveland's admission that he might be the father of an illegitimate child is mocked in this Judge *cartoon of 1884, but the voters recognized his worth and made him President despite his indiscretion.*

One element in presidential folklore persisted. It was not yet essential, though preferable, for a candidate to be a family man: Cleveland was a bachelor, whose campaign survived the scandal of an early liaison with a promiscuous lady of Buffalo. Nor need a candidate be a man of fine appearance and easy manners: a touch of the rough diamond did not come amiss. But he must at all costs be a *serious* person. The ideal figure of the nineteenth century was James A. Garfield, self-made but eminently respectable. Garfield, in his 1880 speaking tour, made a profound impression upon young Robert M. LaFollette of Wisconsin, himself a future aspirant for the Presidency. "I heard him at Madison." LaFollette recalled in his autobiography:

> He was a very handsome man, of fine presence, dignity and power; splendid diction and rather lofty eloquence. I do not remember a suggestion of humor. . . . I remember he im-

pressed me more as a statesman and less as a politician than any of the men I had heard up to that time.

Candidates who indulged in humor, at least on public occasions, were suspect. Not one of the Presidents of the nineteenth century was known as a humorist except Abraham Lincoln; and though we admire his drollery most of his contemporaries did not. Even as late as 1894, Professor Woodrow Wilson wrote primly in an otherwise enthusiastic magazine sketch that Lincoln's "mind never lost the vein of coarseness that marked him grossly when a youth."[18] Genial humor was all very well in local politics. A quick witticism on the floor of Congress was acceptable. One of the Whig leaders, Thomas Corwin of Ohio, acquired a national reputation for humor on the strength of a burlesquing speech in the House of Representatives. But it should be added that he later believed his delight in humor had weakened his political reputation. If Lincoln had been known as Humorous Abe instead of Honest Abe he would never have reached the White House. His presidential prestige was threatened by his rumored fondness for "little jokes." Walt Whitman, who was living in Washington and sometimes caught glimpses of Lincoln, had to reassure friends in 1863 that the President was really a wise person "underneath his outside smutched mannerism, and stories from third-class country barrooms (it is his humor)." Hostile commentators dwelt upon a characteristic that was considered alien to the traditions of the Presidency. James Gordon Bennett's New York *Herald* assailed him in 1864:

> President Lincoln is a joke incarnated. His election was a very sorry joke. The idea that such a man as he should be the President of such a country as this is a very ridiculous joke . . . . His debut in Washington society was a joke; for he introduced himself and Mrs. Lincoln as "the long and short of the Presidency". . . . His conversation is full of jokes. . . . His title of "Honest" is a satirical joke.[19]

Rutherford Hayes recorded in his diary the witticisms of his brilliant Secretary of State, William M. Evarts.[20] He obviously appreciated them, as he did the riddles exchanged by his children, which he also set down. But there is no inkling of one of Hayes's own jokes in his jottings. Presidents even more than candidates were expected to be above frivolity. In domestic life they could behave more relaxedly. Until the end of the century their daily doings in the White House, despite the lack of privacy afforded by the building, were still on the whole concealed from the public. Writing in 1905, in oblique disapproval of Teddy Roosevelt's much-publicized family, Harry Thurston Peck praised President Arthur as a gentleman who "kept the domestic side of his *ménage* a thing entirely apart from his private life":

> Coarse-minded, peeping correspondents, male and female, found scant material here for vulgar paragraphs of kitchen gossip. There were published no foolish, nauseating chronicles of the "daily doings" of the White House. The President's children were not photographed and paragraphed and made the subject of a thousand flat and fatuous stories. Beyond the veil of self-respecting privacy, which was drawn before the President's personal affairs, few ever penetrated .

Peck was a snob. He excluded Jefferson from consideration as a worldly President on the level of Chester A. Arthur because "during his first term, he cultivated an ostentatious boorishness such as would have been impossible in a thoroughbred." Peck said too that probably not "even so great a man as Lincoln could have kept his powerful hold upon the masses had he not possessed some qualities which many of his truest friends deplored." Limited in such insights, Peck also overstated the view that "democracies prefer their idols to have feet of clay." The American people still expected their Presidents to behave as impeccably as in the realms of genteel fiction and campaign biography—realms that had much in common. Toward the end of the century, however, they began to demand more evidence of the human side. When the middle-aged bachelor Grover Cleveland married the daughter of his former law partner, a girl of twenty-one, public curiosity was bound to be stimulated. The appetite was fed by a swarm of newspaper correspondents—the *paparazzi* of 1886—who perched opposite the honeymoon cottage and peered at it through binoculars.

Cleveland was understandably indignant. But he had already fallen foul of the newspaper fraternity. The power of the press to annoy Presidents was no novelty; it had been demonstrated over and over since the 1790's. Cleveland's mistake was in failing to see that American readers were developing more and more interest in the personal aspects of the Presidency. Perhaps this interest was a gauge of the relative insignificance of the public side; perhaps it

The press had a field day when Cleveland married lovely young Frances Folsom, left. The wedding took place in the Blue Room of the White House on June 2, 1886.

foreshadowed the great awakening of interest in a rejuvenated office no longer so subject to the rules of political folklore. Cleveland became a prime target for journalistic censure and ridicule. When he seemed to neglect the obligatory rituals by going fishing on Memorial Day, he was accused of insulting the memory of the Union dead. The rumor that his culinary tastes were primitive led the press to picture him stuffing himself with "pig's feet, fried onions and a bottle of Extra Dry." Editors pretended that his admittedly sententious speeches were plagiarized from an encyclopedia, or written for him by his overeducated sister. He retaliated by sending angry letters to editors. At a banquet to celebrate Harvard's two hundred and fiftieth anniversary (hardly the best moment for an outburst), he denounced the "silly, mean, and cowardly lies that . . . are found in the columns of certain newspapers, which violate every instinct of American manliness, and in ghoulish glee desecrate every sacred relation of private life."[21]

One must have some sympathy for Grover Cleveland. The yellow press *was* offensive and irresponsible. But the press as a whole, though capable of platitudes worse than those perpetrated by any President, had a satirical function that became increasingly evident in the Gilded Age. As we have said, that era gave it plenty to feed on. It is not altogether surprising that Ambrose Bierce, a man trained as a newspaper columnist, should have defined the Presidency in his *Devil's Dictionary* as "the greased pig in the field game of American politics." The rules of Cabinet making, for example, lent themselves to mockery. "Mr. Dooley" (Finley Peter Dunne) had a delicious subject in speculating on the process of selection to be followed, ritually, by the newly elected McKinley:

> It 'twas one of the customs of this great republic of ours, for to appoint the most competent men for the places, he'd have a mighty small lot for to pick from. But, seein' as only them is eligible that are unfit he has the devils own time selectin'. . . . It may be hard for Mack, bein' new at the business, to select the right man for the wrong place. But I'm sure he'll be advised by his friends, and from the list of candidates I've seen he'll have no trouble in findin' timber.[22]

Some of the customs of the country were ripe for alteration. Some would remain unaltered. The folklore of the Presidency was not to change basically for many years after McKinley, although much was to change in the way men acted once they were in office. A good deal of newspaper ridicule was a recognition of a fundamental irreverence that paralleled the rather heavy ideology of Americanism. Americans were of two minds: they wished to respect and almost revere their leaders, but they were also disposed to laugh, to jeer, to deflate the images they had themselves created.

Those fellow citizens who entered the presidential stakes were sometimes tormented and warped by ambition. The good-loser tradition, however, helped the unsuccessful to regain their equilibrium—that, and the double consolation that they had not *appeared* to be coveting the office, and that in four years' time the dice might roll more fortunately. The presidential campaign of 1884, between Cleveland and Blaine, was vicious and heated, and hung upon the slenderest of majorities. A little over a thousand votes in New York State determined the outcome. Blaine, a prominent candidate ever since 1876, had the bitterest of pills to swallow. But custom had prevented the two candidates from abusing one another, though their henchmen did not shrink from the duty. And custom required that they should make gestures of reconciliation. Not long after Cleveland's inauguration, therefore, Blaine paid a courtesy call at the White House. He took the opportunity to ask a small political favor: would the President be so kind as not to remove from office the Republican postmaster of Augusta, Maine, an old friend of Mr. Blaine's? The language of politics could be as delicate as the language of flowers. The beaten candidate was acknowledging the power of the victor—who was correspondingly gracious in return. The postmaster of Augusta kept his job. Some while later it was discovered that a delegation of citizens at the White House included the Reverend Dr. Samuel Burchard, a Republican who had caused a sensation in the recent campaign by damning the Democrats as "the party of Rum, Romanism, and Rebellion." Everyone laughed; the Democratic Cleveland shook hands with Dr. Burchard; and Dr. Burchard expressed his pleasure at finding the President in such good health.[23]

If Cleveland had contrived to be always as genial the press, or the more reputable portion, might have treated him more kindly. For the style demanded of a President, and demanded with mounting insistence, was one of geniality that stopped somewhere short of levity and vulgarity and a long way short of arrogance. In his second term Cleveland struck unsympathetic witnesses as too full of himself, too much given to statements that sounded like edicts. The distinction was nicely put in a speech made by President Wilson in 1916. "Every man who takes office in Washington," he said, "either swells or grows."[24] The reproach against Cleveland, perhaps unfairly, was that he was swelling instead of growing. The unaffected geniality of McKinley exactly caught the pitch of public expectation.

McKinley was not a giant. But then, the American electorate was not interested in gigantic figures. It wanted figures whose capacity was legendary only in the sense of conforming to the familiar legends of national folklore, which were just a little larger than life-size. The process of selection was erratic, as many historians have stated. A more discriminating electorate would probably have given a second term for instance, to John Quincy Adams, and would have preferred Seymour to Grant. In the main the voters got what they deserved. Or rather, the ennobling effect of the presidential office gave them something rather better than they deserved. A Hayes, an Arthur, or a McKinley, commonplace enough in up-bringing and outlook, rose sufficiently above his mediocre milieu to keep alive the democratic trust in the ability of men to transcend themselves. It is a trust that constitutes a magnificent naivete.

The death of a President in office was of all the aspects of the post the one most indicative of its peculiar near-majesty. What the living man is grudged is bestowed on him posthumously. This truth is vividly expressed in Wilfred E. Binkley's *The Man in the White House:*

> The writer can never forget how he found his father, just after hearing the news of McKinley's assassination, weeping as bitterly as if he had lost a child. So it was to others when Lincoln, Garfield, and Harding died in office. The son who protested to his foreign-born mother Harding's lack of merit, when he found her weeping over news of the president's death, got this significant response: *"Ach, aber er ist doch der Präsident"* ["Ah, but he is still the President"].[25]

PART THREE

POWER AND THE TWENTIETH-CENTURY PRESIDENT

WILLIAM MCKINLEY 1897-1901
THEODORE ROOSEVELT 1901-1909
WILLIAM HOWARD TAFT 1909-1913
WOODROW WILSON 1913-1921
WARREN G. HARDING 1921-1923
CALVIN COOLIDGE 1923-1929
HERBERT HOOVER 1929-1933
FRANKLIN D. ROOSEVELT 1933-1945
HARRY S. TRUMAN 1945-1953
DWIGHT D. EISENHOWER 1953-1961
JOHN F. KENNEDY 1961-1963
LYNDON B. JOHNSON 1963-1969
RICHARD M. NIXON 1969-

Judge

ENTERED AT THE POST OFFICE AT NEW YORK AS SECOND CLASS MATTER COPYRIGHT 1904 BY JUDGE COMPANY TITLE REGISTERED AS A TRADE MARK

PACIFIC

PANAMA

CANAL

THE GREATEST ACHIEVEMENT FOR TRADE IN MODERN TIMES

COPYRIGHT 1904 BY JUDGE CO. (?) PANY PUBLISHERS, 225 FOURTH AVE. NEW YORK

A CROWN HE IS ENTITLED TO WEAR.

CHAPTER EIGHT

Changing Factors

IN the thirty years before 1900 little reliance had been placed on the President as a decisive force; at least not as a benevolent force. Even in 1900 it was possible for a Columbia University professor of government, Frank J. Goodnow, to publish *Politics and Administration,* a study that relegated the Chief Executive to merely one of several parts of the nation's administrative system.[1]

A prodigious change was in the making. Woodrow Wilson's early book *Congressional Government,* written while Chester Arthur was in the White House, spoke of the executive as a semi-impotent branch, "taken into partnership with the legislature upon a salary which may be withheld, and . . . allowed no voice in the management of the business. It is," he said, "simply charged with the superintendence of the employees." Though Wilson was critical of the resultant situation—government with no clear party leader-

---

To Teddy Roosevelt the White House was a "bully pulpit"; few men have enjoyed being President as much as T. R. did. At left is a 1904 magazine cover honoring Roosevelt for his key role in bringing the Panama Canal from dream to reality.

ship, no effective executive direction—he did not suggest that any great alteration was likely. Fascinated by the notion that institutions have an organic quality akin to that of living creatures, he portrayed the growth of congressional power as natural and inevitable. Those who believe in such silent, organic developments rarely propose ambitious reforms, for there would be no point in trying to rearrange matters prescribed by the laws of nature. Wilson's early views were therefore limited to an analysis of the regrettable consequences of American political evolution, and a not very sanguine recommendation that something closer to the British method of ministerial responsibility should be aimed at.

In 1900 *Congressional Government* reached its fifteenth reprinting. Wilson wrote a new preface in which he began to sing a different tune. His ideas, he explained, had been set down some years previously: "inasmuch as they describe a living system, like all other living things subject to constant subtle modification . . . of form and function, their description of the government . . . is not as accurate now as I believed it to have been at the time I wrote it . . . ." The President of the United States was now "at the front of affairs, as no president, except Lincoln, has been since the first quarter of the nineteenth century. . . ." His speeches and messages, hitherto often of no great weight with Congress or the public, were suddenly relevant and important. "Upon his choice, his character, his experience hang some of the most weighty issues of the future."[2]

A few years later, when he was President of Princeton University, Wilson expounded his revised conception in a set of published lectures, *Constitutional Government in the United States* (1908). The theme of organic growth was put forward to explain not why Congress was dominant but why the President might be. Government was a living thing, not a machine or a set of abstract principles. The American government had taken shape through many decades of "intimate, almost instinctive, coordination of the organs of life and action"—*and* under the influence of "leadership." The Presidency had thus gone through several different phases; in some the office was powerful, in others passive. Yet in general, Wilson asserted, "we have grown more and more inclined from generation to generation to look to the President as the unifying force in our complex system, the leader both of his party and of the nation." Nor would there be a reverse swing of the pendulum: "We can never again see him the mere executive he was in the thirties and forties." The President must "always stand," said Wilson, repeating a phrase of the 1900 preface, "at the front of our affairs, and the office will be as big and as influential as the man who occupies it."[3]

Wilson's revised opinions had been anticipated in a remarkable book by a Pittsburgh editor, Henry Jones Ford, whom Edward Corwin calls "the real herald of the twentieth-century presidency." In *The Rise and Growth of American Politics* (1898), Ford boldly announced that the rise of presidential authority was preordained:

> It is the product of political conditions which dominate all the departments of government, so that Congress itself shows an unconscious disposition to aggrandize the presidential office. . . .
>
> The truth is that in the presidential office, as it has been constituted since Jackson's time, American democracy has revived the oldest political institution of the race, the elective kingship. It is all there: the precognition of the notables and the tumultuous choice of the freemen, only conformed to modern conditions.[4]

Ford and Wilson sketched the Presidency more or less as it appears today. Yet twenty or even ten years earlier their statements would not have been made, except perhaps as routine denunciations of mildly unorthodox presidential behavior. For example, Grant's readiness to be nominated for a third term in 1876 had aroused some talk of "Caesarism." But neither the arguments of his supporters nor the disapproval of his critics was thunderous. The bid soon collapsed and was soon forgotten. Wilson's analysis in *Congressional Government* was, despite his special pleading on behalf of the British parliamentary system, an accurate version of the federal balance of power in the 1880's. The Presidents of the Gilded Age accepted the situation. Hayes's diary revealed an embryonic sense that there were fresh needs to be satisfied. He favored federal aid for education, federal subsidies for internal improvements, national supervision of state elections. But his horizons were limited like those of nearly all his countrymen. A typical memorandum to himself was this entry of 1879: "While I maintain inflexibly the authority of the executive departments, I must not magnify it at the expense of the just prerogative of either the judicial or legislative departments."[5]

The question of who sank the Maine *was purely academic in the face of press sensationalism and public clamor for war with Spain. McKinley vacillated at first, but then gave in to pressure and opted for war. A quick victory made the United States a world power and changed the Presidency.*

Some observers, particularly if they were Democrats, subsequently held that the Presidency had begun to reawaken in Cleveland's administrations. Woodrow Wilson was among them. In his *Constitutional Government* he praised Grover Cleveland as the only President between 1865 and 1898 who "played a leading and decisive part in the quiet drama of our national life." He added however that Cleveland "owed his great role in affairs rather to his own native force and the confused politics of the time, than to any opportunity of leadership naturally afforded him by a system which had subordinated so many Presidents before him to Congress."

Later, when he was in the White House, Wilson was not ready to give even this much credit to Cleveland. Remarking to a group of senators in 1913 that he himself was actually the first Democratic President since Buchanan, Wilson dismissed Cleveland as "a conservative Republican." (He is said to have been harder still on Chester A. Arthur: "a nonentity with side-whiskers.")[6] Historically, Wilson was more correct than Ford in describing the Presidency as an office that during most of its existence had been somewhat negative and subordinate. From the perspective of Hayes's or Cleveland's day the administrations of a Jackson or a Lincoln were not the norm but departures from the norm.

What then happened at the end of the century to redefine the Presidency, so that before long the admired and expected styles were Jacksonian and Lincolnian, and the long interludes of quietude were regarded as unhealthy? Wilson touched on the obvious explanation in his 1900 preface:

> Much the most important change . . . is the result of the [1898] war with Spain . . .: the greatly increased power and opportunity for constructive statesmanship given to the President, by the plunge into international politics and into the administration of distant dependencies. . . . When foreign affairs play a prominent part in the politics and policy of a nation, its Executive must of necessity be its guide: must utter every initial judgement, take every first step of action, supply the information upon which it is to act, suggest and in large measure control its conduct.[7]

He emphasized the point again in his 1908 book (though in another decade or so the words were to return and haunt him):

> The initiative in foreign affairs, which the President possesses without any restriction whatever, is virtually the power to control them absolutely. The President cannot conclude a treaty with a foreign power without the consent of the Senate, but he may guide every step of diplomacy, and to guide diplomacy is to determine what treaties must be made, if the faith and prestige of the government are to be maintained. He need disclose no step of negotiation until it is complete, and when in any critical matter it is completed the government is virtually committed. Whatever its disinclination, the Senate may feel itself committed also.

The United States had "risen to the first rank in power and resources." Wilson's words again had a prophetic ring: "The other nations of the world look askance upon her, half in envy, half in fear, and wonder with a deep anxiety what she will do with her vast strength." As for the Chief Executive:

> Our President must always henceforth be one of the great powers of the world, whether he act greatly and wisely or not. . . . We have but begun to see the presidential office in this light; but it is the light which will more and more beat upon it. . . . We can never hide our President again as a mere domestic officer.[8]

Wilson was not entirely right: heralds of change frequently exaggerate the completeness and permanence of a new dispensation. But his basic idea was irrefutable, as the early history of the Presidency had demonstrated. A crisis in foreign relations magnified presidential authority. Cleveland, aghast at the prospect of a war with Spain over Cuba, had served notice that he would not countenance such a blunder. McKinley was at first almost as reluctant as his predecessor. Here of course presidential power could be manifested only by acting in a popular direction. John Adams' authority was terminated by electoral defeat when he resisted the pressure to go to war with France in 1797–98. Madison was impelled into war with England by congressional hotheads. Cleveland would have been howled out of office if he had been faced with an acute crisis and had refused to recommend a declaration of war to Congress. McKinley dared not go against public sentiment.

Yet once war had been declared the President was unquestionably "at the front of affairs." The country always insisted upon rapid victory; it was the apparent sluggishness of Lincoln's war measures that provoked Congress into establishing the aggressive "ginger" group known as the Joint Committee on the Conduct of the War. Even so, Congress had to entrust him with the authority to make a good many decisions on his own initiative. In a foreign as distinct from a civil war the President's freedom of action was correspondingly greater. Only he could drive the war machine; he alone held the tangled threads of strategy, supply, and diplomacy. During a war the lights burned late on Capitol Hill; they burned later still in the President's mansion and in the executive departments.

The Spanish-American War was even less essential to America's

The Battle of Manila Bay in 1898 inspired this Japanese print. On May 1 Commodore George Dewey entered the bay, delivered a scathing broadside, and destroyed the Spanish squadron. With the fall of Manila in August, the U.S. proclaimed military occupation of the Philippines.

vital interests than the War of 1812. Viewed, however, merely as a step towards presidential aggrandizement it was highly opportune. As Wilfred E. Binkley observes in *The President and Congress,* the "splendid little war" was over so quickly and so cheaply that it failed to generate any congressional resentment against executive "usurpation." The Anti-Imperialists were unable to sustain a sizable protest movement when the victory seemed so dazzling—indeed, so providential, as if God had willed the events of Manila Bay and San Juan Hill no less firmly than He had willed Andrew Jackson's rout of the British at New Orleans in 1815. Or it was as if the War of 1812 had begun instead of terminating in New Orleans. National and executive aggrandizement coincided, so exactly that the one both disguised and validated the other. Before the majority of Americans had any clear idea of what was afoot their nation had acquired an overseas empire. The Caribbean and the Far East were thenceforward, whether or not this was generally understood, American spheres of influence. The United States was about to become one of the big-navy nations. It too had taken up "the white man's burden" of responsibility for subject peoples in Puerto Rico, Hawaii, and the Philippines. In fact Rudyard Kipling's famous poem on the imperial "burden" was specifically addressed to the

United States. And the chief of the new American empire was the President.

In writing of the transformation Woodrow Wilson did not quite say that *any* President would inevitably become the nation's overlord. Wilson's statement was: "The President is at liberty . . . to be as big a man as he can. His capacity will set the limit. . . ." Wilson's words were obviously composed with the example of Theodore Roosevelt uppermost in his mind, though for equally obvious partisan reasons—Wilson being a staunch Democrat by inheritance from his Southern father—he made almost no direct mention of the Republican President in *Constitutional Government.* Roosevelt was the most restless and flamboyant personality who had ever reached the Presidency. His performance was doubly remarkable because he came to power via the dim shadows of the Vice-Presidency. Other ex-Vice-Presidents were nicknamed "His Accidency" —not Roosevelt.

T. R., himself highly newsworthy, made use of every means of dramatizing his office. The press was of particular importance. Newspaper circulation had more than doubled in the United States between 1870 and 1890, and doubled again in the next twenty years. Mark Sullivan wrote in *Our Times:*

> Roosevelt's fighting was so much a part of the life of the period, was so tied up to the newspapers, so geared into popular literature, and even to the pulpit . . . as to constitute, for the average reader, not merely the high spectacle of the Presidency, in the ordinary sense, but almost the whole of the passing show, the public's principal interest.

He sought to educate and stimulate as well as to entertain. He was the first President to treat the entire press corps as an auxiliary federal information service. Twenty years before his administration, reporters began to hang about the Executive Mansion. McKinley let them have a table and some chairs in an outer reception room. Roosevelt brought them right into the White House (as he described his residence on his new stationery, in place of "Executive Mansion"). When he had an executive office wing added to the building, he made sure that the extension included a properly equipped press room. As soon as he was in office Roosevelt began to cultivate a close understanding with certain Washington correspondents. A later President would have been accused of playing favorites: he had the advantage of pioneering, and the chance therefore to make his own rules. By previous standards the rules were refreshingly informal and generous. He would invite a large group of journalists to hear his views on some topical issue. Half a dozen of the most trusted correspondents often sat and talked with him in the late afternoon while he was being given his daily shave; lather, towel, and razor had no effect on his flow of conversation.

T. R. employed all the attention-getting devices available to him. If radio and television had existed he would undoubtedly have used them to catch the ear and eye of the public. If the telephone had become universal he would surely have played the instrument with a relish equal to that of Lyndon B. Johnson. He did extremely well, however, with the existing media. He would produce stories to fill the newspapers' Monday vacuum. He gained the confidence of the press by off-the-record briefings. Sometimes he leaked information, as when he wished to overcome resistance to the plan to create a Department of Commerce and Labor in 1903. Or he would try out a tentative idea on the newspapers in order to gauge the popular reaction before fully committing himself. His secretary, William Loeb, Jr., became also a skillful press secretary, suggesting lines and limits to the circle of correspondents and co-ordinating the flow of news from the executive departments. And so long as the tone of the reporting was sympathetic, Roosevelt positively welcomed personal stories about himself, his family, their friends, and the procession of callers at the White House.

He was not the first President to travel about the country. Hayes preceded him to the Pacific coast. But unlike his predecessors, Roosevelt took advantage of his frequent tours to bombard the nation with patriotic yet vigorous speeches on matters dear to his heart, including railroad legislation. Those who could not see and hear him in person could promptly read his views, column upon column, in their local newspapers. In the less hectic intervals of his career, T. R. was a ready contributor to magazines, another vital medium. Their editors were sympathetic, for most magazines had become reform-minded. He could therefore count upon a steady flow of encouraging, well-informed articles.

Everything that he said or did intrigued the American public. With his Wild West, Rough Rider's picturesqueness, his multifarious enthusiasms, his short crop of hair, his incongruous spectacles, and his ferocious smile, and the almost absurd vehemence of his life, he was the answer to a cartoonist's prayer. Harrison, Cleveland, McKinley were worthy figures: but how could an artist comment on them without being tedious or else distorting them beyond recognition? Roosevelt was, amazingly enough, perhaps the first man in American history to enjoy being President. He communicated his enjoyment, his bubbling energy, his righteous wrath, his sense of the fitness of all he did. He communicated it in every possible way—not least in the 150,000 letters that he wrote while he was in office. He was accordingly the most visible Chief Executive America had known. So far as Roosevelt was concerned, his capacity to fill the executive role was limitless.

Wilson explained that "leadership" was a necessary ingredient in defining a strong Executive. One wonders what the Presidency would have looked like if by some improbable but not inconceivable chain of circumstances the Democrats had won the 1900 election, and if their candidate had been not William Jennings Bryan but another contender for the nomination, Admiral George Dewey, the hero of Manila Bay, who in announcing that he was prepared to serve said that the office of President was "not such a very difficult one to fill."[9] Assuming a Republican victory, what if instead of a Roosevelt the party chiefs had nominated one of their alternative choices for McKinley's running mate—say Cornelius N. Bliss, the Secretary of the Interior, or Senator William B. Allison of Iowa, both of whom refused to run? Presumably such persons would have fallen far short of Roosevelt in executive leadership. One imagines that they would have more closely resembled William Howard Taft. It is true that Taft suffered from having to follow Roosevelt, and was perhaps driven to formulate a more restricted interpretation of the Presidency than he would otherwise have done. Nevertheless, his opinion that "there is no undefined residuum of power" in the office was deeply held, and deeply grounded in American constitutional dogma. Dewey, Bliss, or Allison would probably have remained within the conventional ramparts. They might well have proved as maladroit as Taft in

The contrasting styles of the mercurial Roosevelt and the thoughtful Taft inspired this 1909 cartoon.

Mr. Roosevelt and Mr. Taft—A Study in Temperaments

handling communications with the public. Archie Butt, the charming military aide who did his best to work loyally for both T. R. and Taft, said: "Mr. Roosevelt understood the necessity of guiding the press to suit one's own ends; President Taft has no conception of the press as an adjunct to his office." Butt had the unhappy duty of shepherding the newspaper reporters who accompanied the President—or as Taft saw it, pursued him—on his summer holiday to Beverly, Massachusetts, in 1909. One of the reporters claims he heard Taft snarl, "Must I see those men again! Didn't I see them just the other day?" He shared Roosevelt's delight in travel, but as an escape from official obligations. "If it were not for the speeches," he significantly confessed on one occasion, "I should look forward with the greatest pleasure to this trip." Taft's inadequacy for this aspect of his job is epitomized in Elmer E. Cornwell, Jr.'s *Presidential Leadership of Public Opinion* (1965):

> He could not be persuaded to return the greetings of a crowd, or even to turn his head . . . for a sign of recognition from the Chief Executive. That he should be unaware of the need for so elementary a gesture, or unwilling to give it . . . suggests how far he was from being able to exploit the potential of the office under the conditions that had obtained since the advent of the new journalism and the White House incumbency of the redoubtable Rough Rider.[10]

Individual temperament made a difference. Governor Roosevelt was after all nominated not with an eye to the Presidency but because the Republican bosses in New York detested him and wanted him out of the way. Still, McKinley himself was anxious to have an able Vice-President in case of accident; and the success of Roosevelt's presidential display proved that he was more in tune with his age than the politicians. He was quick to appreciate a third factor, which, in addition to the importance of foreign affairs and individual toughness, supplied the opportunity for executive vitality. Once again, Wilson touched upon the factor in his *Constitutional Government.* The point was that only the President within the federal government spoke for the whole country. Members of Congress merely represented local and sectional fragments of the nation, and partisan fragments at that. The President was the head of a party, but in becoming President he necessarily took a larger role, as the voice not of a party but of an entire people. In the unending tussle between Executive and legislature, Congress was equipped with formidable constitutional weapons. If it were overborne, said Wilson, this would be "only because the President has the nation behind him, and Congress has not. He has no means of compelling Congress except through public opinion." Discussing the problems of Congress in a later section, Wilson seemed to have abandoned his old preoccupation with Cabinet government. In its place, more or less, he installed public opinion as the only real link between the two houses of Congress and the President. He concluded: "That part of the government . . . which has the most direct access to opinion has the best chance of leadership and mastery; and at present that part is the presidency."[11]

Roosevelt had already based his claims for executive authority on the theory that the President, and only the President, embodied all the people. He and Wilson knew that it was an ancient assertion of presidential prerogative, relied on to the full by Jackson and Lincoln and particularly effective in periods of national emergency. Garfield had almost touched on it during a clash with Senator Conkling over the right to make federal appointments in Conkling's state. The Executive, said Garfield, was "a whole independent function of the government": in a Senate of seventy-six members Conkling was merely "$\frac{1}{76}$ of $\frac{1}{2}$ of another independent branch of the government with which compound fractions the President is asked to compromise." Hayes had claimed in his diary that while he was "not liked as a President by the politicians in office, in the press or in Congress," he was "content to abide the judgement—the sober second thought of the people." At another moment he reminded himself to rebut a congressman by citing "Jackson's claim to *represent* the Nation." But these arguments mean less than they seem to. Garfield's quarrel with Conkling was confined to governmental matters: he did not seek any wider sanction than executive independence in Congress. Hayes was using an old, somewhat conservative expression when he spoke of "sober second thought." In their *Dictionary of American Political Terms,* Hans Sperber and Travis Trittschuh trace the phrase back to the Federalists, indeed as far back as "reminiscences from classical authors like Tacitus' remark that the Germans discussed public affairs at their banquets but made decisions only after a night's rest had restored them to sobriety." That this was the sense Hayes intended seems evident from a subsequent diary notation: "Newspaper and other abuse is not comforting. . . . But the second thought of the best people is I believe with me. . . ." *The people* were the *best people,* those who had second thoughts.

Garfield, as a congressman, had said in 1874 that it was "not part of the functions of the national government to find employment for people." President Garfield held the same view. So did Cleveland, who declared in his second inaugural address: "The lessons of paternalism ought to be unlearned and the better lesson taught that while the people should patriotically support their Government its functions do not include the support of the people."[12] There was no reciprocal bond. Cleveland's laissez-faire aphorism, applauded in the 1880's, would within twenty years sound mean and stony to men of good will. It was a world away from the vocabulary of Theodore Roosevelt. For Garfield and Cleveland "the people" seemed to mean the shiftless poor, those without the moral fiber to fend for themselves. Roosevelt's conception, though not exactly a plea for the underprivileged, was of a stewardship exercised by the President on behalf of the whole people against whatever evils threatened them. "I was bent," he said in his autobiography, "upon making the Government the most efficient possible instrument in helping *the people* to better themselves in every way, politically, socially, and industrially. I believed . . . in real . . . democracy, and I wished to make this democracy industrial as well as political. . . . I believed in *the people's rights*. . ." [italics mine].[13] "Crisis," "leadership," "the people": such words were acquiring new and honorific shades of meaning. They would be used again and again in the twentieth century to justify bold executive action.

A fourth factor may be discerned in Wilson's and in other analyses of the American polity. It is the gradual transformation of party politics. The dominant feature of American politics from Jackson's day to the end of the century was the search for agreement, harmony, balance—what would later be called consensus. Except for brief periods the struggle lay between two parties that maintained an extraordinarily close balance in presidential elections, but that were fluid and miscellaneous in internal composition. Since the control of the Presidency was the apex of the party system, the tendency was to avoid divisive questions and to nominate "available" men. The Democratic party's rule, introduced in

1836, that a successful nominee must receive two thirds of the delegates' votes in the national convention, was an additional guarantee that noncontroversial candidates would be selected. Moderation could be and was overdone. The President was apt to be tucked up in the midst of his following, a symbol rather than a leader. To the extent that politics reduced itself to patronage and pork-barrel operations, and to elections won with "soap" (bribery), the Presidency could preserve its prestige only by seeming removed from the fray—and thus from national life. The dignity of the office was becoming spinsterish.

No total change was wrought at the beginning of the twentieth century. But in the 1890's new economic issues aroused new passions. The Populist Party secured over a million votes in the 1892 presidential election, and though it disintegrated within a few years, some of its reform proposals made their way into the mainstream of national politics. Some scholars suggest that the national party system entered a fourth phase in 1896; the second had begun with Jackson, and the third with the emergence of the Republican party in the 1850's. Paradoxically, the elections of 1896 and 1900 seemed such resounding victories for solid Republican principles that an opportunity for vigorous leadership was created within the more conservative of the two major parties. In other words, the defeat of "Bryanism" gave the Republicans control of both houses of Congress; and McKinley, unlike his recent predecessors, was able to establish both a fruitful relationship with Congress and enough of a hold over his party to ensure that he would be renominated for a second term. (Correspondingly, the Democrats offered a more coherent opposition.) The majorities won by Roosevelt in 1904 and Taft in 1908 were cheeringly substantial; and the Republicans again retained control of both houses of Congress. When faction developed within the Republican party between the conservative and reform wings, it was, though disruptive, at least more meaningful than the Stalwart–Half-Breed split of the 1880's. And when the Democrats recovered and fought back in the 1912 presidential election with Wilson, a candidate as incisive as Roosevelt and a good deal more so than Taft, the party spirit seemed to have borrowed a fresh lease of life from the alliance of the people and the Chief Executive. There was no prodigious difference between the progressivism of Teddy Roosevelt and that of the Wil-

Eugene V. Debs ran for President on the Socialist ticket five times.

sonian Democrats. But there was a considerable difference between them and the "Standpatter" Republicanism represented by Taft in the three-cornered contest of 1912. In fact it was four-cornered: the Socialist party candidate Eugene V. Debs won 900,000 votes, over twice the number given him in 1908. After sluggish decades the parties were trying to outbid one another on the grand scale. Their platforms at last comprised real programs instead of being confined to tariff scales, veterans' benefits, and the like. The rise of Debs was alarming enough to persuade alert politicians that the reforms they offered must be genuine and far-reaching. Wilson was lucky to win in 1912, and again lucky in 1916. No less fortunately for him and for the emergence of a strong Executive, in both elections he brought a Democratic Congress into office with him. The guerrilla warfare of previous party politics seemed to have broadened into something more stable and more significant. It so happened that from 1920 to 1964 every presidential election except those of 1948 and 1960 has been of "landslide" proportions. Winners have had a clear popular mandate—if they cared to assert themselves, and if (unlike Eisenhower in 1956) they also had a congressional majority.

Another related factor takes us back again to Wilson's early *Congressional Government*. He had been sure that American federal government was congressional in the main. The biennial election of the Speaker of the House of Representatives attracted nationwide interest. Newspapers printed almost as much about the rival candidates for the speakership as about presidential candidates, "having come to look upon the selection made as a sure index of the policy to be expected in legislation."[14] Even in his 1908 book, *Constitutional Government*, Wilson devoted several pages to the near-autocratic authority of the Speaker, and he was struck by the "condescension with which the older members of the Senate regard the President":

> Dominate the affairs of the country though he may, he seems to them at most an ephemeral phenomenon. Even if he has continued in his office for the two terms which are the traditional limit of the President's service, he but overlaps a single senatorial term by two years, and a senator who has served several terms has already seen several Presidents come and go . . . A member of long standing in the Senate feels that he is the professional, the President an amateur.

Though by 1908 he classed the President as one of the "active elements" in the federal government, Wilson maintained that there were two other active elements: the Speaker, "with all that he represents as spokesman of the party majority in the popular chamber, with its singularly effective machinery at his disposal," and the "talkative, debating" Senate.[15]

The question is why Congress, so dominant for a generation, did not continue to hold the reins. The answer is that it brought about its own downfall. The Senate grew more pontifical, rather than wiser, and more obstructionist. "Of all things that can be imagined as absurd and inconsistent with . . . the proper operation of our Government," Cleveland once exploded, "the Senate . . . reaches the extreme." Although there were good men in the upper house there were too many Conklings and Platts. The public grew weary and then angry at a legislative body whose complacency and venality mocked the high hopes of the Founding Fathers. The 1892 Populist demand for the direct election of senators (instead of election through state legislatures) was eventually recognized as a reasonable reform, and was put into effect by the Seventeenth Amendment in 1913. As for the House of Representatives, the more apparent authority it accumulated the more unwieldy, discordant, and ludicrous it became. Its calendar was jammed with business that never reached the floor, having been buried in committee or blocked by minority opposition. Things were made even worse by slender party majorities and abrupt shifts in the balance of power. The object of the House rules, said Speaker Thomas B. Reed, "appears to be to prevent the transaction of business." In 1890 the tough-minded Reed, thwarted by Democrats who held up business by refusing to answer voice calls and thus denied the House the necessary quorum, proposed that attendance, not votes, should determine a quorum. McKinley, then in Congress, backed him up by remarking that "sullen silence" was not the way to conduct public business:

> We have done it—all of us. I am not saying that you gentlemen on the other side are doing differently from what we have done for fifteen or twenty years past. I have sat here and filibustered day after day in silence, refusing to vote, but I cannot now recall that I ever did it for a high or a noble or a worthy purpose.

A Texas Democrat, opposing, dragged in our old friend the sober second thought. House rules, he said with more partisan fervor than accuracy, were intended "to cause the House to halt, to pause, to reflect, and in some instances . . . to go back and inquire of the sober second thought of the people again. It is on the sober thought of the people our Government rests."[16]

"Czar" Reed won his battle against the House obstructionists. But the Speaker was only a majority appointee; and the more he sought to assume control of the crazy quilt of committees and coteries the more resentment he aroused. Although Representative George Norris showed courage and tactical skill in depriving the dictatorial Speaker Joe Cannon of his power to appoint the crucial Rules Committee, in 1910, the reform in some ways did more harm than good. The House stood in need of a comprehensive reorganization. To weaken its only unequivocal source of leadership was to encourage fresh abuses in the course of ending old ones.

Congress had, then, proved its inability to provide constructive government. Congressmen in general were, rightly or wrongly, despised and distrusted by the public. Many were in fact ignorant, pompous, corruptible. Those of superior quality were too often preoccupied with factional bickering. The two houses could not function creatively even as single units, let alone work in tandem. An adroit President with the public behind him could, at any rate for a while, force the legislative branch to follow his initiatives or risk defeat the next time their seats were up for election. By 1900 the moment was nearly ripe for an alliance between the President and the People—the People with a capital P.

The impulse did not come from the President or from any branch of the federal government. Roosevelt's enthusiasm for the Progressive cause burgeoned mainly after he had left the White House. Professor Wilson's pronouncements during the Roosevelt years were hardly radical. He disapproved of what he thought Bryan typified within the Democratic party. In 1907, sounding much like Cleveland, he said in a speech that "free men" were better able to take care of themselves "than any government had ever shown or was ever likely to show in taking care of them."[17] The development of the reform spirit was gradual and various. It grew among despairing farmers; among city dwellers appalled by the misery and graft that seemed inseparable from urban living; among intellectuals like Henry George, Edward Bellamy, and Henry Demarest Lloyd, groping for an explanation of America's economic and social ills, and for a cure. There was a revived demand for efficient, honest government: a demand first voiced and first satisfied at the local and state level, for example in Mayor Samuel M. Jones's Toledo, Ohio, and in Robert M. LaFollette's Wisconsin. Here and there, with amazement and then with jubilation and renewed zeal, reformers discovered that boss government could be overthrown. The collective power of the electorate was still irresistible if only it could be harnessed. If legislatures could not be trusted, voters might initiate their own legislation, or show their reaction by means of a referendum, or recall measures they did not like.

The public had been at the mercy of privileged groups, robber barons who established themselves across the pathways of American life and levied a toll on all who came by. The railroads battened upon the farmers, as did the storage men and the mortgage holders and all the other middlemen. Giant industry with its web of combinations and trusts and its tendency to monopoly grew fat at the expense of the consumer. The ordinary citizen paid more than necessary for everyday articles because of the indirect subsidy of high tariffs. He paid more than necessary for sidewalks and water supply and streetcar systems because of crooked bids and franchises. Vested interests were protected by the courts in the sacred name of private property. Or so it seemed to an increasing number of puzzled and exasperated citizens. If the beneficiaries of un-bridled laissez faire had not somehow been held in check the United States would soon have gone the way of every other society in the world's long melancholy history. It would have been not a democracy but a plutocracy; and by a tragic irony the plutocracy would have been created by invoking the catch words of democracy: liberty, individualism, and so on. Some such outcome was predicted in a wave of apocalyptic novels of which Ignatius Donnelly's *Caesar's Column* (1894) and Jack London's *The Iron Heel* (1907) were two examples.

There was much disagreement on how to achieve fundamental improvements. The situation in the House of Representatives posed the problem in miniature. So-called democracy produced corrupt chaos. But strong leaderships might produce dictatorship. Some reformers in the 1890's, as was explained in Chapter 6, tended to lump the Presidency with other dangerous centralizing forces. The remedy appeared to be that proposed by Henry Demarest Lloyd in a Populist speech delivered in Chicago in 1894: "The people [must] get the control of their industries as of the government." Then, he went on in more extreme terms than most would find acceptable, "we will have the judges and the injunctions, the President and the House of Representatives. There will be no Senate; we will have the referendum and the Senate will go out when the people come in."[18] Participatory democracy, in other words, though the exact expression was not used at the time.

The control of industry was more complicated than Lloyd's fiery oratory indicated. The control of government was easier to postulate because of the popular sovereignty of the ballot box. Though Lloyd, not conceiving of the possibility of direct election, would have got rid of the Senate, he was prepared to define the Presidency and the lower house as potentially democratic parts of the government. The next, more positive stage was to recognize that the Chief Executive might be a champion around whom to rally, as the voters of Toledo and Wisconsin rallied around Jones and LaFollette. The idea of the People's President was reborn; and it is no accident that the reputation of Andrew Jackson, occluded for some decades, was now made to shine again in the pages of historians. Frederick Jackson Turner identified Jackson with the quintessential feature of American democracy: its frontier atmosphere. By degrees the

President Roosevelt addresses an enthusiastic crowd in New Castle, Wyoming, in 1903. The enormously popular T. R., the youngest man ever to live in the White House, won re-election easily the following year.

President came to be seen again as the people's advocate within the federal government—the means by which the delays and evasions of Congress could be short-circuited. Participation in the democratic process was necessary but it was not sufficient. There must be leadership and there must be a leader in the federal Capital; for in some way or other the federal government must redress the balance between the too-poor and the too-rich, the underprivileged and the overprivileged.

Agreement that the Executive must accomplish the task was hastened by the drama of the Spanish-American War, which was on the whole a popular war. With Roosevelt in the White House the drama was heightened; the executive office became a continuous theatrical show. A few spectacular performances, notably his handling of the anthracite coal strike of 1902 and his protracted assault on the Northern Securities Company (when he insisted that corporations must "subserve the public good"), convinced Americans of liberal temperament that whatever Roosevelt's deficiencies he was determined to use the Presidency for the general good. His actual achievements were open to dispute. Some reformers felt that he was more bark than bite, and that he was still very much a "regular" politician. One of the "muckraking" journalists, Ray Stannard Baker, who eventually shifted his allegiance to Woodrow Wilson, was enchanted by Roosevelt's "energy and gusto" and flattered to receive letters from the President praising his articles:

> But as the years passed Roosevelt's typical reaction, that of balancing the blame, without going to the root of the matter . . . satisfied me less and less. His actions often seemed . . . to be based not upon principles well thought out, but upon moral judgements which were, or seemed to me to be, too hasty. His notion of a square deal was to cuff the radical on one ear and the conservative on the other, without enlightening either.[19]

Such criticisms should be seen in a larger perspective. An important point about T. R. was that he was a patrician. Of unassailably good family and cushioned by a moderate private income, he had an aristocrat's disdain for *parvenu* wealth. He had also in his early days an unconscious, *de-haut-en-bas* paternalism toward the lower classes. While his invariable "balancing the blame" formula was in part a matter of political calculation, it came naturally to one of his background. He could afford not to be snobbish or unduly genteel. He was genuinely unimpressed by millionaires. The rags-to-riches saga dazzled most Americans, including such self-made men as General Grant and Mark Twain, and disposed them to consider the bonanza as a symbol of Americanism. Roosevelt's symbols of Americanism were of another type, not always more subtle but sometimes more altruistic. Hitherto the nation had tended to believe that presidential candidates ought to be men of humble background who had risen by their own exertions. Roosevelt had certainly exerted himself, from the cowpunching days in the badlands of Dakota to his passage through the political badlands of New York State. But he was not a Jackson, Lincoln, or Garfield character. In the twentieth century Americans would turn increasingly to presidential aspirants—Franklin D. Roosevelt, Adlai Stevenson, Nelson Rockefeller, John F. Kennedy —who could be called patrician in that they were at least one generation removed from the effort to toil for a living and establish a dynasty. Since the cost of campaigning rose astronomically, this was to some extent only to say that wealthy candidates would stand more chance of surviving the expensive ordeal of presidential primary contests. It embodied also, however, a tacit agreement that, other things being equal, a candidate with an assured social position was more likely to have a lofty vision of the United States than a person who was still en route to the country club and the Social Register. Although Woodrow Wilson was not an aristocrat his professional milieu and his demeanor were very much those of a gentleman; he too stood above the daily round.

"Crisis," "leadership," "the people" were key words in the changing conception of the Presidency. So were "nation" and "nationalism." Roosevelt's authentic concern for all the people was not only that of a patrician and a politician but also of an avowed and clamant patriot. "The people" and "the nation" were interchangeable terms for him. He did not fully work out what this entailed until he was no longer President. While he was in the White House, its purest form was perhaps exemplified in his passion to conserve the national domain as steward of the people. Otherwise it tended to encourage the jingo side of T. R. He himself, however, saw no contradiction: a true People's President must be the guardian of every facet of nationhood. He made a revealing statement of this dual conception in an article, "How I Became a Progressive," which was published shortly before the 1912 election:

> I . . . often found that men who were ardent for social and industrial reform would be ignorant of the needs of this nation as a nation, would be ignorant of what the navy meant to the nation, of what it meant to the nation to have and fortify and protect the Panama Canal, of what it meant to the nation to get from the other nations of mankind the respect which comes only to the just, and which is denied to the weaker nation far more quickly than it is denied to the stronger. . . .
>
> I feel that the Progressive party owes no small part of its strength to the fact that it not only stands for . . . measures of social and industrial reform, but . . . also for the right and

duty of this nation to take a position of self-respecting strength among the nations of the world. . . .[20]

As Roosevelt implied, not all Progressives shared his concern for the place of America in the world at large. Some disapproved, with reason, of his pugnacity over Panama. But none could object to his role as mediator in international disputes. There was something grand in the notion of the United States as a virtuous Great Power, implanting a new standard of morality in international affairs. Here as in other ways the idea of nationality struck a responsive chord in the emotions of millions of very different sorts of Americans. There was a readiness to agree that at home as abroad, there was now a need for discipline, for concerted activity, for Presidents who would goven as well as rule. In the revised vocabulary of the era the concepts of "crisis," "leadership," "the people" and "the nation" came together in a sudden fondness for the word "mastery"—meaning benevolent yet energetic leadership of the people. Wilson employed it in 1908 ("That part of the government . . . which has the most direct access to opinion has the best chance of leadership and *mastery*"); Walter Lippmann analyzed the contrast between bad and good in national life in his book *Drift and Mastery* (1913). Lippmann, a brilliant young man recently out of Harvard, was one of a group who should perhaps be called liberals rather than Progressives. He, the journalist Herbert Croly, and a few others were distinctly urban and urbane in outlook. They applauded Roosevelt for his executive assurance, his internationalism, and for his reluctance to lay the blame for the nation's maladies upon any single sector. In *A Preface to Politics* (1914), Lippmann described Roosevelt as a "colossal phenomenon" in American politics, "the working model for a possible American statesman at the beginning of the twentieth century."

These were compliments that might have been proffered by any one of dozens of admirers. The unusual feature of Lippmann's analysis was its cool sophistication. He seemed to blend the amusement of a satirist with the involvement of a prophet. For example:

> Critics have often suggested that Roosevelt stole Bryan's clothes. That is perhaps true, and it suggests a comparison which illuminates both men. It would not be unfair to say that it is always the function of the Roosevelts to take from the Bryans.[21]

The thesis of Lippmann and Croly, who teamed up as editors of the *New Republic,* was that the American republic had to be made new. Croly's book, *The Promise of American Life* (1909), exactly accorded with the emerging Roosevelt variant of progressivism and was read by him with delight. The book explained America's fundamental problem. For over a century Americans of the Jeffersonian persuasion had insisted that democracy was a concomitant of agrarianism and state rights. Americans interested, on the other hand, in a strong federal government had tended to typify selfish business interests. There must now be a realignment. It must be understood that democratic society was best sustained by a powerful regulatory government. What Roosevelt ridiculed as "sincere rural toryism" was an anachronism. Jeffersonian ends must be attained by Hamiltonian means. The ideals upheld by John Quincy Adams, and repudiated by his contemporaries, were at last to be vindicated.

Roosevelt was not alone during the Progressive era in urging the United States forward toward something that sounded disturbingly like a garrison state, animated by the warrior virtues of manliness, discipline, and patriotic ardor. After all, Henry George's *Progress and Poverty* and Edward Bellamy's *Looking Backward* had presupposed a central authority firm enough to introduce and maintain the panaceas they proposed. Bellamy's work had spawned a movement of Bellamy "Nationalist" clubs. Liberals like Croly could talk as unself-consciously as the martial Roosevelt of America's "historic mission," secure in the conviction that their prognosis was economically, intellectually, and emotionally viable. By their methods the United States would substitute "mastery" for the apathy and inefficiency of the old days of "drift." When they and Roosevelt talked of "nationalism" they meant many things rolled into one, each of them good. They were of course not advocating a warrior nation: they were merely reacting against the errors of the past as emphatically as possible.

It followed that Roosevelt's "New Nationalism" made a greater appeal to certain Progressives than the seemingly old-fashioned "New Freedom" of Woodrow Wilson. The Democratic leader appeared to be attempting to turn the clock back: to be pretending that the complex structure of finance and industry could be dismantled, and that a few ethical pronouncements would suffice to

Wilson was optimistic and self-confident when he became President in 1913; he left office a broken man.

restore the country to a Jeffersonian idyll. Wilson was in fact seeking to base his 1912 campaign on other grounds than those of Roosevelt for partly tactical reasons. He was in good Democratic company. The arguments he developed were venerable, and still not without weight. Indeed the polarity between regulation and laissez faire plus moralism has persisted to the present day.

Nevertheless T. R. and Wilson stood on basically similar ground. For somewhat different reasons both could take pride in executive descent from Andrew Jackson. If there was a state rights side to Jackson that particularly pleased the Southern Democrat in Woodrow Wilson, it was the quality of leadership in Jackson's Presidency that inspired him no less than it did Roosevelt. And Wilson too was a stealer of clothes; Arthur S. Link has said of Wilson that his ambition was stronger than his commitment to any given issues. He too meant to be masterful, and had proved to himself and the nation while governor of New Jersey that at his best he was a ruthlessly adroit executive. He too was genuinely moved by the sufferings of America's submerged millions—though in common with the majority of his fellow countrymen he saw no special urgency in the woes of the most submerged group of all, the black Americans. He too could at moments convey with an eloquence and fire as stirring as T. R.'s his determination to fight for a better America. Many who heard his inaugural address in March, 1913, were deeply moved. "This is not a day of triumph," he said; "it is a day of dedication":

> Here muster, not the forces of party, but the forces of humanity. Men's hearts wait upon us; men's lives hang in the balance; men's hopes call upon us to say what we will do. Who shall live up to the great trust? Who dares fail to try? I summon all honest men, all patriotic, all forward-looking men, to my side. God helping me, I will not fail them, if they will but counsel and sustain me![22]

Once in office Wilson plunged into its duties with an unmistakable zest. If Roosevelt was the first President to have truly enjoyed executive responsibility, Wilson was the second. He seized the initiative at once by calling Congress into special session, addressing it in person (which had not been done since John Adams' day), and compelling the legislators to enact the only palpable reduction of the tariff since Jacksonian times. He proceeded to reform the nation's banking system by securing the passage of the Federal Reserve Act in 1913.

President Wilson in due course revealed deficiencies that diminished his effectiveness. He was still half convinced by his own New Freedom slogans. He therefore alarmed Progressive Democrats by seeming ready to abandon further programs of reform. He was addicted to the self-hypnosis of the orator who feels that by delivering a fine, impeccably high-toned speech he has thereby fulfilled his duty to mankind. Croly attacked him in a *New Republic* article, "Presidential Complacency," as the possessor of "a mind which is fully convinced of the everlasting righteousness of its own performances and which surrounds this conviction with a halo of shimmering rhetoric."[23] The accusation had an uncomfortable core of truth when it was written in 1914 and was to seem disquietingly apropos five years later when Wilson was endeavoring to make the Senate "swallow its medicine" by ratifying the Treaty of Versailles. Another weakness of Wilson's was that in adversity he was stubborn

THE CHILD WHO WANTED TO PLAY BY HIMSELF.

PRESIDENT WILSON. "NOW COME ALONG AND ENJOY YOURSELF WITH THE OTHER NICE CHILDREN. I PROMISED THAT YOU'D BE THE LIFE AND SOUL OF THE PARTY."

President Wilson tries to lead a reluctant United States into the League of Nations in this Punch *cartoon of 1919.*

to the point of folly. So long as matters were going his way he was a superb Executive—clear-witted, shrewd, persuasive, even charming. When resistance stiffened, or subordinates like Colonel House began to show signs of independence, Wilson's gaiety and guile disappeared. He was to pay the price in 1919.

It would be a mistake, though, to attribute entirely to Wilson's personality tendencies that lie deep in the American psyche, and that more particularly are characteristic of the Presidency. The presidential term of office is short and its scope limited even in the hands of men as forceful as Roosevelt and Wilson. Those who reach the Presidency have for the most part necessarily achieved a certain oratorical skill. They are apt therefore to exaggerate what has been accomplished in their administration, knowing that they are expected to have brought the millennium overnight, and to proclaim the millennium by fiat. T. R. himself had done this; so would nearly every President after Wilson.

By the same token, even the most popular and favorably situated Chief Executives are restricted in their capacity to act. The Presidency resembles an unwieldy vessel that can navigate only when it has built up a head of steam and is proceeding at a brisk speed. When the pressure is dissipated and the speed drops, the craft is at the mercy of the elements—or in this case, of Congress. The captain is then apt to complain of sabotage. Wilson blundered in his handling of the Senate over the Treaty of Versailles. But by the nature of things he was bound to run into trouble. The domestic crisis of the Progressive years was over, or thought to be over. So was the crisis of the Great War. Leadership no longer seemed so vital. The formulas of laissez faire no longer looked so tarnished. The alliance between the President and the people had lost its clarity. A revived legislative branch was ready to interpose itself between the two, in order to cure the short-circuit. The loss of presidential magic is nicely illustrated in an exchange between Wilson and a hostile member of the Senate Committee on Foreign Relations. The senator asked the President whether the United States could not arrange a bilateral peace with Germany that took no account of the multilateral Treaty of Versailles. "We could, sir," Wilson answered, "but I hope the people . . . will never consent to it." "There is no way," the Senator coldly reminded him, "by which the people can vote on it." Since Congress refused to accept that the President spoke for the people, he had no other recourse but a speaking tour; he discovered to his dismay, however, that his enemies, too, could go on speaking tours.

The nation, a little jaded by crusades, was ready to be told by Warren G. Harding (in his 1921 State of the Union address): "During the anxieties of war, when necessity seemed compelling, there were excessive grants of authority and an extraordinary concentration of powers in the Chief Executive."[24] The intellectuals, disillusioned by the way in which the New Nationalism and the New Freedom appeared to have degenerated into the New Chauvinism and the New Conventionalism of 1917–19, transferred their talents to more private spheres. They could hardly be blamed when the rest of America was doing the same.

Yet the United States was changed, or would thenceforward be more responsive to change when "necessity seemed compelling" once again. The demonstration of executive energy of the Progressive era had left a legacy. There were the examples of Roosevelt and Wilson, examples that posterity would not quite forget though the America of Harding and Coolidge appeared to put them in mothballs. And there were two culminating achievements that would have enormous repercussions. One was the almost unchallenged assumption by Wilson of war powers on a scale that dwarfed anything Lincoln had done. The other Wilsonian transformation took place in 1916, when the Republicans repudiated Progressive principles and left the field open to the Democrats. After that the Democrats could always claim to be the party with a heart; the Republicans could too easily be portrayed as the party with a purse. The distinction was somewhat approximate. Yet it preserved for future occasions something of the spirit of the turn of the century. There was still potentially a People's Party; and its candidate if victorious could again present himself as the People's President.

THE TUMULT AND THE SHOUTING DIES;
THE CAPTAINS AND THE KINGS DEPART

HERBLOCK
©1951 THE WASHINGTON POST

CHAPTER NINE

The Presidency and World Power

In foreign affairs the executive branch has always had considerable scope for action. But traditions of national isolationism and congressional intransigence have limited the executive freedom of maneuver, sometimes drastically. The interaction of these elements—executive initiative and popular or congressional resistance—defines the greater part of the story of the Presidency and foreign policy up to 1945. Traditional attitudes have not entirely disappeared since 1945, but the whole nature of the story has altered. *Power* is the dominant factor. Executive power has enlarged to an extent that would have amazed and possibly dismayed Theodore Roosevelt and Woodrow Wilson. The power of the United States in the world has likewise enlarged on an unbelievable scale and with unbelievable rapidity. New problems, different in kind as well as in degree from those of previous decades, burst upon the postwar scene. "We inhabit a world of original

Harry Truman was the first President in the nuclear age. As this Herblock cartoon of 1951 indicates, the problems confronting him were enormous.

horrors," wrote Edmund Stillman and William Pfaff in their book *The New Politics: America and the End of the Postwar World* (1961).[1] Their title reflected a widespread conviction that an unprecedented situation called for a fresh terminology. Some writers began to distinguish between the "modern" and the "post-modern" world. Some wrote almost with nostalgia of the preatomic days when even a thousand-bomber raid was insufficient to wipe out a city, and when the United States was not blamed for every mischance from China to the Congo.

We may therefore regard 1945 as the great divide in discussing the Presidency and foreign affairs. To go back to the beginning, the Founding Fathers recognized a fact that is still operative. It was undeniable, though somewhat disquieting, that the President had to be given a great deal of discretionary authority. All writers on executive aspects of government agreed that secrecy and dispatch (speed) were essential in certain fields, especially in foreign policy. John Jay used these words in the *Federalist* No. 64 (1788), arguing that in the nature of things the President must have a free hand—even if the other hand was in the grip of the Senate. "Thus," Jay reassured his readers, "we see that the Constitution provides that our negotiations for treaties shall have every advantage which can be derived from talents, information, integrity, and deliberate investigations, on the one hand, and from secrecy and despatch on the other." In 1816, though not always on other occasions, the Senate was in complete accord with this view. Its Foreign Relations Committee declared in a report:

> The President is the constitutional representative of the United States with regard to foreign nations. He manages our concerns with foreign nations and must necessarily be most competent to determine when, how, and upon what subjects negotiations may be urged with the greatest prospect of success. . . . The committee . . . think the interference of the Senate in the direction of foreign negotiations calculated to diminish that responsibility and thereby to impair the best security for the national safety. The nature of transactions with foreign nations . . . requires caution and unity of design, and their success frequently depends upon secrecy and dispatch. . . .

The committee clearly had in mind President Washington's explanation of his refusal to submit papers relating to Jay's Treaty to the House of Representatives, which had demanded them. Nor were these dead precedents in the twentieth century. They were cited in the famous Supreme Court opinion of Mr. Justice Sutherland, *United States v. Curtiss-Wright Export Corporation* (1936): a remarkably positive opinion from a body that had shown no hesitation in striking down the administration's program of domestic legislation. Sutherland's contention was that as a result of the American Revolution, the powers of "external sovereignty" had passed directly to the federal government of the United States and so were not dependent upon the delegation of powers from the states affirmed in the Constitution. "In this vast external realm," said Sutherland, "with its important, complicated, delicate and manifold problems, the President alone has the power to speak or listen as a representative of the nation." In international affairs the President must often be allowed a "freedom from statutory discretion which would not be admissible were domestic affairs alone involved."[2]

Grants of power within the Constitution, or interpreted as derivable from the Constitution, greatly extended the President's control. The clause "he shall receive ambassadors and other public ministers" enabled him to confer recognition upon (or withhold recognition from) other countries. It was T. R. who extended recognition to Panama, two days after the province had staged a rebellion against the parent state, Colombia. It was F.D.R. who entered into diplomatic relations with Russia, in 1933, sixteen years after they had been terminated. The President could on his own initiative bolster up new régimes through immediate recognition. Wilson in 1918 proclaimed the legitimacy of the exiled government of Czechoslovakia: a state that had never existed before and that was still nominally part of the Austro-Hungarian Empire. President Truman made a similarly powerful gesture of friendship when he recognized the state of Israel in 1948.

The President could escape some of the complications in treaty making by entering into the contracts with other nations known as executive agreements. Such agreements were in effect as valid as treaties, though they involved no congressional participation, or required at most a simple majority vote in both houses. They could even be used to replace a treaty defeated by the Senate. This was done in 1845, after the Senate had declined to ratify the treaty be-

Uncle Sam Rooster shelters the Latin American chicks in this 1901 comment on Theodore Roosevelt's corollary to the Monroe Doctrine. The Europeans are cooped up safely away from the Western hemisphere.

tween the United States and the Republic of Texas that annexed Texas to the Union. President Tyler recommended that the Texas treaty be accepted by joint resolution, and after some legislative skirmishing his proposal was adopted. Executive agreements became more and more an accepted practice. From 1789 to 1889 the federal government negotiated 275 treaties, and accepted almost the same number (265) of executive agreements. In the next half-century, to 1939, the balance decisively changed. The total of 524 treaties ratified in that period was outmatched by the total of 917 executive agreements. The trend was to be even more apparent. In the fifteen years between 1940 and 1954 the respective figures were 139 as against 1,948.[3] President Theodore Roosevelt brought Santo Domingo under American jurisdiction in 1905 after the Senate failed to approve a treaty to that effect. And—in perhaps the most famous of all executive agreements—Franklin Roosevelt acted on his own in concluding the deal by which Great Britain, a belligerent, in 1940 acquired fifty destroyers, ostensibly overage, from the neutral United States in return for the right to establish American bases on British territory, from Newfoundland to Trinidad, in the Western hemisphere.

A comparable presidential prerogative resided in the capacity to deliver statements of policy that, though in theory not binding, might well in practice commit the United States as firmly as a treaty. An early instance was the Monroe Doctrine of 1823, announced in the course of President Monroe's annual message to Congress. A later addition, subsequently known as the Roosevelt Corollary, was first aired at a dinner in New York, when Secretary of War Elihu Root read out a letter from the President on the subject of relations with Latin-American republics. "Brutal wrongdoing," the guests heard over coffee and cigars, "or an impotence which results in a general loosening of the ties of civilized society, may finally require intervention by some civilized nation, and in the Western Hemisphere the United States cannot ignore this duty."[4] The dinner took place in May, 1904: not until his annual message in December did Roosevelt officially inform Congress of his view that the nation was thenceforward to be a hemispheric policeman—in virtually the same words as in the letter. His fifth cousin F.D.R. went further still at the beginning of 1942, in signing his name along with the heads of states of twenty-five other nations to the Declaration of Washington. By his act, the United States was committed to a promise that it would wage war against Germany in concert with the rest of the signatories, make no peace until Hitler's Third Reich was destroyed, and then decide upon peace terms jointly, not separately. The President had in effect contracted an alliance without the consent of Congress.

Sundry other devices gave the Chief Executive exceptional freedom of action. Diplomatic appointments were subject to Senate confirmation, and occasionally the Senate had signified its disapproval. This had been done, mainly out of spite, when Andrew Jackson named Van Buren as minister to London. To avoid humiliation or delay, and gain the benefit of personal advice, Presidents have therefore employed private emissaries. President Washington made some use of Gouverneur Morris to confer with the British government. Polk chose Nicholas Trist for a "confidential mission" to negotiate peace terms with Mexico in 1847. Woodrow Wilson sent his confidant Colonel Edward House (whose title, incidentally, was bestowed by the governor of Texas, as a mark of friendship, not of military prowess) on several journeys to Europe, before and during the First World War, and then included him in the American delegation to the Paris peace conference. Franklin Roosevelt, who had grown to lean on Harry Hopkins during the New Deal years, retained him as an unofficial roving ambassador to London and Moscow.

The commander-in-chief clause provided Presidents with still more powers. Control of the Army and Navy permitted Jefferson to wage small undeclared wars against the pirate kingdoms of North Africa, and Polk to bring on the Mexican War by ordering American troops to take up position on disputed terrain. It permitted Theodore Roosevelt, Taft, Wilson, and their successors to land expeditionary forces in various Caribbean countries and to maintain Marines in occupation of Cuba, Haiti, Santo Domingo, and Nicaragua for years at a stretch. T. R. decided to sail the American fleet around the world; when a congressman threatened to withhold a naval appropriation, the President blithely answered that he had sufficient funds on hand to send the fleet halfway, and would leave it to Congress to determine whether to leave the ships stranded on the other side of the globe. President Truman responded to the invasion of South Korea by an immediate order committing American forces to an undeclared war on a far bigger scale than the sanctioned wars of 1846 and 1898.

War powers could in moments of emergency be stretched to astounding limits. In 1917–18 President Wilson asked for and obtained almost totalitarian control of the American economy. He successfully asserted his right to dictate the organization of agriculture, industry, labor, and railroads. When a group of senators, alarmed by evidences of inadequate planning, suggested the establishment of a special war council, Wilson met the challenge to his supreme authority by drafting an alternative bill. The Wilson measure, duly enacted in April, 1918, as the Overman Act, had by chance an appropriately punning name: the President set himself up as the nation's *Übermensch,* empowered to manage the plethora of new executive agencies exactly as he saw fit. As the Second World War loomed ahead, F.D.R. nonchalantly did what he wished and sought sanction afterwards. The "destroyer deal" of 1940 violated at least two American statutes, and, according to critics, usurped power specifically reserved to Congress by the Constitution. Roose-

Teddy Roosevelt's "big stick" went to sea in 1907 when the White Fleet made a "courtesy" cruise to impress world powers. Here American sailors pose with some girls they impressed in Sydney, Australia.

velt's Attorney General, Robert Jackson, pointed to the all-purpose commander-in-chief clause by way of answer: the President was entitled to "dispose" the armed forces to the best of his judgment, and disposing them might include disposing *of* them by executive agreement. Jackson cited other statutes as well, and contended that the bases were more essential to national defense than the destroyers. Congress acquiesced to the extent of overtly handing over its constitutional rights to the President in the Lend-Lease Act of April, 1941, which empowered him to "transfer title, to exchange, lease, lend or otherwise dispose of any defense article" to any country whose survival he deemed vital.

By 1945 F.D.R. wielded greater authority than any elected official on earth. His enemies in the United States asserted that he had trampled on every law and precedent in the nation's history—not least the unwritten law that limited Presidents to two terms in office. Certainly he had gone further than any of his predecessors, but not so very much further, in the circumstances, than Lincoln or

Wilson during earlier wars. He had merely confirmed to the hilt the weight of Jefferson's ancient dictum: "The transaction of business with foreign nations is executive altogether."[5] And since the distinction between foreign and domestic affairs almost disappeared in situations of total war, the President's crisis-jurisdiction reached into every corner of national life. Jefferson would no doubt have stood aghast, but he would have understood.

Jefferson's dictum was of course incorrect. The Executive might be the moving force in foreign policy, he might enlarge his domain, he might demonstrate endless ingenuity in getting his own way. But constitutionally he was held in check by the Senate's voice in the ratification if not the negotiation of treaties, and to a lesser extent in the appointment of officials, and by the control of appropriations exercised by the House of Representatives. Beyond Congress lay the impalpable but overwhelmingly significant factor of public opinion. The President's apparent autonomy was circumscribed. In none of the instances mentioned above was a seemingly autocratic Chief Executive able to depart in any significant way from the route prescribed by congressional sanction, by historic conceptions of policy, and by the popular mood of his immediate day. A "lame-duck" President about to leave the White House in 1845, Tyler could not have imposed upon the Senate the joint resolution annexing Texas if it had not been for the popular mandate that had given Polk victory in the recent presidential election, with the undertaking to seek "the reannexation of Texas." Polk himself would not have risked war with Mexico if he had not been fairly confident that the expansionists were in the ascendant in the United States. Though Lincoln was condemned for acting unconstitutionally, he knew he would earn far more opprobrium if through punctilio he allowed the Union to break up. For all his swagger Theodore Roosevelt had a canny regard for popular support. His Caribbean activities, like some of his other ventures in foreign policy, satisfied the popular appetite for excitement without real involvement. As for Wilson, his fate at the hands of the anti-League members of the Senate was an object lesson to Presidents tempted to overreach themselves. He had failed to make the necessary gestures of compromise and had been punished. The next wartime President, F.D.R., would not have risked the destroyer deal unless he had been confident that most Americans would approve.

This cartoon from the New York Sun *credits Henry Cabot Lodge with the defeat of the peace treaty and the League of Nations.*

In short, the President was like a man fettered to a heavy vehicle. Once the vehicle was moving he could add his own motive force and by so doing increase the speed. He could ease its passage by kicking small obstacles out of the way. He could change its direction a little. But he could not start it moving on his own. Nor could he stop it.

For most of America's history the vehicle was almost stationary, with its movement obstructed by Congress and by the public. The metaphor is unfortunate if it suggests that congressional dissent was invariably obstructionist. The Constitution obliged Congress to act in resistance to the Executive. While Congress could be wrong, so could the President. The Whigs were justified in querying the necessity of the war with Mexico. Grant's administration was so inept that the Senate was probably wise to refuse to sanction the purchase of Santo Domingo, which he recommended. Though Senator Henry Cabot Lodge opposed Wilson's League of Nations out of personal and partisan spite, Wilson had behaved with arrogant rashness; and there were features in the Versailles Treaty that ran counter to cherished notions of America's role in world affairs. The Presidents themselves were not immune to error. After John Quincy Adams few until Theodore Roosevelt's day showed much knowledge of foreign affairs, or had had occasion to travel abroad for private purposes, let alone on official business. The comment made about Calvin Coolidge, that he had "not an international hair on his head," could have been applied to several nineteenth-century Presidents. Their inexperience was, moreover, not always remedied by their Secretaries of State. As the senior post in the Cabinet, the Secretaryship was often regarded as a sop to a disappointed rival whom it was important to placate. Lincoln chose William H. Seward for this reason (though the appointment proved a good one). Political necessity induced Wilson to make William Jennings Bryan his first Secretary of State, although he had considered Bryan a reckless and unreliable politician and might well— if he had been a Republican opposition figure instead of Democratic President—have echoed the view of a New York newspaper that Bryan was "about as well fitted to be Secretary of State as a cherub is to skate or a merman to play football." In the event Bryan performed quite creditably. But the appointment could have turned out lamentably, as did McKinley's selection of John Sherman. McKinley picked Sherman, a man on the verge of senility, because he wanted to offer a fitting reward to Mark Hanna, his Ohio guide, philosopher, and friend. When Hanna declined the Secretaryship, indicating that he preferred to enter the Senate, McKinley's solution was to move Sherman (also of Ohio) into the Cabinet and arrange for his Senate seat to be filled by Hanna. In the mercifully brief period of his Secretaryship, Sherman was a liability whose work had to be done by an assistant.[6]

Nevertheless the broad statement holds true: executive liberty of action was frequently nullified by legislative and national tendencies to inaction—or reaction. John Hay, Secretary of State from 1898 to 1905, found the task of educating congressmen in the new realities of American commitments extremely painful. At one point he wondered whether the Senate would ever consent to ratify another treaty. A man with little stomach for the fray, Hay complained that a treaty entering the Senate resembled a bull entering the arena in a bullfight. The animal's death was certain; the only question was the precise manner and timing of the slaughter. Hay's friend Henry Adams said disdainfully:

The Secretary of State exists only to recognize the existence of a world which Congress would rather ignore; of obligations which Congress repudiates whenever it can; of bargains which Congress distrusts and tries to turn to its advantage or reject. Since the first day the Senate existed it has always intrigued against the Secretary of State whenever the Secretary has been obliged to extend his functions beyond the appointments of Consuls in Senators' service.[7]

The United States as a whole was profoundly isolationist. The only alliance of its early history, that with France, was formally terminated in 1800, and for some years previous had been regarded as a dangerous liability. Not until 1942 did Americans enter into another full alliance; during the First World War the nation fought with the "Allies," but technically as only an "associated power." The average American believed that foreign nations were corrupt, unstable, class-ridden, selfish, and trapped in a cycle of dynastic wars. His own country must beware of becoming caught in the same snares; it belonged spiritually as well as geographically to another hemisphere. The Monroe Doctrine epitomized the sense of separation, and the determination to remain separate from Europe's entanglements. A mild, fairly genial form of xenophobia was endemic in nineteenth-century America. To call something un-American was not merely to note its strangeness but to pass judgment on its depravity. Radical ideas were commonly thought of as foreign in origin. Suspicion of Britain, the nation with whom the United States had the most dealings, was heightened by the American Civil War, in which both North and South believed the British were behaving with a hostile bias. Irish-American enmity toward England supplied another stimulus to Anglophobia. Not until the twentieth century, when Britain's authority was waning rapidly, was it widely understood that the security of the United States had in fact been strengthened by British seapower.

Anxious to avoid Europe's errors, and believing itself liberated from Old World necessities, the United States maintained a relatively tiny Army and Navy. Some citizens argued that by the same token the nation ought to dispense with a foreign service. Consular appointments might be retained, since the United States was engaged in world trade; but conventional diplomacy with its apparatus of functionaries seemed an unnecessary extravagance. Such was the view expressed, for instance, by Henry George in his *Social*

Problems (1884). America stopped short of outright abolition, but the level of diplomatic and consular appointments remained extremely low, as it had been since the end of the War of 1812. A career service never properly developed in the nineteenth century. Salaries were too low—and were to continue so until well after the First World War—to attract men who had no private income. Appointments were generally regarded as party awards, made either to politicians like James Buchanan or, increasingly, to wealthy citizens who had contributed to party funds. Every major power was represented by an ambassador at the capital city of other major powers, and by a minister or charge d'affaires in countries of lesser importance, on a reciprocal basis. But until 1893 no American diplomat ranked higher than a minister. In London, Paris, Berlin, or Rome the American minister would find himself outranked by numerous ambassadors from other countries. Belatedly the United States began to acknowledge that if it viewed itself as an important nation it must make sure that others saw it in the same light. The American missions in Britain, France, Germany, and Italy were raised to embassies in 1893. In the next dozen years the United States upgraded her diplomats in Russia, Mexico, Austria-Hungary, Brazil, Japan, and Turkey.

The slow growth of professionalism in diplomacy was not accompanied by any apparent growth of internationalism in the American people. The Allies owed much to the United States for aid in the First World War. Indeed this was their subsequent grievance: they felt they owed *too* much, in the concrete form of war and postwar debts. Even the much-traveled and reputedly philanthropic Herbert Hoover, who had toiled to organize relief programs in Europe, became convinced that the Old World was a source of little but trouble. American doughboys reached the same conclusion. So in the 1920's did the average civilian. Europeans were dirty, ungrateful, dishonest. Uncle Sam had been taken for a ride. Let there be no more "foreign wars" for the United States, no more Presidents like Wilson, re-elected because "he kept us out of war" only to drag his country into the war within a few months. At the next presidential election the voters by an overwhelming majority indicated their preference for Warren G. Harding, who campaigned on the slogan "America First," and was sustained by Republican publicity that declared: "This country will remain American. Its next Presi-

UNDER WHICH FLAG?

During the presidential campaign of 1920 Democrat James Cox supported the League, but voters preferred Warren G. Harding's isolationism. Cox's running mate that year was young Franklin Delano Roosevelt.

dent will remain in our own country. . . . We decided long ago that we objected to foreign government of our people."[8] The flow of immigrants to the United States was now drastically—and selectively—reduced by the Acts of 1921 and 1924. In this respect it could be contended that America was more isolationist than ever before. Nor was there any basic difference of outlook between the Republicans and the Democrats. A small minority of liberals, including ex-Secretary of State Elihu Root and Walter Lippmann, strove to remind their countrymen of the folly committed in repudiating the Treaty of Versailles. The majority remained indifferent. President-elect Franklin D. Roosevelt expressed the common attitude when in 1932 he announced on behalf of the Democrats: "We are opposed to any official participation in purely European affairs or to committing ourselves to act in unknown contingencies."[9]

Though Roosevelt's words were probably not weighed with any

particular care it is worth pointing out that he referred to aloofness from *European* affairs. American isolationism was in fact qualified. The Monroe Doctrine, which proclaimed American noninterference in Europe, also warned Europe against interference in the Western hemisphere. It is unlikely that Monroe or his Secretary of State John Quincy Adams meant at that stage to define the entire hemisphere as a United States sphere of influence. Certainly their country ignored for half a century and more the possibility, elusive though it may have been, of offering a lead in the establishment of the entity known as Pan-America. The actions of Polk and others, however, revealed that the United States did assert a special claim to territory in *North* America. By degrees the claim spread farther south, into the Caribbean. It hung equivocally over Cuba, though no President except Grant committed himself to the firm proposition that Cuba should become an American possession. It encouraged Cleveland and his Secretary of State Richard Olney to take a pugnacious tone with Britain during the Venezuela dispute of 1895. Theodore Roosevelt felt that it justified him in engineering the creation of Panama as well as of the Panama Canal. It led to the Roosevelt Corollary, and to a series of interventions in Caribbean affairs that persisted well into the limp administrations of Harding and Coolidge. Only in 1927 did the United States begin the serious attempt to institute friendly instead of hectoring relations with Latin America; and by then, unfortunately, the damage had been done. Pan-America was a chimera; talk of Good-Neighbor policy provoked cynical disbelief even when it was sincere. Perhaps the narrow, high-minded isolationism of a Senator Borah or a Senator Norris was preferable to this brand of American involvement. To resentful Latin Americans and to some European critics, the United States seemed unable to discern a middle ground between self-righteous neutrality and the blatant "dollar diplomacy" practiced around the waters of the Caribbean. The other exception to isolationism concerned the Pacific. An American, not a British or French, naval expedition opened Japan to the outside world in 1853. The first American doctrinal contribution to international affairs (excluding the Monroe Doctrine, which was merely a unilateral declaration) was the "Open Door" policy of 1899–1900 with regard to China. Thereafter the United States, which had taken possession of the Philippines, part of Samoa, and Hawaii, liked to think of itself as a Pacific power, and believed with some reason that it had treated China more benevolently than the European nations, each jostling for special rights within the Chinese domain. Except for the relatively brief presence of the A.E.F. in France, service overseas for the armed forces came to mean service in the Pacific or the Caribbean (including the Panama Canal Zone). During the years of mounting tension in Europe, from 1935 to 1939, Major Dwight D. Eisenhower was stationed in the Philippines as assistant to General Douglas MacArthur. However, only a small section of the American public had more than a vague awareness of conditions in the contemptuously named "banana republics" of Central America, or of what was going on in the Far East. The editor of the Brooklyn *Daily Eagle* in the 1930's kept on his desk a memo that read: "Always remember that a dogfight in Brooklyn is more important than a revolution in China." A California editor, changing "Brooklyn" to "Oakland," might have substituted "Europe" for "China." An editor in Kansas or Illinois might have been happy with either "Europe" or "China."

There is no need to dwell upon the change that took place. After the First World War the United States retreated psychologically within its frontiers, with the exceptions noted above. On the approach of the Second World War President Roosevelt, engrossed in domestic emergencies, had to educate himself in foreign problems before he could begin to educate the public. Previous American initiatives such as the "cooling-off" treaties devised by Bryan, and the Kellogg-Briand Pact of 1928 (formulated by Coolidge's Secretary of State, Frank B. Kellogg), followed John Hay's Open Door letter in being virtuous mutual declarations that negotiation was preferable to warfare. They suffered from the same weakness that afflicted Wilson's League of Nations—still further debilitated by American abstention—and the later United Nations organization, in entailing no real surrender of national sovereignty. The most admirable of the American initiatives, the summoning of an international conference in Washington at the end of 1921, led to some actual disarmament and to a number of treaties, including a four-power agreement on consultation in the event of "aggressive action" in the Pacific. The Senate ratified all the treaties. But it attached to the four-power agreement with Britain, France, and Japan a reservation that "there is no commitment to armed force, no alliance, no obligation to join in any defense." The subsequent aggressions of Japan in the Far East, of Italy in Africa, and of Germany in Europe made the pious hopes of the Bryans and Kelloggs appear pathetically optimistic. Moreover, they were not even presidential inspirations. Harding did not grasp the fine points of international diplomacy. When queried as President-elect on what his foreign policy would be, he replied, "You must ask Mr. Hughes about that." His Secretary of State, Charles Evans Hughes, was the formulator of whatever was done.[10]

On the eve of the Second World War the United States was easily the greatest industrial power in the world and had one of the largest navies. But the nation counted for disproportionately little in the places where momentous decisions were being reached. No American representative was invited to attend the fateful meeting between Hitler, Chamberlain, and Daladier at Munich in 1938. In the previous four years Congress had passed various Neutrality Acts designed to keep the United States out of war. Even when war broke out in Europe, and Hitler won victory after victory, many reputable Americans strove to maintain neutrality. Peace-minded citizens equally anxious to avoid embroilment with Japan so much resented Roosevelt's undisguised aversion to the Axis Powers that they afterward accused him of having dragged America into war by obliging the Japanese to attack Pearl Harbor. Isolationist motives had always been mixed. It is only fair to observe that not all so-called isolationists were purblind. Some feared that war would breed war—that conflict would acquire a ghastly momentum and become an addictive habit. Some pointed to the First World War as proof that wars solved nothing. Some mourned the loss of the peaceable virtuous tradition of America at its best. If they were softheaded, they feared the results of a national indulgence in hardheadedness; and they had some cause.

But the war came. By the spring of 1945 it was almost won in Europe and the end was in sight in the Far East. The death of Roosevelt in April shocked the world. But the extent of the shock was a measure of the dependence of the Allies upon the United States; and Harry Truman's manful assumption of presidential responsibility left no serious hiatus in leadership. Moreover, he had inherited a secret weapon, the atomic bomb, which was to end Japanese resistance almost overnight. The bomb appeared to

Prime Minister Winston Churchill, President Harry S. Truman, and Marshal Joseph Stalin pose happily after the Potsdam Conference of 1945.

endow America with prodigious power for good. In 1889 an American writer, Frank R. Stockton, had produced a fantasy entitled *The Great War Syndicate* Stockton envisaged a future war in which American scientists invented an invincible weapon called the instantaneous motor. This early version of the atomic bomb, in his tale, is used to win a war against Britain, decisively but without loss of life, and then to form the basis of an Anglo-American alliance that guarantees global peace.

In 1945 it was possible to dream a comparable dream. The United Nations organization took shape in that year as the result of a meeting held in San Francisco. The headquarters of the old League of Nations, which it superseded, had been at Geneva: the headquarters of the United Nations would be on American soil, in New York. Optimists could fancy that a better world was genuinely in the making. The defect of previous American proposals for disarmament, arbitration, and the like had been that while apparently internationalist, they were at heart isolationist. They sought paper solutions that would permit the United States to remain detached from world concerns. They decreed peace but had no force with which to deter aggression. Now, however, the traditional benevolence of American policy was backed by overwhelming power. With America in the lead, working through the United Nations and other international agencies, the world might at last be made truly safe for democracy.

The dream quickly faded. The triumphant months of 1945 set in train a host of intractable problems, any one of which was enough to occupy the full energies of the President. Instead of peace America faced an apparently interminable cold war, at times terrifyingly close to full-scale war and always perplexing and frustrating. International communism confronted the American vision of international democracy. Before long Russia too had an atomic bomb. From the horrible missiles of Hiroshima and Nagasaki the two superpowers developed thermonuclear weapons of still more nightmarish destructive capacity. Lesser powers following in their wake began to acquire nuclear warheads of their own. Ultimate weapon succeeded ultimate weapon. The American defense budget, amounting to $11 billion in 1948, had more than quadrupled by 1953. Though President Eisenhower was able to reduce the figure at the close of the Korean war, it crept upward again to over $40 billion before he left the White House. During his Presidency military spending accounted for at least half of the federal budget.

Such astronomical outlays proved unavailing, or so it seemed. Here and there it was possible to say, especially in the immediate postwar years, that American action had achieved decisive results. European recovery was no doubt hastened by the Marshall Plan. Greece would almost certainly have become Communist if the United States had not taken over Britain's defense role in the eastern Mediterranean. The vigorous policy of containment, spelled out under President Truman, was at least negatively effective. But in general the situation was comfortless. The Communist bloc interpreted American activity as aggressive imperialism. Non-Communist countries, especially those such as Britain and France, which had until recently themselves been first-rate powers, were resentful of American hegemony. Before the war the difficulty had been to persuade the United States to enter into international agreements for collective security. It was now the United States, immensely richer and stronger than other "free" nations, that had the task of persuading them to join and support defense pacts. Everything had happened too quickly. During the Second World War Roosevelt was critical of British and French "imperialism." Within a few years the United States was compelled to try and prop up former European possessions whose society and economy were alarmingly precarious. The "uncommitted" nations, well aware of the competing claims of America and Russia, naturally endeavored to play one against the other. Everything was expected of the United States, yet every sign of "interference" provoked hostility.

The situation was deeply disappointing to Americans. Accustomed to thinking of themselves as the anti-imperialist, democratic wave of the future, they were now treated in some quarters as bloated reactionaries. Here, said Reinhold Niebuhr, lay "the irony of American history": their ideology was apparently outmatched by that of communism; and the very proofs of free society cited by the Americans—wealth and stability—were both envied and despised by much of the rest of the world. Angered and impatient, some Americans, briefly led by Senator Joseph McCarthy of Wisconsin, hunted for scapegoats within the federal government. Others, briefly enthused by the dicta of General MacArthur, became "hawks," urging what they called preventive war. The United States, they said, held a temporary superiority in nuclear weapons: why not use them before it was too late?

Only a dozen or so years after the Korean War died down, the United States was more heavily committed than ever in the Far East, this time in Vietnam. An easing of the tension with Russia, inhibited by the Vietnam conflict, was more than offset by the increasing hostility of Communist China. The rehabilitation of Europe's economic strength prompted America's allies to question the further usefulness of the North Atlantic Treaty Organization. General de Gaulle, more intransigent, or at any rate more blunt, evicted NATO forces from France. There was increasing talk of Europe as a "third force," poised between America and Soviet Russia and affiliated to neither. Yesterday's innovation in foreign policy became today's orthodoxy and tomorrow's straightjacket. The containment theory sketched out by Truman's advisers hardened into the brinkmanship of the Eisenhower era. Fidel Castro's Cuba accused the United States of every crime in the calendar. In

1967 the Arab countries convinced themselves for a while that their defeat in the Six-Day War with Israel had been brought about through American (and British) intrigue.

Such were the predicaments of the United States, and therefore of the Presidency, in the postmodern world. They profoundly affected the executive branch of government and its response to global crisis (the adjective "global" was now part of everyday American discourse). The most obvious effect was the vesting of still more power in the President. As the advance warning of enemy attack dwindled in defense calculations from days to hours, and from hours to minutes, the need for secrecy and dispatch was the more readily acknowledged. The intricacy of foreign affairs baffled the ordinary citizen. The electorate, and even Congress, seemed obliged to entrust decisions to the President, for only he with his access to fresh, detailed, and confidential information could be presumed to know what was going on in Cuba, Iran, Guatemala, and all the other places that suddenly claimed the headlines.

For long stretches of the nineteenth century one-term Presidencies were the norm. The desire for continuity of leadership in external policy, and the prestige accruing to the Executive, now made it almost impossible to defeat a President seeking re-election — and it was assumed that each President would expect to be renominated. General Eisenhower's prominence as the former head of multinational armies gave him an immense advantage over Governor Stevenson of Illinois in the 1952 election, though Stevenson himself had served in the State Department and had been actively involved in the United Nations. As a candidate again in 1956, and a possible candidate in 1960, Adlai Stevenson necessarily made himself a foreign policy expert. After the Democratic victory in 1960 he hoped to become Secretary of State and was in fact appointed ambassador to the United Nations. Any presidential aspirant strove to demonstrate his firsthand knowledge of international issues. In the 1960 campaign the Republican candidate Richard M. Nixon frequently referred to his Moscow visit, in which he had

---

Eisenhower, who believed in summitry and face-to-face conferences, traveled widely during his Presidency. In this photograph the Chief Executive bows to admirers in the Philippines.

publicly argued with Premier Khrushchev. Though F.D.R.'s one-time Vice-President John Nance Garner had remarked that the office was "not worth a pitcher of warm spit," his successors after 1953—Nixon, Lyndon B. Johnson, Hubert Humphrey—began to travel abroad so often on official business that at least in this sphere they ceased to be negligible functionaries. As Vice-President, Truman had known nothing of the atomic-bomb project. Subsequent Vice-Presidents could no longer be left in the dark on vital matters affecting national security. The office therefore now promised again to become a route to the Presidency, as it had been in the early days of the republic. There were signs too, to judge from the careers of Nixon, John F. Kennedy, Lyndon Johnson, and Barry Goldwater, that membership in the Senate—and especially in its Foreign Relations Committee—formed a more attractive qualification for presidential nomination than the governorship of a state. Governor Romney of Michigan, hoping for the Republican nomination in 1968 (in vain as it turned out), planned to overcome his ignorance of world affairs by means of preliminary tours of Europe, the Soviet Union, Vietnam, and the Far East.

As in earlier decades, the President's relations with Congress were sometimes strained. He tended to bypass the legislative branch through executive agreements. Presidents and their emissaries traveled abroad with increasing readiness. Eisenhower inaugurated a new postwar era of summit diplomacy, particularly in his second administration. He attended the Geneva disarmament conference in 1955. In 1959, having flown to the capitals of Western Europe beforehand to explain his purpose, he invited Premier Khrushchev to the United States and in September held private talks with the Russian leader at his summer retreat, Camp David. At the end of the year President Eisenhower visited eleven nations —Italy, Turkey, Pakistan, Afghanistan, India, Iran, Greece, Tunisia, France, Spain, and Morocco—in less than three weeks, on an errand of good will. The display was both personal and symbolic of America's purposes. He distributed scores of gold medallions inscribed on one side "In Appreciation, D.D.E.," and on the other "Peace and Friendship in Freedom." In February, 1960, he flew fifteen thousand miles on a similar good will tour of Latin America. He had already prevailed upon Khrushchev to attend the first of a possible series of multinational summit meetings, in Paris, and was

The world held its breath during the Cuban Missile Crisis of 1962, when John F. Kennedy and Nikita Khrushchev locked horns.

himself preparing to visit the Soviet Union when Russian-American relations were abruptly jarred by the news that Soviet antiaircraft gunners had shot down an American U-2 reconnaissance plane engaged on a secret and illicit mission over Russian territory.

President Kennedy was somewhat skeptical of the value of summit meetings. But he too appeared in Europe's capitals, to wild acclaim, and peered across the Berlin Wall. He too was forced to reckon with the harsh truth announced by Khrushchev: "There are only two nations which are powerful—the Soviet Union and the U.S."[11] In the Cuban Missile Crisis of October, 1962, the American President and the Russian Premier were linked in an ambivalent intimacy. They were as close as two chess players, each contributing to the pattern of play and each endeavoring to read the other's mind. The hot line from Washington to Moscow, with its telephone on the President's desk, was a constant reminder that in moments of supreme emergency, decision rested with the White House, not with Congress. Whether or not Presidents wished to treat directly with other heads of state, circumstances dictated conduct. The need for tact, if nothing else, in dealing with friendly or uncommitted nations obliged Presidents to include them in travel itineraries. Conversely, the White House was obliged to act as host to a stream of visits from foreign heads of state, each anxious to convince his own people of his privileged standing with the United States.

It was inevitable that Congress should at times react sharply to executive dominance in foreign affairs. President Truman and Secretary of State Dean Acheson were assailed by neo-isolationists who disapproved of foreign aid, or of involvement in Korea, or of the government's apparent failure to gain immediate victory in the cold war. This national mood found expression in a 1951 proposal by Senator John Bricker of Ohio to prevent the President from making executive agreements without previous congressional authorization. The Bricker Amendment, as it became known, also voiced a more judicial uneasiness that treaties might be enforced as domestic law without sanction of Congress. But in essence it was an attempt to reduce presidential authority and reclaim the rights of Congress; and it was enthusiastically supported by the Chicago *Tribune,* the Daughters of the American Revolution, and other guardians of patriotism. Discussion dragged on for three years. According to Emmet Hughes, a White House adviser under Eisenhower, the President became seriously worried. "The whole damn thing," he exclaimed at one point, "is senseless and plain damaging to the prestige of the United States. We talk about the French not being able to govern themselves—and we sit here wrestling with a *Bricker* Amendment." Not least among Eisenhower's irritations was the inability of otherwise amiable Senators to see the problem through the President's eyes. The Republican majority leader,

Senator William Knowland of California, voted for a substitute version of the amendment even after receiving a note from the President that he was "unalterably opposed" to it, and that it would constitute a declaration that "our country intends to withdraw from its leadership in world affairs." Eisenhower's alarm was understandable: the diluted version of the Bricker Amendment was approved by the Senate in February, 1954, by sixty votes to thirty-one—only one short of the necessary two-thirds majority. Vice-President Nixon reported that among those in favor was Senator Lyndon B. Johnson: "He says he doesn't think it's wise at all, but he's going to vote for it. And you ask him why, and he says simply: 'Because all my people in Texas want it.'"[12]

The controversy gradually abated, but the basic issue was still liable to revive. In his presidential incarnation Lyndon Johnson found himself on the receiving end. During the summer of 1967 Senator J. William Fulbright, chairman of the Foreign Relations Committee, submitted a resolution that would require any American overseas commitment to be approved beforehand by Congress. Introducing his resolution, he said that the executive branch had acquired "virtually unrestricted power to commit the U.S. abroad politically and militarily." He maintained that if Congress had been consulted, American intervention in Vietnam and the Dominican Republic might have been avoided, and so might the 1961 Bay of Pigs fiasco, in which the United States connived at an invasion of Cuba by anti-Republic Castro exiles.

One reason for the Senate's annoyance was that in actuality recent Presidents have, far from ignoring Congress, made increasing use of congressionally approved executive agreements in international affairs. The procedure eliminated the traditional treaty-making procedure; and it gave a stronger voice to the House of Representatives, which formerly could participate only obliquely by giving or withholding appropriations. For the same reason a concerted assault on executive prerogative was unlikely to come from Congress as a whole. Moreover, beginning with President Truman, there was a marked tendency to formulate policy on bipartisan lines. The Republican Senator Arthur J. Vandenberg of Michigan led the way by staunchly supporting the overseas programs of Truman's Democratic administration. Eisenhower and his successors were careful to consult prominent congressmen, including the minority as well as the majority members of the Senate's Foreign Relations and the House's Foreign Affairs committees. Such treatment raised a problem for congressmen. Though it gave them a better grasp of certain matters it drew them into a more consenting rapport with the White House than they might wish. If the price of confidential briefing was legislative silence, some of them would rather not pay it. A dilemma developed. Eisenhower had a genuine wish to curb what he regarded as the executive "usurpations" of F.D.R. But when he therefore from the best of motives sought to involve Congress in decision making, the legislators from a mixture of motives revealed that they would rather not be implicated.

Some congressional resolutions, such as one in 1955 that allowed the President discretionary authority to respond to Communist China's threatened assault on Formosa, muffled debate instead of promoting it. A disquieting feature of the cold war was that perpetual crisis deadened discussion. Criticism of the administration was apt to be interpreted by the public as evidence of disloyalty. It was condemned as bringing aid and comfort to the enemy. The either-for-or-against psychology of actual war was applied to a situation that continued year after year. Congressmen who sought to prove their patriotic energy were liable to repent when it was too late. President Johnson's response to the attacks by Senator Fulbright and others was to argue that he had not exceeded his powers in sending half a million Americans to fight in Vietnam. He had merely followed out the implications of the 1964 Tonkin Bay Resolution, which had received almost unanimous approval—and which Fulbright himself had piloted through Congress. The President, knowing that he held the whip hand, challenged Congress to rescind the resolution. Unless public opinion swung toward his Senate critics, their gesture against him was doomed to failure. Testifying before the Foreign Relations Committee, the Under Secretary of State, Nicholas Katzenbach, made two points. One was that throughout American history "the voice of the United States in foreign affairs was that of the President." The second was that "whatever the powers of the President to act alone on his own authority . . . there can be no question that he acts most effectively when he acts with the support and authority of the Congress." While these assertions were true they did not really answer the congressional complaint, which was that more and more the President determined policy and Congress made this effective by voting favorably—a vote it dare not refuse.[13] As the "credibility gap" widened under Johnson and Nixon, the Senate became more and more angry at successive revelations of the extent to which, over the Tonkin Bay and other issues, Congress and the public had been manipulated by the White House.

In a climate of protracted crisis, attitudes hardened and became cliché-ridden. Both the executive and the legislative branches developed the habit of overdramatizing problems. Their intention in part was no doubt to convey complex ideas in the simplest possible way, so as to render·them intelligible to the electorate. They also felt that public approval, and congressional appropriations, would be more easily secured if needs were presented as crash programs designed to combat some immediate menace to the free world offered by diabolical Communists. Sometimes legislation not directly related to international problems was given a crisis coloration. A bill of 1958, for example, though stimulated by the shock of Russia's successful launching of Sputnik I, was largely a step towards federal support for education. But it was christened the National *Defense* Education Act. Foreign observers, misinterpreting such domestic nuances, were given additional reason to believe that the United States, from the President downward, was in the grip of an anti-Communist hysteria. It is likely that men in Washington, D.C., underestimated the sophistication of the public. They might gain short-run advantages from playing upon the hopes and fears of the electorate. In the long run, however, they risked extending the dangerous "credibility gap" between official language and actuality.

If the President's tasks were complicated by his relations with Congress, they were also complicated by his relations with the executive branch. In theory he *was* the Executive, but he was only the chief figure in a welter of agencies and bureaus concerned with foreign affairs in one way or another. There was the State Department with its vastly expanded realm.[14] There was the great secret domain of the CIA (Central Intelligence Agency). There was the USIA (United States Information Agency). There was the Defense Department, established in 1947 as a consolidation of the old War and Navy departments. There were the Army, Navy, Air Force, and Marine Corps chiefs of staff, each representing his military constituency with competitive zeal. There was, in President Eisenhower's words, a "permanent armaments industry of vast proportions," employing three and a half million men by 1961. In 1956 the sociologist C. Wright Mills published a study called *The Power Elite,* in which he argued that Congress and the public had ceased to have any effective voice in American affairs: the nation was run by an interlocking directorate of "warlords" and executive officials, most of whom—like Eisenhower's Defense Secretary Charles E. Wilson—were corporation heads. Eisenhower was sufficiently concerned, just before leaving the Presidency in 1961, to warn America of the dangerous potential of "the military-industrial complex"; a typically "civilian" response from this former "warlord."[15]

The Secretary of Defense had undeniably become a major executive figure. Robert S. McNamara, holding the post under Presidents Kennedy and Johnson, wielded a formidable authority in his dealings with the Pentagon on the one hand and Congress on the other. But the chief Cabinet office, in protocol and in practice, was still that of the Secretary of State. Ever since Herbert Hoover's day the State Department had been headed by men of some stature: Henry L. Stimson, Cordell Hull, James F. Byrnes, George C. Marshall, Dean Acheson, John Foster Dulles, Christian Herter, Dean Rusk. But the relationship between the President and the Secretary was not simple. President Truman was irked by Byrnes's disdainful view of himself as "an Assistant President in full charge of foreign policy." He failed to realize, said Truman, that the President is responsible for foreign affairs: "The President cannot abdicate that responsibility, and he cannot turn it over to anyone else." Truman was particularly annoyed when Byrnes, on his return from a foreign ministers' conference held in Moscow in December, 1945, prepared to discuss his experiences over national radio before reporting on it to the White House.[16]

At the other extreme, though President Eisenhower would not accept this interpretation, came the cordial relationship between him and Dulles, which rested on the Secretary's virtual autonomy in determining policy. True, the two operated in close harmony, conferring almost daily when Dulles was in Washington. Dulles was tremendously industrious, and a tireless advocate of the idea of personal contact: he traveled over half a million miles in his six years at the State Department. He was courteous in his contacts with the President. When Eisenhower's heart attack in 1955 made him

George C. Marshall (left), architect of the Marshall Plan, Dean Acheson (center), and John Foster Dulles (right), were all strong Secretaries of State.

more or less a passenger in the executive branch for six months, Dulles was able to continue without difficulty. The reason for this smooth transition seems, however, to have been that Dulles' policies were the President's, rather than vice versa. At any rate, Dulles was the conspicuous architect of "massive retaliation" and brinkmanship—policies that appeared too rigidly doctrinaire to have been conceived by a man of Eisenhower's temperament. While somewhat narrowly conservative on domestic issues, Eisenhower was, generally speaking, liberal, if naïvely so, in foreign policy. It seems more than coincidence that he embarked on his sequence of travels and summit meetings almost immediately after the death of Dulles in 1959.

Between the extremes of attempted dominance and accepted dominance lay the impeccable conduct of General Marshall and Dean Acheson, men of strong will and bold ideas who enjoyed considerable freedom of action but who managed to efface themselves in the interests of presidential prerogative. They were fortunate in working with President Truman, who repaid their loyalty with generous appreciation: it was he who insisted that the European recovery program should be called the Marshall Plan because he wanted the Secretary to be given "full credit for his brilliant contributions."[17] They were in this respect luckier than F.D.R.'s Secretary Cordell Hull, who for nearly twelve years endured the humiliation of being left out in the cold. On the pretense that the wartime summit meetings at Casablanca, Cairo, and Teheran were military, not diplomatic, in emphasis, Roosevelt did not take Hull with him. Worse still, Hull was not even informed of the result of the conferences. He was not told of the atomic bomb project. He had almost no idea of the vital matters discussed between the President and his Lend-Lease "expediter" Averell Harriman. Nor were Cabinet meetings of value to him (or to most other executive heads in the past twenty-five years: the real business was nearly always transacted elsewhere). Roosevelt Cabinets, another official said, were "a solo performance by the President, interspersed with some questions and very few debates."[18]

Hull was treated thus because the President regarded him as unduly conservative. What he gained from relative obscurity was immunity from the kind of malevolent hostility that enveloped Marshall and Acheson. Hull's recourse was a familiar one in the executive milieu: debarred from the chance to shape policy, he became a champion of the career diplomats congregated in the State Department—a bureaucrat instead of a decision maker. Though they were loyal to their subordinates as well as to the President, Marshall and Acheson had to witness a drastic slump in the prestige and the morale of the State Department, for they bore the brunt of the McCarthyite attack on "striped-pants diplomats" with "phony British accents." Dulles' intransigent position on communism may have been unconsciously conditioned by a desire to protect the department against a recurrence of the onslaught. At any rate it was several years before professional diplomacy was again securely established in the United States.

Even then there was a fundamental difficulty in the position of the Secretary of State *vis-à-vis* the President (comparable to that of the British Foreign Secretary in relation to the Prime Minister). The preponderance of foreign affairs meant that it was essential to appoint a distinguished public servant to the post and keep him in it to develop his grasp of the great range of tangled responsibilities. But, as Harry Truman said, the President could not abdicate responsibility. The Secretary of State was therefore apt to be a frustrated figure, treated with more respect than Cordell Hull and yet still left to work out the almost impossible compromise between overassertion and a meek retreat into the fastnesses of executive bureaucracy. Dean Rusk, Kennedy's Secretary of State, had a somewhat thankless tenure: he was not merely obliged to shape a proper relationship with the President; he had to compete with other advisers on the White House staff such as the forceful, clear-witted McGeorge Bundy, the President's special assistant for national security affairs. Holding the same office under President Johnson, Rusk again endured the inevitable lot of Secretaries of State appointed by strong-minded Presidents in periods of international tension. He resembled Tantalus in the old fable: each time he was about to drink, the water was apt to recede. Secretary William Rogers suffered the same humiliating eclipse under Nixon. In comparison with Nixon's special assistant Henry Kissinger he was a nobody, an outsider, excluded from the inner process of policy making.

Earnest endeavors were made to think out the implications of executive proliferation. It was agreed that there were too many competing agencies, some alarmingly autonomous (the CIA operated without reference to the State Department, with a somewhat nominal responsibility to the National Security Council), none with a sufficiently comprehensive grasp of the whole picture of situations overseas. A survey made in 1968, to act as a guide for the incoming President, reviewed the rival claims of a system centered upon the State Department, one emanating from the White House, and one combining both. In no very euphoric mood it recommended the combination. The White House should control the allocation of resources. The State Department should have primacy in coordinating and monitoring operations. The President must continue as main policy maker, but was inevitably and perhaps increasingly dependent upon expert advisers. This survey and others also recommended the extension of small executive committees (SIG's—Senior Interdepartmental Groups) for special purposes. In effect it emphasized the irrelevance of the President's Cabinet, and the at best secondary role of the old State Department. It noted wistfully, too, the impossibility of finding executive assistants in real life who possessed the mythical omnicompetence of Sherlock Holmes's mysterious brother Mycroft:

> Well, his position is unique. . . . He has the tidiest and most orderly brain, with the greatest capacity for storing facts, of any man living. . . . The conclusions of every department are passed to him, and he is the central exchange, the clearing-

Embarking on their trip to China in 1972, President and Mrs. Nixon are followed by Secretary of State William Rogers and special assistant Henry Kissinger. Most observers of the Washington scene believed that Kissinger was far more influential than Rogers in forming American foreign policy.

house, which makes out the balance. All other men are specialists, but his specialism is omniscience. . . . In that great brain of his everything is pigeon-holed and can be handed out in an instant. Again and again his word has decided the national policy.

Yet the Bundys and Kissingers were in conception at least analogues to the mysterious Mycroft Holmes. And to the extent that their activities depended on secrecy they were, outside the White House, objects of automatic suspicion.[19]

Perhaps the exact balance between the President and his crop of advisers depended upon the chemistry of temperament rather than upon organization charts. The President sought out those whose ideas and style most pleased him. Though there was nothing intentionally devious in the process, the President's entourage was reminiscent of the court of Versailles in the days of Louis XIV. Those who had his ear acquired renown; those who were not in the running occupied themselves with obsessive speculation on the inner history of the foremost courtiers.

Certainly the organization charts lacked permanence. President Eisenhower, accustomed to a military command structure, liked to have issues presented via a neat committee hierarchy and a chief of staff (his ex-campaign manager, Sherman Adams, from 1953 until 1958). He held weekly meetings of the National Security Council, a body established in Truman's time. He was probably more systematic than his successor John F. Kennedy, though the incoming Democratic administration announced its intention to make the mechanism function more efficiently. Kennedy arranged fewer meetings of the NSC than Eisenhower—sixteen in the first six months—and sometimes encouraged the council to deliberate in his absence, in order to promote uninhibited argument. McGeorge Bundy explained in September, 1961:

> Much that used to flow routinely to the weekly meetings of the Council is now settled in other ways—by separate meetings with the President, by letters, by written memorandums, and at levels below that of the President. President Kennedy has preferred to call meetings of the NSC only after determining that a particular issue is ready for discussion in this particular forum.

Another of Kennedy's advisers, Theodore C. Sorensen, shed light on the matter in his witty little book *Decision-Making in the White House* (1963):

> For years agencies and individuals all over town have felt affronted if not invited to a National Security Council session. The press leaps to conclusions as to who is in favor and who is not by scanning the attendance lists of meetings, speculating in much the same fashion . . . as the Kremlinologists who study the reviewing stand at the Russian May Day Parade. . . .
> Yet in truth attendance at a White House meeting is not necessarily a matter of logic. Protocol, personal relations, and the nature of the forum may all affect the list. Some basic foreign policy issue, for example, may be largely decided before it comes to the National Security Council—by the appoint-

ment of a key official, or by the President's response at a press conference, or by the funds allocated in the budget.[20]

Like Kennedy, Johnson too was impatient with formal NSC meetings.

Presidents who might once have had difficulty in procuring expert advice on esoteric international questions were now swamped with guidance from a plethora of executive offices. Often it was bewilderingly various, or highly technical in form. As Kennedy remarked in the course of a television address, "No matter how many advisers you have, the President must finally choose." The burden is his: "The advisers may," he said with dry wit, "move on to new advice."[21] By the mid-1960's the burden was nearly intolerable. However devoted and wise his assistants, at the moment of decision the President was alone. Most of his decisions were, fortunately, less than cataclysmic. But always in a corner of his mind was the knowledge that he might some day feel impelled to press the button that would spell the destruction of our civilization. The aim of his foreign policy must be to see that he never had to press it. Beneath this supreme negation came all the other negations of a power seemingly illimitable and yet circumscribed by the actions of his predecessors, by public opinion and national habit, by Congress, by the sensibilities of allied nations, by sudden developments outside his ken. His principal nightmare between 1967 and 1971 was the American commitment in Vietnam, embarked upon in Kennedy's administration. Neither swift withdrawal nor further involvement appeared acceptable.

On the whole the Presidents of the postmodern era achieved the abrupt transition from isolation to total responsibility with dignity and moderation. In an imperfect world it was unlikely that the leader of any other nation placed in America's shoes would have performed as creditably. They had made mistakes. The nation had not always appreciated what was at stake. Flexibility had sometimes been lacking. The experts on holocaustic war revealed an almost excessive readiness to think the unthinkable—talking airily of casualties measured in tens of millions. But in retrospect the Truman policies seemed firm without being unduly truculent, the Eisenhower ones ponderous without being disastrous, the Kennedy initiatives intelligent and mature. Kennedy's handling of the Cuba crisis stood out as a high point of crisis diplomacy; imaginative ex-

During a press conference in 1961, President Kennedy points to a map of Indochina while discussing that troubled region.

periments such as his Peace Corps showed the world that there was more to the United States than dollars and ballistic missiles. Until the escalation ("escalation"—that most ominous of words in the vocabulary of the postmodern era) of the war in Vietnam, there was light ahead. The cold war was dissolving into new alignments; given flexibility and good sense on both sides, not all of these were unpromising. Though very far from real friendship, the United States and Soviet Russia seemed to be within reach of a sort of weary truce, or at least of a superpowers' willingness to recognize one another's spheres of influence. The understatement of America's reaction to Russian intervention in Czechoslovakia, during the summer of 1968 would have seemed unthinkable ten or fifteen years earlier when John Foster Dulles was occupied in brinkmanship.

Or so it could seem to a sympathetic witness who declined to believe that if the United States could have remained isolationist, the world since 1945 would have been a better place. There were signs of a nationwide readiness to draw back from the policies of the previous twenty years—to repudiate the automatic assumption that the United States had a stake in every corner of the world. Cynics might insist that President Nixon's secretly engineered invitation to visit China was more of an election stunt, looking ahead to the 1972 presidential campaign, than a genuinely peaceable move. But at the very least it revealed the readiness of a professional politician to pay attention to public opinion, and to abandon without apparent qualm what might have been regarded as his previous inflexibly anti-Communist "principles." Radical critics, however, inside as well as outside the United States, portrayed the nation as power-mad, brutal, imperialistic. New Left historians, looking back upon a generation of active American engagement (during which the CIA had swollen into a half-sinister, half-absurd task force of two hundred thousand men), accused their leaders of vicious hyperactivity. Less radical observers, probably with more justice, began to suggest that the executive branch suffered from too little autonomy in domestic affairs and too much in foreign affairs.[22] Lyndon Johnson, so bruised by unpopularity that he declined to seek re-election in 1968 and longing to bring off a statesmanlike peacemaking *coup* in Vietnam, may have inclined privately to agree with some of these views. In the meantime, the President as director of foreign policy seemed to possess power without glory: power to destroy rather than power to preserve, to pacify, to reconcile.

CHAPTER TEN

The Presidency and the American Union

In a sense it is impossible to separate the external and internal responsibilities of the Presidency. During the twentieth century they have become inextricably related. Eisenhower's warning against the "military-industrial complex" is a conspicuous instance; some commentators believe that the Great Depression of the 1930's was solved only by the compulsions of world crisis, which forced the United States into a wartime economy, and that the cold war has been the main *economic* safeguard against another sizable depression. Within the executive branch, the Departments of the Treasury, Agriculture, Commerce, and even the Interior (through its control of petroleum uses) all may have an important say in foreign policy. Conversely, of course, foreign affairs may determine the shape of America's domestic development. Premier Khrushchev certainly thought that his activities could sway the American electorate; and it is at least conceiv-

---

F.D.R. exuded confidence and charm, as this photograph taken toward the end of his second term reveals.

able that if the U-2 piloted by Francis Gary Powers had eluded the Soviet antiaircraft gunners in May, 1960, the Republican candidate, Vice-President Richard Nixon, might have won the presidential election of the following November, for the incident was a serious embarrassment to the Eisenhower administration. It is also arguable that John F. Kennedy, the Democratic candidate in 1960, would not have been elected, or indeed nominated, if Americans had not been prepared to discard one of their ancient isolationist fears: fear, that is, of the alleged determination of the Roman Catholic Church to sway the loyalties of adherents in the United States. Foreign and domestic crises have usually kept step with one another, especially since 1945. The extension of presidential authority has constituted a response to both, equally and inseparably. It has been one of the indicators of a transformation in the whole tone of the American union.

However, there is a range of internal issues mainly conditioned by domestic considerations. The stock market crash of 1929 and the decade of economic adversity that ensued were part of a worldwide malaise. But the Depression naturally turned the gaze of Americans inward. A breadline in Brooklyn had an understandable, in fact a necessary priority in the newspapers over a revolution in China. It was near at hand, it was urgent, and it was doubly grim after the complacent assurances of the 1920's that an era of permanent American prosperity was in sight. President Hoover was booed for telling audiences that the national economy was basically sound, that federal regimentation would destroy liberty, and that (as he later phrased the matter in his memoirs) the Depression had been caused by "miasmic infections" from "the boiling social and economic caldron of Europe."[1]

The presidential memory was longer than that of the average citizen. Hoover could have found sanction for his outlook in the words of several previous Chief Executives, including Garfield and Cleveland. Franklin D. Roosevelt, elected in 1932, deliberately reached back to a conception of his office defined between the Garfield-Cleveland epoch and what he called the "hear-nothing, see-nothing, do-nothing" administrations of the 1920's.[2] Pledging himself and the nation to a New Deal in his acceptance speech at the Democratic convention, he adapted the Square Deal formula of his fifth cousin Theodore Roosevelt. During a 1932 campaign address

Roosevelt was Assistant Secretary of the Navy when this picture was taken in 1913; he is at the far right. To the left are Secretary of State William Jennings Bryan, Secretary of the Navy Josephus Daniels, and President Woodrow Wilson.

he reiterated T. R.'s view that the Presidency was a pulpit—"a bully pulpit," in T. R.'s breezy phrase—from which to reach and educate the nation. Many of his speeches were couched in the idiom of "Roosevelt the First" and of Woodrow Wilson, and evoked the precedents of Jackson and Lincoln. F.D.R.'s first inaugural address called for "a leadership of frankness and vigor." He was to be again a People's President, representing all the country but especially the poor.

Nor was his sense of the past confined to rhetoric. F.D.R. had served in Wilson's administration. Many of the men who came to work for him in Washington were veterans of the old Progressive crusades. Some of the sweeping measures that passed through Congress with dazing rapidity in 1933, and at subsequent stages of Roosevelt's Presidency, derived their sanction from the control of the American economy entrusted to Wilson in such measures as the Overman Act of 1918. Roosevelt's methods of communicating with the public were for the most part those already exploited by predecessors. Even Calvin Coolidge, who is said to have succeeded in his

Calvin Coolidge posed in cowboy costume during the 1927 Independence Day celebration in Rapid City, South Dakota.

ambition to be "the least President" the United States had ever had, was shrewdly aware of the value of good publicity. He held press conferences with even greater frequency than F.D.R., was always willing to have his photograph taken, and exploited the novel possibilities of radio broadcasting. "I am very fortunate," he told a senator, "that I came in with the radio. I can't make an engaging, rousing, or oratorical speech to a crowd as you can . . . but I have a good radio voice, and now I can get my messages across to them without acquainting them with my lack of oratorical ability."[3] Coolidge's message to Congress in December, 1923, was broadcast, and he delivered several well-received talks from time to time. President Hoover made twenty-one radio addresses in his four-year term.

Nevertheless F.D.R. went beyond anything that his predecessor had done to energize and dramatize the Presidency. The contrast with Hoover's dour manner was amazingly marked. One of Roosevelt's 'brain trust' advisers, Rexford Tugwell, described him as "not a made President, but a born one":

> No monarch . . . unless it may have been Elizabeth or her magnificent Tudor father, or maybe Alexander or Augustus Caesar, can have given quite that sense of serene presiding, of gathering up into himself, of really representing, a whole people. He had a right to his leeways, he had a right to use everyone in his own way, he had every right to manage and manipulate the palpables and impalpables. . . . He had touch with something deeper than reason. . . .[4]

The Roosevelt touch was brilliantly demonstrated in his relations with the press. Coolidge had been considerate with newspapermen; Hoover attempted to convey information efficiently. Roosevelt treated them with affection, informality, and humor, but with a basic respect. His mastery of the press conference, at which he abolished the previous practice of demanding written questions, was such that his critics said he had bemused the fourth estate and turned hardened journalists into gushing sycophants. Whatever the truth of this, he certainly succeeded in keeping them informed of what his administration was doing. The result was apparent in the fullness of reporting; Roosevelt's name was rarely absent from the front pages. Nor in general did he use his press contacts to nag Congress, though he employed every means at his disposal to attract public interest in and support for his programs. His references to the legislative branch were usually in the best traditions of executive courtesy. Indeed, oddly enough, F.D.R. prodded Congress in public somewhat less than the "do-nothing" Coolidge, despite the latter's claim in his autobiography that "I have never felt it my duty to attempt to coerce Senators or Representatives. . . ."[5]

Roosevelt's rapport with the nation was still more triumphantly demonstrated in his radio broadcasts. As governor of New York he had already begun to anticipate the famous "fireside chats" of the New Deal era. He was keenly aware that most newspaper publishers were Republican, whatever the sympathies of their reporters. Unlike newspapers, Roosevelt told an N.B.C. official in 1933, radio "can not misrepresent or misquote. It is far reaching and simultaneous in releasing messages given it for transmission. . . ."[6] Many members of his administration, including the forceful Harold Ickes, were also frequent and skillful broadcasters. He devised his annual messages with quite as much attention to their radio audience as to his live audience in Congress. The fireside talks were, however, the high point of Roosevelt's contacts with the American public. Coolidge and Hoover had sounded stiff, and their remarks platitudinous. F.D.R. perfected a style that was direct, lucid, friendly, and informative. Anxious not to blunt their effect by overdoing them, he gave only twenty-seven fireside chats in his twelve White House years, six of them in the first eighteen months of the New Deal. So great was the impression they created that many people believed in retrospect that they had been almost weekly occurrences. His voice could be heard in every street in the land and his words lingered in the nation's imagination. His concern was that the federal government, under a Democratic administration, should not only be active, but be *known* as active.

The activity was undeniable, above all in the first Hundred Days of March–June, 1933, which witnessed an unparalleled quantity of legislation. These saw the beginning of the "alphabet soup" of New Deal agencies and acts—CCC (the Civilian Conservation Corps), FERA (the Federal Emergency Relief Administration), AAA (the Agricultural Adjustment Administration), TVA (the Tennessee Valley Authority), NRA (the National Recovery Administration), PWA (the Public Works Administration), and so on. Some, like the NRA, fell by the wayside; others, such as WPA (the Works Progress Administration), were created later.

The result was an immense extension of federal power and of executive functions. Roosevelt outlined the change in his April, 1939, message to Congress:

> Forty years ago in 1899 President McKinley could deal with the whole machinery of the Executive Branch through his eight cabinet secretaries and the heads of two commissions and there was but one commission of the so-called quasi-judicial type in existence. He could keep in touch with all the work through eight or ten persons.
>
> Now, forty years later, not only do some thirty major agen-

cies (to say nothing of the minor ones) report directly to the President, but there are several quasi-judicial bodies which have enough administrative work to require them also to see him on important executive matters.[7]

The first of these bodies were the Civil Service Commission (1883) and the Interstate Commerce Commission, dating back to 1887. In Wilson's time came the Tariff Commission, the Federal Reserve apparatus, the Federal Trade and Power Commissions, and various war agencies, including the War Industries Board. Under Hoover were formed the Reconstruction Finance Corporation and the Federal Farm Board. The New Deal added a swarm of other corporations, agencies, commissions, and banking organizations.

Some of F.D.R.'s predecessors had tried to reform the increasingly cumbersome structure of the executive branch, but with little success. He himself had a great deal of trouble before Congress finally passed the Reorganization Act of 1939, which enabled him to divide the Executive Office of the President into five main groups. One of these, the Bureau of the Budget, had been set up in 1921 within the Treasury Department: it was now moved into the immediate orbit of the President. Another division, the White House Office, was to include a number of secretaries and personal assistants. A third was designated as the National Resources Planning Board. At the end of the list provision was made "in the event of a national emergency, or threat of a national emergency," for "such Office for Emergency Management as the President shall determine."[8] This sixth division, the OEM, was in fact created in 1940. Like his strong predecessors, Roosevelt had stressed the existence of a "crisis" to justify bold executive measures. He went on to use the word "emergency" to define a supercrisis. Under the OEM were eventually massed the panoply of bodies that helped to make wartime Washington so hectically busy—and so bewildering to the casual visitor. There were under the umbrella of the OEM, for instance, the Office of Production Management, the Defense Communication Board, the Council of National Defense, the Central Administrative Services, the Office of Price Administration, and the National Defense Mediation Board. Every bit of this mushrooming administrative empire, it is worth reiterating, lay within the Executive Office of the President. No wonder that as Roosevelt was renominated for a third and then a fourth term, he was increasingly referred to by his opponents as a dictator.

During and since his administrations there have been spectacular demonstrations of presidential authority. One of the most extreme claims of presidential prerogative ever propounded was that of F.D.R. in September, 1942. Congress had passed an Emergency Price Control Act, and incorporated a farm parity provision to which the President objected. In fact he threatened to repeal the act on his own if Congress failed to meet his wishes within the near future. The legislators bowed to his will—a will expressed by Roosevelt in these words:

> The President has the powers, under the Constitution and under Congressional acts, to take measures necessary to avert a disaster which would interfere with the winning of the war .... When the war is won, the powers under which I act automatically revert to the people—to whom they belong.

As John P. Roche has remarked, such a claim was essentially the same as that advanced by Locke in the seventeenth century on behalf of royal prerogative ("the power to act according to discretion for the public good, without the prescription of the law and sometimes even against it").[9] In less sensational episodes F.D.R., followed in the same spirit by Truman, was prompt to veto bills he did not like. There is a story that Roosevelt used to ask his aides to look out for a piece of legislation he could veto, in order to remind Congress that they were being watched.

In every subsequent administration a President has aroused a clamor of excitement over some sudden demonstration of his supremacy. Truman electrified the nation, and infuriated a fair portion of it, when he dismissed General MacArthur in April, 1951. MacArthur was the most eminent American soldier of his day. He had been allowed considerable latitude in expounding his views on the need for the United States to give priority to Asian affairs, and to substitute all-out war for the limited strategy being pursued in Korea. He returned home to a hero's welcome, and the rare compliment of an invitation, which he accepted, to address Congress. But the dismissal stood; there was no way of getting around Truman's decision. MacArthur was General of the Army,

The Arkansas National Guard, federalized by President Eisenhower, keeps the peace at Central High School in Little Rock in September, 1957.

but the President was still the Commander in Chief. "It is fundamental," said Truman, "that military commanders must be governed by the policies and directives issued to them in the manner provided by our laws and Constitution. In time of crisis, this consideration is particularly compelling."[10] If anyone was to justify actions unsanctioned by the law on the grounds that there was a crisis, it was the President. This was a game that only one could play at.

In September, 1957, Eisenhower appeared on television to announce another critical decision:

> Whenever normal agencies prove inadequate to the task and it becomes necessary for the Executive Branch of the Federal Government to use its powers and authority to uphold Federal Courts, the President's responsibility is inescapable. In accordance with that responsibility, I have today issued an Executive Order directing the use of troops under Federal authority to aid in the execution of Federal law at Little Rock, Arkansas. . . .[11]

Governor Orval Faubus of Arkansas, supported by the state legislature, had refused to abide by the ruling of a federal court that under a Supreme Court ruling of 1954, racial segregation must end in the public schools of Little Rock. The federal government, upheld by the Court, had for a decade honorably attempted to combat racial discrimination. The Little Rock school board was among those in the South that had begun to move toward integration, only to be thwarted by what Eisenhower described as "certain misguided persons." American rights, he said, depended upon "the certainty that the President and the Executive Branch of Government will . . . insure the carrying out of the decisions of the Federal Courts, even, when necessary, with all the means at the President's command." Federal authority was paramount, at least in the circumstances outlined by him. State-righters might fulminate, but the day after Eisenhower explained his action, paratroopers were patrolling the streets of Little Rock. President Kennedy similarly employed federal marshals to enforce the law at the University of Mississippi in 1962.

One of Kennedy's boldest exercises of authority was his handling of the steel industry in April, 1962. Delicate negotiations were in progress to persuade the steelworkers to accept a wage increase

During the Depression it was easy to blame everything on President Herbert Hoover—and people did.

modest enough to avoid inflationary consequences for the national economy. Kennedy had been actively involved in these consultations. At the moment when matters seemed to be under control the steel companies suddenly announced a substantial increase in the price of steel. The episode illustrates the spread of executive responsibility as well as of the executive capacity to maneuver. The President, Herbert Hoover gloomily observed in 1933, "has become increasingly the repository of all national ills, especially if things go wrong." What was true then was even truer thirty years later. The President was the person to whom everyone looked to rectify wrongs, indeed to prevent the very existence of wrongs. The health of the economy had become his charge. Prices and wages and taxes and tariffs and stockpiles were his daily diet. It is not surprising that Presidents should sometimes appear to devote a disproportionate amount of energy and enthusiasm to small, noncontroversial questions. The sheer relief was akin to that of a circus lion tamer, playing with a puppy after his act was over.

On this occasion Kennedy made his intention to tame the steel companies unmistakable. He deployed the whole arsenal of executive weapons. The Attorney General (the President's brother, Robert F. Kennedy) threatened antitrust proceedings. The Defense Department declared that federal contracts would be given only to companies that had not raised their prices. Democratic spokesmen from both houses of Congress announced that judiciary committees were to investigate the steel companies' machinations. The President discussed the situation at length and with scathing eloquence at a press conference—in the knowledge that it was an excellent method of mobilizing public opinion. His introductory statement invoked the national emergency as his reason for insisting that the new prices "constitute a wholly unjustifiable and irresponsible defiance of the public interest." The emergency was manifold: Kennedy referred to "grave crises in Berlin and Southeast Asia," to the sacrifices expected of American servicemen, and to the struggle for "economic recovery and stability." He implied that "the tiny handful of steel executives," in their "pursuit of private power and profit" were a disloyal bunch of Benedict Arnolds.[12] The price increases were swiftly canceled; Kennedy had used executive pressure in lieu of the statutory authority that he did not possess.

Every President since F.D.R., with the exception of General Eisenhower, has been among other things an experienced politician with a keen appreciation of the congressional viewpoint. Though Eisenhower was much criticized for political naïveté, he too was by temperament and training an advocate of executive-legislative consensus. "Consensus," one of Lyndon B. Johnson's favorite words, was equally applicable to the Eisenhower techniques, at least in his conception of them. A President, he would explain to his associates,

> does not lead by hitting people over the head. Any damn fool can do that, but it's usually called "assault"—not "leadership." . . . I'll tell you what leadership is. It's *persuasion*—and *conciliation*—and *education*—and *patience*. It's long, slow, tough work. That's the only kind of leadership I know—or believe in—or will practice.[13]

In his book *Presidential Power* (1960), which is said to have been carefully read by President-elect John F. Kennedy, Richard E. Neustadt emphasizes that the Founding Fathers did not create a government of "separated powers," but a government of "separated institutions *sharing* powers."[14]

By the middle of the twentieth century the executive and legislative branches were well aware of the complexity of their relationship. The level of congressional sophistication was raised by such devices as the establishment in 1946 of the Legislative Reference Service, and by making heavy demands on executive officers, some of whom spent much of their time in testifying before congressional committees. Congress was reconciled to the fact that some four fifths of the thousands of bills and resolutions coming before it in each session would have emanated from the executive branch. The majority and minority leaders in both houses were closely involved in the shepherding of legislation. Mike Mansfield, the Democratic majority leader in the Senate, said in 1962 that his chief function was "to interpret the President's program to Members of the Senate . . . to interpret the attitudes of the Senate with respect to his program to the President and to try to obtain a definite decision on the legislation the President desires." The minority leader, Senator Everett Dirksen, sounded equally compliant. "The majority leader and I," he recalled of the operations of the Eighty-seventh Congress, "used to go to the telephone, or to the White House. When the President of the United States said, 'There is no further business,' Congress went home. But if the President said, 'You did not finish your business,' we remained. The Congress would not dare to go home if the President said the job had not been finished."[15]

For their part Presidents took great trouble to maintain amicable relations with Congress. Lyndon Johnson frequently stressed his determination to avoid the mistakes made by Woodrow Wilson in 1918–19 in failing to name Senate spokesmen to his team of peace negotiators, and by F.D.R. in 1937, when he alienated Congress in attempting to create a more liberal Supreme Court. Other Presidents were no less familiar with such cautionary tales. Eisenhower instituted a series of breakfast meetings for congressmen. Anxious to consolidate his slender electoral victory in the 1960 election (the Democrats lost twenty seats in the House of Representatives), Kennedy held individual discussions at the White House with every committee chairman, briefing sessions on important bills for Democratic supporters, and foreign policy briefings for bipartisan groups. He entertained batches of congressmen for morning coffee.

Johnson surpassed his predecessors in demonstrations of esteem. He attended the funerals of Senator Harry Byrd's wife in Virginia and Representative Emanuel Celler's wife in New York, and even managed to fly to Georgia for the funeral of a nephew of his old associate Senator Richard Russell. At the close of the Eighty-eighth Congress he invited the entire membership to a gala White House occasion that included a specially produced Broadway show. Kennedy and Johnson prided themselves on their intimate links with Capitol Hill, maintained through the activities of a squad of liaison assistants. The columnist Joseph Alsop, explaining Johnson's success in securing the passage of the Civil Rights Bill of 1964, said that in addition to indefatigable executive lobbying by staff aides, "the President . . . left no Congressman unturned. . . . presidential telephone calls to individual members . . . of both houses . . . have been almost incessant."[16]

The highly professional Chief Executives of the mid-twentieth century likewise recognized the importance of capitalizing on party loyalty, no matter how imperfect this might be. President Kennedy rewarded a Tennessee New Frontier congressman, who was running for election in 1962, by appointing him special ambassador to represent the United States at the independence ceremonies in Trinidad: an exotic gesture, but one that would bring valuable publicity to the Tennessean. The whole Kennedy family lavished praise upon Representative Charles A. Buckley of New York. Buckley was temperamentally poles apart from the New Frontier; but as chairman of the House Public Works Committee he was too important to be flouted. And it is significant that President Kennedy's final, fatal visit to Texas in November, 1963, was on party business: his aim was to patch up the bitter quarrel between the Texas Democratic factions identified with Senator Ralph Yarborough and the then Vice-President Lyndon Johnson.[17]

Yet every technique, every pressure exerted by the President was often inadequate. The central thesis of Richard Neustadt's book *Presidential Power* is suggested by its subtitle: *The Politics of Leadership*. Professor Neustadt quotes two revealing observations by President Truman. The first was an epitome of his White House experiences: "I sit here all day trying to persuade people to do the things they ought to have sense enough to do without my persuading them. . . . That's all the powers of the President amount to." The second was a comment made in 1952 on the fate awaiting General Eisenhower if he won the forthcoming election: "He'll sit here, and he'll say, 'Do this! Do that!' *And nothing will happen.* Poor Ike — it won't be a bit like the Army. He'll find it very frustrating."[18]

Neustadt analyzes some of the apparent demonstrations of presidential authority, such as the dismissal of MacArthur and the dispatch of federal troops to Little Rock. His point is that though in a sense decisive, they were actually confessions of failure, or steps taken reluctantly when more satisfactory expedients had failed. Presidential power is severely limited; in domestic as in foreign affairs, frustration has been more usual than triumph. Although Kennedy on the face of it abased the steel industry, steel price increases were in fact introduced a year later. Neustadt's conclusion is that consummate political skill is required of the Chief Executive; General Eisenhower was an unsuccessful President because he failed to grasp the essential balance between persuasion and leadership. But mere political skills are not enough; some extra quality of charm, magnetism, imagination must disclose itself.

Looking back over the Presidency in the final third of the twentieth century, it becomes clear that despite the vast growth in the activities of the federal government, and of the executive branch, the Presidency has not escaped its traditional shackles. In fact, the President has in some respects been still further hemmed in through the spread of executive offices. As Neustadt insists, Congress and the President still have different "constituencies," and different ideas as to why certain things should be done (or not done). The President in general has come to stand for "liberal" and "international" ideas, while Congress—particularly the House of Representatives—has in general continued to be "conservative" and "national" (or "local") in outlook. A recent example is the blocking by the House in 1967 of a reciprocal arms arrangement between the American and British defense departments. This would have enabled Britain to offset some of the costs of purchasing United States military aircraft by selling British military and naval equipment to the United States. The agreement was largely nullified by an amendment to the Defense Appropriations Bill requiring all naval vessels to be built in American yards. The amendment was introduced by Representative John W. Byrnes of Wisconsin, who was determined that an order for seven minesweepers should go not to a foreign country but to yards in his own state.[19]

Plenty of other examples may be cited. One of the most resounding setbacks to presidential authority was suffered by Franklin Roosevelt in 1938. Until that time, backed by a handsome Demo-

*Accustomed to a cooperative Congress,
F.D.R. was startled by the independence
of the legislators elected in 1938.*

cratic majority in Congress, he had seemed invulnerable. Suddenly
he was in trouble, over the Executive Reorganization Bill submitted to Congress in the previous year. Most of its proposals were
sensible, and a new bill was approved in 1939. But the first one
seemed to disgruntled legislators and citizens to confer altogether
too many powers on Roosevelt. For example, he proposed to absorb
some of the independent regulatory commissions within the executive branch. Though the Senate reluctantly passed the bill, the
President enraged the Upper House by suggesting at a press conference that the votes of some Senators were open to "purchase." In
the House of Representatives a hundred Democrats, including the
powerful chairman of the Rules Committee, deserted the administration. A Missouri Democrat, who had been begged to trust the

President, shouted out: "Assurances are not worth a continental when they come from men who care no more for their word than a tomcat cares for a marriage license in a back alley on a dark night." A Kentucky representative cried: "Let us tell the world that the Congress is not impotent." If Congress did not resist Roosevelt's dictatorial tendencies, declared another speaker, members "might just as well stay at home and endorse Executive desires by mail."[20] In April, 1938, after the House defeated the bill, F.D.R.'s whole New Deal government seemed in disarray. Everyone was angry with everyone else—except jubilant Republicans. Underlying resentments burst to the surface. The fragility of presidential rule was all at once painfully apparent. As often in such crises, the President struck his associates as a gambler who had lost his touch: he ignored warnings and advice, he confused his followers, his words were maladroit. One recurrent problem that led to such blunders was explained in the memoirs of F.D.R.'s successor Harry Truman. The President, said Truman,

> will hear a hundred voices telling him that he is the greatest man in the world for every one that tells him he is not. A President, if he is to have a clear perspective and never get out of touch, must cut through the voices around him, know his history and make certain of the reliability of the information he gets.[21]

Truman himself had a hard time with Congress. He lacked the Rooseveltian aura, his ambitious legislative programs were challenged, and for the first time since 1932 the Republicans controlled both houses of Congress after the 1946 election. He fought back boldly. A clever stratagem, announced in his acceptance speech at the Democratic nominating convention in 1948, was to summon the "last, worst 80th Congress" back into special session:

> On the 26th day of July, which out in Missouri we call "Turnip Day," I am going to call Congress back and ask them to pass laws to halt rising prices, to meet the housing crisis— which they say they are for in their [Republican] platform.
> At the same time I shall ask them to act upon other vitally needed measures such as aid to education, which they say they are for; a national health program; civil rights legislation, which they say they are for; an increase in the minimum wage, which I doubt very much they are for; extension of the social security coverage and increased benefits, which

they say they are for. . . .

The tactic worked. Truman won election as President in his own right, and the Democrats regained control of Congress. But the Eighty-first Congress proved as intransigent on some points as the Eightieth, especially on the vexed question of policy toward communism. The President maintained a robustly "liberal" and "international" position: Congress by contrast seemed ready to give credence to wild theories of conspiracy and subversion. Thus Congress passed the Internal Security Act of 1950, which attempted to curb Communist (or other radical or totalitarian) activities in the United States, and to debar suspect aliens. Truman vetoed the bill in an eloquent message:

> Our position in the vanguard of freedom rests largely on our demonstration that the free expression of opinion, coupled with government by popular consent, leads to national strength and human advancement. Let us not, in cowering and foolish fear, throw away the ideals which are the fundamental basis of our free society.

His appeal was brushed aside; the next day his veto was overridden. The bill, slightly amended, emerged in 1951 as the McCarran Act. Senator Pat McCarran (Democrat, of Nevada) also sponsored the McCarran-Walter Act of 1952, which virtually retained the discriminatory provisions of immigration legislation of the 1920's, proposed complex screening methods to keep out "subversives," and empowered the Attorney General to deport unwelcome immigrants. Again, President Truman sent the bill back with a rousing veto. "In no other realm of our national life," he declared, "are we so . . . stultified by the dead hand of the past as we are in this field of immigration. We do not limit our cities to their 1920 boundaries; we do not hold corporations to their 1920 capitalizations; we welcome progress and change . . . in every sphere of life except in the field of immigration. . . ." Again, however, Congress overrode his veto.[22]

Nor were more placatory methods invariably successful. President Eisenhower gained such favor with the public during his first administration that he was re-elected in 1956 by a margin of over nine million votes. But the Democrats were returned to power in Congress, and increased their hold in the mid-term elections of

Pollsters and newspapers predicted Truman's defeat in the election of 1948, and the Chicago Tribune *went so far as to put out an early edition on election night trumpeting Dewey's victory.*

1958. Throughout his Presidency he sought to cooperate with the legislative branch. Yet legislators, journalists, and all the other President watchers in Washington soon perceived that he was more likable than formidable. He made no move to dissociate himself from the excesses of Senator Joseph McCarthy. Exasperated by the unresponsiveness of congressional Republicans, in 1953 he pondered whether it might not be better to form a new party. But he took no steps toward this—and in any case the dream was unrealistic. One of his associates noted that congressmen "were scared of Roosevelt, and even Truman. They're not scared of Ike." More assertive in his last two years, he was nevertheless too negatively inclined to clash head-on with Congress. So, what he gained in popularity among congressmen he lost in authority.[23]

John F. Kennedy obliquely attacked the Eisenhower conception of the Presidency in a speech at the National Press Club in January, 1960. The nation, he said, could not "afford a Chief Executive who is praised primarily for what he did not do, the disasters he prevented, the bills he vetoed." The President "must know when to lead Congress, when to consult it and when he should act alone." Bold words. But Kennedy himself, once in the White House, came under criticism for failure to dominate Congress. Carroll Kilpatrick, a sympathetic Washington correspondent, maintained that while the record of Kennedy's first two years with Congress "was not without notable successes . . . there were notable failures as well, and the amount of energy he expended in gaining as much as he did was enormous. The President's power struggle with Congress was almost equal to that of his struggle with the Communist leaders abroad." Despite a substantial Democratic majority, the administration's omnibus farm bill was killed in the House by ten votes, and the Medicare bill was lost in the Senate by five votes. Among other defeated pieces of presidential legislation were bills to create a Department of Urban Affairs and to provide federal aid for public schools and for higher education. Contemplating the disappointments of this couple of years, Kennedy's able assistant Theodore Sorensen wryly remarked that a President "is free to choose only within the limits of permissibility, within the limits of available resources, within the limits of available time, within the limits of previous commitments, and within the limits of available information." Congress might contribute to each of these limits. In 1962 Sidney Hyman, an expert on the Presidency, predicted that in domestic affairs the legislative branch would continue to claim dominance "in defiance of the President, in defiance of the public opinion he mobilizes, and in defiance of the fact that the sum of all local and regional interests do not necessarily add up these days to the national interest."[24]

His prediction was borne out by the legislative history of Lyndon Johnson's administration. True, Johnson established an astonishing record in his first year; he persuaded Congress to enact most of the principal measures desired by Kennedy, and promised the legislators "the full co-operation and support of the Executive branch":

> As one who has long served in both Houses of Congress, I firmly believe in the independence and integrity of the Legislative branch. . . . I shall always respect this. It is deep in the marrow of my bones. With equal firmness, I believe in the capacity and the ability of Congress, despite the divisions of opinion which characterize our nation, to act wisely, vigorous-

ly, and speedily when the need arises. The need is here. The need is now. I ask your help.

The appeal succeeded. And having gained a crushing victory over Senator Goldwater in the 1964 election, President Johnson moved on to his own Great Society with its far-reaching schedule of plans for social justice, economic improvement, beautification of the landscape, and so on. Portions of his program, including an increased and extended national minimum wage and the establishment of a new Department of Transportation, were quite briskly enacted. Professor Robert Lekachman wrote in June, 1965: "Lyndon B. Johnson is without question more lovingly immersed in domestic issues, and more effective in getting his programs through Congress, than any American President since Franklin Roosevelt in his first term of office."

The statement is, however, qualified. Lekachman went on to say that President Johnson's prescription for the Great Society "is the drive not toward the transformation of society but toward the expansion of the economic machine. This is not an ignoble vision. But it is a highly conservative one." The reforms he proposed were, in other words, relatively modest, relatively inexpensive, and relatively superficial. There was little to raise the hackles of Congress. Lekachman concluded his survey: "Although there is no special reason to condemn a conservative politician for choosing the path of conciliation, there is every reason to avoid confusing rhetoric with the program of social action that is desperately needed."[25]

By 1967 there was widespread criticism of Lyndon Johnson's domestic legislation for being more shadow than substance. The "Great Society" was derided as a catch phrase. Preoccupied by the agonizing dilemma of Vietnam, the President had ceased his previous barrage of flattery and cajolery on Capitol Hill. Executive-legislative relationships require constant attention: like plants in a hot, arid zone they wilt away unless watered daily. Congress complained of neglect and hostility, and responded with comparable hostility. Its rough handling of the Defense Appropriations Bill was in part a way of showing its displeasure with the Johnson administration. By 1968 there was almost no more talk of the Great Society, and Johnson had announced his impending withdrawal from the White House.

After the relative good humor of the first honeymoon year

Richard M. Nixon had an equally rough passage. Struggling to free the nation from the Vietnam nightmare, and harassed by a Democratic majority in both houses of Congress, he met with increasing resistance and unpopularity. This was true of commendable items in his program, such as welfare legislation, as well as of his calamitous failure to persuade the Senate to approve either of two bad nominations to a Supreme Court justiceship.[26] His intervention in the mid-term elections, with the aim of returning Republicans who would support administration policies, was as unsuccessful as similar attempts made by Wilson in 1918, Roosevelt in 1938 and 1942, Truman in 1950, and Eisenhower in 1954, and was conducted with such partisan spleen that it infuriated the liberal wing of his party in Congress. He suffered a further ignominious defeat when Congress refused funds to continue development of the SST aircraft—America's answer to the Concorde. This was hardly the record of a crushingly powerful autocrat, whether or not he had himself to blame for most of his failures.

The problems engendered by the spread of the executive side of the federal government have been mentioned.[27] Nineteenth-century Presidents were sometimes irritated by the devious resistance encountered among federal bureaucrats. The situation was far worse by the 1930's. "Half of a President's suggestions," according to Jonathan Daniels, a former aide of Franklin D. Roosevelt's, "which theoretically carry the weight of orders, can be safely forgotten by a Cabinet member. And if the President asks about a suggestion a second time, he can be told that it is being investigated. If he asks a third time, a wise Cabinet officer will give him at least part of what he suggests. But only occasionally, except about the most important matters, do Presidents ever get around to asking three times." Permanent officials were often able to impose their own ideas on executive heads, or at least to prevent them from making changes. F.D.R. had to recognize this as a fact of life:

> The Treasury is so large and . . . ingrained in its practices that I find it is almost impossible to get the action . . . I want. . . . But the Treasury is not to be compared with the State Department. You should go through the experience of trying to get any changes in the thinking . . . of the career diplomats and then you'd know what a real problem was. But the Treasury and the State Department put together are nothing compared with the Na-a-vy. . . . To change anything in the Na-a-vy is

like punching a feather bed. You punch it . . . until you are finally exhausted, and then you find the damn bed just as it was before you started punching.[28]

President Truman encountered the same difficulty. Career officials, he said in his memoirs, "regard themselves as the men who really make policy and run the Government. They look upon the elected officials as just temporary occupants. . . . It has often happened in the War and Navy Departments that the generals and the admirals, instead of working for and under the Secretaries, succeeded in having the Secretaries act for and under them. And it has happened in the Department of State."[29]

Different Presidents tried different expedients to solve the difficulty. Congress also took the initiative in introducing administrative changes. Starting with Roosevelt's Executive Reorganization Bill, a steady stream of proposals were considered. In 1947 Congress established a twelve-man Commission on Reorganization of the Executive Branch, with the approval of President Truman, who named ex-President Herbert Hoover to head it. The Hoover Commission plunged into the bureaucratic warren and emerged again in 1949 with a detailed report. As often happens with such reports, the diagnosis of deficiencies was rather more impressive than the list of suggested palliatives. The main trouble was the sheer spread of federal involvements. Under President Hoover the executive branch had 570,000 employees and cost $3.6 billion a year: a reminder that even in the 1920's the days of unregulated enterprise were already over. But twenty years later the number of employees had soared to over two million, and the annual cost to over $42 billion, spread out among more than 1,800 "assorted departments, bureaus, sections, divisions, administrations, etc." As a result of "depression, war, new needs for defense, and our greater responsibilities in the foreign field," the federal government had become "the most gigantic business on earth." The Hoover report implied that it was also one of the worst-run businesses. Unable to exercise any real control over the immense complex, the President was "forced either to delegate unofficially or neglect completely." The inevitable result was "overlapping, and administrative turmoil." The executive branch was "cut up into a large number of agencies, which divide responsibility and are too great in number for effective direction from the top." The chain of command downward

335

from the President, and of responsibility upward to him, had been "weakened, or actually broken, in many places and in many ways." There were not enough competent administrators. The rules of procedure were cumbersome and stultifying. It was a picture of a Parkinsonian universe: a universe so pervasive in spirit that the Hoover report was couched in its peculiarly leaden, circumlocutory prose.[30]

Helpless to offer any basic remedy, the commission recommended various realignments and the provision of more staff and funds for the President, as well as greater flexibility in running his immediate entourage. Congress responded, less generously than the commission had suggested, through the Administrative Reorganization Act of 1949. It was conceded that the President must have more genuine authority over his own branch. As another kind of recognition, the President's annual salary was increased in 1949 to $100,000 (plus a tax-free allowance of $50,000), and that of the Vice-President to $30,000 plus a $10,000 allowance. (In 1955 the Vice-President's salary was raised to $35,000. Possibly this was a gauge of his somewhat improved status. From 1789 to 1909 the Vice-President's salary had been only one fifth of that of the President, and from 1909 to 1949 less than one sixth.)

But even the limited reforms of the Hoover Commission met with a major snag. Congress, understandably anxious to retain a degree of control, restricted the act to a four-year span, and renewed it for shorter periods of two years in 1953, 1957, and 1959. It stipulated that plans for executive reorganization must be submitted for congressional approval. The renewal proposal of 1959 was defeated in the Senate, and the President's grant of authority therefore lapsed. The reason was that Congress had grown more and more uneasy at the implications of permitting the President to run his own household, when that household was "the most gigantic business on earth." It rejected twelve of the fifty-one reorganization plans submitted by Truman, and three of the seventeen devised by Eisenhower. On request from President Kennedy, Congress consented in 1961 to a further vesting of authority for a two-year period. Four of Kennedy's nine plans were rejected. One of these would have established the new Cabinet-rank Department of Urban Affairs. Many congressmen were suspicious of such a creation; some were hostile because the President had intimated

The first black Cabinet member was Robert Weaver (left), who was appointed Secretary of Housing and Urban Development by President Lyndon Johnson after that department was created in 1965.

that he intended to appoint a Negro, Robert Weaver, as Secretary of the Department.[31]

When the Reorganization Act was given a further two-year lease of life in 1963, Congress denied to the President authority to institute new departments of Cabinet rank. President Johnson managed to carry through the Kennedy scheme by establishing the Department of Housing and Urban Development in 1965, and to place Robert Weaver at its head. But he had to promote a separate bill to get his way; and—perhaps prudently—he did not name Mr. Weaver until the bill became law. He got nowhere in 1967 with a proposal to merge the Departments of Labor and Commerce.

In 1971 President Nixon, as part of the "New Revolution" outlined in his previous State of the Union address, disclosed his plan to reduce the number of Cabinet posts from twelve to eight. The scheme had been worked out by a special commission over a two-year period. It would leave the Departments of State, Treasury, Defense, and Justice intact. The Post Office was already being recast as a government corporation (in the hope of making it more businesslike and less unprofitable). That left the seven Departments of Agriculture, Labor, Commerce, Housing and Urban Development, Transportation, Interior, and Health, Education, and Welfare. In a complicated reshuffle the seven would be amalgamated into four new Departments: Natural Resources, Human Resources, Economic Affairs, and Community Development. Much thought had gone into the plan and its new shape looked attractively "streamlined." As an exercise in logic and a challenge to the cozy network of affiliations among politicians, bureaucrats, and businessmen it was commendable. Alas for paper schemes—congressmen in key positions soon made known that they preferred the old structure. Washington pundits argued that the Nixon regrouping might do as much harm as good. HEW (Health, Education, and Welfare), for example, already was bogged down in administering over two hundred programs. To merge its one hundred thousand employees with a huge mass of civil servants in the new Department of Human Resources might prove distinctly inhuman. And other critics of Nixon grumbled that even if approved, such tinkering with organization tables was almost totally irrelevant to the nation's fundamental problems—poverty, injustice, pollution, overseas embroilment.[32]

The executive branch, or at least the Executive Office centered in the White House, was more adequately staffed than in the past. But the mushrooming of functions and personnel tended to cancel out the "streamlining" theoretically achieved. More than ever the President's problem was to recognize key issues among the immense quantity of documents moving about the so-called corridors of power in Washington. Eisenhower's solution was to rely on his executive heads, and especially upon his assistant Sherman Adams, to preselect and digest such issues for him. He kept a clean desk and a tidy organization chart. The disadvantage was that he risked isolating himself unduly: how could he be sure that the proper issues were reaching him? Cabinet and committee meetings were supposed to bring him in contact with all his chief officials and their areas of responsibility. But were committees a satisfactory way of handling executive business? President Kennedy thought not. Reverting to styles reminiscent of F.D.R., though with considerably greater concern for administrative clarity, he sought to break through the elaborate hierarchy of the federal government. Kennedy sought advice from a wide variety of sources, often drawing upon the views of men outside the government. He would telephone directly to an official, bypassing the head of the department or agency; he encouraged energetic subordinates to communicate directly with him. Up to the moment of his death the technique was working reasonably well, because so many of his officials respected and admired him. If he had continued, however, he might have exposed his administration to some of the defects complained of by F.D.R.'s underlings—confusion, duplication of effort, factionalism, undermining of authority. There was no perfect way for a President to pick his way through the mazes of Washington. If he could work a twenty-four-hour day, seven days a week, he would still not have time for more than a fraction of the matters demanding his attention.

No theoretical clarification of structure made much difference. Only Eisenhower among postwar Presidents used the National Security Council in the ways in which planners had intended. Most Presidents found committee meetings, including those of the Cabinet, more of a public relations device than a means of reaching decisions. (The laudable readiness of government officials to explain themselves to journalists and to the public—a matter in which the American government compared very well with that of almost every other in the world—was apt to be self-defeating. No one, for example, was greatly impressed by a televised Eisenhower Cabinet meeting; to the layman the executive heads around the table appeared to have neither opinions nor knowledge.)

Each President tended to lean upon a few individuals whose personality was congenial, or whose discretion and intelligence he respected. The process went exceptionally far in the case of Sherman Adams, a Republican ex-governor of New Hampshire, who served as "Assistant to the President" from 1953 until compelled to resign over a minor impropriety in 1958. Some observers felt that he had more authority than many an actual President of the old days. One joke in Washington circles was: "What if Adams should die, and Eisenhower should become President?"[33] Adams—laconic, unimpressable, compulsively industrious—was a remarkable man. His notation, "O.K., S.A.," on a document was equivalent to presidential approval. But as the joke indicates, he owed his extraordinary position to his chief. Eisenhower detested unpleasantness. Years of high military rank had accustomed him to sheltering behind hard-working, loyal staff officers; the authority he delegated could be wielded by subordinates more ruthlessly than he was prepared to wield it himself.

However, every President has had his intimates. Occasionally they have been department heads or other senior officials, like Attorney General Mitchell in the Nixon administration. More often they have been supernumerary figures, like Wilson's Colonel House or F.D.R.'s Harry Hopkins (nicknamed Lord Root of the Matter). The postwar years brought increased reliance on press secretaries, such as Kennedy's Pierre Salinger, and on White House assistants. McGeorge Bundy, for instance, performed a vital function as special assistant for national security affairs, first for Kennedy and then (before leaving to become head of the Ford Foundation) for Lyndon Johnson. With the 1960's there was a revival of the New Deal practice of drawing upon academics. Bundy, Arthur Schlesinger, Jr., Eric Goldman, John P. Roche, and Walt Rostow, who all served in Washington under Kennedy or Johnson, or both, were all college professors—though Bundy had left teaching to be an academic administrator. President Nixon's extremely influential adviser on foreign affairs, Henry Kissinger, was a former Harvard scholar. Perhaps the trend would be reversed in the 1970's. Even so, it pointed to the acute shortage, noted in the Hoover report, of able men who were prepared to exchange the relative peace of campus life or the relative affluence of the business corporation for the hectic frustrations of life in the nation's Capital. In their search for executive talent and shrewd counsel the Democratic administrations of the 1960's showed a sensible willingness to ignore previous party allegiance: Bundy had been a Republican.

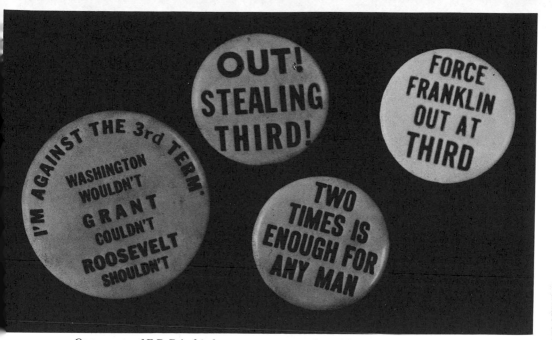

Opponents of F.D.R.'s third term were outnumbered by voters who wanted the President to remain at the nation's helm during a frightening period of international crisis.

There were signs of the evolution of a new type of presidential confidant-adviser. A few men, such as Clark Clifford, who succeeded Robert S. McNamara as Johnson's Defense Secretary, seemed resilient enough to survive whole decades of continuous service in Washington. But the strain was considerable, for the President's associates as well as for himself. For many, a twelve-hour working day was the norm.

Even in less burdensome periods most Presidents professed to have been overworked. In a private memorandum that Truman wrote in April, 1950, he observed that "eight years as President is enough and sometimes too much for any man to serve in that capacity." It was not merely that executive heads become fatigued. There was, he felt, a subtler difficulty. Presidents were too subject to the lure of power, by which he presumably meant the glamour of the office: "It can get into a man's blood just as gambling and lust for money have been known to do." Truman seems to have thought F.D.R. wrong to have broken with precedent by running for a third term; unless Chief Executives honored the code of restraint followed by Washington, Jefferson, and Jackson, he said, "we will start down the road to dictatorship and ruin." Though he could have sought and probably secured renomination in 1952, he decided not to; he would already have been in office for nearly eight years.

The same thoughts had occurred to Congress, which had proposed what in 1951 became the Twenty-second Amendment to the Constitution:

> No person shall be elected to the office of the President more than twice, and no person who has held the office of President, or acted as President, for more than two years of a term to which some other person was elected President shall be elected to the office of the President more than once.

The amendment had not yet been adopted when Truman set down his views, and he was specifically exempted from its ruling. But he knew it was likely to be ratified and was opposed: the two-term tradition, he said, "should continue not by a Constitutional amendment, but by custom based on the honor of the man in the office." The logic of this statement is not altogether clear. President Truman may have felt that decisions on re-election were best left between the Executive and the electorate. No doubt he considered the amendment a posthumous revenge exacted by a Republican Congress upon the dead Democratic leader F.D.R. A further tactical aspect undoubtedly struck him. He said in his memoirs that while he had decided as early as 1949 not to run again in 1952, "I could not share this decision with anyone. By the very nature of his office this is one secret a President must keep to himself to the last possible moment."[34] If he disclosed it prematurely he was liable to set off a furious contest among aspirants for the succession; and his own influence would dwindle, since party men would have nothing to hope for from a lame-duck President. Most commentators have agreed with Truman that the Twenty-second Amendment was a mistake. Whether or not they are correct, it should be added to the list of factors that circumscribed presidential potency in the second third of the twentieth century.

The President must reckon with every branch of government. Apart from legislative and executive complications, he might also run into difficulties with the third branch—the judiciary. Much of F.D.R.'s New Deal legislation was invalidated by a Supreme Court of whom the majority did not share his social and political attitudes. His scheme of 1937–38 to end the deadlock by threatening to alter the composition of the Court aroused violent opposition and alienated even some of his liberal admirers. He discovered to his cost that the Court enjoyed as much prestige as the Presidency—in fact perhaps more, in being further removed from the huckster world of politics. Roosevelt's exasperation with the Supreme Court was well founded. But in questioning the impartiality of the judiciary he unwittingly laid open to question the rectitude of the President. Here was another of the paradoxes of executive prerogative. Leadership depended upon vigorous presidential activity. Activity was, however, not always compatible with the appearance of rectitude. The standing of the office rested partly on the notion that he must be in some sense an "appellate" President, a Chief Magistrate with a magistrate's dispassionate aloofness. To attack the excessive power vested in the "nine old men" was to invite the response that they were guardians, not aggressors, and so less dangerous than *one* man, the President, whose power might take aggressive forms.

By the end of the F.D.R.'s administration, and with remarkable strength and near-unanimity after the appointment of Chief Justice Earl Warren in 1953, the Supreme Court moved into an era of positive liberalism. It thus became an ally of the almost innately liberal executive branch, especially in the realm of civil rights. Before this happened, however, President Truman suffered a sharp reminder that the Court as well as Congress might on occasion resist executive decrees. During the Second World War Roosevelt had now and then taken over factories in order to avert strikes and maintain essential production. In 1952 President Truman was faced with a strike in the steel industry. The Korean War was in progress, and Truman's advisers agreed with him that the threatened strike—brought on in his view by the obstinacy of the steel companies—constituted a national emergency. He therefore issued an executive order for the seizure of the steel mills by the government, and on the same day delivered an explanatory radio address to the nation. "I believe," he said afterward, "that the power of the President should be used in the interest of the people, and in order to do that the President must use whatever power the Constitution does not expressly deny him." Congress, he insisted, had obliged him to step in by refusing to act constructively in the dispute.

The steel owners and most of the newspapers disagreed. The volume of protest was so great that the Supreme Court decided to hear testimony in a suit challenging the President's authority. Chief Justice Fred Vinson declared that Truman had simply performed his constitutional duty "to take Care that the Laws be faithfully executed," and had sustained the tradition of Washington, Jefferson, Jackson, Lincoln, Wilson, and the two Roosevelts. Only two justices sided with him. The other six, including Hugo Black and Felix Frankfurter, ruled that the President had exceeded his powers. Frankfurter approvingly cited the opinion of Justice Brandeis in *Myers v. United States* (1926):

> The doctrine of the separation of powers was adopted by the Convention of 1787, not to promote efficiency but to preclude the exercise of arbitrary power. The purpose was, not to avoid friction, but, by means of the inevitable friction incident to the distribution of the governmental powers among three departments, to save the people from autocracy.[35]

The irony of this statement was that the majority opinion in *Myers v. United States* upheld presidential authority against that of Congress. The majority opinion in the 1952 steel case obliged the President to hand the companies back to their operators; he was rapped on the knuckles for dictatorial conduct.

Neither the man nor the institution was crushed. President Truman continued to believe he had been right. Within a couple of years the Warren Court was beginning to rule in case after case that America's interests were best served by a strong, benevolent federal Executive, rather than by private enterprise or state and local autonomy. The action of the 1952 Court revealed, however, that the third branch was still capable of contesting the prerogatives of the executive branch, and that constitutional precedents were still susceptible of more than one interpretation. Moreover, the "activism" of the Warren Court, though far preferable to the stubbornness of the New Deal Court, was not an unmixed blessing for the Presidency. Some perceptive commentators thought it was tending to weaken its own prestige by venturing into areas best left to Congress and the White House. And a President like Eisenhower, with passive or "appellate" inclinations, showed a disturbing readiness to shelter behind the armor of the Court instead of himself leading public opinion. His argument in justifying his intervention at Little Rock was that the President was merely enforcing a Supreme Court decision. "Our personal opinions about the decision," he said, apparently including the Executive in the word "our" and not affirming any executive attitude, "have no bearing on the matters of enforcement."[36] The danger was that the White House might abdicate responsibility, shifting to the Court a burden it should not be expected to carry. The hostile reaction of the Senate judiciary committee in 1968, when Johnson nominated Justice Abe Fortas to succeed Earl Warren, showed how much the Court had become resented as a supposed ally of liberal administration policies.

In the mid-twentieth century the news media were often referred to as the fourth branch of government. Newspapers, periodicals, radio, and television performed important if miscellaneous functions. Not least of these was the presentation to the public of the views of the man in the White House. As we have seen, Presidents became increasingly alert to the opportunities afforded by the news media. A President was now guaranteed immediate and comprehensive coverage of everything he did and said. The partisan political advantages were great. In the mid-term elections of 1962, as Louis Koenig points out, President Kennedy could set out on a campaigning tour with three airliners, four helicopters, a fleet of White House automobiles, five press assistants, and a squad of forty-four reporters plus attendant photographers and technicians.[37]

Yet no twentieth century President, not even F.D.R., was altogether happy with the outcome. For one thing, the influence of the media was not as significant as some journalists liked to think. President Truman won the 1948 election despite a mainly hostile (and predominantly Republican) press. The public, used to a diet of entertainment, tended to be bored by presidential exhortations on television. Relations between the White House and the press corps were apt to wear thin. If the President was uncommunicative, the newspapermen complained of being shut out; if he took trouble to keep them informed, they complained of being taken in—in other words, spoon-fed. The televised press conference exemplified the frustrating situation of the fourth branch in Washington. It was far too large, too staged, too public to offer genuine contact with the President. The interview conventions of the mass media required journalists to ask about matters on which they could not hope to be given a candid answer. Public figures, above all the President, often struck the ordinary citizens as men with nothing to say because discretion compelled them to respond evasively. Journalists, in search of good copy, usually exaggerated the fascination of new Presidents, and before long would start to exaggerate the failings of the incumbent. For their part, Presidents often proved oversensitive to press reports. Harry Truman occasionally lost his temper with journalists and told them so. Kennedy, while less peppery, was sufficiently annoyed by the New York *Herald Tribune* to cancel the White House subscription to the paper. Lyndon Johnson was markedly resentful of unfavourable publicity. The news media, in common with the general public, began to complain that instead of guidance by and information about the President they were being fobbed off with bland substitutes fashioned by public relations officers. They sensed obscurely that in an era of ghost-writing and publicity releases Presidents were too concerned with their images and too little concerned with reality. Some observers believed that the "cult of consensus" had led the whole nation, including the Presidency, into an obsession with polls and ratings, with the photogenic, with the pseudo-event, and that this must have damaging consequences for the nation. In the Nixon administration Vice-President Agnew, presumably with presidential approval, went out of his way to attack *The New York Times* and other papers deemed hostile to the administration. This mutual antipathy reached an extraordinary culmination in 1971 when the *Times,* followed by the Washington *Post* and other "liberal" newspapers, defied presidential anger and a Justice Department attempt to enjoin their activities by publishing confidential government documents on Vietnam policy. They won a notable victory in July, 1971, on appeal to the Supreme Court.[38]

There was, of course, nothing new in the tendency of journalists to become disenchanted with each President once his novelty wore off. They typified a national habit almost as old as the Presidency, to expect too much and react too harshly. Mid-term elections usually showed a swing away from the President's party after the brief honeymoon period. The disenchantment was usually even greater during a President's second term. Calvin Coolidge said in his autobiography: "An examination of the records of those Presidents who have served eight years will disclose in almost every instance the latter part of their term has shown very little in the way of constructive accomplishment."[39] This is not invariably true—it did not

Associated Press Wirephoto

President Johnson at his news conference yesterday. His manner led many people to phone White House in praise.

With a microphone concealed in his coat, the President could leave lectern. Sometimes he gestured and frowned.

United Press International Telephoto

He waved his arms. His voice ranged from angry volume to modest gentleness. This, some said, was "the real Johnson."

A New Presidential Style: That Was 'the Real Johnson,' His Old Friends Say

By ROY REED

Special to The New York Times

WASHINGTON, Nov. 17— President Johnson unveiled a new, free-swinging television style at his White House news conference today and set Washington talking.

Some old friends said that "the real Johnson," as they had seen him in private, had at last come through on the screen.

Wearing a portable micro-phone under his coat, the President stepped out from behind the podium and walked up and down in front of the camera like a revival preacher.

He waved his arms, chopped the air, drew imagi-nary lines with his fingers, clutched his glasses, scowled, laughed and ran his voice through a range of sound from high-volume anger to quiet, self-deprecating gentle-ness. Beyond the theatrics, he enlivened the content of the news conference with his-torical comparisons, scrip-tural quotations, jokes and a bit of sarcasm.

Political friends and ene-mies speculated that the President's new style signaled the beginning of an offensive pointed toward next year's election.

One Republican Congress-man, who asked not to be quoted by name, called Mr. Johnson's performance at the news conference "pretty darned effective."

"I keep telling our boys," he said, "not to count the chickens before they're hatched."

To some of his former col-leagues on Capitol Hill it ap-peared that Mr. Johnson had finally discovered how to be as effectively persuasive with a mass audience as with a private gathering.

A number of persons tele-phoned the White House from other cities to congratulate the President on his improved television delivery.

The new style is the visible part of what apparently is to become a major theme with the President between now and next year's election, a shift from the defensive to the offensive as he begins trying to convince the public that the Vietnam war is being won, that the Administration is in good shape and that things are going well all around.

Last night, discussing poli-tics at a White House brief-ing, Mr. Johnson had said that he was ready to come out fighting. Today he did.

The new technique became apparent about eight minutes

Continued on Page 19, Column 3

Uncomfortable in his early confrontations with the press, Lyndon B. Johnson avoided televised news conferences for some time; but in 1967 the Chief Executive tried to project a new, more sympathetic image, as The New York Times *reported.*

happen in the closing stages of Eisenhower's Presidency — but it has by and large been the case. F.D.R.'s administration reached a low point in 1937–38. Truman's government, despite his personal resilience, had lost most of its impetus by 1950 or 1951. Though Kennedy might have been an exception, most Washington observ-ers of his post-honeymoon administration noted a disparity between what one of them, the journalist Douglass Cater, has called "coura-geous expectations" and "cautious operations." Comments by con-gressmen in the wake of the 1966 mid-term elections indicated a drastic swing away from Lyndon Johnson. "We've had our bellyful of new legislation," said a Democratic leader. "The pendulum has swung too far in the direction of the White House, and now it's time for it to swing back. This will be a people's Congress." The House Republican leader, Gerald R. Ford, Jr., announced that his party's gains were "a repudiation of the President's domestic policies. . . . It's going to be rough going for him around here. Congress will write the laws, not the executive branch."[40]

The post-1945 President, everyone concurred, was the most powerful person in the most powerful nation on earth. Historically speaking, there was no doubt that an aggrandizing office had taken an almost total responsibility, not only for the well-being of the American nation but for that of half the globe. This much was cumulative, and possibly irreversible. On another scale, however, the office seemed to face a principle of diminution. Enlarged executive powers evoked increased congressional uneasiness. The response to Truman's seizure of the steel mills implied that Presidents could no longer count on being able to impose their will upon the nation by claiming "emergency" powers. A state of permanent emergency seemed to amount to no emergency at all. In spite of the links between the White House and Capitol Hill, they remained separate political realms.

What then was presidential "power" or "authority"? A contradictory affair, compounded of celebrity, frustration, and crushing responsibility. The President was the person of whom too much was expected and on whom everything could be blamed. John F. Kennedy dealt with the predicament at a meeting of newspaper editors in April, 1963, when he was asked for his policy on a possible wage increase for steelworkers. "I know," he said, "that there are important editorial interests . . . who really don't feel that this is the President's business. They have never really defined what his business is, but it is not this. I take a somewhat different view . . . in that if there is a wage demand, it has a number of effects upon the public interest. . . . I find that when things go badly, it becomes our business. When the stock market goes down, letters are addressed to the White House. When it goes up, we get comparatively few letters of appreciation. But when you have high unemployment, it is because the President hasn't gotten the country moving again."[41] He was the symbol of national pride, but also the nation's scapegoat. He might be widely popular, like Harding, yet weak and mediocre as Harding was. He might be widely unpopular, like Truman, yet combative and able as Truman was. He might be both popular and competent, as Kennedy would probably have been had he lived. He might be both unpopular and mediocre. In the eyes of posterity he would be liable to be held at fault for errors beyond his ken, though he might also be given credit for achievements that in truth were rather those of his executive associates, or of good men in Congress, or of the nation as a whole. Perhaps it was more accurate to talk of presidential "responsibility" than of presidential "power." At least this was how it seemed to the White House occupants of the

1950's and 1960's. "All Presidents," the journalist Alistair Cooke remarked in 1963, "start out pretending to run a crusade, but after a couple of years they find they are running something much less heroic, much more intractable: namely, the Presidency."[42]

CHAPTER ELEVEN

The Future of the Presidency

EVER since the Presidency was instituted its working has been under discussion. Some critics, at one extreme, have echoed the belief of certain delegates to the 1787 Constitutional Convention that a single Executive placed too much power in the hands of one man. Such was the view, for example, of Augustus B. Woodward, who in his *Considerations on the Executive Government of the United States* (1809) proposed a plural executive of five men, to be elected and to preside in annual sequence. This was more or less the plan adopted in the Swiss constitution of 1848. Henry C. Lockwood's *The Abolition of the Presidency* (1884) expressed a similar alarm and likewise recommended government by an executive council. At the other extreme, especially in the first half of the twentieth century, it has been argued that the problem is not to curb the President but to remove some of the factors that make his leadership ineffective. In the previous two

---

The immense burdens of the Presidency are symbolized by this photograph of John F. Kennedy, taken in his office at the White House.

chapters we have seen that even in the field of foreign affairs the President is not a free agent, while in domestic matters he is still more hampered.

Are reforms desirable? Are they feasible? Are they likely? The common response is unenthusiastic. As Theodore C. Sorensen observed in 1963: "There are already enough proposals to reorganize the Presidency to stretch from here to Utopia. . . ."[1]

One obvious consideration is that essentially the problems of post-1945 Presidents are the problems of a nation with an advanced economy and a polyglot society compelled to play a principal world role in a world that is undergoing rapid and prodigious transformation. No amount of administrative regrouping would return the United States to the old days of laissez faire and isolationism. Truman grasped this harsh fact when he placed on his desk the reminder that "the buck stops here." Whether there were a single desk or five or fifty desks, the executive would still have to exert itself to the utmost.

A second consideration is that whatever the theoretical shortcomings of the American system of government, those of other countries are no better. Woodrow Wilson dreamed of reforms on the British model. But the British scholar Harold Laski, lecturing on the Presidency at the University of Indiana in 1938–39, maintained that "anyone who knows the life of a political party from within Great Britain will not feel inclined to cast a stone at the American system." Judged by results, American methods were quite as likely to produce outstanding leaders when the hour demanded them. As for the interference of Congress in foreign policy, Laski said:

> A president eager for imperialistic adventure . . . might easily in the absence of Senate control, be a source of grave danger to the American people. And this view is, I suggest, reinforced by experience of systems like that of Great Britain where the control of foreign affairs is, in fact, "executive altogether." For the only real control of the House of Commons is of a *post-mortem* nature. It is presented by the cabinet with a *fait accompli*, rejection of which involves the defeat of the government and a subsequent general election. There is no instance in modern times where the government has had an assured majority, upon which its supporters have been willing to take that risk.[2]

More recent observations would seem to confirm Laski's skepticism. In *The Chief Executive* (1964) Louis W. Koenig devotes a chapter to comparisons with Chief Executives in other countries. He points out defects in British practice that worry the British themselves. Prime ministers may be mediocre figures. The method of selecting a prime minister, as revealed in 1963 when Harold Macmillan made way for Sir Alec Douglas-Home, was clumsy, slow, and somewhat secretive. The House of Commons, Professor Koenig asserts, "has been reduced to a passivity which even the most resolute critic of Congress would not wish upon it. In its tightly restricted capacity, the House resembles the American electoral college, registering the popular will in choosing a government and then automatically ratifying its program and voting the funds it asks for." The British civil service, once the envy of American political scientists, is now seen as "ingrown, uninspired, uncreative, and out of step with the fast pace of Britain's problems."[3] Developments in former colonies such as Nigeria suggest that even if the British model were ideal for the mother country it is not necessarily suitable for export. As for non-English-speaking nations, none seems to offer executive styles alluring enough for the United States to try to copy them.

Putting the matter more positively, a third common line of reasoning is that the American Presidency in fact works well. The process of selection is thorough and democratic. Aspirants have little chance to hide their weaknesses in the preconvention months, and none once the major parties have chosen their candidates. Only men of rare stamina and political maturity, it is argued, can survive the gruelling test of presidential campaigns. In office, the President has as much power as is good for any man. It is necessary in a federal government—so the argument goes—that Congress should represent local attitudes. If it did not the administration in Washington might become dangerously remote and monolithic. Moreover, the United States has fifty mini-Presidents—the governors of its fifty states and numerous mayors of large cities. That each of these tends to act as a reduced-scale President is held to prove that the real Presidency is an office well adapted to American needs. The states and cities serve too as laboratories for political experiment. Some suggested reforms, including types of plural executive, have been tried and found wanting at the local level.

A fourth contention is that even if the Presidency did not work reasonably well, it would be naïve to suppose that any fundamental revision of the executive office could be introduced at this late stage in the nation's development. The federal government has been in existence for nearly two hundred years. Far from crumbling through the decades it has been hardened by the cement of tradition. The nation is deeply averse to revolutionary political change. National as well as world history appears to bear out the practical wisdom of the almost unanimous popular feeling that any change should be gradual and organic, and that it should be introduced by the men who have to live with it at either end of Pennsylvania Avenue, not by theoreticians. Indeed, most of the academics who specialize in American government would agree with the conclusion of one of their number, Professor Arthur N. Holcombe, in his *Our More Perfect Union* (1950), that "there is no rational basis for loss of confidence in the soundness and practical utility of the . . . great principles upon which the government . . . was established . . . . They have given character to a system of government under which the men in power have been able to control one another without losing their ability to control the governed."[4] Professor Clinton Rossiter, who like Holcombe would like to see improvements here and there, thinks that "Leave your Presidency alone!" is a sensible slogan. Constitution-mongering strikes him as a futile occupation in the American context: "The Presidency is in a state of sturdy health, and that is why we should not give way easily to despair over the defects men of too much zeal or too little courage claim to discover in it." Sir Denis Brogan, a distinguished British student of American politics, felt in 1933 that it was necessary to give the President a more compelling mandate for action, and that a national referendum on each major issue would be the way to accomplish it. But he wrote at a time of exceptional crisis and would presumably not now wish to be held to an idea of half a lifetime ago.

By the same token, yesterday's actual reforms are often today's nuisances. The presidential primary seemed in the Progressive Era a valuable means of enabling ordinary citizens to voice their sentiments on possible candidates. By the 1950's, however, Clinton Rossiter wrote:

I am inclined to agree with Adlai Stevenson, who speaks to

the point with matchless authority, that the presidential primaries are a "very, very questionable method of selecting presidential candidates." Rather than have a handful of primaries spread carelessly over the months between February and July, it might be the wiser and even more democratic thing to have none at all. . . . It is, by almost any standard, one of the failures of our political system.[5]

Reforms are apt to misfire. The primary contest may, for instance, give an unfair advantage to a candidate with abundant personal resources over one of limited means. This could well be said of John F. Kennedy in relation to Hubert Humphrey in 1960. Though he might have defeated Senator Humphrey in the primaries in any case, Kennedy and his family left nothing to chance. So, all in all, the presidential primary was a mixed blessing. In 1972 the string of primary contests was so long it began to seem ridiculous. Reformers now started to propose abolishing presidential primaries or limiting them all to a few specific dates—perhaps three, perhaps only one.

Wisdom aside, self-interest is too much involved to encourage reform. Any executive-legislative regrouping would entail a loss of prerogative for someone or for some institution. Why *should* the President, or the independent regulatory commissions, or the Senate, or the House of Representatives, acquiesce in a diminution of their authority? The 1946 mid-term elections confronted President Truman with a Republican majority in both houses of Congress. Senator Fulbright, predicting with some justification that the result would be legislative stalemate, suggested a way out and subsequently tried to implement the idea as a constitutional amendment. His solution was that Truman should appoint a Republican as his Secretary of State and then immediately resign from the Presidency. There was at the time no Vice-President; the Secretary of State was next in succession for the Chief Executiveship. If Truman had been ready to oblige, the country would have had a unified Republican government—at any rate in theory. Not surprisingly, Truman ignored Fulbright's plan; nor did Congress or the public show any sympathy for the senator's eccentric panacea.

A fifth answer to criticisms of the *status quo* is that modest revisions are actually being made, or are likely to be made in the

"Lyndon Johnson says you're out of date!"

This cartoon appeared in the Baltimore Sun *in 1965, after Lyndon Johnson said that the Electoral College was outmoded.*

not-distant future. Thus, no significant group defends the operations of the Electoral College, or rather insists that it operates faultlessly. In 1950 there was considerable support in the Senate for a proposed constitutional amendment that would have abolished the Electoral College altogether. The electoral vote would remain but would be divided within each state according to the proportion of the popular votes cast in the state for presidential candidates. As Rossiter explains, "If the electors are puppets, they are useless; if they are free agents, as several Southern states have tried to make them, they are 175 years out of date."[6] It is uncertain whether the nation will go the whole way in this direction, if only because the present method of giving the entire electoral vote in a state to the leading candidate pleases the Northern urban interest, which would therefore be reluctant to yield. But in 1969 the House of Representatives did pass a bill to do away with the Electoral College and replace it with a direct popular vote. The candidate securing a majority of the votes, if this is more than 40 per cent of the total number cast, would become President. If no candidate secured 40 per cent there would be a runoff contest between the two leading contenders.[7]

One of the acknowledged weaknesses of the mechanism for electing a President prescribed in the Twelfth Amendment is the hiatus between the casting of popular votes early in November and the formal meeting of the Electoral College six weeks later. Chaos could result if the winning candidate were to die in the interval. There is a further lame-duck gap between the meeting of the college and the inauguration of the President. This transitional period has however been shortened, by the Twentieth Amendment (1933), from early March to January 20. A good deal of thought has been given to the problem of a smooth transition from one administration to the next. Abraham Lincoln, contemplating the likelihood of defeat in the 1864 election, decided that if necessary in order to avert a breakdown of the war effort he would resign immediately after the election and yield the office to his rival, General McClellan. In 1916 Woodrow Wilson, faced with a comparable defeat at the hands of the Republican candidate, Charles Evans Hughes, might have resigned (and persuaded his Vice-President to do the same) after nominating Hughes as Secretary of State. After the Democrats lost the 1920 presidential election, his former Secretary of State William Jennings Bryan publicly urged Wilson—an exhausted invalid—to follow the precedure in handing over the White House to the victorious Warren G. Harding. No doubt these precedents, if precedents they were, were known to Senator Fulbright when he requested President Truman to abdicate.

Future Presidents will probably be no more compliant than Truman was. But the expedient is there in case of emergency. Certainly Truman is likely to be the last Vice-President to be hurled into the Presidency without previous introduction. Since the 1950's, Vice-Presidents have been kept informed of vital business. In Truman's own words:

It is a terrible handicap for a new President to step into office and be confronted with a whole series of critical decisions without adequate briefing. I thought it was an omission in our political tradition that a retiring President did not make it his business to facilitate the transfer of the Government to his successor.[8]

President Hoover did make the attempt to consult with President-elect Roosevelt at the end of 1932, though he met with a rather evasive response. Truman was determined to avoid the errors of the past. In 1952 he arranged for the Democratic candidate, Adlai Stevenson, to attend Cabinet meetings and be regularly briefed on foreign affairs by the CIA. He offered the same facilities to the Republican contender, Dwight D. Eisenhower. Although Eisenhower declined the invitation (wishing like F.D.R. to preserve his freedom of maneuver), he readily accepted a postelection invitation to name deputies who would liaise with the outgoing administration on budgetary and other matters. President Eisenhower in turn provided facilities for President-elect Kennedy at the end of 1960, and met him twice at the White House. The value of such transitional discussions is limited, especially when the change of President is also a change of party. The incoming Chief Executive is understandably anxious not to appear to be in accord with an administration whose programs he has just finished denouncing. Nevertheless, on major foreign issues and on certain domestic matters a degree of bipartisan continuity has now been established. The expenses of the transition have been provided for by Congress, in answer to a request by President Kennedy. It seems certain that such behind-the-scenes collaboration will increase, within modest limits.

The sudden deaths of F.D.R. in 1945 and of John F. Kennedy in 1963, and the illnesses suffered by Eisenhower and Lyndon Johnson, have directed attention to the related problems of presidential succession and disability. Succession at the time of Roosevelt's death was governed by an act of 1886 that designated the Secretary of State as next in succession after the President and Vice-President, followed in order of seniority by the remaining Cabinet secretaries: Treasury, War, and so on. It was pointed out in 1945 that Truman, a former Vice-President, would be able to designate his own immediate successor through his right of Cabinet appointment. This seemed undemocratic, to Congress and to Truman himself. After some complex skirmishing between the parties and the two houses

The public was kept well informed of President Eisenhower's progress during the medical crises of his two terms. Here the commandant of Walter Reed Hospital, General Leonard Heaton, explains the President's ileitis operation of 1956 to a group of reporters.

of Congress, the 1947 Succession Act interposed the Speaker of the House and then the president pro tempore of the Senate between the Vice-President and the Secretary of State. The Speaker was given preference because he was thought to be a person who had already won the suffrage of his own congressional district and that of a majority of the 435 members of the House of Representatives. But the change illustrates the dangers of well-meant reforms. Doubt has been expressed as to whether either figure can be deemed to be an "Officer of the United States." Constitutionally, if the verdict were negative, he might not be entitled to assume the full powers of the Presidency for the whole of the term remaining to him.[9] If President Johnson had died in the year between the assassination of Kennedy and his own election, he would have been followed in the White House by Speaker John W. McCormack, a man of seventy-two who, whatever his other qualifications, was hardly presidential timber. Both the Speaker and the Senate president pro tempore are likely to be elderly figures chosen through seniority and for party loyalty rather than because they are outstanding. Statisticians offer the consolation that the death of both President and Vice-President in the same administration should not occur more than once in every 840 years.

Presidential disability has been treated with remarkable nonchalance until recently. It has been more than merely an academic question, with four Presidents assassinated, four others (William H. Harrison, Taylor, Harding, Franklin D. Roosevelt) dying in office, and several seriously incapacitated through illness. Garfield, after being shot by Guiteau, lingered for two and a half months during which there was virtually no President. Woodrow Wilson, having suffered a paralytic stroke in September, 1919, was a bedridden invalid for most of the eighteen months remaining to him in the White House. The malevolent Senator Albert Fall of New Mexico was not far wrong when he told colleagues in the Foreign Relations Committee, "We have petticoat Government! Mrs. Wilson is President!"[10] The President was paralyzed: so was the United States government. President Eisenhower's three illnesses, although he made excellent recoveries, were further indications that it was time to clarify the problem. In his second annual message, of January, 1965, Lyndon Johnson referred to the need for "laws to insure the necessary continuity of leadership should the President become disabled or die." In the summer of that year Congress approved a new constitutional provision (which became law as the Twenty-Fifth Amendment in February, 1967). The amendment entitles the President to nominate a Vice-President whenever the office is vacant, subject to confirmation by Congress. The Vice-President is empowered to assume the duties of President whenever the President declares himself disabled, or is ruled by the Vice-President and a respectable contingent of department heads or other prominent persons to be so disabled. The amendment likewise describes the procedure by which a President may resume his office.

Harry Truman, much exercised by these important considerations, also had views on the employability of ex-Presidents. He was impressed by Herbert Hoover's wide knowledge of men and affairs, as revealed in the work of the Hoover Commission. Ex-Presidents were the people, he said, "to whom we must look for help and counsel. That is why we must not shelve or thrust into obscurity men with such unique experience." (Former Vice-Presidents and Speakers might also, he thought, have a useful part to play.) Truman therefore suggested that "Congress should pass enabling legislation designating former Presidents of the United States as *Free Members of the Congress,*" with the right to attend sessions or committees of either house, though with no voting right. Part of his proposal has found sanction. In 1963 three Democratic Senators and one Republican sponsored a proposal that ex-Presidents should be regarded as "Senators-at-Large" and given seats in the Senate. Their scheme was reduced to an agreement—reached a few weeks before the death of President Kennedy—to change the rules of the Senate in order to permit ex-Presidents to address the Senate, which could be arranged by notifying the presiding officer.[11]

Other connections, previously mentioned, have developed between Congress and Presidents in office. A Chief Executive who takes sufficient trouble can maintain close contact with the legislative branch. If the tendency continues to nominate for the Presidency men who are serving or have served in Congress—Truman, Nixon, Kennedy, Goldwater, Johnson—it is possible that prior service in Congress, especially in the Upper House, might become an unwritten law of the American federal system.

It is arguable too that Congress may undergo changes that will improve the quality of membership, or at least make members more representative of public opinion. If the electoral-college method of choosing a President gives an advantage to large, urban states, each with its big bloc of electoral votes, election to Congress has been overweighted in the interests of small states and of rural areas. Though empowered to compel reapportionment so as to take account of shifts in population, the House was too influenced by parochialism to take action. There was, for example, no redistricting in Illinois from 1901 until 1948. When changes were finally made, the Chicago area contained over half the population of the state but had only ten representatives as against fifteen for the rest of Illinois. A special message to Congress from President Truman in January, 1951, requesting legislation to provide for more equal districts, failed to accomplish reorganization. Similar proposals again failed to pass Congress in 1959. The 1960 census disclosed glaring discrepancies. One congressional district in Michigan, which included part of Detroit, had 803,000 inhabitants, while another in the rural north of the state had only 177,000.

The Supreme Court stepped into the breach with a series of decisions involving federal as well as state legislative districting. In *Wesberry v. Saunders* (1964) the Court ruled that although "it may not be possible to draw congressional districts with mathematical precision," this was "no excuse for ignoring our Constitution's plain objective of making equal representation for equal numbers of people the fundamental goal for the House of Representatives."[12] If the winds of change keep blowing, the Congress of A.D. 2000 could be a considerably more alert body with less of a standpat and more of a contemporary outlook upon the nation's needs.

Signs of change are apparent also in the conception of the kind of person who may be eligible for the Presidency. Until the 1960's a set of implicit assumptions narrowed the field of candidates. Professor Sidney Hyman, writing in 1959, listed "Nine Tests for the Presidential Hopeful":

1. The rule of political talent and experience.
2. The rule of governors.
3. The rule of big swing states.
4. The rule of northern monopoly.
5. The rule of multiple economic interests.
6. The rule of happy family life.
7. The rule of the small town.
8. The rule of English stock.
9. The rule of Protestantism.[13]

He did not suggest that all nine would have to be or could all be fulfilled by major party nominees. General Eisenhower was not politically experienced in federal or state government, and like Herbert Hoover was not of English but of Swiss-German ancestry. Adlai Stevenson might seem to have broken Rule 6 by having been divorced. Nevertheless, political astrologers did once pay keen attention to such considerations. As Clinton Rossiter notes, they were also hesitant to back aspirants who were conspicuously wealthy.

It is too early to suggest that the rules will alter fundamentally. Yet the events of the 1960's have made some of them appear relatively unimportant. John F. Kennedy was not the first Roman Catholic candidate, or the first to exemplify a big-city background. Al Smith, nominated by the Democrats in 1928, was a Catholic and a New Yorker. But unlike Smith, Kennedy won; and he was wealthy, as were the two contenders in 1964, Lyndon Johnson and

No first lady was more active, more admired, or more controversial than Eleanor Roosevelt, seen here with a group of soldiers on the White House lawn early in World War II.

Barry Goldwater. Johnson, a Texan, was acutely aware that Southerners were virtually ineligible for nomination; the desire to break out of the "Texas trap" seems to have had much to do with his acceptance of the vice-presidential nomination in 1960. Only accident made him the Democratic nominee for President in 1964. Again, however, he won. And in the same year the Republicans chose a candidate of Jewish descent.

None of the things feared of Presidents who were members of minorities or special-interest groups happened. General Eisenhower displayed no bias towards the armed services; indeed, he was probably more impartial than F.D.R., who had manifested a boyish attachment to the United States Navy that sometimes irked Army spokesmen. Kennedy revealed so little evidence of his personal religious affiliation that some Catholic leaders accused him of prejudice *against* the Roman faith. Lyndon Johnson suppressed all trace of Southernness in securing the passage of the Civil Rights Act of 1964. In fact, it would seem that a minority-group President, out of caution, is even more likely than a centrally placed incumbent to behave with judicial impartiality.

The rules will not disappear altogether. Candidates will still have to be widely acceptable and have a power base from which to operate. Wealth has become an asset rather than a liability, for the grace, the cosmopolitan style, and the aura of success it confers upon a candidate, as well as its obvious other advantages. If present tendencies persist, divorce may be no great handicap, but a candidate will benefit from having an attractive and intelligent wife, and preferably some young children. Franklin Roosevelt gained greatly from the activities of his wife, Eleanor. The personalities of Mrs. Kennedy and Mrs. Johnson have reinforced the expectation that the First Lady will contribute appreciably to life in the White House and in the nation.

In a speech to Chicago Populists, Henry Demarest Lloyd prophesied in 1894: "Women will vote, and some day we will have a woman president when the people come in."[14] Women do have the vote, but the odds are that they will prefer to give it to a male candidate. To the extent that women are a minority group, they are however powerful and respected. They have achieved recognition, somewhat as Catholicism and Judaism have achieved a near-parity of *official* esteem in American public discourse. It is quite likely that the major parties will in future as often as not deliberately pick someone Catholic or Jewish as a vice-presidential candidate, and conceivable that they will one day choose a woman for the second office. The chances would be increased if women had as prominent a place in public life as they have in some other countries. The same may be said of black Americans. They are not likely to be nominated for the Presidency before A.D. 2000. But a Negro Vice-President could conceivably be put forward, especially by the Republican party; and the chances will be much increased if and when there are several black senators and governors to choose from. Nor would the relegation of such minority figures to the vice-presidential office be evidence of discrimination. In the next generation the majority of Americans will after all continue to be white Protestants. There is nothing sinister in expecting the man in the White House to be drawn from the majority, so long as there is what might be called a sporting chance of his being replaced by a minority deputy.

The fluidity of the situation has stimulated some speculation in fiction. Eugene Burdick's novel *The 480* (1964) has as its hero a

Hoping to attract the support of women and black Americans, Congresswoman Shirley Chisholm of New York campaigned for the Democratic presidential nomination in 1972.

tough, capable American engineer, vaguely reminiscent of the young Hoover, who becomes a presidential candidate. His beautiful Eurasian wife, who was interned by the Japanese during the war, survived imprisonment only by prostituting herself to the camp guards. When his enemies discover this they attempt to use the information as blackmail, to compel him to abandon his campaign. At the end of the novel Thatch, the hero, has made the surrender announcement to spare his wife's feelings; but she tells him he must stick to his guns. An equally equivocal theme is that of Irving Wallace's *The Man* (1965). Wallace imagines a United States not very different from that of the 1960's. The Vice-President dies of a heart attack. Named president pro tempore of the Senate is Douglass Dilman, a Negro, selected for the empty honor in an effort to appease the Negro protest movement. The President of the United States and the Speaker of the House of Representatives travel overseas to attend a Russo-American conference. They are both accidentally killed. According to the succession law of 1947, Dilman is now President. Next in line would be the Secretary of State, an intimate friend to the dead President. But for the 1947 act he would now be President. He wants the office. Dilman's enemies scheme against him and finally impeach him. Having demonstrated his integrity of character, and his capacity to handle a series of domestic and foreign crises, Dilman is acquitted. When popular novelists begin to exploit a theme, we may be sure the general public is almost ready to accept the theme as actuality.

Criticisms of the Presidency, to repeat, are usually met with the answers that the office is adversely affected by difficulties, national and international, which would exist in any case; that although executive government has unsatisfactory features in other countries, in America it works well; that even if it did not, sweeping reforms are neither feasible nor desirable; and that modest improvements are being gradually introduced.

This would be a cheerful note to end on. But if we really wish to look into the future it is necessary to envisage pessimistic as well as optimistic developments. The American political system is certainly resistant to change. An admirer would say that it is "organic," "stable," and so on. A critic would say that, being so highly conservative, it is anachronistic, and dangerously so in a world of constant, rapid change. The problem of the Presidency is thus dual. The federal government needs to strike a balance between executive efficiency and legislative democracy. It also needs to be stable —effective, systematic, dignified, respected—and yet to be swiftly and sensitively responsive to an unstable national and international situation. Most reform proposals focus upon the first of these aspects—the balance between executive and legislature, efficiency and democracy, authority and consent. In doing so they naturally tend to the verdict that matters are as satisfactory as could be expected.

If, however, we emphasize the second aspect, matters look less rosy. The governmental conservatism of Americans is then seen not as a cause for congratulation but for alarm. The parade, year after year and decade after decade, of reform recommendations appears as a proof not of the simple-mindedness of professors of political science but of the real need for reform. After all, it is not only academics who want improvement: Presidents and congressmen often share their views. President Johnson has been described as "a political animal"—a man steeped in practical politics, which is defined as "the art of the possible." We ought to be able to assume that he was not shadow-boxing in his annual message of January, 1966, when he asked that the term of representatives be extended to four years. The change had already been advocated by many political scientists. Books such as Senator Joseph S. Clark's *The Senate Establishment* (1963) and Representative Richard Bolling's *House Out of Order* (1965) provide firsthand evidence of the grave defects of Congress. The Presidency also has come in for some fairly basic criticism from liberals for almost the first time this century. One does not have to be a Jeremiah to maintain that the United States faces the 1970's with impaired confidence in its economic, social, and political soundness. Radicals such as Abbie Hoffman (*Steal This Book,* 1971) preach ribald, contemptuous rebellion. Nonradical critics such as Andrew Hacker (*The End of the American Era,* 1970) and Gary Wills (*Nixon Agonistes,* 1970) likewise suggest the moral bankruptcy of the United States. The mood of national alarm and despondency may turn out to be temporary, especially if Nixon succeeds in withdrawing from Vietnam and reaching an entente with China. If not, and if the uneasiness increases, the nation might seek far-reaching remedies that would be bound to embrace the federal government.

It is therefore worthwhile to take a look at some of the analyses of the Presidency made in the past quarter of a century, and to reflect on which of them might before A.D. 2000 be actually applied.

The majority are concerned with strengthening the Presidency by bringing it into harmony with Congress. Most of these proposals look towards a parliamentary system roughly akin to that of Britain. Thomas K. Finletter, for example, in his book *Can Representative Government Do The Job?* (1945), recommends lengthening the term of the President and of representatives, and providing for a dissolution of the federal government, to be followed by a national election, if the President and Congress fail to reach agreement on crucial elements of the legislative program. Professor C. Perry Paterson, in *Presidential Government in the United States: The Unwritten Constitution* (1947) advocates the creation of a Cabinet executive council chosen by Congress from among its membership and headed by a prime minister. Though the President would

Even back in 1928, when this cartoon first appeared, the Presidency seemed too big a job for any single man to fill.

continue to supervise administration and to initiate policy, his views would be mediated by the Cabinet, which would be directly responsible to Congress. Professor Charles S. Hyneman (*Bureaucracy in a Democracy*, 1950) suggests the establishment of a central advisory council selected by the President from among congressional leaders of his own party, certain executive officials, and a few prominent citizens from outside the government.

Professor Herman Finer's *The Presidency: Crisis and Regeneration* (1960) would go much further. Finer feels that "the gravest problem of America's government is the inadequacy of the President, any President." He would have all executive heads and members of Congress elected simultaneously for a four-year period. The executive branch would consist of a President and eleven Vice-Presidents (all eligible for re-election), who must all be past or present members of Congress. The President and his eleven associates would function as the Cabinet. The Cabinet would have collective responsibility for executive decisions, whereas the existing principle, says Finer, is that "the President alone is responsible and that his convictions are to dominate the administration; but if he lacks the personal qualities, and has not the kind of assistance such a man would need, he will surely fail." Congress under his scheme would cease to be "a congeries of local interests" and become a truly national legislative body, with the majority party genuinely in accord with the party executive as represented by the presidential dozen.[15]

Professor James MacGregor Burns, in *The Deadlock of Democracy: Four-Party Politics in America* (1963), focuses upon the weaknesses of the party structure. He believes that "to see the pattern of power at the national level only in terms of two parties is grossly misleading. The balance between one or two parties . . . and over a thousand personal parties (one for the President, one for each member of Congress, and at least one for each rival for the office, in both parties) . . . has been struck not in a two-party system but in what is essentially a four-party system. The four national parties are the presidential Democrats, the presidential Republicans, the congressional Democrats, and the congressional Republicans." The presidential party of the defeated candidate is woefully weak. The party aligned with the victorious candidate is powerful within limits, and especially dominant for the brief period of the national party convention. The congressional parties have very different outlooks from the presidential parties:

> An executive impulse and a legislative tendency confront each other at every junction. The executive impetus is to combine legislative and administrative power, to coordinate functions, to exert control from the top. . . . The legislative instinct is pluralistic. Congress and the state legislatures, under the control of the legislative parties, seek to fragmentize the executive, by means of individual or committee influence over administrative units, or control of specific budgetary items, or through holding the executive's power to reorganize. . . . This bewildering array of countervailing and over-lapping powers compels American political leaders to piece together a new patchwork of party fragments, factional chieftains, congressional votes, constitutional usage, and bureaucratic officials in order to put through each major new program. . . .[16]

Burns's hope is for an integration of the four-party system into a two-party system. He would end the seniority principle in Congress and seek to place effective control in the hands of leaders and whips elected for ability instead of availability. He proposes constitutional amendments that include a four-year term for representatives and a repeal of the Twenty-second Amendment (the anti-third-term rule). Though no President would be indiscreet enough to ask for the repeal of the Twenty-second Amendment, the four-year term for the House has obvious attractions for the House and for the executive branch. Hence Lyndon Johnson's words to Congress in January, 1966:

> . . . I strongly urge an amendment to provide a 4-year term for Members of the House of Representatives which should not begin before 1972.
> The present 2-year term requires most Members of Congress to divert enormous energies to an almost constant process of campaigning. . . . Today, too, the work of government is far more complex than in our early years, requiring more time to . . . master the technical tasks of legislating. And a longer term will serve to attract more men of the highest quality to political life. The Nation, the principle of democracy, and I think each congressional district, will all be better served by a 4-year term for Members of the House, and I urge your swift action.[17]

The aim of such proposals is to overcome the excessive separation and mutual institutional antipathy of President and Congress. Some would argue that only Constitution-worship blinds us from perceiving that the Founding Fathers erred from the start. Less radical critics maintain that while the delegates at Philadelphia built extremely well, they could not be expected to devise a government suitable to the needs of a totally different society. And some of the ancillary devices they did not contemplate—the party system, the Cabinet—have likewise grown hoary and require revision.

Another contention is that the framers of the Constitution failed to conceive clearly what the role of the Executive should be, and that this basic ambiguity has persisted ever since. Some of the implications have been discussed in Chapter 5. Our own thinking on the matter has been shaped by twentieth-century experience, which has then been read back into American history by scholars. The lessons presented to us in the dominant liberal style may be summed up as follows:

—"Strong" Presidents (Washington, Jefferson, Jackson, Lincoln, Wilson, the two Roosevelts) have promoted national unity, prosperity, democracy, and responsibility.

—"Weak" Presidents, (Pierce, Buchanan, Grant, Harding, Coolidge) have, no doubt unwittingly, countenanced national disunity, economic selfishness, social conservatism, and irresponsibility in both domestic and international affairs.

—The "Whig" conception of the Presidency is therefore unsound.

—A "strong" Executive must be a single Executive: schemes for a plural Executive threaten a reversion to the parlous days of America under the Articles of Confederation.

—Historically, the legislative branch has sought to weaken executive authority through jealous obstructionism.

—The executive branch is the hero of the story of American federal government: Congress is the villain.

An example of this attitude is revealed in Emmet Hughes's account of the Eisenhower administration, *The Ordeal of Power.* Asked on one occasion to characterize his great predecessor Abraham Lincoln, Eisenhower praised his "modesty and his humility," and cited with approval Lincoln's meek remark, after he had been slighted by his Army commander: "I would hold General McClellan's horse if he would just win the Union a victory." For John F. Kennedy, Hughes points out, "the Civil War President excited a wholly different image." Kennedy, as President-elect, cited Lincoln's instruction to his Cabinet, when he had decided to issue the Emancipation Proclamation: "I have gathered you together to hear what I have written down. I do not wish your advice about the main matter—that I have determined for myself." For Eisenhower, says Hughes, the supreme symbol of the Presidency "would be not the sword of authority but the shield of rectitude."[18]

Which of the two attitudes to the Presidency is preferable? Our knowledge of American history and our present expectations make us opt for authority. We note that "strong" Presidents have often been less popular during their own time than "weak" Presidents. Lincoln was execrated, Harding applauded. The judgment that counts is that of posterity; and posterity is probably right. If decisive leadership had been lacking in the White House, the United States might have become another sort of country, an inferior one, pervaded by the spirit of what Emerson termed "village littleness." This is the spirit that infuses much of the activities (or inactivities) of Congress at its narrowest. It is expressed in such legislative slogans as "To get along, go along" (go along, that is, with the rest) and "Vote your district first."[19]

But there are drawbacks to the display of presidential authority. "Strong" Presidents run a far greater risk of assassination, or at least of provoking unhealthily fierce opposition on Capitol Hill and among the population. Most of this opposition is irrational and deplorable; yet not all. One French writer, Amaury de Riencourt, claims in *The Coming Caesars* (1957) that "it is in Washington and not in London, Paris, or Berlin that the Caesars of the future will arise. It will not be the result of conspiracy, revolution, or personal ambition. It will be the end result of an instinctive revolution in which we are all taking part like somnambulists." His thesis is that "as society becomes more equalitarian, it tends increasingly to concentrate absolute power in the hands of one single man." He believes that Americans are particularly disposed to accept the rule of a Caesar: "They always tend to personalize issues, and in every walk of life they look up to the 'boss'." And "wars are the main harbingers of Caesarism. . . . In grave emergencies, leadership can never be collective, and we are now living in an age of permanent emergency. Presidential power in America has grown as American power and expansion have grown, one developing within the other." Today, says Riencourt, "one man is directly in command . . . of more than half the world's economic and technical power." He wields an imperial prerogative as vast as that of the Roman emperors in the ancient world. The chief factor, this writer emphasizes, is psychological, not political or strategic. "It is the growing 'father complex' . . . the willingness to follow . . . the leadership of one man. It is the growing distrust of parliaments, congresses, and all other representative assemblies, the growing impatience of Western public opinion at their irresponsibility, lack of foresight, sluggishness, indecisiveness."[20]

Riencourt's thesis consists of half-truths and need not be accepted as a convincing prophecy. Even in the executive branch government proceeds largely by committee bureaucracy. In Congress the committee structure is almost the whole of the story; and some, though mercifully not all, of the committee chairmen wield power not by taking action but by impeding it. The federal government combines dashes of Caesarism with quantities of inertia. The worst threats to American democracy have not come from Presidents but from demagogues of the McCarthyite variety. Yet there is a measure of truth in Riencourt's account. The situation is dangerous not so much because of absolute executive prerogative but rather because it seems erratic, discontinuous, capricious—even in the hands of a first-rate President, and still more in the hands of a mediocrity. One source of danger lies in the American *fear* of Caesarism, a fear that might induce self-appointed patriots to re-enact the tale of Brutus and Cassius (or, in the American context, of John Wilkes Booth or Lee Harvey Oswald). Another undoubted danger is that a President might, with the best of intentions, commit the world to catastrophe. This, the work of a moment, could be called Caesarism, but the word is not really applicable: such a possibility is the supreme nightmare of our time, for which the past provides no parallel. The danger that comes nearest to Caesarism in Riencourt's use of the expression is of involvements on the Vietnam scale. Their most terrifying feature, however, is not that they may be wished upon the American people by a despotic President, but that public and congressional sentiment may accord so readily with that of the Executive, and even impel him towards belligerence.

There are other elements of presidential power to which less apocalyptic commentators have addressed themselves. Finer, Edward S. Corwin, and a few other mid-twentieth-century scholars have tried to go beyond the simple reassurances of the "liberal" idea that the stronger the President the better. They maintain, as did Henry C. Lockwood in *The Abolition of the Presidency* (1884), that the American public is too ready to entrust the Presidency to men whom they have endowed with superhuman attributes. Along with Woodrow Wilson in his first book, *Congressional Government* (1885), they hold that no one man is capable of reaching wise decisions on all the issues that confront him. "A quiet voice in the White House is all to the good," the historian Eugene Genovese said of Nixon's first year in office. Another historian of radical bent, Stuart Hughes, agreed: "The President's quiet, reassuring tone, the way he's tried to de-escalate political passions, is a welcome change over the frenetic style of LBJ."[21] Finer's plan to institute more effective party government is also a plan to diminish the power of the single Executive. He would ask why we applaud an anecdote which shows that Lincoln took no notice of the Cabinet on a matter of such prime importance as the Emancipation Proclama-

During the 1944 campaign, Socialist candidate Norman Thomas complained that President Roosevelt's "nonpolitical" speeches were really campaign oratory.

tion. He would no doubt agree with General Eisenhower's view that the prestige of the Presidency is based upon rectitude as well as authority. It is often said that the Presidency is an "ennobling" office, whose occupants behave with a dignity one might not have expected in all cases, to judge from their previous conduct. Chester Arthur's new-found probity may have owed more to his sense of the elevation of the office than of its powerfulness. The Whig conception cannot be entirely dismissed. Presidents who descend from their eminence to give legislative or partisan battle may bring the Chief Magistracy into disrepute; or so such Presidents as Taft and Eisenhower have honestly believed.

The modern President, says Finer, is given more advice than he can assimilate, and responsibility for more decisions than any single person ought to possess. His veto power is excessive. Worse still, he is "chosen by the most ramshackle, the flimsiest method ever used to select the supreme leader of a nation." The electorate seeks impossible qualities in its candidates, and admires them for the wrong reasons:

> Because the President is expected to play a dual role, demi-god and astute politician, the voters disregard the immensity of the responsibilities with which he is vested as they seek to assess his charm. . . . The combination of the two roles, national symbol and political leader, is too emollient, too disarming, to be healthy for the mightiest democracy in the world.

Corwin, too, feels that "presidential power has been at times dangerously *personalized*," in making leadership subject to the particular personality of whatever President happened to be selected by "our haphazard method."[22]

The Presidency has undoubtedly suffered from the cult of personality, a cult intensified by the inordinate publicity given to the Chief Executive and his entourage. This in itself is no proof of Caesarism. American popular interest in the occupants of the White House is about on the same level as British interest in the occupants of Buckingham Palace, which is of course not the center of power in British government. But the American appetite for gossipy information about the President, harmless in itself, is related to a disquieting exaggeration. There is a tinge of hysteria in the quadrennial excitements that attend each new administration. It is somehow expected that with each new President the office will undergo a transfiguration. The limitations of his role are temporarily forgotten. The immensely complex federal structure is dramatized and personalized as if it consisted of only one man, remotely attended by shadowy subordinates and challenged only by a rabble of scheming congressmen. Ex-Presidents minister to the tendency by carrying off the papers of their administration, mingling these with personal files, and establishing them in separate archives. The most grandiose to date, "Lyndon's Pyramid" to house thirty-one million documents relating to the political saga of Lyndon B. Johnson, was opened at the University of Texas. A mausoleum in marble, it had cost $16,800,000. Under the Presidential Library Law of 1955 the operating costs of such archives ($720,-000 a year in this case) will be borne by the federal government.

The inevitable letdown is the more painful in consequence. Having failed to be all things to all men, the President is condemned both for weakness and for arrogance. Paradoxically, the more contemporary Presidents respond to the public demand for a dazzlingly attractive executive image the less likely they are to attempt genuinely forceful leadership. The trenchancy of Harry Truman's utterances comes as a shock when we read them again, having grown accustomed to the judicious, affable words of his successors. The American people, vaguely worried by the vast potential of executive power, is also vaguely disappointed that power is so blandly wielded. If the worst has not befallen the nation, neither has the best. Yet such apparent mildness ought to be comforting. Corwin, in the 1957 revision of his influential book *The President: Office and Powers,* was induced to modify previous strictures. He had called for an executive council; by 1957 an "institutionalized Presidency" seemed to be actually coming into existence, with the President "merged with—albeit not submerged in—a cluster of institutions designed to base government . . . on conference and consensus." Perhaps Dwight D. Eisenhower was more sensible than some of his critics realized; perhaps a dose of modesty and humility was not such a bad prescription for the White House of the future.

Corwin ended his 1957 edition by refusing to predict whether the "institutionalized Presidency" would become permanent. In our changing world, he said, "the incalculables are too many and too formidable."[23] Since 1957 the liberal view of the Presidency has wavered somewhat. It is still maintained that the country needs first-rate men on the Lincoln-Roosevelt model. On the other hand worries have been expressed of the kind that dominated liberal discussion in the last third of the nineteenth century—misgivings that in our century have until now mainly been confined to conservatives. They are more or less epitomized in Herman Finer's analysis. Underlying them is the reflection that no one man should be either expected or empowered to bear so much responsibility. It has been assumed as a liberal axiom that presidential authority would always be benevolent. Now, pondering the awful dilemmas of the contemporary scene, Americans of good will wonder if a President might not also use his authority in harmful ways, and if so how he could be stopped. They talk again of the brake instead of the accelerator—not surprisingly in view of the velocity of modern events. Disability amendments are all very well. But a close reading of Gene Smith's excellent account of Woodrow Wilson's illness, *When The Cheering Stopped* (1964), suggests that the national government could still be paralyzed or warped if something went wrong at the top. Suppose the President were not physically incapacitated, nor certifiably insane, but became by degrees increasingly jaded, increasingly exasperated by Congress, increasingly apathetic? Or increasingly truculent? He could of course be removed at the next election, but possibly not until serious harm had been done. *It hasn't happened yet* is only a partial consolation: *it can't happen here* is a foolish form of optimism.

Which, then, is the better guide to future developments, optimism or pessimism? If the latter, there is still a dilemma. Reformers offer two propositions: that the federal government, Congress in particular, is slow, overcautious, and negative; and that the President is given too much isolated authority. How is it possible to remedy the one without making the other worse? The optimistic recommendation for the future of the Presidency is that things should be left alone because things are fine. The pessimistic conclusion may be that things should be left alone because changes might aggravate an already unsatisfactory situation. The wisdom of optimism might, via a different route, arrive at the same result as the wisdom of pessimism.

All books about the Presidency, including this one, conclude inconclusively. It can never be an ideal institution. So far, in comparison with chief executives in other countries, it has been a success. Its future success, like its past development, involves many factors—among them the fundamental decency of American life, the devotion of many thousands of executive officials, and the labors of Congress when the legislators are in a constructive, responsible mood. This is not to say that Capitol Hill is constructive only when agreeing with the White House: the important thing is that Congress should agree or disagree for the right reasons, not through narrow partisanship or excessive touchiness.

Reform *is* needed. Whatever the precise shape, thoughtful citizens seem to concur that one need is for a closer link between the executive and legislative branches. Congress has perhaps unfairly been dubbed the "sapless branch." The metaphor may be extended. Can there be a tree that has branches but no trunk? Which is the trunk of the federal government? Should there not be less reference to *separation* of powers and more to *association* of powers?[24]

Another need is for improved counseling within the executive, and if possible a more visible sharing of executive responsibility. If this change were to lead to a slight diminution of the Presidency it would be beneficial for everyone. The presidential limelight is too glaring and makes other governmental figures too penumbral. There is much to be said for a House of Representatives elected quadrennially; a good deal of the present Capitol-White House animosity is futile. Cabinet-type reforms are a more dubious proposition, though worth aiming at. Professor Finer, for instance, would empower the President to dismiss any of his eleven vice-presidential Cabinet members, having also provided that they should be popularly elected to their office. One can imagine the constitutional wrangling that would arise from this feature alone in his scheme.

Among the shrewdest comments on attitudes to government is Alexis de Tocqueville's:

> I have come across men of letters who have written history without taking part in public affairs, and politicians who have concerned themselves with producing events without thinking about them. I have observed that the first are always inclined to find general causes, whereas the second, living in the midst of disconnected daily facts, are prone to imagine that everything is attributable to particular incidents, and that the wires they pull are the same as those that move the world. It is to be presumed that both are equally deceived.[25]

Neither the reformers nor the pragmatists are entirely correct in their estimates of the Presidency; neither liberals nor conservatives, neither optimists nor pessimists. Changes are worth introducing; the climate of reform is valuable. But the most ingenious of paper reforms amount to nothing, and so do the most sophisticated attempts at consensus, voter satisfaction, and the like, unless certain broad considerations are given weight. Although the Presidency has altered profoundly since George Washington's day, these considerations are still true; they are truisms, but they can bear reiterating.

A conundrum remains. Harry Truman said that the President must wear six hats: those of commander-in-chief, party leader, legislative leader, director of foreign policy, chief of the executive branch, and head of state. The last of these, the most obviously "monarchical," conflicts with most of the others in being general, ceremonial, symbolic, and nonpartisan. There is a danger—indeed almost a certainty, in the light of past experience—that a President who emphasizes rectitude at the expense of authority will be ineffectual. A purveyor of moralistic platitudes, lacking in guile and personal ambition, could well diminish the office in all the wrong ways. We may ponder the remark attributed to Senator Eugene McCarthy, an unsuccessful contender for the Democratic nomination in 1968, that if elected to the Presidency he might be satisfied with a single term: "If you can't do it in four [years], you can't do it in eight." The later stages of McCarthy's attractively unorthodox campaign suggested that, though intelligent and unusually candid, he was deficient in that brand of indispensable political gumption that is not to be confused with mere timeserving and gladhanding.[26]

Still, Andrew Jackson initially advocated a single term for the Presidency. And Senator McCarthy is symptomatic of a widespread new conviction that the United States must revivify its politics, and must engage in a limited withdrawal—from acting as world policeman (world burglar, in the eyes of enemies), from extreme assertions of certain kinds of centralized federal authority, and therefore also from excessive assertions of presidential authority. Significantly, men as dissimilar as Barry Goldwater and Eugene McCarthy, while for somewhat different reasons, concur in the view that there has been too much encroachment by the executive on the legislative branch. McCarthy, moreover, along with a growing number of liberal Americans, perceives that it is just not feasible to expect one man in the White House to go it alone. The Presidency, he added to his comment on a single term, is not "an incarnation of all the hopes and aspirations of the country. I think that is to put too much of a burden on the office."

The basic dilemma will persist. As executive head the President cannot be a withdrawn, austere figure. He is bound to continue to be selected from among the ranks of active politicians, not from clergymen or academics or professional lawyers. He will always be overworked. He will probably always be expected to give up time to ceremonial duties, such as entertaining foreign heads of state, and to making himself accessible to sections of the public. Thus on one average day (March 25, 1971) President Nixon, apart from attending a meeting of the National Security Council and a session with thirteen Negro congressmen, "met informally with student body presidents of five colleges" and with his wife "acted as host of a reception for publishers of small newspapers."[27] Yet large numbers of Americans, at least temporarily, are tired of conventional politics and politicians. The enthusiasm for McCarthy in 1968, the contempt expressed for the Republican nominee Richard M. Nixon and his Democratic opponent Hubert H. Humphrey, and the disgust aroused by the spectacles of the two party conventions at Miami and Chicago, reveal this clearly. Americans by the millions are suspicious of old slogans, especially when seemingly employed to justify delusions of imperial grandeur. Protracted world crisis may prevent American disengagements of any kind, foreign or domestic. But if there should be a relaxation, it is quite possible that among other things American liberals might pursue their recent tendency to adopt formerly conservative positions. They might make a concerted effort to reduce the theoretical, folklore dimensions of presidential power in the interests of a more compact yet more genuinely effective office. In any case, they will probably insist that they want as President a man who is capable of transcending his administrative functions; who is imaginative and humane; who in some sense can be the nation's conscience, its chief teacher, a seer rather than a Caesar. Such figures are rare. The obligation of the United States is to nurture some, within the apparently unpromising field of national politics, and to bring forward at least one in every four years.

The nation gets the President it deserves. An America obsessed with popularity ratings will pick a Chief Executive because he looks the part—and get a man who in turn is obsessed with popularity ratings. A brutal nation merits a brutal Executive. A complacent, mindless country ought not to be surprised if the White House is occupied by a garrulous bore. Only if Americans seek and value excellence in their own lives have they the right to hope for an excellent President.

Epilogue

AFTER the first version of this book was finished there came the 1968 presidential campaign, culminating in the victory of the Republican candidate, Richard M. Nixon, and the subsequent early stages of his administration — Cabinet making, the inaugural ceremony, the first press conferences, the first sketchings of foreign policy.

Commentators in 1968 tended to assume that all previous guidelines were abolished. Journalists as well as cartoonists, apparently feeling that truth was stranger than fiction, presented the candidates as puppets or grotesques or demons. The novelist Norman Mailer indeed seemed to catch the "truth" of Nixon and Hubert Humphrey, Eugene McCarthy and George Wallace (in his *Miami and the Siege of Chicago*) with more lurid verisimilitude than the soberer professional journalists. If any figure was more derided than Nixon or Humphrey, it was the reigning demon, President Lyndon Johnson.

With the actual election the American mood started to alter. Humphrey's critics began grudgingly to admit that whatever his previous equivocations, the desire for votes was bringing out the best in the man. His last-minute fight, viewed merely as a fight or endurance contest, was now seen to display a certain gallantry. That he should have narrowed the gap in the popular vote to a mere third of a million votes—despite his late start, his unheroic image to the young who had gone out for McCarthy, and the inroads made by Wallace—was a solace to the Democratic party, whose tattered banner he bore. Perhaps all was not lost. Perhaps 1972 would bring a Democrat back into the White House. As for Wallace, there was relief on two grounds. First, he had not done as well as the polls predicted. Though not far short of ten million people voted for him, they constituted less than 14 per cent of the total, against an anticipated 20 per cent. Second, as a result his third-party candidacy had not disrupted the usual electoral mechanism. There was no deadlock, no resort to the House of Representatives. The threat no doubt remained; Wallace was still very much alive and kicking, and a small reminder of the potential weakness of the system came with the formal meeting of the Electoral College, when an elector from North Carolina who was pledged to Nixon insisted on shifting his vote to Wallace. But such isolated gestures of independence had occurred before. The mechanism could apparently take them in its stride.

Other traditional harmonies likewise seemed to assert their effect. The good-loser convention was handsomely displayed by Hubert Humphrey. President Johnson bowed out gracefully, possibly consoled by the knowledge that his and Mrs. Johnson's memoirs—eagerly bid for by publishers—would bring in well over a million dollars. In the closing days of his administration Congress voted increases that would raise the annual salary of future Presidents to $200,000, and that of the Vice-President to $67,500. Almost overnight Johnson's unpopularity dwindled. The spotlight had shifted away from him. A group of historians, invited to rate his performance, differed in their estimates but gave him generally high marks for his domestic program, as if the Great Society had been praiseworthy after all. One or two of the group went so far as to bracket him with Lincoln and the Roosevelts.

In this characteristic honeymoon phase Richard Nixon also lost, if only temporarily, his own aura of second-rate villainy. There took place, in the term of one journalist, a "demonsterization" of Nixon. His inaugural address was cordially received; so were some of his executive appointments. His visit to Europe at the end of

President Nixon and China's Premier Chou En-lai cross a bridge in Peking's Forbidden City during Nixon's precedent shattering visit to China in 1972.

February, 1969, was almost a triumph; he obviously struck the European heads of state as shrewd and well-briefed.

A few analysts, having reversed themselves, were probably glad for once that public memory is so short. A few, trying once more to cast the political horoscope, sought larger significances. Mailer's *Miami and the Siege of Chicago* discerned a revival of America's old but still powerful and sizable Wasp (white Anglo-Saxon Protestant) culture. Others, following this line in sundry magazine articles, agreed, though they defined "Waspishness" with a breadth that would have been unthinkable a generation ago. A Wasp, it now appeared, could easily be a Catholic: hardly anyone seemed to notice that Humphrey's popular running mate Governor Edmund Muskie was a Catholic, and his Polish origins counted against him no more than did the Greek origins of Nixon's Vice-President, Spiro Agnew. Efforts to trace major new patterns failed to convince, since the circumstances of 1968 were so peculiar, and since the presidential contest is so much a matter of personality. Thus, it was suggested that Nixon represented a victory of the West over the East, in line with the nation's westward trend. But would Nixon have defeated Lyndon Johnson without the Vietnam imbroglio, or Robert Kennedy if Kennedy had not been assassinated? And could one say that Nixon symbolized any broad political shift toward Republicanism when he faced Democratic majorities in both houses of Congress?

It was tempting therefore to argue that in perspective, the presidential crisis of 1968–69 would fall into shape. There had been crises before. Nothing likely to happen in the future, including the quite swift end of Nixon's honeymoon era, would be unprecedented. The probable survival of the Electoral College could be placed in this context. At the time of the election, in November, 1968, four fifths of the nation was reported to favor electoral reform. In both houses of Congress committee hearings were arranged, to discuss a constitutional amendment that would provide for the direct popular election of the President and Vice-President. Yet inertia, and the prospect of resistance from sundry groups, were immediately evident. "Even with the closeness of the last election," a congressman remarked, "you're already hearing people say: 'It worked last time and we got a President.'" A New England elector said: "It's an antiquated process, but I feel the Founding Fathers gave it a lot of thought. . . . The tradition is nice."[1] In September, 1970, the Senate at length refused to commit itself to the scheme for direct popular election that had already passed the House of Representatives.

Two factors seemed however to be different. World instability in all its manifestations showed no sign of abatement in 1969–70. On such a scale the inauguration of a new President was of little or no significance. Second, there were indications that Richard Nixon recognized the need to make the Presidency a less conspicuously activist office. This modest conception lay within the recent Republican memory: it had been the mark of every Republican President from Harding to Eisenhower. But now it was also a liberal, reformist goal. A colloquium led by Rexford Tugwell, at the lively Center for the Study of Democratic Institutions in Santa Barbara, California, was rewriting the American Constitution. Among their proposals were a single six-year term for Presidents; the confining of presidential authority mainly to defense and foreign policy; and the creation of a new executive branch, with two Vice-Presidents, to handle domestic affairs. "This means," they said, "the President loses much of his power as a legislator. But he gains stature as a statesman and leader." Their report was too sweeping to have much chance of being implemented (it would among other things abolish the existing states and replace them with a dozen or so regional areas, or "republics").[2] The recommendations were in some ways curiously reminiscent of the Articles of Confederation of the 1780's. But the document testified to the widespread conviction, in 1969, that the Presidency was not a satisfactory office. In changing the office to meet present-day problems—problems of devolution, de-escalation, de-emphasis— the reformers might well find themselves repeating things that had been said long ago. Agreement as to the exact desirable scope of the Presidency has never been unanimous: that has been a main theme of this book. The initial tactics of Richard Nixon—the prominence given to executive officers, his deliberatedly circumspect style— indicated that he and his advisers might have come to the conclusion that the United States ought to think again about the advantages of the Whig view of the Presidency.

Yet the subsequent progress of the Nixon administration showed how complex and contrary the situation was. His first appointment was an assistant to liaise with Congress. But his relations with Congress gradually deteriorated, in large part—it was said—because of his personal remoteness and secretiveness, and because of his tendency to solicit votes in Congress too blatantly on behalf of ill-chosen administration measures. Nixon undertook to devolve authority wherever feasible. But he showed scant consideration for his Cabinet as a whole, and got rid of the one or two executive heads who showed a disposition to think for themselves. He allowed far more prominence to his Vice-President than had been usual. But Agnew's brash attacks on television, the press, and on radical youth divided the country and puzzled presidential commentators. Did he represent Nixon? If so, it seemed highly unwise of the President to be so truculently conservative. Was he acting on his own initiative? Then it seemed the President was allowing far too much prominence to his deputy. There was similar uneasiness at Nixon's evident dependence on the companionship and advice—almost invariably bad advice—of his former law partner, Attorney General Mitchell. To hostile observers, whose number steadily grew in 1970–71, Nixon appeared to have no consistent conception of the duties of his office, but to veer with circumstance and the state of the opinion polls between delusions of grandeur and "low-profile" inactivity. His professionalism often seemed too close to partisan politics, as when he threw himself into the support of candidates of his own presumed persuasion in the 1970 mid-term elections.

In all this, it must be said, public expectation was equally contrary. There was good reason to complain that Nixon created distrust by certain acts and statements: candor might have served him far better than equivocation. But his critics did not always recognize how intractable the Vietnam problem was, or how limited his room for maneuver. His most spectacular move, persuading Communist China to let him visit Peking, was an undoubted coup, which might win him the 1972 election. Yet it perhaps represented the limit of what a President could do: make one isolated gesture, not fundamentally different from the summitry favored by President Eisenhower—and a gesture not capable in itself of transforming the world scene. Perhaps significantly, Rexford Tugwell's new Constitution, as finally revised in 1970, called for a more powerful and less politically vulnerable Chief Executive, to hold office for a single term of nine years (though removable by a 60 per cent referendum after three years), backed by a permanent Senate on the lines of the House of Lords. There would be some twenty "republics" in the final Tugwell scheme, instead of the present fifty states; but in this new federal structure the authority of the federal Executive would be paramount. After much cogitation the Tugwell group returns to the conventional propositions of the Roosevelt era: "We live in an almost continuous state of emergency and the saying is quite true that crises belong to the Executive" (Tugwell in *The New York Times,* October 3, 1970). For at least one experienced observer we are back where we started a generation ago, indeed nearly two hundred years ago: the ball is in the presidential court. As with tennis, the only certainty is that it will not remain long in either court.

Appendixes

Presidential Elections, 1789-1968

Successful candidates are capitalized. Candidates receiving less than 1 per cent of the popular vote are not included; hence the percentage of popular vote for any given election year may not total 100.

Before the passage of the Twelfth Amendment in 1804, the Electoral College voted for two presidential candidates; the runner-up became Vice-President.

Year	No. of states	Candidates	Parties*	Pop. vote	Elec. vote	% of pop. vote
1789	11	GEORGE WASHINGTON	NPD		69	
		John Adams			34	
		Minor Candidates			35	
1792	15	GEORGE WASHINGTON	NPD		132	
		John Adams			77	
		George Clinton			50	
		Minor Candidates			5	
1796	16	JOHN ADAMS	F		71	
		Thomas Jefferson	D-R		68	
		Thomas Pinckney	F		59	
		Aaron Burr	D-R		30	
		Minor Candidates			48	

*The following abbreviations have been used for political parties:
NPD: *No party designations*   F: *Federalist*   D-R: *Democratic-Republican*
I-R: *Independent-Republican*   D: *Democratic*   NR: *National Republican*
Am: *Antimasonic*   W: *Whig*   L: *Liberty*   FS: *Free Soil*   A: *American*
R: *Republican*   CU: *Constitutional Union*   G-L: *Greenback-Labor*   PR: *Prohibition*   UL: *Union Labor*   Pe: *People's*   Po: *Populist*   S: *Socialist*
Pr: *Progressive*   F-L: *Farmer-Labor*   U: *Union*   SR: *States' Rights*   AI: *American Independent*

Year	No. of states	Candidates	Parties*	Pop. vote	Elec. vote	% of pop. vote
1800	16	THOMAS JEFFERSON	D-R		73	
		Aaron Burr	D-R		73	
		John Adams	F		65	
		Charles C. Pinckney	F		64	
		John Jay	F		1	
1804	17	THOMAS JEFFERSON	D-R		162	
		Charles C. Pinckney	F		14	
1808	17	JAMES MADISON	D-R		122	
		Charles C. Pinckney	F		47	
		George Clinton	D-R		6	
1812	18	JAMES MADISON	D-R		128	
		DeWitt Clinton	F		89	
1816	19	JAMES MONROE	D-R		183	
		Rufus King	F		34	
1820	24	JAMES MONROE	D-R		231	
		John Quincy Adams	I-R		1	
1824	24	JOHN QUINCY ADAMS	D-R	108,740	84	30.5
		Andrew Jackson	D-R	153,544	99	43.1
		William H. Crawford	D-R	46,618	41	13.1
		Henry Clay	D-R	47,136	37	13.2
1828	24	ANDREW JACKSON	D	647,286	178	56.0
		John Quincy Adams	NR	508,064	83	44.0
1832	24	ANDREW JACKSON	D	687,502	219	55.0
		Henry Clay	NR	530,189	49	42.4
		William Wirt	Am	33,108	7	2.6
		John Floyd	NR		11	
1836	26	MARTIN VAN BUREN	D	756,483	170	50.9
		William H. Harrison	W		73	
		William L. White	W	} 739,795	26	} 49.1
		Daniel Webster	W		14	
		W. P. Mangum	W		11	
1840	26	WILLIAM H. HARRISON	W	1,274,624	234	53.1
		Martin Van Buren	D	1,127,781	60	46.9
1844	26	JAMES K. POLK	D	1,338,464	170	49.6
		Henry Clay	W	1,300,097	105	48.1
		James G. Birney	L	62,300		2.3

Year	No. of states	Candidates	Parties*	Pop. vote	Elec. vote	% of pop. vote
1848	30	ZACHARY TAYLOR	W	1,360,967	163	47.4
		Lewis Cass	D	1,222,342	127	42.5
		Martin Van Buren	FS	291,263		10.1
1852	31	FRANKLIN PIERCE	D	1,601,117	254	50.9
		Winfield Scott	W	1,385,453	42	44.1
		John P. Hale	FS	155,825		5.0
1856	31	JAMES BUCHANAN	D	1,832,955	174	45.3
		John C. Frémont	R	1,339,932	114	33.1
		Millard Fillmore	A	871,731	8	21.6
1860	33	ABRAHAM LINCOLN	R	1,865,593	180	39.8
		Stephen A. Douglas	D	1,382,713	12	29.5
		John C. Breckinridge	D	848,356	72	18.1
		John Bell	CU	592,906	39	12.6
1864	36	ABRAHAM LINCOLN	R	2,206,938	212	55.0
		George B. McClellan	D	1,803,787	21	45.0
1868	37	ULYSSES S. GRANT	R	3,013,421	214	52.7
		Horatio Seymour	D	2,706,829	80	47.3
1872	37	ULYSSES S. GRANT	R	3,596,745	286	55.6
		Horace Greeley[1]	D	2,843,446		43.9
1876	38	RUTHERFORD B. HAYES	R	4,036,572	185	48.0
		Samuel J. Tilden	D	4,284,020	184	51.0
1880	38	JAMES A. GARFIELD	R	4,453,295	214	48.5
		Winfield S. Hancock	D	4,414,082	155	48.1
		James B. Weaver	G-L	308,578		3.4
1884	38	GROVER CLEVELAND	D	4,879,507	219	48.5
		James G. Blaine	R	4,850,293	182	48.2
		Benjamin F. Butler	G-L	175,270		1.8
		John P. St. John	PR	150,369		1.5
1888	38	BENJAMIN HARRISON	R	5,447,129	233	47.9
		Grover Cleveland	D	5,537,857	168	48.6
		Clinton B. Fisk	PR	249,506		2.2
		Anson J. Streeter	UL	146,935		1.3
1892	44	GROVER CLEVELAND	D	5,555,426	277	46.1
		Benjamin Harrison	R	5,182,690	145	43.0
		James B. Weaver	Pe	1,029,846	22	8.5
		John Bidwell	PR	246,133		2.2

[1] Greeley died shortly after the election; the electors supporting him then divided their votes among minor candidates.

Year	No. of states	Candidates	Parties*	Pop. vote	Elec. vote	% of pop. vote
1896	45	WILLIAM MCKINLEY	R	7,102,246	271	51.1
		William J. Bryan	D	6,492,559	176	47.7
1900	45	WILLIAM MCKINLEY	R	7,218,491	292	51.7
		William J. Bryan	D;Po	6,356,734	155	45.5
		John C. Wooley	PR	208,914		1.5
1904	45	THEODORE ROOSEVELT	R	7,628,461	336	57.4
		Alton B. Parker	D	5,084,223	140	37.6
		Eugene V. Debs	S	402,283		3.0
		Silas C. Swallow	PR	258,536		1.9
1908	46	WILLIAM H. TAFT	R	7,675,320	321	51.6
		William J. Bryan	D	6,412,294	162	43.1
		Eugene V. Debs	S	420,793		2.8
		Eugene W. Chafin	PR	253,840		1.7
1912	48	WOODROW WILSON	D	6,296,547	435	41.9
		Theodore Roosevelt	Pr	4,118,571	88	27.4
		William H. Taft	R	3,486,720	8	23.2
		Eugene V. Debs	S	900,672		6.0
		Eugene W. Chafin	PR	206,275		1.4
1916	48	WOODROW WILSON	D	9,127,695	277	49.4
		Charles E. Hughes	R	8,533,507	254	46.2
		A. L. Benson	S	585,113		3.2
		J. Frank Hanly	PR	220.506		1.2
1920	48	WARREN G. HARDING	R	16,143,407	404	60.4
		James N. Cox	D	9,130,328	127	34.2
		Eugene V. Debs	S	919,799		3.4
		P. P. Christensen	F-L	265,411		1.0
1924	48	CALVIN COOLIDGE	R	15,718,211	382	54.0
		John W. Davis	D	8,385,283	136	28.8
		Robert M. La Follette	Pr	4,831,289	13	16.6
1928	48	HERBERT C. HOOVER	R	21,391,993	444	58.2
		Alfred E. Smith	D	15,016,169	87	40.9
1932	48	FRANKLIN D. ROOSEVELT	D	22,809,638	472	57.4
		Herbert C. Hoover	R	15,758,901	59	39.7
		Norman Thomas	S	881,951		2.2
1936	48	FRANKLIN D. ROOSEVELT	D	27,752,869	523	60.8
		Alfred M. Landon	R	16,674,665	8	36.5
		William Lemke	U	882,479		1.9
1940	48	FRANKLIN D. ROOSEVELT	D	27,307,819	449	54.8
		Wendell L. Willkie	R	22,321,018	82	44.8

Year	No. of states	Candidates	Parties*	Pop. vote	Elec. vote	% of pop. vote
1944	48	FRANKLIN D. ROOSEVELT	D	25,606,685	432	53.5
		Thomas E. Dewey	R	22,014,745	99	46.0
1948	48	HARRY S. TRUMAN	D	24,105,812	303	49.5
		Thomas E. Dewey	R	21,970,065	189	45.1
		J. Strom Thurmond	SR	1,169,063	39	2.4
		Henry A. Wallace	Pr	1,157,172		2.4
1952	48	DWIGHT D. EISENHOWER	R	33,936,234	442	55.1
		Adlai E. Stevenson	D	27,314,992	89	44.4
1956	48	DWIGHT D. EISENHOWER	R	35,590,472	457	57.6
		Adlai E. Stevenson	D	26,022,752	73	42.1
1960	50	JOHN F. KENNEDY	D	34,227,096	303	49.9
		Richard M. Nixon	R	34,108,546	219	49.6
1964	50	LYNDON B. JOHNSON	D	43,126,506	486	61.1
		Barry M. Goldwater	R	27,176,799	52	38.5
1968	50	RICHARD M. NIXON	R	31,785,480	301	43.5
		Hubert H. Humphrey	D	31,275,165	191	42.9
		George Wallace	AI	9,906,473	46	13.5

The American Party System

1. BIBLIOGRAPHY

Among the most thoughtful general studies are James M. Burns, *The Deadlock of Democracy: Four-Party Politics in America* (Englewood Cliffs, N.J., Prentice-Hall, 1963); William N. Chambers, *Political Parties in a New Nation* (New York, Oxford University Press, 1963); William N. Chambers and Walter D. Burnham, eds., *The American Party Systems* (New York, Oxford University Press, 1967); Robert A. Goldwin, ed., *Political Parties, U.S.A.* (Chicago, Rand McNally, 1964); V. O. Key, Jr., *Politics, Parties, and Pressure Groups* (5th edn., New York, Crowell, 1964); Seymour M. Lipset, *Political Man* (Garden City, N.Y., Doubleday, 1960), Part III; and Clinton Rossiter, *Parties and Politics in America* (Ithaca, N.Y., Cornell University Press, 1960; repr. New York, Signet, 1964). On the major parties see William N. Chambers, *The Democrats,* 1789–1964 (New York and London, Van Nostrand, 1964), a historical essay with readings, and Charles O. Jones, *The Republican Party in American Politics* (New York, Macmillan; London, Collier-Macmillan, 1965). Minor parties are covered in William B. Hesseltine, *Third-Party Movements in the United States* (New York and London, Van Nostrand, 1962) and Fred A. Shannon, *American Farmers' Movements* (Van Nostrand, 1957). Most of these books contain bibliographies.

2. ESSENTIAL FEATURES

Political parties began to emerge in the early days of American independence. Their structure was often complex, and was much influenced by local issues and personalities. But they have shown a tendency to form into two major groupings or coalitions; to operate at local, state, and national level; and to organize themselves in a competition for control of the federal government—executive and legislative. Neither major party has exhibited any clear, coherent "ideology," except possibly for short periods. Some observers have doubted whether they deserve to be regarded as parties in the European sense. James Bryce, writing in the 1880's, said that they were like two identical bottles bearing different labels. In defense, it is argued that

(a) two-party systems provide greater stability than multiparty ones; and that their existence (confined at the present time to about 15 of the world's 130 or more nation-states) is itself a measure of the stability of a nation;

(b) the multiplicity of interests to be accommodated within each party make it impossible that either should represent a distinct viewpoint;

(c) sharply divided parties are not necessarily desirable: the closeness of the two parties means that each may plausibly outbid the other and

that each is genuinely capable of providing a national government;
(d) within these limits, there has in fact been a division of sentiment between the two parties ever since the 1790's, with one leaning toward the "haves" and the other toward the "have-nots."

3. A MAJOR-PARTY GENEALOGY

Some historians see a continuous evolution along these lines:

HAVES		HAVE-NOTS
Federalists	c. 1787	Antifederalists
Federalists	c. 1790–1820	Democratic-Republicans
National Republicans	1820's	Republicans
Whigs (1834–56)		Democrats (1828)
Republicans (1856–)		

According to this picture, the first party division was aroused by debates over the Constitution of 1787. The Federalists represented property interests and favored 'centralized government. The Antifederalists represented less privileged groups and were suspicious of centralized government. The alignment persisted, despite the disintegration of the Federalist party in the first two decades of the nineteenth century. Their heirs, the Whig party, likewise catered to the well-to-do, and recommended national economic policies. Their Jeffersonian and Jacksonian opponents continued to defend the conception of a nation of "little men" and semiautonomous states. Arguments over slavery confused the pattern; they shattered the Whig party and gave rise to a new Republican party, which though again a coalition was in conception hostile to the institution of slavery. In consequence, the early Republican party was a *sectional* party, drawing its strength from the North; and though the Democrats remained alive as a Union party during the Civil War of 1861–65, the South then began its long, sterile political tradition as a one-party region dominated by the Democrats. Hence the peculiar spectacle in our times of a Democratic party combining a conservative, race-supremacist Southern wing and a relatively liberal Northern urban wing. Nevertheless, during the generation after the Civil War the Republicans ceased to be a reforming party and instead served—as they do today—as the party of the businessman. (Like the Democrats, the Republicans have conservative and liberal wings, divided somewhat sectionally, with the conservative wing Western and the liberal one Eastern.)

The confusion of the story is thus sometimes explained as more apparent than real. It may be seen as a confusion of nomenclature rather than of viewpoint. The two major parties have each at different periods laid claim to the label of "Republican." The designation of "Democrat" was originally meant to be pejorative, at a time when democracy was usually defined as an unworkable system. Attributed by rival politicians, it was at length assumed as a badge of honor. The Whigs adopted their party name to free themselves from the "Federalist" stigma, and to seek credit for libertarian impulses.

4. THIRD PARTIES

This term is something of a misnomer. There have sometimes been fourth and even fifth or sixth parties. They have included Prohibition as well as more overtly political movements. Their variety is suggested by the following selective chronology:

1826–32	Antimasonic party
1830–36	Liberty (antislavery) party
1848	Free Soil (antislavery) party
1852–56	Native American, or "Know-Nothing," party
1854–56	Republican party (originally a challenger to the two established parties, Whigs and Democrats)
1872	Labor Reform party
	Prohibition party (still notionally in existence)
1876–84	Independent, or "Greenback," party
1892–96	People's, or Populist, party
1897	Socialist party (still more or less in being)
1912–16	National Progressive party
1924	La Follette Progressives
1948	Henry Wallace Progressives
	States' Rights Democrats, or "Dixiecrats"
1968	George Wallace Independents

Only the Republicans have moved from minor to major party status. Minor parties have managed in certain elections (1844, 1848, 1884, 1912) to secure enough votes to affect the choice of a presidential candidate. But this has not been a deliberate or usually a desirable result for them. Third parties have emerged at times when the two-party structure was in disrepair because of sectional and other divisions. Sometimes they have seemed eccentric improvisations, notably in the case of the Antimasons, whose rationale was narrow and negative (opposition to privilege, opposition to Andrew Jackson).

5. A SEQUENCE OF PARTY SYSTEMS

Unsympathetic accounts of American party politics make the situation sound so daftly corrupt that they fail to explain its real advantages. Sympathetic accounts are apt, on the other hand, to exaggerate continuity, to read back into the past a symmetry not always actually present, and to minimize the discontents that give rise to third parties. Thus, an alternative interpretation might concede the recurrent tendency to develop a two-party alignment, but stress the discontinuity of party evolution. Why, when the first party systems were created, did the two-party pattern disappear from about 1815 to 1825? Was there really a stable two-party alignment between then and the end of the Civil War? Is there not too great a gulf between the "ideology" politics of, say, the American Socialist party and the "consensus," horse-trading politics of the major parties?

A more satisfactory way of looking at the matter is to see American political history as falling into a series of phases, each with its special features (see Chambers and Burnham, *American Party Systems*, Chs. 1 and 10):

(a) 1789–1815: *the experimental system* (parties organized from the center outward; heavily influenced by foreign-policy controversy; survival of deference habits; reluctance of the "ins" to recognize the legitimacy of opposition by the "outs");

(b) 1828–54: *the democratizing system* (parties organized at all levels, focusing on the capture of the Presidency; creation of national nominating conventions; disappearance of deference habits; widened voter participation; professionalization of political activity);

(c) 1860–93: *The Civil War system* (sectional politics; dominance of the Republican party; abandonment of reform ethic by both major parties; creation of the "Solid South" as Democratic stronghold);

(d) 1894–1932: *the industrialist system* (continuing sectionalism—Democratic bastion in the South, Republican in the Northeast, debatable ground in the West from which abortive protest movements develop; general Republican domination, weakening in the 1920's);

(e) 1932–?: *the New Deal system* (Democrats replace Republicans as the "normal" majority party, through forging of alliance between South and urban Northeast; possible change of direction after 1950, as South becomes less solid, the nationwide suburban vote tends to go Republican, and party divisions appear less meaningful).

Other names and slightly different dates could be allotted to these systems. Note that there was a distinct hiatus from about 1815 to 1825 or 1828, and another during the 1850's. At almost every period of modulation to another system, third parties appear: the Antimasonic party before the establishment of the second system, the Know-Nothings and Republicans before the third, the Populists before the fourth. The 1932 election is perhaps an exception; but it should be remembered that the Socialist and Communist parties waged active presidential campaigns in that year and secured nearly a million popular votes in spite of the manifest disadvantages under which the two-party system placed them.

Presidential Election Costs

1. Two guides to this vexed question are Alexander Heard, *The Costs of Democracy* (Chapel Hill, University of North Carolina Press, 1960), and *Financing Presidential Campaigns,* Report of the President's Commission on Campaign Costs (Washington, D.C., Government Printing Office, 1962)—an inquiry instituted by President Kennedy, under the chairmanship of Professor Heard. There is an excellent condensed article, "Financing Presidential Campaigns," by Herbert E. Alexander, in Arthur M. Schlesinger, Jr., and Fred L. Israel, eds., *History of American Presidential Elections* (New York, Chelsea House and McGraw-Hill, 1971), IV, 3869–97.

2. The costs of presidential electioneering in the United States are impossible to estimate exactly; but they are gigantic and are increasing at an alarming rate. Money has long been a problem for aspirants not personally affluent and for the Democrats in relation to the Republicans. The Democratic candidate in 1896, William Jennings Bryan, was certainly at a disadvantage because his party lacked the resources available to his opponent William McKinley. Reform-minded candidates, such as Woodrow Wilson in 1912, run the embarrassment of having to raise funds from the very sources they may have been denouncing.[1] Minor-party campaigns are of course at a still greater disadvantage; only passionate conviction can draw contributions for a candidate who is a sure loser. But in the inflationary 1960's even this does not seem to have hampered all minor candidates: ex-Governor George Wallace of Alabama, drawing shamelessly upon the resources of his state for his nationwide 1968 campaign, also successfully adopted the fund-raising techniques long familiar to revivalist preachers in order to extract a mass of small donations from a multitude of followers.

The costs of presidential campaigning can only vaguely be estimated, partly because amounts are not always known, or declared, and partly because of the difficulty of distinguishing between what is spent on the actual presidential and vice-presidential candidates and what is spent for the party as a whole or upon gubernatorial, local, and congressional campaigns in a presidential election year. Nor is it possible to determine the exact amounts spent by *individual* candidates, in the primaries and in other campaigning before the party nominating conventions. There is, moreover, a great deal of unpaid voluntary labor. In addition to the party

---

[1] "Woodrow Wilson's initial needs were provided for by several well-heeled old Princeton friends. . . . Wilson's manager . . . excelled at collecting large sums from Wall Street contributors while simultaneously crying, whenever Wilson was attacked, that 'Wall Street' was behind the dastardly deed." Louis W. Koenig, *The Chief Executive* (New York, Harcourt, Brace and World, 1964), 37.

national committees, there are fifty *state* committees for each party, independent committees for each candidate, and sundry other *ad hoc* bodies such as cross-party committees (for example, to persuade Democratic votes to switch to the Republicans, or vice versa) and independent national committees.

For what the figures are worth, the President's 1962 commission estimated joint expenditure on presidential and vice-presidential candidates by the national committees of the two major parties as follows:

1952	$11.6 million
1956	$12.9 million
1960	$20 million

The commission estimated the total expenditure on all candidates in 1960 at $165 million to $175 million. A survey by the Citizens' Research Bureau (quoted in *The Times,* August 7, 1968) calculated the cost *per vote* in a presidential election year as:

1952	$0.18
1964	$0.41
1968	$0.50

(approximately; compare the costs of the British general election of 1966, which worked out at 9½ cents per vote. The actual American figure for 1968 seems to have been not 50 cents but 60 cents).

3. The basic difficulty, both in estimating and in restricting expenditure, is that it has not yet proved feasible to limit individual or corporate contributions. Many efforts have been made through national and state legislation. The best-known federal law is the Hatch Act (1939). The Hatch Act laid down that no person or organization may contribute more than $5,000, in any single year, to a political organization or to a presidential candidate. It also restricted each *political group* to an expenditure of not more than $3 *million* in any one presidential campaign. Though well-intentioned, the Hatch Act has proved almost meaningless:
(a) anyone may legally contribute to ostensibly different organizations, which, though going by different names, have in fact the same purpose;
(b) any *member of a family* may contribute up to $5,000 to each of these front organizations. A rich and enthusiastic partisan with several children may indulge himself lavishly, within the law;
(c) where the range of "political organizations" (national, state, independent, etc.) is so large, the upper limit of $3 million can be and is multiplied many times over.

4. The results could easily be seen, though not precisely calculated, in the 1968 contest. Dr. Herbert Alexander of the Citizens' Research Foundation

put the *preconvention* spending of all the assorted candidates at somewhere between $15 million and $21 million (television time, travel, staff salaries, opinion surveys, promotional literature, stickers, buttons, fancy hats, etc.). In an unsuccessful last-minute bid to gain the Republican nomination at the Miami convention, Governor Nelson Rockefeller of New York gave a party for 8,000 delegates and others whose cost was reckoned at $50,000. He and the successful candidate, Richard Nixon, vied with one another in producing daily convention newspapers, distributed free. It was assumed that Nixon and Rockefeller would each have laid out $3 million to $5 million in contesting the nomination, and that ex-Governor Wallace's campaign expenses up to the election would be in the region of $7 million. After the Miami convention the Republican national committee announced a budget of $20 million, of which $8 million would be allotted to television. In addition, of course, there is the enormous outlay incurred by the three principal television networks in covering the party conventions, and the cost of providing bodyguards for candidates (not to mention police and even the National Guard, to head off demonstrations). The defeated Democrats emerged from the 1968 campaign with a debt of $8 million.

5. *Reforms.* The Kennedy commission of 1962 tried to make realistic recommendations. It wished to abolish the theoretical *maximum* contributions, as unworkable. At the same time it aimed at prohibiting partisan block contributions by labor unions or by corporations. In order to encourage the truthful disclosure of what was being spent, and to achieve a larger number of modest contributions, it recommended that individual contributions to a particular *party* should be tax-deductable up to a total of $1,000.

Congress unfortunately showed only mild interest in these proposals and took no action on them. In 1970 Nixon vetoed a bill to limit political television advertising, with the dubious argument that it was wrong to single out one medium (even though it was by far the most expensive). He showed little enthusiasm for various other proposals that were scrutinized by a Senate subcommittee in March, 1971. These included free or reduced postage for candidates, and free air travel for presidential nominees.

Prospects for genuine reform seem poor. The process is expensive, and wastefully so. It grows ever more expensive with the professionalization of electioneering and the costliness of the media employed. Batteries of speech writers, public relations teams, advance men, and the like swell the bill prodigiously; so do chartered jets, and similar facilities for journalists. One apparently hopeful sign has been the readiness of the major parties to postpone their conventions by about a month, thus shortening the campaign season for party nominees. But this change has also the contrary effect of lengthening the preconvention campaigns of presidential aspirants. It also intensifies the strain upon the party national committees, which in the nature of American presidential politics have to be built overnight up from almost nothing. With only three months or so in which to fashion immense organizations, they are obliged to rely upon money to produce an instant result, instead of mounting careful, prudent, economical campaigns. So the posters get bigger, the advertisements more prolific, the television plugs longer and more and more spectacular.

Notes

FOREWORD

[1] e.g., Anthony Howard in *The Observer,* September 8, 1968.

[2] "The average vote for all minor party candidates taken together in presidential elections from 1828 through 1964 has only been 5.2 per cent of the total popular vote." William N. Chambers in Chambers and Burnham, eds., *The American Party Systems* (New York, Oxford University Press, 1967), p. 31.

[3] *Sketches of Public Characters,* pp. 112–13.

CHAPTER ONE

[1] Joseph E. Kallenbach, *The American Chief Executive* (New York, Harper & Row, 1966), pp. 39, 65–66; Kate M. Rowland, *Life and Correspondence of George Mason* (New York, Russell & Russell, 1964), II, pp. 388–89; James Monroe, *Writings,* S. M. Hamilton, ed. (1898), I, pp 336–37, quoted in Stuart G. Brown, *The First Republicans* (Syracuse University Press, 1954), pp. 31–32.

[2] *Papers of Thomas Jefferson,* Julian P. Boyd, ed. (Princeton University Press), XII, pp. 350–51, 439–40.

[3] On Clinton and Workman, see Morton Borden, ed., *The Antifederalist Papers* (East Lansing, Michigan State University Press, 1965), pp. 197–99, 212–13, and E. W. Spaulding, *His Excellency George Clinton* (New York, Macmillan Co., 1938), pp. 175–83.

[4] *The Federalist Papers,* Clinton Rossiter, ed. (New York, Mentor, 1961), pp. 312–14, 422–23.

[5] *Papers of Jefferson,* Boyd, ed., XIV, pp. 650–51; *Writings of Thomas Jefferson,* P. L. Ford, ed. (New York, Federal edn.), XI, p. 58 (letter to John Taylor, January 6, 1805).

[6] R. R. Palmer, *Age of Democratic Revolution, 1760–1800* (Princeton University Press, 1959), pp. 30–33. Louise Dunbar, *A Study of Monarchical Tendencies in the United States, 1776 to 1801* (University of Illinois Press, 1923), p. 18, gives examples of hostile American reactions to European absolutism: "Prussia . . . as absolute as any monarch of the East. . . ."

[7] Paine quotations from Leonard Kriegel, ed., *Essential Works of the Founding Fathers* (New York, Bantam, 1964), pp. 138, 147.

[8] *Writings,* Ford, ed., V, p. 256 (letter of January 30, 1787); *Papers,* Boyd,

ed., XII, pp. 356–57 (letter to William Stephens Smith of November 13, 1787).

[9] *Writings of George Washington,* J. C. Fitzpatrick, ed. (Washington, 1939), XXIX, p. 52 (letter dated November 5, 1786).

[10] John D. Feerick, *From Failing Hands: The Story of Presidential Succession* (New York, Fordham University Press, 1965), pp. 24–26, 36–37; Charles Thach, Jr., *The Creation of the Presidency, 1775–1789* (Baltimore, Johns Hopkins University Press, 1922), Chs. 2–3; Louis W. Koenig, *The Chief Executive* (New York, Harcourt, Brace, 1964), p. 17.

[11] Quoted in Koenig, *Chief Executive,* p. 27.

[12] On Hamilton's speech, Jay's query, and the Connecticut royalists see Koenig, *Chief Executive,* pp. 16, 20–22; Kallenbach, *American Chief Executive,* p. 34; and Dunbar, *Monarchical Tendencies,* pp. 74–75. On Nicola, see Dunbar, pp. 40–46, and Douglas Southall Freeman, *George Washington* (London, Eyre & Spottiswoode, 1952), V, pp. 416, 429–37. On Webster and Mrs. Warren see Louis Smith, *American Democracy and Military Power* (Chicago University Press, 1951), pp. 23–24.

[13] Butler quotation in Kallenbach, p. 35n., from which other material in this and succeeding paragraphs is drawn.

[14] Saul Padover, ed., *The Forging of American Federalism* (New York, Harper Torchbooks, 1965), pp. 199–200 (letter to Jefferson, October 24, 1787).

[15] Quoted in Koenig, *Chief Executive,* p. 20.

[16] Baron de Montesquieu, *The Spirit of the Laws,* Book XI, Ch. 6 "Of the Constitution of England" (London, G. Bell, 1906), p. 163.

[17] Padover, *Forging of Federalism,* p. 200 (letter of May 31, 1789).

[18] Edward S. Corwin, *The President: Office and Powers* (New York, New York University Press, 4th edn., 1957), p. 9; J. R. Pole, *Political Representation in England and the Origins of the American Republic* (London, Macmillan, 1966), pp. 369–70, 511–13. A Massachusetts Federalist, commenting with satisfaction on the re-election of Washington and John Adams in 1792, said that the "old King and his second" were in again (W. Bernhard, *Fisher Ames,* Chapel Hill, University of North Carolina Press, 1965, pp. 209–10). But when James Madison won re-election in 1812 a Federalist journal used the analogy accusingly. It printed a verse probably intended to be sung to a tune of the period:

> *The day is past–the election o'er*
> *And Madison is King once more!*

(Denis T. Lynch, *An Epoch and a Man,* New York, Liveright, 1929, p. 114).

[19] Franklin anecdote in Kallenbach, p. 566; Butler quotation in Max Farrand, ed., *Records of the Federal Convention* (4 vols., New Haven and London, Yale University Press, 1937, repr. 1966) III, p. 302 (letter of May 5, 1788, to Weedon Butler).

CHAPTER TWO

[1] Rexford G. Tugwell, *The Enlargement of the Presidency* (Garden City,

N.Y., Doubleday, 1960), p. 35; Washington letters to Lafayette, February 7, and April 28, 1788, in *Writings,* Fitzpatrick, ed., XXIX, pp. 409–11, 479–80.

² Hamilton letter (August 13, 1788) quoted in *Writings of George Washington,* XXX, pp. 66–67. Washington letters to Samuel Hanson (January 10, 1789), *Writings,* XXX, pp. 177–78 and John Armstrong (April 25, 1788), *Writings,* XXIX, pp. 464–65.

³ Quoted in Koenig, *Chief Executive,* p. 28.

⁴ Quoted in A. B. Tourtellot, ed., *The Presidents on the Presidency* (Garden City, N.Y., Doubleday, 1960), pp. 29–30.

⁵ Quoted in Marcus Cunliffe, *The Nation Takes Shape* (Chicago University Press, 1959), p. 174.

⁶ Marcus Cunliffe, *George Washington: Man and Monument* (New York, Mentor, 1960), p. 134; Wilfred E. Binkley, *The Man in the White House* (New York, Harper Colophon), p. 246. Note that Adams added in a tone of ironic detachment: "This is all nonsense to the philosopher, but so is all government whatever." G. Chinard, *Honest John Adams* (Boston, Little, Brown, 1933), p. 226. As late as the 1890's Americans writing to the President showed much uncertainty about how to address him. Quite often, perhaps out of a wish to flatter, they resorted to modes suggested and rejected a century earlier: "Sometimes he is addressed by letter writers as plain 'Mister,' sometimes as 'His Majesty,' or 'His Lordship,' and very often as 'His Excellency.'" Benjamin Harrison, *The Constitution and Administration of the United States of America* (London, David Nutt, 1897), p. 165.

⁷ On the Jackson tour see Binkley, p. 248, and John W. Ward, *Andrew Jackson: Symbol for an Age* (New York, Oxford University Press, 1955), pp. 115–17.

⁸ Packing-case anecdote cited by Stephen K. Bailey in D. B. Johnson and J. L. Walker, eds., *Dynamics of the American Presidency* (New York, Wiley, 1964), p. 239 n. 3. Other information from Leonard D. White, *The Federalists: A Study in Administrative History* (New York, Macmillan, 1948), pp. 31–37.

⁹ Richard F. Fenno, Jr., *The President's Cabinet* (New York, Vintage), pp. 17–18.

¹⁰ Fenno, p. 14.

¹¹ Quoted in Tourtellot, pp. 80–81.

¹² Fenno, p. 18.

¹³ Stephen G. Kurtz, *The Presidency of John Adams* (Philadelphia, University of Pennsylvania Press, 1957), pp. 266–69.

¹⁴ Jackson protest and Adams comment in Tourtellot, pp. 147–51, and Tugwell, p. 40.

¹⁵ "Mr. Adams chose wisely and according to his constitution, when, on leaving the Presidency, he went into Congress. He is no literary old gentleman, but a bruiser, and loves the *mêlée.*" Ralph Waldo Emerson, *Journals,* February 8, 1843.

¹⁶ Corwin, *The President,* pp. 177–84; Wilfred E. Binkley, *The President and Congress* (New York, Vintage, 1962), pp. 51–55.

[17] Citations chiefly from Lucius Wilmerding, Jr., *The Electoral College* (Boston, Beacon Press, 1964), Ch. 2.

[18] John to Abigail Adams, December 19, 1789, in Caroline T. Harnsberger, ed., *Treasury of Presidential Quotations* (Chicago, Follett Publishing Co., 1964), p. 326.

[19] Wilmerding, p. 40.

[20] Jefferson to Elbridge Gerry, May 13, 1797, in Harnsberger, p. 326.

[21] See comments by James M. Burns, *New York Times,* October 9, 1955, repr. in Johnson and Walker, *Dynamics,* pp. 261–62.

[22] Mrs. Adams' letter (November 21, 1800) cited in J. N. Kane, *Facts About the Presidents* (New York, Pocket Books, 1960), pp. 34–35; and see Page Smith, *John Adams* (Garden City, N.Y., Doubleday, 1962), pp. 1049–50.

[23] Ruth C. Silva, in Johnson and Walker, *Dynamics,* pp. 156–57.

[24] Tugwell, *Enlargement of the Presidency,* pp. 83–86.

[25] John Quincy Adams went through a bad patch as ex-President before he entered Congress. "My father seems . . . to be exceeding heavy," his son noted in June, 1830, "and not to take as well as he did the leisure with which he is perhaps overburdened. He thinks more of politics than I wish he did." *Diary of Charles Francis Adams,* Marc Friedlaender and L. H. Butterfield, eds. (Cambridge, Mass., Harvard University Press, 1968), III, p. 264.

[26] Quotations from D. C. Coyle, *Ordeal of the Presidency* (Washington, Public Affairs Press, 1960), pp. 19–20, and Harnsberger, p. 238.

CHAPTER THREE

[1] Quoted in W. E. Binkley, *The Man in the White House,* p. 65.

[2] Quoted in Robert and Leona Rienow, *The Lonely Quest: The Evolution of Presidential Leadership* (Chicago, Follett, 1966), p. 37.

[3] Henry Adams, *The Education of Henry Adams* (New York, Modern Library, 1931), p. 107. Henry was the grandson of President John Quincy Adams and the great-grandson of President John Adams.

[4] They are further discussed in Chapters 5 and 6.

[5] *The State of the Union Messages of the Presidents,* Fred L. Israel, ed. (New York, Chelsea House, 1966), I, pp. 63–64.

[6] Quoted in Corwin, *The President* (1957 edn.), pp. 319–20.

[7] Jefferson to G. Hay, June 20, 1807, quoted in Tourtellot, *Presidents on the Presidency,* p. 267.

[8] Quoted in Morton Borden, ed., *America's Ten Greatest Presidents* (Chicago, Rand McNally, 1961), pp. 79–80. On the whole subject of the Virginia Dynasty, see James S. Young, *The Washington Community, 1800–1828* (New York, Columbia University Press, 1966).

[9] Cunliffe, *The Nation Takes Shape,* p. 141; Charles M. Wiltse, *John C. Calhoun, Nationalist, 1782–1828* (Indianapolis, Bobbs-Merrill, 1944–49), I, p. 137.

[10] Adams quotations from Herbert Agar, *The Price of Union* (Boston, Houghton Mifflin, 1966), pp. 225–30.

[11] R. P. McCormick, "New Perspectives on Jacksonian Politics," *American Historical Review*, 65 (1960), p. 288.

[12] Harold C. Syrett, *Andrew Jackson: His Contribution to the American Tradition* (Indianapolis, Bobbs-Merrill, 1953), pp. 256–57.

[13] Joseph G. Baldwin, *Party Leaders* (1855), quoted in George E. Probst, ed., *The Happy Republic: A Reader in Tocqueville's America* (New York, Harper Torchbooks, 1962), pp. 119–37.

[14] Quoted in Rienow, *Lonely Quest*, p. 87.

[15] "When one is presented to [the electorate] possessed of an ardent temperament who adopts their cause, they return sympathy for sympathy . . . and are always ready to place the most favourable construction on his actions and slow to withdraw their confidence however exceptionable his conduct in many respects may be." Martin Van Buren, *Autobiography*, J. C. Fitzpatrick, ed. (American Historical Association, *Annual Report for 1918*, 2, Washington, D.C., 1920), p. 168.

[16] Jackson's special contribution to the idea of a people's President was perhaps above all his theory that re-election in 1832 gave him a plebiscitary mandate to carry out his policies. Robert V. Remini in *History of American Presidential Elections*, Arthur M. Schlesinger, Jr. and Fred L. Israel, eds. (New York, Chelsea House and McGraw-Hill, 1971), I, p. 516. The broad idea had of course been mooted before. One delegate at Philadelphia in 1787 had declared that "the Executive Magistrate should be the guardian of the people . . . against the Great and the wealthy. . . ." (Farrand, II, p. 52), and see Correa M. Walsh, *The Political Science of John Adams* (New York, Putnam's, 1915), pp. 276–78.

[17] Where the sources are not made plain, quotations in the previous few paragraphs are mainly from Leonard D. White, *The Jacksonians* (New York, Macmillan, 1954), pp. 23–28.

[18] Quoted in Agar, *Price of Union*, p. 313.

[19] White, *The Jacksonians*, p. 50.

[20] See Norman Graebner, "James K. Polk," in Borden, *Ten Greatest Presidents*, pp. 115, 138.

[21] Margaret Leech, *In the Days of McKinley* (New York, Harper, 1959), p. 463.

[22] White, *The Jacksonians*, p. 84.

[23] David Donald, *Lincoln Reconsidered* (New York, Vintage, 1956), pp. 187 ff; Tourtellot, p. 312.

[24] Corwin, *The President*, pp. 232–33, 449, 452.

CHAPTER FOUR

[1] Farrand, II, p. 104.

[2] Richard Hofstadter, *The Idea of a Party System: The Rise of Legitimate Opposition in the United States, 1780–1840* (Berkeley and Los Angeles, University of California Press, 1969), pp. 40–73.

[3] Harnsberger, *Presidential Quotations*, p. 220; Agar, *Price of Union*, p. 80.

[4] Cunliffe, *George Washington,* p. 151.

[5] Jefferson to William B. Giles, December 31, 1795, and to John Taylor, 1798, both cited in William N. Chambers, *Political Parties in a New Nation* (New York, Oxford University Press, 1963), pp. 93, 149.

[6] Agar, *Price of Union;* Joseph Charles, Jr., *Origins of the American Party System* (Williamsburg, Va., Institute of Early American History & Culture, 1956); Chambers, *Political Parties;* Richard P. McCormick, *The Second American Party System* (Chapel Hill, University of North Carolina Press, 1966).

[7] Quoted in Kallenbach, *American Chief Executive,* p. 288.

[8] Agar, *Price of Union,* p. 201.

[9] Adams to Josiah Quincy, February 18, 1811, in Tourtellot, pp. 376–77.

[10] Quoted in Binkley, *The President and Congress,* p. 74.

[11] Chambers, *Political Parties,* pp. 199–200.

[12] Binkley, *The Man in the White House,* p. 94.

[13] Adams, diary for March 5, 1827, in Tourtellot, p. 349; S. F. Bemis, *John Quincy Adams and the Union* (New York, Knopf, 1956), pp. 71–91, 99–103.

[14] Indeed the idea took root earlier still. It often came up at the Philadelphia Constitutional Convention in 1787: see the references under "rotation" in the index to Max Farrand, ed., *Records of the Federal Convention.*

[15] Leonard D. White, *The Jacksonians,* p. 317.

[16] White, *The Jacksonians,* pp. 321–22.

[17] Cunliffe, *The Nation Takes Shape,* p. 162.

[18] For an account of his consular experiences, see Hawthorne's *Our Old Home* (2 vols., London, Smith, Elder, 1863), I, pp. 1–59.

[19] White, *Jacksonians,* pp. 304–5; Tourtellot, pp. 155–57.

[20] White, *Jacksonians,* pp. 72, 312.

[21] Undated, unaddressed autograph letter formerly in the possession of the author.

[22] Quoted in Louis W. Koenig, *The Invisible Presidency* (New York, Holt, Rinehart & Winston, 1960), pp. 92–93.

CHAPTER FIVE

[1] Corwin, *The President,* pp. 29–30, 307. The term "aggrandizement" seems to have been introduced by Henry Jones Ford in *The Rise and Growth of American Politics* (New York, Macmillan Co., 1898), p. 287.

[2] Goldwater address, *Saturday Review,* October 17, 1964, quoted in Kallenbach, *American Chief Executive,* p. 568.

[3] Goldwater, "Powers of the Presidency," quoted in James M. Burns, *Presidential Government: The Crucible of Leadership* (Boston, Houghton Mifflin, 1965), p. 276.

[4] From Sidney Hyman, "What Is the President's True Role?" *New York Times,* September 7, 1958, repr. in Johnson and Walker, *Dynamics of the Presidency,* p. 134.

[5] A technique mocked in this limerick about James G. Blaine from the American *Punch* (May 19, 1880):

> *There was an old stalwart named Blaine,*
> *Who hailed from the region of Maine.*
> *When he felt badly hurt*
> *He would cry "Bloody Shirt"*
> *And slay over the already slain.*

[6] *Thomas Paine: Representative Selections,* Harry Hayden Clark, ed. (revised edn., New York, Hill and Wang, 1961), p. 392.

[7] Claude M. Fuess, *Calvin Coolidge* (Boston, Little, Brown, 1940), p. 342.

[8] James M. Burns, *The Deadlock of Democracy: Four-Party Politics in America* (Englewood Cliffs, N.J., Prentice-Hall, Spectrum, 1963).

[9] Quotations from Marcus Cunliffe, "Madison: 1812–1815," in Ernest R. May, ed., *The Ultimate Decision: The President as Commander in Chief* (New York, Braziller, 1960), pp. 25–53.

[10] Speech of Washington Barrow of Tennessee, House of Representatives, January 24, 1848.

[11] These are conveniently summarized in an article by Wiltse repr. in A. S. Eisenstadt, ed., *American History: Recent Interpretations,* Book I (New York, Crowell, 1962), pp. 311–13.

[12] William N. Chambers, *Old Bullion Benton: . . . Thomas Hart Benton, 1782–1858* (Boston, Little, Brown, 1956), pp. 218–19.

[13] Eugene H. Roseboom, *A History of Presidential Elections* (New York, Macmillan, 1964), pp. 112–13; Robert V. Remini, "Election of 1836," in Schlesinger and Israel, eds., *History of American Presidential Elections,* I, pp. 577–600.

[14] Arthur M. Schlesinger, Jr., *The Age of Jackson* (Boston, Little, Brown, 1945), pp. 275–77.

[15] Corwin, *The President,* pp. 21–22; Nathan Sargent, *Public Men and Events* (New York, 1875), I, pp. 258–60.

[16] Schlesinger and Israel, eds., *History of American Presidential Elections,* I, pp. 695–96.

[17] Edwin C. Rozwenc, ed., *Ideology and Power in the Age of Jackson* (Garden City, N.Y., Doubleday Anchor, 1964), pp. 336–38.

[18] David B. Davis, *Homicide in American Fiction: A Study in Social Values* (Ithaca, N.Y., Cornell University Press, 1957), pp. 237–90.

[19] Edmund Wilson, *Patriotic Gore* (New York, Oxford University Press, 1962), p. 108.

[20] Coyle, *Ordeal of the Presidency,* pp. 142–43.

[21] In the two years before the Dallas murder the Secret Service had investigated thirty-four threats against the President's life from the state of Texas alone. There had already been ninety-eight murders within the city of Dallas, Texas, during the first ten months of 1963. Arthur M. Schlesinger, Jr., *A Thousand Days: John F. Kennedy in the White House* (London, André Deutsch, 1965), pp. 648, 864–65.

[22] On Bean, see J. W. Dodds, *The Age of Paradox* (London, Gollancz,

1953), pp. 67–68. Bean's attack took place in July, 1842. It had been preceded by two attempts to shoot the Queen: in June, 1840, by a potboy named Edward Oxford, and in May, 1842, by an unemployed man named John Francis. Bean and Oxford were judged insane: Francis was transported for life. A special act was passed in 1842 "to punish those who attacked her Majesty with intent to alarm." The first man tried under the act, and the last to offer a serious threat to the Queen's life, was an Irish bricklayer named Hamilton, who fired a pistol at her coach in May, 1849. He was sentenced to seven years' transportation. So was Robert Pate, a former lieutenant of the 10th Hussars, who in May, 1850, struck Queen Victoria on the head with a stick. The judge in Pate's case "so far gave effect to the plea of insanity as to omit whipping from the punishment the court might have awarded." Joseph Irving, *Annals of Our Times* (London, Macmillan, 1880), pp. 68, 111, 113, 277, 300, 305. On presidential assassinations generally see Robert J. Donovan, *The Assassins* (New York, Harper, 1955). One of the few thoughtful discussions on this theme, written after the death of McKinley, is an essay by Charles Francis Adams, Jr., "A National Change of Heart," repr. in his *Lee at Appomattox and Other Papers* (Boston, Houghton Mifflin, 1902), pp. 256–60. A recent study suggests that in the United States, "the higher the office, the more impersonal and political the motive for assassination." But this does not seem to probe very deep. James F. Kirkham, S. G. Levy, and W. J. Crotty, *Assassination and Political Violence* (New York and London, *New York Times*/Bantam, 1970), p. 57.

[23] William Manchester, *Death of a President* (London, Michael Joseph, 1967), p. 67; Tugwell, *Enlargement of the Presidency*, pp. 265–66.

[24] Edward Hyams, *Killing No Murder: A Study of Assassination as a Political Means* (Edinburgh, Thomas Nelson, 1969; Panther edn., 1970); Ali A. Mazrui, "Thoughts on Assassination in Africa," *Political Science Quarterly*, 83 (March, 1968), pp. 40–58.

[25] Louis Brownlow, *The President and the Presidency* (Chicago, Public Service Administration, 1949), pp. 17–18.

[26] Glyndon G. Van Deusen, *The Jacksonian Era, 1828–1848* (New York, Harper, 1959), pp. 99–100; and see Edwin A. Miles, *Jacksonian Democracy in Mississippi* (Chapel Hill, University of North Carolina Press, 1960), pp. 103–4, on Jackson's charges against "that damned rascal" Senator Poindexter.

[27] William H. Crook, *Through Five Administrations* (New York and London, Harper's, 1910), pp. 92–93.

[28] W. A. Swanberg, *Citizen Hearst* (New York, Bantam, 1963), pp. 214, 227, 229–32, 299.

[29] *Franklin D. Roosevelt: Selected Speeches,* Basil Rauch, ed. (New York, Rinehart, 1957), pp. 182–84.

[30] Manchester, *Death of a President*, p. 70.

[31] Henry Dwight Sedgwick, *The New American Type and Other Essays* (London and Boston, 1908), pp. 317–43.

[32] According to Roosevelt's secretary, William Loeb, there were two

possible threats to T. R.'s life in 1905 and 1906—after he had won renewed tenure of the White House through the election of 1904. Roosevelt was not told of them. The first involved an excitable lady who demanded to see the President. Frustrated by Loeb, "she opened up a large reticule she carried on the top of which reposed a pearl handled revolver which I grabbed before she could reach it." In the second instance, "A Slav tailor turned up at the White House office, but was so incoherent and wild that the officers at once took charge of him. On the way to the police wagon, he whipped from the sleeve of his coat one of the blades of a tailor's shears which had been sharpened to a needle-point and he severely cut up one of the officers. . . ." This disclosure from Loeb is quoted in Owen Wister, *Roosevelt: The Story of a Friendship* (New York, 1930), pp. 238–39. Anti-Roosevelt material is illustrated in Arthur S. Link, *Woodrow Wilson and the Progressive Era, 1910–1917* (New York and London, Harper Torchbooks, 1963), p. 17, and in Coyle, *Ordeal of the Presidency,* pp. 259, 284.

[33] *Frank Leslie's Illustrated,* July 16, 1881.

[34] John P. Roche and Leonard W. Levy, eds., *The Presidency* (New York, Harcourt, Brace, 1964), pp. 22, 37.

[35] Harold Laski, *The American Presidency: An Interpretation* (New York, Harper, 1940), p. 132.

[36] Thomas J. Pressly, *Americans Interpret Their Civil War* (Princeton University Press, 1954), p. 25.

[37] William B. Hesseltine, *Lincoln and the War Governors* (New York, Knopf, 1948), pp. 379–83.

CHAPTER SIX

[1] Quoted in Corwin, *The President,* pp. 22, 25–26.

[2] *The Education of Henry Adams* (Modern Library edn.), pp. 261–62.

[3] To Buchanan, Lincoln's immediate predecessor, "a 'strong' president, one who overpowered or ignored the Congress and the courts, meant an executive who would destroy the republican form." Philip S. Klein, *President James Buchanan* (University Park, Pennsylvania State University Press, 1962), p. 428.

[4] Quoted in Roche and Levy, *The Presidency,* pp. 25–28.

[5] Binkley, *The President and Congress,* p. 173.

[6] Binkley, *President and Congress,* pp. 184–85. Leonard D. White, *The Republican Era 1869–1901* (New York, Macmillan, 1958), p. 24.

[7] White, *Republican Era,* p. 34.

[8] Binkley, *President and Congress,* p. 196.

[9] Binkley, *President and Congress,* p. 203; Harry Thurston Peck, *Democrats and Republicans,* Louis Filler, ed. (New York, Capricorn, 1964), pp. 72, 76, 88.

[10] April 29, 1879, quoted in White, *Republican Era,* p. 36.

[11] Binkley, *President and Congress,* pp. 166, 203, 212.

[12] Peck, *Democrats and Republicans,* p. 128.

[13] Peck, *Democrats and Republicans,* p. 140.

[14] Cox article in *Atlantic Monthly,* 71 (1893), p. 831, quoted in White, *Republican Era,* p. 107; and see Vincent P. De Santis, "The Republican Party Revisited," in Wayne Morgan, ed., *The Gilded Age* (Syracuse University Press, 1963), pp. 92–104.

[15] James Bryce, *The American Commonwealth* (London, Macmillan, 1888), II, p. 20.

[16] *State of the Union Messages of the Presidents,* Israel, ed., II, pp. 1598–1604.

[17] White, *Republican Era,* p. 106; Harnsberger, *Presidential Quotations,* pp. 242–43.

[18] The idea of course readily occurred to British visitors to the U.S. Here is an example: "The career of one of the President's ministers is not a very high career as things now stand; nor is the man supposed to have achieved much who has achieved that position. I think it would be otherwise if the ministers were the leaders of the legislative Houses. . . . The power of the President would no doubt be diminished as that of Congress would be increased. But an alteration in that direction is in itself desirable." Anthony Trollope, *North America* (2 vols., London, Chapman & Hall, 1862), II, p. 316.

[19] Peck, *Democrats and Republicans,* pp. 245–46.

[20] Ernest Samuels, *Henry Adams: The Middle Years* (Cambridge, Mass., Harvard University Press, 1965), pp. 24, 32, 93, 168–69.

[21] Woodrow Wilson, *Congressional Government* (New York, Meridian, 1956), pp. 48–49, 140–42, 169–70, 181. *Congressional Government* was on the whole enthusiastically received. A writer in the *Nation* said that Wilson was the first to explain "the real working" of the federal government. Some of the more sophisticated reviewers complained however that he was too much influenced by "Anglomaniac" visions of Cabinet responsibility. It was also said — interestingly, in view of Wilson's latter development — that he was too much committed to a belief in energetic government serving as the expression of a vaguely defined popular will. Henry W. Bragdon, *Woodrow Wilson: The Academic Years* (Cambridge, Mass., Harvard University Press, 1967), pp. 134–39.

[22] Walter Clark, *The Arena,* 10 (September, 1894), pp. 460–61; Schlesinger and Israel, eds., *History of American Presidential Elections,* II, pp. 1742–44.

[23] William D. P. Bliss, ed., *The Encyclopedia of Social Reform* (New York, Funk & Wagnalls, 1897), pp. 1080–86. Advocates of proportional and other voting reforms in the United States often use the 1896 election to make a case. What they fail to point out is that even with a small shift McKinley was still the "democratic" victor, since he received 600,000 more popular votes than Bryan.

CHAPTER SEVEN

[1] Lincoln to Ward Lamon, in Tourtellot, p. 353. "In the nervous struggles for that high honour even the best man loses faith in others, and forgets his

own obligations in his distrust of his supporters. The vast patronage of the office, and the vexations and heart-burnings of those who seek place, open a wide avenue to intrigue and deception." J. W. Forney, *Anecdotes of Public Men* (New York, 1873), p. 325.

[2] Wilson, *Congressional Government* (Meridian edn.), p. 162.

[3] Michael V. Di Salle, *Second Choice* (New York, Hawthorn Books, 1966), p. 14; Michael Harwood, *In the Shadow of Presidents: The American Vice-Presidency and Succession System* (Philadelphia, Lippincott, 1966), pp. 109–10.

[4] Frank J. Cavaioli, *West Point and the Presidency* (New York, St. John's University Press, 1962), pp. 55–59.

[5] Cavaioli, pp. 85–86.

[6] Old styles lingered on. *The Nixon Yearbook 1968*, in its biographical notes, said: "Mr. Nixon's mother was a Quaker and the tenets of that faith have played a major part in the Nixon story. A belief in the virtue of hard work (he worked in the family store as a boy) and a strong desire for peace and true social justice, both part of the Quaker philosophy, have been part of his life since his days in Yorba Linda and Whittier [California]." A later paragraph injects a more modern note: "Since he became a senior partner in his law firm, Mr. Nixon has made approximately $200,000 a year, from practicing law and from writing."

[7] The humble-origins theme goes a long way back. As early as 1837 a St. Louis newspaper published an article entitled "The Poorest Boy May Be President." It noted that Jackson and Van Buren were both self-made; Van Buren was "the son of a farmer, who was obliged to till the soil with his own hands, for means of support." So the Presidency was "within the reach of the humblest urchin that roams the streets of our villages. . . . *Liberty and Equality* is the glorious motto of our republic." William N. Chambers, *Old Bullion Benton: . . . Thomas Hart Benton, 1782–1858,* p. 223n.

[8] Examples in the previous paragraphs are taken from W. Burlie Brown, *The People's Choice: The Presidential Image in the Campaign Biography* (Baton Rouge, Louisiana State University Press, 1960), pp. 18, 20, 27–28, 41, 52, 86–87.

[9] *Hayes: The Diary of a President, 1875–1881,* T. Harry Williams, ed. (New York, David McKay, 1964), pp. 278–79 (entry for June 11, 1880).

[10] Binkley, *The Man in the White House,* p. 79; Henry Ward Beecher, "The Reign of the Common People" (London, James Clarke, c. 1886), pp. 12–13.

[11] Cavaioli, pp. 61–64.

[12] Seymour quotations from Irving Stone, *They Also Ran* (New York, Pyramid, 1964), pp. 303, 318–19.

[13] Gouverneur Kemble to Joel R. Poinsett, June 7, 1839, Poinsett Papers, Historical Society of Pennsylvania, quoted in Marcus Cunliffe, *Soldiers and Civilians: The Martial Spirit in America, 1775–1865* (Boston, Little, Brown, 1968; London, Eyre & Spottiswoode, 1969), p. 304.

[14] *Hayes: Diary of a President,* xvi, pp. 10, 15–16, 18, 19–21.

[15] Quoted in excerpt from Alexander Heard, *The Costs of Democracy*, in Johnson and Walker, *Dynamics of the Presidency*, p. 52. But Adams' own father had taken to the stump, unavailingly, in the presidential election of 1800: Stephen G. Kurtz, *The Presidency of John Adams*, pp. 397–98.

[16] Robert F. Durden, *The Climax of Populism: The Election of 1896* (Lexington, University of Kentucky Press, 1965), pp. 81–82.

[17] Johnson and Walker, eds., *Dynamics of the American Presidency*, p. 53; Schlesinger and Israel, eds., *History of American Presidential Elections*, II, 1816–19.

[18] La Follette, *Autobiography* (Madison, Wis., La Follette Company, 1911), pp. 16–17; *Forum*, February, 1894; cited in Donald Day, ed., *Woodrow Wilson's Own Story* (Boston, Little, Brown, 1952), pp. 41–42.

[19] See James G. Randall, *Lincoln the Liberal Statesman* (New York, 1947), pp. 82–83.

[20] Evarts' humor was not always suitable for or known to the President. "In the White House the water flowed like champagne": this *mot* of his on the temperance-minded Hayeses would hardly have amused them. Another story about Hayes, possibly untrue, was that he now and then managed to visit a Philadelphia club as the guest of a friend; once safely inside the club he would exclaim, "For God's sake, Patterson, give me a drink!" Owen Wister, *Roosevelt: The Story of a Friendship*, p. 17.

[21] Peck, *Democrats and Republicans*, pp. 9, 119–21.

[22] Quoted in Richard F. Fenno, Jr., *The President's Cabinet* (Vintage edn.), p. 52.

[23] Peck, pp. 56–57.

[24] Speech in Washington, D.C., May 16, 1916, in Harnsberger, *Presidential Quotations*, pp. 264–65.

[25] Binkley, *Man in the White House*, p. 251.

CHAPTER EIGHT

[1] James M. Burns, *Presidential Government* (Boston, Houghton Mifflin, 1965), p. 94.

[2] Wilson, *Congressional Government*, pp. 19, 22. Some scholars have traced Wilson's vision of a powerful Executive further back than 1900. Even in an article published in 1879—his first venture into print—as well as in *Congressional Government*, he had stressed the importance of bold, efficient direction of national affairs. Walter Lippmann suggests, in his introduction to the 1956 Meridian edition of *Congressional Government*, that Wilson had begun to take a new view of the Presidency under the inspiration of Grover Cleveland. True, in the 1880's and 1890's he admired the courage of this fellow Democrat. In an *Atlantic Monthly* article of July, 1897, praising the examples set by Andrew Jackson and Abraham Lincoln, he demanded a "new national leadership"; and in a lecture delivered shortly afterward he defined the American system as a "Leaderless Government." But James M. Burns (*Presidential Government*, pp. 94–95) shows that the Lippmann theory is unsound: Wilson sent the manuscript of *Con-*

gressional Government to the publisher in October, 1884, before Cleveland had even been elected President. Examined closely, the book makes clear that all Wilson's pronouncements before 1900 looked to a partnership, more or less on the British model, between the President, his Cabinet, and Congress. Power, Wilson assumed, really resided in congressional committees or among the executive officers as a group. "Leadership" for him appeared in practice to be a collective activity; by "executive" he understood the whole executive branch, rather than the President as "Chief Executive." This is not to deny that Wilson often spoke in general terms about leadership. In common with a great many other people of his day he strongly believed in the need for personal strength. But he was also, like them, slow to apply such generalities to the actual office of the Presidency.

[3] Woodrow Wilson, *Constitutional Government in the United States* (New York, Columbia University Press, 1908, repr. 1961), pp. 56–57, 60, 79.

[4] Henry Jones Ford, *The Rise and Growth of American Politics* (New York, Macmillan, 1898; repr. New York, Da Capo Press, 1967), pp. 279–93; Corwin, *The President*, pp. 27–28.

[5] *Hayes: The Diary of a President* (July 19, 1879), p. 240.

[6] Wilson, *Constitutional Government*, pp. 58–59; Cleveland and Arthur anecdotes in T. A. Bailey, *Presidential Greatness: The Image and the Man from George Washington to the Present* (New York, Appleton-Century, 1966), pp. 299, 302.

[7] *Congressional Government*, p. 22.

[8] *Constitutional Government*, pp. 77–78.

[9] Eugene H. Roseboom, *A History of Presidential Elections*, p. 326.

[10] Elmer E. Cornwell, Jr., *Presidential Leadership of Public Opinion* (Bloomington, Indiana University Press, 1965), pp. 26–30.

[11] *Constitutional Government*, pp. 70–71, 110.

[12] Agar, *The Price of Union*, p. 531; *Hayes: Diary*, pp. 123, 128, 192; Leonard D. White, *The Republican Era*, p. 4; Sperber and Trittschuh, *Dictionary of American Political Terms* (New York, McGraw-Hill, 1964), p. 412. Martin Van Buren also spoke of "sober second thought" in a letter of 1829; Arthur M. Schlesinger, Jr., *The Age of Jackson*, p. 392 n. 5.

[13] Theodore Roosevelt, *An Autobiography* (New York, Scribner's, 1920), pp. 420–21.

[14] *Congressional Government*, p. 85.

[15] *Constitutional Government*, pp. 99, 130. There is also some force in the argument that Congress was beginning to improve in the 1890's, and that party discipline was gradually strengthened in beneficial ways. By the next decade, vigorous Presidents could count on the support of a number of sensible, well-informed politicians in both houses. John A. Garraty, *The New Commonwealth, 1877–1890* (New York and London, Harper & Row, 1968), pp. 306–8.

[16] Binkley, *President and Congress*, p. 219; Harold U. Faulkner, *Politics, Reform and Expansion, 1890–1900* (New York, Harper, 1959), pp. 98–99.

[17] Agar, *Price of Union*, p. 662.

[18] Quoted in Chester McA. Destler, *American Radicalism, 1865–1901* (Chicago, Quadrangle, 1966), p. 220.

[19] Ray Stannard Baker, *American Chronicle,* quoted in Carl Resek, ed., *The Progressives* (Indianapolis, Bobbs-Merrill, 1967), p. 163.

[20] Quoted in Resek, *The Progressives,* p. 336.

[21] Lippmann, *A Preface to Politics* (repr. Ann Arbor, University of Michigan Press, 1962), p. 79.

[22] Quoted in Arthur S. Link, *Woodrow Wilson and the Progressive Era, 1910–1917,* p. 34.

[23] Link, *Wilson and the Progressive Era,* p. 80.

[24] John M. Blum, *Woodrow Wilson and the Politics of Morality* (Boston, Little, Brown, 1956), p. 182; *State of the Union Messages of the Presidents,* Israel, ed., III, pp. 2616–17, 2621.

CHAPTER NINE

[1] *The New Politics 1961* (New York, Harper Colophon, 1962), p. 181.

[2] Roche and Levy, eds., *The Presidency,* pp. 125–27; Allen M. Potter, *American Government and Politics* (London, Faber, 1956), pp. 211–13.

[3] Kallenbach, *American Chief Executive,* pp. 504–5.

[4] George E. Mowry, *The Era of Theodore Roosevelt, 1900–1912* (New York, Harper, 1958), p. 159; Albert K. Weinberg, *Manifest Destiny* (Baltimore, Johns Hopkins Press, 1935; repr. Chicago, Quadrangle Books, 1963), pp. 427–31.

[5] Harold Laski, *The American Presidency,* p. 168.

[6] Alexander De Conde, *The American Secretary of State: An Interpretation* (New York, Praeger, 1962), pp. 50–55.

[7] De Conde, p. 137.

[8] Andrew Sinclair, *The Available Man: . . . Warren Gamaliel Harding* (New York, Macmillan; London, Collier-Macmillan, 1965), p. 162.

[9] See entry on "Isolation," *Concise Dictionary of American History,* Wayne Andrews, ed. (New York, Scribner's, 1962), p. 495.

[10] De Conde, *The American Secretary of State,* p. 82.

[11] Emmet J. Hughes, *The Ordeal of Power* (New York, Dell, 1964), pp. 252–53.

[12] Hughes, *Ordeal of Power,* pp. 126–27.

[13] Quotations from Fulbright and Katzenbach in *The Guardian,* August 18 and 21, 1967.

[14] Arnold Beichman, in *The "Other" State Department* (New York, Basic Books, 1968), shows that we should also take into account the United States Mission to the United Nations (USUN), which owes allegiance both to the executive branch in Washington and—ideologically at least—to the UN headquarters in New York. He argues that Henry Cabot Lodge as American ambassador to the UN, through his resolute resistance to Secretary of State Dulles, established USUN as a semiautonomous body within the State Department; and that Lodge's successors, Adlai Stevenson and Arthur Goldberg, built on his foundations.

[15] Eisenhower address of January 17, 1961, quoted in Johnson and Walker, *Dynamics of the American Presidency*, p. 312. The speech was drafted for him, however, by an entirely "civilian" speechwriter, Malcolm Moos. For a cool, well-documented analysis see Adam Yarmolinsky, *The Military Establishment: Its Impacts on American Society* (New York and London, Harper & Row, 1971).

[16] De Conde, *The American Secretary of State*, pp. 125–27.

[17] De Conde, p. 121.

[18] De Conde, p. 108.

[19] Keith C. Clark and Laurence J. Legere, *The President and the Management of National Security* (New York and London, Praeger, 1969), pp. 170–71; and see Charles Maechling, Jr., "Our Foreign Affairs Establishment: The Need for Reform," *Virginia Quarterly Review,* 45 (Spring, 1969), repr. in William R. Nelson, ed., *American Government and Political Change* (New York and London, Oxford University Press, 1970), pp. 347–56.

[20] Bundy in Johnson and Walker, *Dynamics,* p. 329; Theodore C. Sorensen, *Decision-Making in the White House: The Olive Branch or the Arrows* (New York, Columbia University Press, 1963), pp. 63–64.

[21] Sorensen, *Decision-Making,* p. 82.

[22] Foreign policy, complex enough to start with, was also hideously confused by the plurality of executive agencies in Washington—their ignorance of one another's activities aggravated by President Johnson's secretiveness. Sometimes the President himself was alarmingly out of touch. See David Kraslow and Stuart H. Loory, *The Secret Search for Peace in Vietnam* (New York, Random House, 1968).

CHAPTER TEN

[1] Quoted in Walter Johnson, *1600 Pennsylvania Avenue* (Boston, Little, Brown, 1963 edn.), p. 28.

[2] Madison Square address, October 31, 1936, in Edwin C. Rozwenc and Thomas T. Lyons, eds., *Presidential Power in the New Deal* (Boston, Heath, 1964), p. 16.

[3] Cornwell, *Presidential Leadership of Public Opinion,* p. 90.

[4] William E. Leuchtenburg, ed., *Franklin D. Roosevelt: A Profile* (New York, Hill & Wang, 1967), p. 86.

[5] Calvin Coolidge, *Autobiography* (London, Chatto & Windus, 1929), pp. 231–34.

[6] Cornwell, *Presidential Leadership of Public Opinion,* p. 255.

[7] Quoted in Tourtellot, *Presidents on the Presidency,* p. 126.

[8] Executive Order No. 8248 of September 8, 1939, *Public Papers and Addresses of Franklin D. Roosevelt, 1939* (London, Macmillan, 1941), pp. 490–96; Tugwell, *Enlargement of the Presidency,* pp. 435–36.

[9] See Johnson and Walker, eds., *Dynamics of the American Presidency,* pp. 340–55.

[10] Quoted in John P. Roche, *The Presidency* (New York, Harcourt, Brace, 1964), p. 104.

[11] Roche, *The Presidency*, pp. 62–63.

[12] Roche, *The Presidency*, pp. 111–12.

[13] Emmet J. Hughes, *The Ordeal of Power*, p. 108.

[14] Richard E. Neustadt, *Presidential Power: The Politics of Leadership* (New York, Wiley, 1960), p. 33.

[15] Richard H. Leach, *Governing the American Nation* (Boston, Allyn & Bacon, 1967), pp. 268–69, 337.

[16] Leach, p. 334; Robert Sherrill, *The Accidental President* (New York, Grossman, 1967), p. 18; Philip Geyelin, *Lyndon B. Johnson and the World* (New York, Praeger, 1966), p. 146; Aida Di Pace Donald, ed., *John F. Kennedy and the New Frontier* (New York, Hill & Wang, 1966), p. 55.

[17] Donald, *Kennedy and the New Frontier*, pp. 28–31.

[18] Neustadt, *Presidential Power*, p. 9.

[19] *The Times* (London), September 14, 1967.

[20] Richard Polenberg, *Reorganizing Roosevelt's Government, . . . 1936–1939* (Cambridge, Mass., Harvard University Press, 1966), pp. 164, 166.

[21] Harry S. Truman, *Memoirs*, Vol. 2: *Years of Trial and Hope, 1946–1952*, (New York, Signet, 1965), p. 556.

[22] Barton J. Bernstein and Allen J. Matusow, eds., *The Truman Administration* (New York, Harper & Row, 1966), pp. 146, 153, 389.

[23] Walter Johnson, *1600 Pennsylvania Avenue*, p. 325.

[24] Walter Johnson, pp. 328, 332; Donald, *Kennedy*, pp. 51–53, 220.

[25] Robert Lekachman, "Johnson So Far: The Great Society," *Commentary*, 39 (June, 1965), pp. 37–42.

[26] On the second Nixon nomination see Richard Harris, *Decision* (New York, E. P. Dutton, 1971): "Of all the actions that President Richard Nixon took during his first two years in office, probably none more clearly revealed the character of his Presidency—the regional and class appeals that divided the nation, the disregard for the constitutional separation of powers, the embittered relations between the Administration and the Senate, the apparent confidence that the people would sleep through even the noisiest raid of their liberties, and the belief that members of Congress could be counted on to put their own political interest above the public interest—than his nomination of George Harrold Carswell of Florida to be an Associate Justice of the Supreme Court."

[27] See Chapter 9.

[28] Neustadt, pp. 41–42.

[29] Truman, *Years of Trial*, pp. 193–94.

[30] *Hoover Commission Report* (New York, McGraw-Hill, 1949), pp. v–xiii, 4–19. Another twenty years later, bureaucratic language had grown still more obscure and markedly more portentous. At least bureaucrats could perceive the humor of their enthrallment. In 1968 a "Systematic Buzz

Phrase Projector," apparently a Canadian invention, was being circulated among Washington civil servants. It consists of three columns each of ten words. An official in search of a sonorous phrase need only choose a random three-digit number, apply it to the table, and insert the result in his own memorandum. Thus, 803 would give him "compatible management capability," and 999 "balanced policy contingency":

	A	B	C
0	Integrated	Management	Options
1	Total	Organizational	Flexibility
2	Systematized	Monitored	Capability
3	Parallel	Reciprocal	Mobility
4	Functional	Digital	Programming
5	Responsive	Logistical	Concept
6	Optional	Transitional	Time-Phase
7	Synchronized	Incremental	Projection
8	Compatible	Third-Generation	Hardware
9	Balanced	Policy	Contingency

(*Time*, September 13, 1968.)

[31] Kallenbach, *American Chief Executive*, pp. 384–85.

[32] For a clear, sophisticated, insider's view by a scholar who formerly worked in the Bureau of the Budget, see Harold Seidman, *Politics, Position and Power: The Dynamics of Federal Organization* (New York and London, Oxford University Press, 1970).

[33] Louis W. Koenig, *The Invisible Presidency*, pp. 338–39.

[34] Truman, *Years of Trial*, pp. 551–52.

[35] Truman, *Years of Trial*, p. 535; Roche, *The Presidency*, p. 84.

[36] Roche, *The Presidency*, p. 63.

[37] Louis W. Koenig, *The Chief Executive*, p. 120.

[38] Neil Sheehan *et al.*, *The Pentagon Papers* (New York and London, Bantam, 1971).

[39] Calvin Coolidge, *Autobiography*, p. 242.

[40] Douglass Cater, *Power in Washington* (London, Collins, 1965), p. 82; *Newsweek*, International edn., November 21, 1966, p. 29.

[41] Harold W. Chase and Allen H. Lerman, eds., *Kennedy and the Press* (New York, Crowell, 1965), pp. 426–27.

[42] Quoted in Cater, *Power in Washington*, p. 72.

CHAPTER ELEVEN

[1] Sorensen, *Decision-Making in the White House*, p. 3.

[2] Harold Laski, *The American Presidency: An Interpretation*, pp. 52, 200–201.

[3] The reforms proposed by the Fulton Commission (1968), designed to revivify the British civil service through broader recruitment and a lowering of the barriers between one grade and another, may accomplish something but have no obvious relevance for what Arthur Schlesinger, Jr., has

called the "permanent government"—the administrative departments—of the United States (Schlesinger, *A Thousand Days,* pp. 589–95).

However, a reverse influence is more noticeable. Where once American reformers cited British practice, there is now a tendency in Britain—deprecatingly or admiringly—to perceive American analogies. Recent prime ministers such as Harold Macmillan and Harold Wilson have, to judge from their references to "new frontiers" and so on, seemed perhaps unwittingly to visualize themselves as national leaders on the presidential model. Some students of parliamentary government in contemporary Britain, including Professor Max Beloff and (at one stage) Mr. Richard Crossman, discern a distinct drift toward a "presidential" style of executive conduct—for example, in the diminution of the role of the cabinet, the widening of the gulf between the executive and the legislature, and the increasing readiness of the executive to take Parliament for granted. Some critics appear to find the remedy as well as the malady in the American model. Early in 1963 a number of correspondents to *The Times,* Lord Boothby among them, argued that Parliament might recover its lost authority *vis-à-vis* the prime minister and the cabinet by establishing powerful investigatory committees like those of Congress. Boothby suggested four select committees, to cover defense, foreign, Commonwealth, and economic policy.

Parliament, like Congress, though to a lesser extent, is in need of reform. Very little scope for inquiry and initiative is provided by such devices as question time, or private members' bills. The two systems, British and American, may be growing to resemble one another. But they are still too far apart for either to be used as an object lesson for the other. Party discipline, campaign techniques, methods of choosing leaders are very different in the two countries. The most crucial difference of all lies in the British association between cabinet responsibility and majority party rule. As a result, prime ministers in some ways enjoy more genuine, clear-cut authority than do Presidents. For this very reason, according to Henry Fairlie (*The Life of Politics,* New York, Basic Books, 1968, pp. 221–25), the congressional committee pattern could not function in the House of Commons. American legislative committees operate with little reference to the executive branch; their independence is an aspect of the American separation of powers. British parliamentary committees, Fairlie plausibly contends, would lack such independence. They would if instituted either become mere fact-finding and rubber-stamping bodies, or—if more assertive—would quickly feel the force of party and ministerial disapproval. In a struggle of that nature, a parliamentary committee would have little chance of successfully challenging governmental decisions.

(For a good brief summary of similarities and dissimilarities, see Malcolm Shaw, *Anglo-American Democracy,* London, Routledge & Kegan Paul, 1968.)

[4] Arthur N. Holcombe, *Our More Perfect Union* (Cambridge, Mass., Harvard University Press, 1950), p. 422.

[5] Clinton Rossiter, *The American Presidency* (New York, Harvest, 1960), pp. 194, 258–59.

[6] Rossiter, *American Presidency,* p. 199.

[7] See James A. Michener, *Presidential Lottery* (London, Secker & Warburg, 1970).

[8] Truman, *Years of Trial,* p. 573.

[9] Ruth C. Silva, *Presidential Succession* (Ann Arbor, University of Michigan Press, 1951), p. 131 ff.

[10] Gene Smith, *When the Cheering Stopped: The Last Years of Woodrow Wilson* (New York, Bantam, 1965), p. 110.

[11] Harry S. Truman, *Mr. Citizen* (London, Hutchinson, 1961), pp. 109–12; *Keesing's Contemporary Archives,* XIV (1963–64), p. 19714. Ex-Presidents, under a presidential retirement law of 1958, have the additional comfort of a $25,000 yearly annuity, free office space, and up to $65,000 a year for office staff. On his retirement in January, 1969, Lyndon B. Johnson became entitled to an annual congressional pension of $24,000—thus giving him a total government pension of $49,000 per annum. See *Newsweek,* September 9, 1968, which notes that Truman was also in receipt of a double pension; ex-President Eisenhower, on the other hand, was not entitled to receive both a presidential and his military pension, and so lost the benefit of the latter. One conclusion is that a congressman or senator with a fairly safe seat can count on a pension rivaling that of the President in adequacy.

[12] Guy B. Hathorn, H. R. Penniman, and M. F. Ferber, *Government and Politics in the United States* (New York, 2nd edn., Van Nostrand, 1966), pp. 278–79.

[13] Sidney Hyman, *New York Times Magazine,* January 4, 1959, p. 50, quoted in Richard H. Leach, *Governing the American Nation,* p. 343.

[14] Quoted in Chester McA. Destler, *American Radicalism, 1865–1901,* p. 220.

[15] Herman Finer, *The Presidency: Crisis and Regeneration. An Essay in Possibilities* (Chicago, University Press, 1960), pp. 21, 49, 67.

[16] James M. Burns, *The Deadlock of Democracy,* pp. 196–97, 262.

[17] *State of the Union Messages of the Presidents,* Israel, ed., III, p. 3176.

[18] Hughes, *Ordeal of Power,* pp. 300–301, 305.

[19] David T. Bazelon, *Power in America: The Politics of the New Class* (New York, New American Library, 1967), p. 82. Note however that Robert K. Murray, *The Harding Era* (Minneapolis, University of Minnesota Press, 1969), goes some way toward the rehabilitation of a President usually deemed the weakest in the entire sequence. There are signs too of a revival in the reputation of Herbert Hoover.

[20] Amaury de Riencourt, *The Coming Caesars* (London, Cape, 1957), pp. 5–7; and see Willmoore Kendall and George W. Carey, eds., *Liberalism versus Conservatism: The Continuing Debate in American Government* (New York and London, Van Nostrand, 1966).

[21] *Newsweek,* January 26, 1970.

[22] Finer, *The Presidency: Crisis and Regeneration,* pp. 23, 112–13; Corwin, *The President,* p. 312.

[23] Corwin, *The President,* p. 313.

[24] Franklin D. Roosevelt well understood this, at least in the critical month of March, 1933, when he had just been inaugurated. The influential columnist Walter Lippmann had expressed impatience at the indecision and stupidity of Congress in the face of national economic emergency. With the President's approval, his friend and adviser Felix Frankfurter answered Lippmann: "Of course there are times for summary action and the pace for devising policies is properly more rapid at one time than at another. But all this is a very different thing from educating the public into the psychology of dictatorship. I know your phrase has been concentration of authority, but the result is the same. We have not, and ought not to have, government by Presidential decree. . . . And I strongly deplore the current tendency to assume that power as such generates wisdom and that the deliberative processes are drags upon wise action." *Roosevelt and Frankfurter: Their Correspondence, 1928–1945,* Max Freedman, ed. (London, Bodley Head, 1968), pp. 115–20. Frankfurter and F. D. R. had a tactical no less than an ethical concern. They wanted to ensure that the President would not at some later stage be left to bear the whole brunt for policies that had misfired — which a proportion of policies are bound to do. Tactically and ethically, they were wise.

[25] Quoted in W. H. Auden and Louis Kronenberger, eds., *The Faber Book of Aphorisms* (London, Faber, 1964), p. 233.

[26] McCarthy as quoted in *Time,* July 26, 1968. On the need for rectitude, see Arnold A. Rogow and Harold D. Lasswell, *Power, Corruption and Rectitude* (Englewood Cliffs, N.J., Prentice-Hall, 1963).

[27] *New York Times,* March 26, 1971.

EPILOGUE

[1] *Newsweek* (international edn.), December 30, 1968, p. 17.

[2] *Time* (international edn.), January 24, 1969, p. 26.

Bibliography

REFERENCE

HARNSBERGER, CAROLINE T., ed., *Treasury of Presidential Quotations.* Chicago: Follett Publishing Co., 1964.

ISRAEL, FRED L., ed., *The State of the Union Messages of the Presidents,* 3 vols. New York: Chelsea House, 1966.

A larger collection of documents may be found in the old 10-volume compilation by James D. Richardson, *Messages and Papers of the Presidents, 1789–1897.*

KANE, JOSEPH N., *Facts About the Presidents: A Compilation of Biographical and Historical Data.* New York: H. W. Wilson, 1959; abridged edn., New York, Pocket Books, 1960.

MCCARTHY, EUGENE, *The Crescent Dictionary of American Politics.* New York and London: Macmillan, 1962; Penguin, 1969.

A handy dispassionate little guide, offering few clues to the temperament of its compiler.

SCHLESINGER, ARTHUR M., JR., and ISRAEL, FRED L., eds., *History of American Presidential Elections,* 4 vols., New York: Chelsea House and McGraw-Hill, 1971. (One-volume condensed edition, *The Coming to Power.* New York: McGraw-Hill, 1972.)

A huge work, with an original essay and a selection of relevant documents for every election from 1789 to 1968.

SPERBER, HANS, and TRITTSCHUH, TRAVIS, *Dictionary of American Political Terms.* New York and London: McGraw-Hill, 1964.

Interesting historical etymologies.

TOURTELLOT, ARTHUR B., ed., *The Presidents on the Presidency.* Garden City, N.Y.: Doubleday, 1960.

Intelligently arranged; less snippety than Harnsberger.

GENERAL WORKS

AGAR, HERBERT, *The Price of Union.* Boston: Houghton Mifflin, 1950; also Sentry edn., 1966.

A well-written survey of American history that pays particular attention to political aspects.

BARBER, JAMES D., "Adult Identity and Presidential Style: The Rhetorical Emphasis." *Daedalus,* Summer, 1968.

A step toward a theory of personality analysis, based on the case of Andrew Johnson.

BINKLEY, WILFRED E., *The President and Congress*. New York: Knopf, 1947; New York: Vintage, 1962.

——*The Man in the White House*. Baltimore: Johns Hopkins University Press, 1959.

BORDEN, MORTON, ed., *America's Ten Greatest Presidents*. Chicago: Rand McNally, 1961.

BROWN, W. BURLIE, *The People's Choice: The Presidential Image in the Campaign Biography*. Baton Rouge: Louisiana State University Press, 1960.

BROWNLOW, LOUIS, *The President and the Presidency*. Chicago: Public Service Administration, 1949.

BRYCE, JAMES, *The American Commonwealth*, 2 vols., 3rd edn. London: Macmillan, 1893–95.

BURNS, JAMES MCGREGOR, *The Deadlock of Democracy: Four-Party Politics in America*. Englewood Cliffs, N.J.: Prentice-Hall, 1963.

——*Presidential Government: The Crucible of Leadership*. Boston: Houghton Mifflin, 1965.

CAVAIOLI, FRANK J., *West Point and the Presidency*. New York: St. John's University Press, 1962.

CHAMBERS, WILLIAM N., *Political Parties in a New Nation: The American Experience, 1776–1809*. New York: Oxford University Press, 1963.

CHAMBERS, WILLIAM N., and BURNHAM, WALTER D., eds., *The American Party Systems: Stages of Political Development*. New York: Oxford University Press, 1967.

CLARK, KEITH C., and LEGERE, LAURENCE J., *The President and the Management of National Security*. New York and London: Praeger, 1969.

CORNWELL, ELMER E., JR., *Presidential Leadership of Public Opinion*. Bloomington: Indiana University Press, 1965.

CORWIN, EDWARD S., *The President: Office and Powers*, 4th edn. New York: New York University Press, 1957.

COYLE, DAVID C., *Ordeal of the Presidency*. Washington, D.C.: Public Affairs Press, 1960.

DONOVAN, ROBERT J., *The Assassins*. New York: Harper, 1955. Attempts on the lives of Presidents.

FEERICK, JOHN D., *From Failing Hands: The Story of Presidential Succession*. New York: Fordham University Press, 1965.

FENNO, RICHARD F., JR., *The President's Cabinet: An Analysis in the Period from Wilson to Eisenhower*. Cambridge, Mass.: Harvard University Press, 1959; New York: Vintage.

FINER, HERMAN, *The Presidency: Crisis and Regeneration*. Chicago: Chicago University Press, 1960.

FORD, HENRY JONES, *The Rise and Growth of American Politics: A Sketch of Constitutional Developments*. New York: Macmillan, 1898; repr. New York, Da Capo Press, 1967.

HEREN, LOUIS, *The New American Commonwealth*. London: Weidenfeld & Nicolson, 1968.

Sees the modern President as analogous to an English medieval king.

HESS, STEPHEN, *America's Political Dynasties: From Adams to Kennedy.* Garden City, N.Y.: Doubleday, 1966.
The activities of sixteen families, several of which have produced presidential candidates.

HOFSTADTER, RICHARD, *The American Political Tradition.* New York: Knopf, 1948; London, Cape, 1966.
Includes coolly excellent essays on Jackson, Lincoln, Theodore Roosevelt, Wilson, and Franklin D. Roosevelt.

——— *The Idea of a Party System: The Rise of Legitimate Opposition in the United States, 1780–1840.* Berkeley and Los Angeles: University of California Press, 1969.

HOLCOMBE, ARTHUR N., *Our More Perfect Union: From Eighteenth-Century Principles to Twentieth-Century Practice.* Cambridge, Mass.: Harvard University Press, 1950.

JOHNSON, DONALD B., and WALKER, J. L., eds., *Dynamics of the American Presidency.* New York and London: Wiley, 1964.
Well-chosen readings.

JOHNSON, WALTER, *1600 Pennsylvania Avenue: Presidents and the People Since 1929.* Boston: Little, Brown, 1960; repr. 1963.

KALLENBACH, JOSEPH E., *The American Chief Executive: The Presidency and the Governorship.* New York: Harper & Row, 1966.

KOENIG, LOUIS W., *The Invisible Presidency.* New York: Holt, Rinehart & Winston, 1960.
An historical survey of presidential cronies, advisers, and assistants.

——— *The Chief Executive.* New York: Harcourt, Brace & World, 1964.

LASKI, HAROLD J., *The American Presidency: An Interpretation.* New York: Harper, 1940.

LIPSET, SEYMOUR M., *The First New Nation.* New York: Basic Books, 1963.

LOCKWOOD, HENRY C., *The Abolition of the Presidency.* New York: Worthington, 1884.

McCORMICK, RICHARD P., *The Second American Party System: Party Formation in the Jacksonian Era.* Chapel Hill: University of North Carolina Press, 1966.

MAILER, NORMAN, *The Presidential Papers.* New York: Bantam, 1964; Harmondsworth: Penguin Books, 1968.
Brilliantly wild yet precise journalism on the Kennedy years.

MARTIN, RALPH G., *Ballots and Bandwagons.* Chicago: Rand McNally, 1964; New York: Signet, 1964.
National conventions of 1912 (Republican), and 1932 and 1956 (Democratic).

MAY, ERNEST R., ed., *The Ultimate Decision: The President as Commander in Chief.* New York: Braziller, 1960.

NEUSTADT, RICHARD E., *Presidential Power: The Politics of Leadership.* New York: Wiley, 1960; Signet, 1964.

PECK, HARRY THURSTON, *Twenty Years of the Republic, 1885–1905.* New

York: Dodd, Mead, 1906; abridged edn., Louis Filler, ed., *Democrats and Republicans: Ten Years of the Republic.* New York: Capricorn, 1964.

POLLARD, JAMES E., *The Presidents and the Press: Truman to Johnson.* Washington, D.C.: Public Affairs Press, 1964.

A sequel to Pollard's earlier *Presidents and the Press.* New York: Macmillan, 1947.

POLSBY, NELSON W., and WILDAVSKY, AARON B., *Presidential Elections: Strategies of American Electoral Politics.* New York: Scribner's, 1964.

RIENCOURT, AMAURY DE, *The Coming Caesars.* London: Cape, 1957.

ROCHE, JOHN P., and LEVY, LEONARD W., eds., *The Presidency.* New York: Harcourt, Brace & World, 1964.

A brisk, competent collection of readings.

ROSEBOOM, EUGENE H., *A History of Presidential Elections,* 2nd edn. New York: Macmillan, 1964.

ROSSITER, CLINTON, *The American Presidency,* revised edn. New York: New American Library, 1960.

SEIDMAN, HAROLD, *Politics, Position and Power: The Dynamics of Federal Organization.* New York and London: Oxford University Press, 1970.

SILVA, RUTH C., *Presidential Succession.* Ann Arbor: University of Michigan Press, 1951.

SORENSEN, THEODORE C., *Decision-Making in the White House: The Olive Branch or the Arrows.* New York: Columbia University Press, 1963.

STILLMAN, EDMUND, and PFAFF, WILLIAM, *The New Politics: America and the End of the Postwar World.* New York: Coward McCann, 1961; New York: Harper Colophon, 1962.

THACH, CHARLES, JR., *The Creation of the Presidency, 1775–1789.* Baltimore: Johns Hopkins University Press, 1922; repr. 1969.

TUGWELL, REXFORD G., *The Enlargement of the Presidency.* Garden City, N.Y.: Doubleday, 1960.

VILE, M. J. C., *Politics in the U.S.A.* London: Allen Lane The Penguin Press, 1970.

WARREN, SIDNEY, *The Battle for the Presidency.* Philadelphia: Lippincott, 1968.

WHITE, LEONARD D., *The Federalists: A Study in Administrative History.* New York: Macmillan, 1948.

—— *The Jeffersonians . . . 1801–1829.* 1951.

—— *The Jacksonians . . . 1829–1861.* 1954.

—— *The Republican Era . . . 1869–1901.* 1958.

WHITE, THEODORE H., *The Making of the President, 1960.* New York: Atheneum, 1960; London: Cape, 1962.

—— *The Making of the President, 1964.* New York: Atheneum, 1965.

—— *The Making of the President, 1968.*

WILMERDING, LUCIUS, JR., *The Electoral College.* New Brunswick, N.J.: Rutgers University Press, 1959; Boston: Beacon Press, 1964.

WILSON, WOODROW, *Congressional Government.* Boston: 1885; repr.

Cleveland, Ohio: Meridian Books, 1956.

———*Constitutional Government in the United States.* New York: Columbia University Press, 1908; repr. 1961.

WOLL, PETER, *American Bureaucracy.* New York: Norton, 1963.

See especially Chapter 5, "The President and Bureaucracy."

WRIGHT, BENJAMIN F., ed., *The Federalist.* Cambridge, Mass.: Harvard University Press, 1961.

Among the best of many editions.

YARMOLINSKY, ADAM, *The Military Establishment: Its Impacts on American Society.* New York and London: 1971.

INDIVIDUAL PRESIDENTS

This is a highly selective list. Nearly all the twentieth-century Presidents who survived the office in reasonable health have written their memoirs: Theodore Roosevelt, Coolidge, Hoover, Truman, Eisenhower, Lyndon Johnson. Though Taft did not produce memoirs, he did publish sundry reflections on the Presidency. The memoir-writing habit was less common in the nineteenth century; one of the few examples, the autobiography of Martin Van Buren, is unrevealing and says little about Van Buren's own administration. Fortunately several of these earlier Presidents kept diaries or were copious letter writers. There are substantial editions of the papers of Washington, John and John Quincy Adams, Thomas Jefferson, James Madison, Andrew Jackson, James Buchanan, Lincoln, and Theodore Roosevelt. James K. Polk's *Diary* is available in a good four-volume edition. There are also several important new scholarly editions in progress. These include the writings of the Adamses, Jefferson, Madison, Andrew Johnson, and Woodrow Wilson. Here follows a sampling of biographical studies, in alphabetical order by President:

KURTZ, STEPHEN G., *The Presidency of John Adams.* Philadelphia: University of Pennsylvania Press, 1957.

SMITH, PAGE, *John Adams,* 2 vols. Garden City, N.Y.: Doubleday, 1962.

BEMIS, SAMUEL F., *John Quincy Adams and the Union.* New York: Knopf, 1956.

KLEIN, PHILIP S., *President James Buchanan: A Biography.* University Park: Pennsylvania State University Press, 1962.

MERRILL, HORACE S., *Bourbon Leader: Grover Cleveland and the Democratic Party.* Boston: Little, Brown, 1957.

MCCOY, DONALD R., *Calvin Coolidge: The Quiet President.* New York: Macmillan, 1967.

WHITE, WILLIAM A., *A Puritan in Babylon: The Story of Calvin Coolidge.* New York: Macmillan, 1938; repr. New York: Capricorn, 1965.

ALBERTSON, DEAN, ed., *Eisenhower as President.* New York: Hill & Wang, 1963.

HUGHES, EMMET J., *The Ordeal of Power: A Political Memoir of the Eisenhower Years.* New York: Atheneum, 1963; New York: Dell, 1964.

MURRAY, ROBERT K., *The Harding Era: Warren G. Harding and His Ad-*

ministration. Minneapolis: University of Minnesota Press, 1969.

RUSSELL, FRANCIS, *President Harding: His Life and Times, 1865–1923*. London: Eyre & Spottiswoode, 1969.

SINCLAIR, ANDREW, *The Available Man: The Life Behind the Masks of Warren Gamaliel Harding*. New York: Macmillan; London: Collier-Macmillan, 1965.

BASSETT, JOHN S., *The Life of Andrew Jackson*, revised edn. New York: Macmillan, 1916.

REMINI, ROBERT V., *The Election of Andrew Jackson*. Philadelphia: Lippincott, 1963.

SCHLESINGER, ARTHUR M., JR., *The Age of Jackson*. Boston: Little, Brown, 1945.

MALONE, DUMAS, *Jefferson and His Time*, 5 vols. Boston: Little, Brown, 1948, 1951.

PETERSON, MERRILL, *The Jefferson Image in the American Mind*. New York: Oxford University Press, 1960.

EVANS, ROWLAND, and NOVAK, ROBERT, *Lyndon B. Johnson: The Exercise of Power*. New York: New American Library, 1966.

GEYELIN, PHILIP, *Lyndon B. Johnson and the World*. New York: Praeger, 1966.

SHERRILL, ROBERT, *The Accidental President*. New York: Grossman, 1967.

CHASE, HAROLD W., and LERMAN, ALLEN H., eds., *Kennedy and the Press: The News Conferences*. New York: Crowell, 1965.

DONALD, AIDA DI PACE, ed., *John F. Kennedy and the New Frontier*. New York: Hill & Wang, 1966.

FUCHS, LAWRENCE H., *John F. Kennedy and American Catholicism*. New York: Meredith, 1967.

MANCHESTER, WILLIAM, *Death of a President: November, 1963*. London: Michael Joseph, 1967; New York: Harper & Row, 1967.

SCHLESINGER, ARTHUR M., JR., *A Thousand Days: John F. Kennedy in the White House*. London: Andre Deutsch, 1965; New York: Houghton Mifflin, 1965.

SORENSEN, THEODORE C., *Kennedy*. New York: Harper & Row, 1965.

CURRENT, RICHARD N., *The Lincoln Nobody Knows*. New York: McGraw-Hill, 1958; Hill & Wang: 1963.

DONALD, DAVID, *Lincoln Reconsidered*. New York: Knopf Vintage, 1956.

FEHRENBACHER, DON E., ed., *Abraham Lincoln: A Documentary Portrait*. New York: Signet, 1964.

RANDALL, JAMES G., *Lincoln the Liberal Statesman*. New York: Dodd, Mead, 1947; repr. New York: Apollo.

BRANT, IRVING, *The Fourth President: A Life of James Madison*. London: Eyre & Spottiswoode, 1970.

MCGINNISS, JOE, *The Selling of the President*. Harmondsworth: Penguin, 1970.

On the "marketing" of Richard Nixon in 1968.

WILLS, GARRY, *Nixon Agonistes: The Crisis of the Self-Made Man*. Boston:

Houghton Mifflin, 1970.

SELLERS, CHARLES G., JR., *James K. Polk: Continentalist.* Princeton: Princeton University Press, 1966.

FREIDEL, FRANK, *Franklin D. Roosevelt: The Apprenticeship; The Ordeal; The Triumph,* 3 vols. Boston: Little, Brown, 1952, 1954, 1956.

LEUCHTENBURG, WILLIAM E., ed., *Franklin D. Roosevelt: A Profile.* New York: Hill & Wang, 1967.

MAJOR, JOHN, ed., *The New Deal.* London, Longmans, Green, 1968.

SCHLESINGER, ARTHUR M., JR., *The Age of Roosevelt: The Crisis of the Old Order; The Coming of the New Deal; The Politics of Upheaval,* 3 vols. London: Heinemann, 1957, 1958, 1960.

BLUM, JOHN M., *The Republican Roosevelt* [T.R.] Cambridge, Mass.: Harvard University Press, 1954; New York: Atheneum, 1962.

HARBAUGH, WILLIAM H., *The Life and Times of Theodore Roosevelt,* revised edn. New York: Collier, 1963.

KELLER, MORTON, ed., *Theodore Roosevelt: A Profile.* New York: Hill & Wang, 1967.

PRINGLE, HOWARD F., *The Life and Times of William Howard Taft,* 2 vols. New York: Holt, 1939; repr. Hamden, Conn.: Archon Books, 1964.

BERNSTEIN, BARTON J., and MATUSOW, ALLEN J., eds., *The Truman Administration: A Documentary History.* New York and London: Harper & Row, 1966.

PHILLIPS, CABELL, *The Truman Presidency: The History of a Triumphant Succession.* London: Collier-Macmillan, 1966.

ROSS, IRWIN, *The Loneliest Campaign: The Truman Victory of 1948.* New York: New American Library, 1968.

CURTIS, JAMES C., *The Fox at Bay: Martin Van Buren and the Presidency, 1837–1841.* Lexington: University of Kentucky Press, 1970.

CUNLIFFE, MARCUS, *George Washington: Man and Monument.* New York: Mentor, 1960.

WRIGHT, ESMOND, *Washington and the American Revolution.* London: English Universities Press, 1957.

BLUM, JOHN M., *Woodrow Wilson and the Politics of Morality.* Boston: Little, Brown, 1956.

LINK, ARTHUR S., *Woodrow Wilson and the Progressive Era, 1910-1917.* New York: Harper & Row, 1954; New York: Harper Torchbooks, 1963.

Picture Credits

Index

178, 190; as President, 185, 235, 374; vetoed restriction of Chinese immigration, 186, *187*
Articles of Confederation, 9, 10, 18, 19, 21, 25, 31, 41, 371, 385
Atlantic Monthly, 412n.
Atomic weapons, 276, 290–91, 292, 296, 304
Attorney General, 46; *See also* Justice, U.S. Department of
Austria-Hungary, 286
Autobiography of Martin Van Buren, The, 154

Bagehot, Walter, 75
Baker, Ray Stannard, 264
Baldwin, J. G., 88, 90, 91, 92
Baltimore Sun, 356
Bancroft, George, 201
Bandaranaike, Solomon, 162
Bank of the U.S.: First, 48, 87; Second, 86, 87, 88, 91, 93, 124, 150, 154, 157, 158, 163
Barkley, Alben W., *167*
Barry, William T., 123
Bean (assassin), 161, 407n.
Beard, Charles A., 30
Beckley, John, 112
Beecher, Henry Ward, 224
Beichman, Arnold, 413n.
Bell, John, 230
Bellamy, Edward, 202, 261, 267
Beloff, Max, 417n.
Bennett, James Gordon, 234
Benton, Thomas Hart, 88, 90, 124, 136, 152, 153
Biddle, Nicholas, 86, 87, 93, *125*
Bierce, Ambrose G., 164, 166, 172, 237
Binkley, Wilfred E., 239, 249
Bismarck, Otto von, 162
Black, Hugo L., 344
Blackstone, William, 19, 20, 32
Blaine, James G., 197, 202, 212, 216, 221, 226, 229, 237–38, 406n.
Bliss, Cornelius N., 252
Bliss, William D. P., 206–7
Bolling, Richard, 367
Booth, John Wilkes, *159,* 160, 162, 163, 373
Boothby, Lord, 417n.
Borah, William E., 288

Boudinot, Elias, 63
Bowdoin, James, *22*
Brandeis, Louis D., 344
Brazil, 286
Breckinridge, John, 230
Bricker, John, 298
Bricker Amendment, 298–99
Brogan, Sir Denis W., 354
Brooklyn *Daily Eagle,* 289
Brown, W. Burlie, 219–20
Brownlow, Louis, 163
Bryan, William Jennings, 261, 266, 357; as a candidate, *231*–32, 252, 396; and election of 1896, 128, 207, 410n.; as an orator, 88, 202, 232; as Secretary of State, 284, 289, *315*
Bryce, James, 192–93, 207, 392
Buchanan, James, *131,* 172, 212, 286, 408n.; campaign literature on, 222; and patronage, 132–33; as President, 170, 371
Buckley, Charles A., 326
Bundy, McGeorge, 305, 307, 340
Burchard, Dr. Samuel, 238
Burdick, Eugene, 365
Bureaucracy in a Democracy (Hyneman), 368
Burns, James MacGregor, 147, 369–70, 412n.
Burr, Aaron, *64*–65
Butler, Benjamin F., 182
Butler, Pierce, 28, 35, 61
Butt, Archie, 252, 254
Byrd, Harry, 325
Byrnes, James F., 302
Byrnes, John, 327

Cabinet, 105, 199, 305, 334–39 *passim,* 370, 378, 409n.; Congress and, 198, 204; forming of, 48–51, 237; as route to Presidency, 212; tenure of, 118, 122. *See also* Federal bureaucracy; individual departments; individual Presidents
"Cabinet Government in the United States" (Wilson), 198
Caesar's Column (Donnelly), 262
Calhoun, John C., 83, 88, 116, 117, 134, 149, 150, 151, 153, 155, 158, 163, 171, 210, *211*
California, 98
Cameron, Simon, 183

55, 271, 284, 324–26, 366, 371, 378;
reorganization of, 319, 327–28; and
separation of powers, 15, 23–24, 32,
47–48, 59, 100, 128, 143, 193. *See
also* Constitution, the; Federal
bureaucracy; Presidency, the;
President, the
Executive Reorganization Act, 319,
328–29, 335

Fairlie, Henry, 417n.
Fall, Albert, 360
Faubus, Orval, 322
Federal bureaucracy, 46, 51–52, 198,
327, 334–41, 372, 379, 416n; anti-
communist crusade and, 293, 304;
appointments to, 51; civil service
reform and, 133, 150, 185, 190, 196;
and foreign affairs, 301–8; Hoover
Commission and, 335–36, 340;
laxity in, 96–97; and New Deal,
318–19; reorganization of, 319, 335–
38; rotation in office. *See* Spoils
system; salaries of, 44, 51; and
spoils system, 52, 91, 121–24, 128,
129–30, 132–34, 150, 154, 183, 185,
190, 192, 193, 197. *See also*
Cabinet; Executive branch
"Federal Government" (Upshur), 177
Federal Reserve Act, 269
Federalist, The, 15, 26, 33, 106–7,
276
Federalists, 10, 16, 19, 23, 28–29, 33,
34, 58, 62, 64–65, 67, 70, 73, 75,
83, 108, 110, 113, 114, 120, 147, 393,
394
Ferdinand, archduke of Austria, 162
Ferdinand IV, king of Naples, 19
Fillmore, Millard, 212, 213
Finer, Herman, 368–69, 373–75, 376,
378
Finletter, Thomas K., 367
First lady: social responsibilities
of, 70. *See also* individual first
ladies
First New Nation, The (Lipset), 74
Florida, 113
Foraker, Joseph B., 192
Ford, Gerald R., Jr., 347
Ford, Henry Jones, 245, 247
Foreign affairs, 275–310; bipartisan-
ship in, 299–300; Congress and, 58–

60, 275, 280–281, 282, 283, 284–85,
290, 294, 296, 298–301, 352; and
domestic issues, 313–14; foreign aid,
298; and Presidential power, 58–60,
247–48, 275–310 *passim,* 352; secrecy
in, 276, 294, 414n.; U-2 incident,
297, 314. *See also* individual
countries; individual Presidents
Fortas, Abe, 345
480, The (Burdick), 365·
France, 4, 60, 61, 285, 286, 289;
assisted in American Revolution,
58; and French Revolution, 58;
and Napoleon, 58; postwar, 292–93
Francis, John, 407n.
Frank Leslie's Illustrated Newspaper,
169
Frankfurter, Felix, 344, 419n.
Franklin, Benjamin, 46, 214; as
delegate to Constitutional
Convention, 14, *31, 35,* 44
Frederick II, king of Prussia, 19
Frederick Augustus (duke of York),
25
*Freeman's Journal: Or, the North-
American Intelligencer, The,* 14
Frémont, John C., 215, 218, 221
Fulbright, J. William, 299, 300, 355,
357

Galbraith, John K., 85
Gallatin, Albert, 59, *111,* 112, 113
Gandhi, Mohandas, 162
Garfield, James A., 172, 173, *191,*
212, 215, 219, 222, 228, 256, 314;
appointments of, 184–85, 255;
assassination of, 159, 160, 162, 169,
185, 192, 213, 239, 360; campaign
biography of, *208,* 223–24; as a
candidate, 231, 233; Congress and,
184–85, 197, 198; as an orator, 88,
231
Garner, John Nance, 296
Garson, Barbara, 171
Genet, Edmond, 58
Genovese, Eugene, 373
George, Henry, 195, 202, 261, 267,
285
George III, king of England, 20, 25,
34, 74, *114,* 155
Georgia, 25, 148–49
Germany, 286; in World War II,

279, 290
Gerry, Elbridge, 28
Godkin, Edwin L., 200
Goebel, William, 166
Goldberg, Arthur, 414n.
Goldman, Eric, 340
Goldwater, Barry M., 3, 142–43, 146, 156, 296, 333, 361, 363, 379
Goodnow, Frank J., 243
Gorham, Nathaniel, 24
Grant, Ulysses S., 195, 198, 200, 212, 239, 245, 264; Cabinet of, 179, 180; campaign biography of, 221, *225;* as a candidate, 224–46, 227, 230–31; Congress and, 178, 179, 180, 182–83, 186, 190; as President, 169, 170, 178–79, 283, 288, 371; as professional soldier, 215, 216, 218, 219; second term of, 192
Great Britain, 95, 286, 288, 289, 327; and American Civil War, 285; and destroyer deal with U.S., 278–79, 280–81; government of, 15–16, 20, 24, 34, 43, 53, 56, 352–53, 367, 397, 412n., 417n.; political parties in, 105, 110; postwar, 292–93; violence in, 161
Great War Syndicate, The (Stockton), 291
Greece, 292
Greeley, Horace, 198, 200, 226
Guiteau, Charles J., *159,* 160, 169, 360
Gulliver's Travels (Swift), 105
Gustavus III, king of Sweden, 19

Hacker, Andrew, 367
Haiti, 280
Hamilton (assassin), 407n.
Hamilton, Alexander, 40, 60, 73, 78, 79, 109; as delegate to Constitutional Convention, *12,* 14, 18, 19, 24, 25, *27,* 28, 29, *31,* 32, 33, 146; and *The Federalist,* 15–16; and foreign affairs, 59; Jefferson and, 49, 50, 53–54, 108; as Secretary of the Treasury, 41–42, 46, 48, *49,* 50, 51, 53–55, 56, 87, 97
Hamlin, Hannibal, 66
Hancock, Winfield Scott, 173, 215, 216, 219, 222, 226, 229
Hanna, Marcus A., 284
Harding, Warren G., 357; death of,

239, 360; as President, 18, 81, 271, 272, 286–*87,* 288, 290, 348, 371, 419n.
Harper's Weekly, 219, 224
Harriman, Averell, 304
Harrison, Benjamin, 173, *191,* 192, 201, 212, 213, 215, *222;* Congress and, 190; as President, 199, 252
Harrison, William H., *127, 131,* 134, 171, 212, 215; as a candidate, *222,* 229; death of, 67, *69,* 76, 163, 360; and election of 1840, 85, 126, 128, 155–56, 223–24; and patronage, 130
Harvard University, 45
Hatch Act, 397
Hawaii, 249, 288
Hawthorne, Nathaniel, 129, 220
Hay, John, 284, 289
Hayes, Rutherford B., 172, *174, 184, 201,* 212–13, 214, 215, *217;* appointments of, 183–84, 190; Cabinet of, 183; campaign biographies of, 220, 221; Congress and, 178, 183–84, 186, 187, 189, 197; and labor strikes, 188, 201–2; as a politician, 223–24, 226, 227–28, 231; as President, 198, 200, 201, 234, 245, 251, 255–56, 411n.; vetoed restriction of Chinese immigration, 186; vetoes of, 186, 187
Hayes, Mrs. Rutherford (Lucy), 200, *201,* 214, 411n.
Health, Education, and Welfare, U.S. Department of, 338
Hearst, William Randolph, 166
Heaton, Gen. Leonard, *359*
Henry, Patrick, 11, 16, *17,* 40, 51
Herblock cartoon, *274*
Herter, Christian, 302
Hillhouse, James, 65
Hitler, Adolf, 279, 290
Hoar, George F., 183
Hoban, James, *66*
Hoffman, Abbie, 367
Holcombe, Arthur N., 354
Holland, 19
Hoover, Herbert Clark, *323,* 358, 362, 419n.; and economy, 314; and foreign affairs, 286; Hoover Commission, 335–36, 340, 360; on Presidency, 323; and press, 317; and radio, 317, 318
Hoover Commission, 335–36, 340, 360
Hopkins, Harry, 280, 340

on Presidency, 65, 70, 71, 101; as
President, 47, 50, 67, 78–82, *104,
109,* 120, 141, 344, 370; reputation
of, 77, 78, 102; second term of, 65,
70; as Secretary of State, 34, 46,
48, *49,* 50; and states' rights, 79,
82–83, 91, 148; supported higher
education, 83; as Vice-President,
64, 65, 109
Johnson, Andrew, *165,* 200–201, 213;
Congress and, 182, 187, 194;
impeachment of, 53, 170, *176,* 178,
*179–*80; as President, 164, 180–81,
187, 201; as Vice-President, 137,
161
Johnson, Lyndon B., *171,* 251, 296,
299, 302, 361, 363, 418n.; and civil
rights, 326, 363; Congress and, 299,
325–26, 332–33, 337–38, 347; criticism of, 171, 381, 382; Great Society
of, 333, 382; illness of, 358; Library
of, 375–76; as President, 305, 308,
324, *347, 356,* 360, 367, 370, 373,
414n.; and press, 346; special assistants to, 340, 341; as Vice-President,
161, 296, 326; and Vietnam, 300,
301, 310, 333, 384; withdrawal of, 1,
2, 4, 310, 333
Johnson, Mrs. Lyndon B. (Claudia),
171, 364, 382
Johnson, Richard M., 65, 153
Jones, Samuel M., 261, 262
Jubilee of the Constitution (Adams),
53
Judiciary Acts, 46, 113
Justice, U.S. Department of, 338,
346. *See also* Attorney General

Katzenbach, Nicholas, 300
Kellogg, Frank E., 289
Kellogg-Briand Pact, 289
Kennedy, Edward, 3
Kennedy, John F., 161, 170–71, 173,
296, 302, *309,* 324, 358, 361;
assassination of, 159, 160, 167–68,
169, 171, 358; Congress and, 325,
326, 331–32, 336; criticism of, 332;
and Cuba, *297,* 298, 308; and foreign affairs, 297–98, 308–9;
patrician background of, 265, 355;
and Peace Corps, 309; as a
politician, 326, 345; on Presidency,

348; as President, 154, 170, 304–5,
307–8, 339, 347, 348, *350,* 371; and
press, 324, 346; and religion, 314,
362, 363; special assistants to, 305,
307, 340; and steel industry, 322–24,
327; trips of, 297; and University of
Mississippi incident, 322; and
Vietnam, 308, 309
Kennedy, Mrs. John F. (Jacqueline
Bouvier), 364
Kennedy, Robert, 1, 3, 323, 384
Kent, James, 154
Khruschchev, Nikita S., 296, *297,*
298, 313
Kilpatrick, Carroll, 332
King, Dr. Martin Luther, 1
King, Rufus, *27,* 28, 29
King, William R., 65
Kinsman, Seth, *184*
Kipling, Rudyard, 249
Kissinger, Henry, 305, *306,* 340
Knowland, William, 299
Know-Nothing party, 394, 395
Knox, Henry, 46, 48, *49*
Koenig, Louis W., 345, 353
Korean War, 280, 292, 298, 320, 343
Kurtz, Stephen G., 51

Labor, *188,* 201–2, 343
Labor, U.S. Department of, 338
Lafayette, Marquis de, 39, 40
LaFollette, Robert M., 233–34, 261,
262, 394
Lamon, Ward, 101
Laski, Harold J., 170, 352–53
Latin America, *278,* 279, 280, 288,
289, 296; and dollar diplomacy, 288;
and Good-Neighbor policy, 288
Lawrence (assassin), 160, 163, 172
Lawrie, Lee, *31*
Legislative branch, 18, 194, 301;
corruption in, 197; and executive
branch, 11, 15, 26, 33, 56, 79, 91,
117, 142–43, 146–47, 151, 178, 180,
182–88, 190, 198, 203–7, 254–55,
271, 284, 324–26, 366, 371, 378; and
separation of powers, 15, 23–24,
32, 47–48, 59, 100, 128, 143, 193.
See also Congress, U.S.; House of
Representatives, U.S.; Senate, U.S.
Lekachman, Robert, 333
Lend-Lease Act, 281

Leopold I, grand duke of Tuscany, 19
Lincoln, Abraham, 4, 33, 65–66, *99,*
161, 172, 173, 210; administrative
problems of, 96; against Mexican
War, 98; assassination of, 159, 160,
162, 169, 170, 239; Cabinet of, 102,
284; as a candidate, 220, 222, 224,
229, 230, 410n.; and Civil War, 76,
96, 98, 100–101, *103,* 136, 158, 218,
248, 282, 357; as Commander in
Chief, 18, 98, 101; Congress and,
100–101, 102, 137; as a congressman,
98, 212; criticism of, 76, 101, 164;
and Emancipation Proclamation,
102, 371, 374; humor of, 234;
inauguration of, 76; and law and
order, 157; as an orator, 88; and
patronage, 132, 137; and politics,
136–37; on Presidency, 101; as
President, 98, 101–2, 170, 178, 180–
81, 209, 235, 244, 247, 255, 315, 344,
370, 371, 412n.; reputation of, 102;
rumored plot against, 76–77;
second term of, 170, 192; and
slavery, 101; in state legislature,
212; and the Union, 76, 101; war
powers of, 98, 100–101, 164, 282
Link, Arthur S., 268
Lippmann, Walter, 266–67, 287, 411n.,
412n., 419n.
Lipset, Seymour M., 74
Little Rock, Ark., *321,* 322, 327, 344–
45
Livingston, Edward, 88
Livingston, Robert R., *38*
Livingston, William, 26
Lloyd, Henry Demarest, 261, 262,
364
Locke, John, 19, 20, 32, 320
Lockwood, Henry C., 177–78, 180,
181, 351, 373
Lodge, Henry Cabot, *283,* 414n.
Loeb, William, Jr., 251, 408n.
Logan, John A., 183
Logan Act, 60
London, Jack, 262
Looking Backward (Bellamy), 202,
267
Louis XIV, king of France, 71, 307
Louis XVI, king of France, 19, 58
Louisiana Purchase, 79–80
Lowndes, Rawlin, 11

MacArthur, Douglas, 289, 293, 320,
327
MacBird, 171
Maclay, William, 43, 48
Macmillan, Harold, 353, 417n.
Madison, James, 13, 47, 49, 50, 54,
57, *81,* 212; as delegate to
Constitutional Convention, 9, 10,
14, 21, 28, 29–30, *31,* 34, 146; and
The Federalist, 15, 26; and foreign
affairs, 58; on political parties,
106–7, 109, 116; as President, 18,
62, 70, 78, 79, 81, 113; on rotation
in office, 123; second term of, 70,
114, 401n.; and states' rights, 83,
148; and War of 1812, 80, 147, 248
Mailer, Norman, 381, 383
Malone, Dumas, 80
Man, The (Wallace), 365–66
Man in the White House, The (Bink-
ley), 239
Mansfield, Mike, 325
"March of Anarchy, The," 157
Marcy, William L., 95, 96, 122
Marie Antoinette, queen of France, 58
Marshall, George C., 302, *303,* 304
Marshall, John, 51, 60, 75, 78, 79,
148, 152
Marshall Plan, 292, 303
Martin, Luther, 9, 25
Mason, George, 10–11, *17*
Massachusetts, 10, 25, 148
McCarran, Pat, 330
McCarran-Walter Act, 330
McCarthy, Eugene, 1, 379, 380, 381,
382
McCarthy, Joseph, 293, 304, 331, 373
McClellan, George B., 173, 215, 216,
218–19, 357, 371
McClure Syndicate, 166
McCormack, John W., 359
McCormick, Richard P., 85, 110, 111,
128
McCulloch v. Maryland, 151
McKinley, William, 212, 213, 215,
254, 260, 318; assassination of, 159,
160, 161, 166, 169, 170, 239, 407n.;
campaign biography of, 221; as a
candidate, *231,* 232; Congress and,
205, 257; and election of 1896, 128,
207, 396, 409n.; on Presidency, 96;
as President, *205,* 237, 238, 250,

252, 284; second term of, 192; and
Spanish-American War, *246,* 248
McLean, John, 122
McNamara, Robert S., 302, 341
Mencken, H. L., 2
Mexican War, 95, 97, 98, 134, *135,*
136, 147, 279, 280, 282, 283
Mexico, 286
Miami and the Siege of Chicago
(Mailer), 381, 383
Miami Beach, Fla., 2, 380
Michael, prince of Serbia, 162
Mills, C. Wright, 302
Mississippi, University of, 322
Missouri Compromise, 118
Mitchell, John, 340, 386
M'Naghten, Daniel, 161
Monarchies, 19–20, 111; and aristo-
cracy, 19; fear of an American,
10–11, 13–16, 20, 24–25, 33, 34,
145–46, 154; 157, 158, 169–71, 172,
173
Monroe, James, 57, *81,* 147, 212;
appointments of, 115–16, 117;
Cabinet of, 116, 117, 118; as
delegate to Constitutional Conven-
tion, 11, 15, 16, 18; and political
parties, 115, 137; as President, 62,
70, 79, 81, 97, 113, 117, 118, 120,
279, 288; and states' rights, 83, 148;
trips of, 44–45
Monroe Doctrine, 31, 80, 115, 279,
285, 288
Montesquieu, Charles Louis de
Secondat, baron de La Brède et de,
19, 20, 32, 33
Moos, Malcolm, 414n.
Morris, Gouverneur, 24, *27,* 28, 29,
32, 59, 106, 279
Morris, Robert, 14
Murray, Robert K., 419n.
Muskie, Edmund, 2, 383
Myers v. United States, 344

Napoleon I, 32, 58, *114*
Napoleon III, 162
Nast, Thomas, 225–26
Nation, 224
National Republic party. *See* Whig
party
National Security Council, 305, 307–8,
339
Navy, U.S., 193, 249, *281,* 285, 290
Navy, U.S. Department of, 47, 96,
301, 334–35
Negro, the, 194, 269; in Cabinet, 337–
38; and franchise, 210; and Vice-
Presidency, 364; vote of, during
Reconstruction, 195. *See also* Civil
rights
Neustadt, Richard E., 324, 326–27
Neutrality Acts, 59, 290
Neutrality Proclamation of 1793, 48,
58
New Deal, 314, 318–19. *See also*
Roosevelt, Franklin Delano
New Hampshire, 10, 23
New Jersey, 26
New Mexico, 98
*New Politics: America and the End of
the Postwar World, The* (Stillman
and Pfaff), 276
New Republic, 267, 269
New York City, 41, 66, 229, 291
New York Custom House, 183, 184
New York *Herald,* 234
New York *Herald Tribune,* 346
New-York Journal, 13
New York *Journal,* 164, 166
New York State, 10, *12,* 18, 23, 25–26,
30–31, 32, 213
New York *Sun,* 224, *283*
New York Times, The, 346, *347,* 386
New York *Tribune,* 224
Nicaragua, 280
Nicola, Lewis, 24
Niebuhr, Reinhold, 293
Niles, Hezekiah, 159
Niles' Register, 157, 159
Nixon, Richard M., 173, 296, 361,
401n.; appointments of, 382, 385;
Cabinet of, 385; 1960 campaign of,
294, 296, 314; China trip of, *306,*
310, 367, *383,* 386; Congress and,
334, 385; criticism of, 2, 338, 380,
386; European trip of, 382–83; and
foreign affairs, 294, 296; nomination
and election of, 1, 2, 382, 398; as
President, 373, 380, 381, 382–86,
398, 415n.; and reorganization of
executive, 338; special assistants
to, 305, 340; and Supreme Court
nominations, 334, 415n.; as Vice-

President, 296, 299; and Vietnam, 301, 334, 367, 386

Nixon, Mrs. Richard M. (Patricia), *306*, 380

Nixon Agonistes (Wills), 367

Norris, George, 260, 288

North American Review, 218

North Atlantic Treaty Organization (NATO), 293

North Carolina, 10, 23

Nullification Proclamation, 88, 148, 158

Ohio, 213

Olney, Richard, 288

Open Door policy, 288, 289

Ordeal of Power, The (Hughes), 371

Oregon, 95, 98

Orsini, Felice, 162

Osborn v. Bank of the U.S., 151

Osgood, Samuel, 46

Ostrogorski, Moisei, 133

Oswald, Lee Harvey, 160, 373

Otis, James, 24

Our Chief Magistrate and His Powers (Taft), 181

Our More Perfect Union (Holcombe), 354

Our Times (Sullivan), 250

Overman Act, 280, 315

Oxford, Edward, 407n.

Paine, Thomas, 20, 145–46

Panama, 266, 277, 288, 289

"Pandora" (James), 200

Partisan Leader, The (Tucker), 155

Parton, James, 89

Pate, Robert, 407n.

Paterson, C. Perry, 367–68

Paterson, William, 25

Patriotic Gore (Wilson), 157

Peale, Rembrandt, *81*

Peck, Harry Thurston, 199, 235

Peel, Sir Robert, 161

Pegler, Westbrook, 166

Pendleton Act, 185, 190

Pennsylvania, 23, 29

People's Choice: The Presidential Image in the Campaign Biography, The (Brown), 219–20

People's party. *See* Populist party

Peterson, Merrill, 78

Pfaff, William, 276

Philadelphia, Pa., *8,* 9, 66

Philadelphiensis. *See* Workman, Benjamin

Philip Dru: Administrator; A Story of Tomorrow (House), 168

Philippines, 249, 288, 289, *295*

Pierce, Franklin, *131, 133,* 134, 212, 215, 371; campaign biography of, 220, 221, 222; and election of 1852, 129

Pillow, Gideon, 136

Pinckney, Charles C., 28, 29, 49, 51

Pitt, William, 53

Platt, Thomas C., 184–85, 192, 213

Plehve, Vyacheslav, 162

Poindexter, George, 150

Poland, 19–20, 34

Political parties, 3, 73, 89, 105–37, 256–58, 370, 392–95; advantages of, 392–93, 394; bribery and fraud in, 189, 257; and campaign biographies, 219–24; and clubs, 73, 224; "coattail" phenomenon of, 112; Congress and, 108, 111–13, 181, 413n.; consensus in, 256, 346; conventions of, 2, 85, 94, 121, 128, 210, 225, 228–29, 380, 395; cost of campaigns, 396–98; and criticism of Presidents, 145, 146, 147, 181; decline of, 114–17; early leaders against, 105–10; and government, 193–94, 197, 392–93; and Hatch Act, 397; and issues, 124; and military candidates, 216, 218; origin of, 110; and the people, 194; and platforms, 121, 124, 128, 224, 258; and Presidency, 110–16, 119–20, 121, 126, 128–29, 130, 134, 137, 172, 188–89, 190, 200, 209, 256–57, 326, 395; reformers in, 185, 200, 258; and search for presidential candidates, 192, 194, 209–10; and spoils system, 122–24, 128, 129–30, 132–34, 183; and third parties, 3, 194, 200, 209, 394, 395, 396, 400n.; two major, 107, 126, 128, 147, 173, 392–93, 394; and unrest in America, 157; and Vice-Presidency, 214. *See also* Elections and election campaigns; individual parties

Politics and Administration (Goodnow), 243

Polk, James K., *94,* 120, 212, 213;

Cabinet of, 95, 96–98, 102, 212; and election of 1844, 94, 129, 172; final message of, 92; and Mexican War, 95, 97, 98, 134, 136, 147, 158, 279, 280, 282; and Oregon settlement, 95; and patronage, 130, 133, 147, 192; on Presidency, 96, 98, 130; as President, 92, 94–98, 141, 288; and veto power, 92–93

Polk, Mrs. James K., 95–96

Populist Party, 199, 202, 206, 257, 259, 262, 394, 395

Postage, U.S., 56

Postmaster General, 46, 48, 123, 338

Power Elite, The (Mills), 302

Powers, Francis Gary, 314

Preface to Politics, A (Lippmann), 266

Presidency, the 78, 410n; burdens of, 65, 70–71, 96, 98, 101, 118, 130, 326, 348, 379; ennobling effect of, 239, 374; in Gilded Age, 192–207 *passim,* 237, 245; as liberal and international, 327, 330; and political parties, 110–16, 119–20, 121, 126, 128–29, 130, 134, 137, 172, 188–89, 190, 200, 209, 256–57, 326, 395; power of, 79, 80, 87, 98, 120, 126, 141–43, 146, 148–58, 164, 168–74, 177–78, 180–82, 252, 254–55, 266, 294, 298–301, 308, 310, 320, 322–24, 327, 343, 347–49, 351–52, 354, 372–77, 379, 380, 411n., 412n., 419n; and precedents, 44–61 *passim,* 65, 402n.; and protocol, 41–44, 70; reforms in, 352–80 *passim,* 385, rise of authority of, 245–50 *passim,* 263, 266, 314; routes to, 210, 212, 296; and single Executive, 10, 25, 26, 33, 178, 180, 351, 353, 371; social aspects of, 70, 200–201, 379–80; succession in, 62–65, 67–68, 70, 76, 117, 213, 358–60; transition in, 357–58. *See also* Executive branch; President, the; individual Presidents

Presidency: Crisis and Regeneration, The (Finer), 368–69

President, the, 39, 128, 204; administrative problems of, 96, 199, 301–8, 327, 334–42, 378; appointive power of, 51, 52, 182–85, 206, 279; and assassinations and attempts at, 76, 159–64, 166–74, 406n., 407n.; and Cabinets, 48–51, 204, 305, 409n.; and campaigns and campaign costs, 219–24, 235, 353, 396–98; candidates for, 192, 194, 209–10, 220–23, 233–35, 362–64, 375, 380; candidates for, coyness in, 226–28; chart of, 387–91; as Commander in Chief, 10, 15–16, 18, 98, 280–81; Congress and, 56, 70, 79, 190, 192, 284, 296, 299–301, 324–34 *passim,* 336–38, 348, 361, 370; and credibility gap, 301; criticism and suspicion of, 143, 145–58, 163–64, 166–74, 181, 204–7, 300, 366, 367, 376; disability and death of, 239, 358–60, 377; elected without popular majority, 172–73, 189–90; election of, 3, 11, 15, 93, 106, 111, 120–21, 206, 207, 356–57, 375, 384; and executive agreements, 277–78, 296, 298, 299; ex-Presidents, 128–29, 360–61, 418n.; and foreign affairs, 58–60, 247–48, 275–310 *passim,* 352; humor in, 234; impeachment of, 15, 25; lame-duck, 342; and law background, 210; and military heroes, 134, 214–19; and pardons granting of, 18, 25; and patronage, 112, 115, 117, 120, 121–24, 128, 130, 132–34, 147, 190, 192, 198, 206; pensions for, 57, 418n.; and the people, 90, 92–93, 187–88, 194, 197, 199, 201, 235, 237, 238–39, 254–56, 257, 260–63, 271, 272, 282, 284, 404n.; and primaries, 354–55; private emissaries of, 279; and publicity, 315–18, 345–46, 375; reluctance to run, 226–27; removal power of, 52–53, 156, 182; reticence in candidates in 1800's, 229–32; salary of, 44, 336, 382; second terms of, 70, 169, 170, 173, 192, 346–47, 401n.; and Secret Service, 161; and Secretary of State, 302–5; special assistants of, 305–8, 338–41; and statements of policy, 279; strong vs. weak, 77, 371–75, 379; and strong predecessor, 180–81, 408n.; as symbol, 172, 209, 257, 375–76; term of office of, 11, 13–15, 16, 25, 29–30, 33, 39, 70, 111, 156, 198, 202, 206, 207, 270, 281, 294, 341–42, 379; and treaties, 16, 276, 277–78, 299;

trips of, 42, 44–45, 296, 298; and
veto power, 25, 56, 197, 206, 375;
war and emergency powers of, 95,
98, 100–101, 248–49, 272, 280, 320,
343–44; and wealth, 355, 362, 363,
364. *See also* Executive branch;
Presidency, the; individual
Presidents
President and Congress, The (Binkley), 249
President: Office and Powers, The
(Corwin), 376
*Presidential Government in the
United States: The Unwritten Constitution* (Paterson), 367–68
*Presidential Leadership of Public
Opinion* (Cornwell), 254
Presidential Power (Neustadt), 324,
326
Presidential Problems (Cleveland),
188
Press, 154, 345–46; Agnew and, 346,
385–86; and assassins, 162, 163,
164, 166–68, 174; Cleveland and,
235–37, 238; conferences, 316, 317,
324, 345; Coolidge and, 315–16, 317;
Hoover and, 317; Johnson and, 346;
Kennedy and, 324, 346; leaks to,
251; politics and, 128, 150, 151,
232, 234; F. D. Roosevelt and, 317–
18; T. Roosevelt and, 250–51, 254;
and satire, 189, 237; secretaries,
340; and Supreme Court, 346; Taft
and, 254; Truman and, 345, 346. *See
also* Communications; individual
papers
Progress and Poverty (George), 195,
202, 267
Progressive party, 160, 265–66, 271,
315, 354, 394
Promise of American Life, The
(Croly), 267
Puerto Rico, 249
Punch, 270

Quincy, Josiah, 147

Randolph, Edmund, 10, *17,* 23, 28,
34, 46, 48, *49,* 50
Randolph, John, *111,* 112–13, 147
Reconstruction, 164, 194–95

Reed, Thomas B., 260
Republican party, 2–3, 101, 143, 232,
257, 394, 395; and business, 393;
in Congress, 189, 257, 329;
conservative wing of, 181, 257, 393;
conventions of, 2, 225–26, 229, 380;
fraud in, 189; liberal wing of,
198, 200, 202, 257, 393; Lincoln and,
136; money problems of, 396, 398;
and Presidency, 180, 206; and
Reconstruction, 145, 194–95; re-
pudiated Progressive principles,
272, 393; and slavery, 393. *See also*
Political parties
Republicans, Jeffersonian, 51, 58,
62, 64–65, 67, 73, 78–79, 92, 108,
110, 112–15, 117, 120. *See also*
Democratic party
Rhode Island, 10, 44
Richmond *Enquirer,* 123
Riencourt, Amaury de, 372–73
*Rise and Growth of American
Politics, The* (Ford), 245
Ritchie, Thomas, 123
Robertson, Ignatius Loyola, 3
Roche, John P., 320, 340
Rockefeller, Nelson, 265, 397–98
Rogers, William, 305, *306*
Romney, George, 296
Roosevelt, Franklin Delano, 39, *287,
315,* 358; attempted assassination
of, 160, 166, 169; brain trust of, 317;
Cabinet of, 304, 334–35; Congress
and, 317, 320, 325, 328–29, 331;
criticism of, 166–67, 281, 320;
death of, 290, 358, 360; and destroyer deal with Britain, 278–79,
280–81, 282; fireside chats of, 317–
18; first Hundred Days of, 318;
and foreign affairs, 277, 279, 280,
287–88, 289, 293, 303–4; New Deal
of, 314, 318–19; and Office for
Emergency Management, 319;
patrician background of, 265; and
the people, 315; as President, 154,
167, 170, 181, 281, 300, *312,* 317,
328, 339, 340, *341,* 344, 363, 364,
371, 419n.; and press, 317–18, 345;
and reorganization of executive,
319, 327–29, 335; and Supreme
Court, 325, 342–43; term of office
of, 158, 281, 319, 341, 342, 347; and
veto power, 320; war powers of,

Nor need we shrink from ~~being~~

~~of~~ our country today.   This

as it has endured, will reviv

first of all let me assert my

thing we have to fear is fear

unjustified terror which paral

convert retreat into a~~~~

~~to bring about prosperity once~~

~~in the midst of our war~~